The
NOVEL CURE

An A~Z of
Literary
Remedies

ELLA BERTHOUD and **SUSAN ELDERKIN**

CANONGATE
Edinburgh · London

To Carl and Ash
and in memory of Marguerite Berthoud and David Elderkin
who taught us to love books – and build the bookshelves

This paperback edition first published by Canongate Books
in 2015

First published in Great Britain in 2013 by Canongate Books Ltd,
14 High Street, Edinburgh EH1 1TE

www.canongate.tv

Copyright © Ella Berthoud and Susan Elderkin, 2013

The moral right of the authors has been asserted

British Library Cataloguing-in-Publication Data
A catalogue record for this book is available on
request from the British Library

ISBN 978 0 85786 421 5

Designed by Here Design

Printed and bound in Great Britain by Clays Ltd, St Ives plc

CONTENTS

INTRODUCTION

This is a medical handbook – with a difference.

First of all, it does not discriminate between emotional pain and physical pain; you're as likely to find a cure within these pages for a broken heart as a broken leg. It also includes common predicaments you might find yourself in, such as moving house, looking for Mr/Mrs Right, or having a midlife crisis. Life's bigger challenges such as losing a loved one or becoming a single parent are in here too. Whether you've got the hiccups or a hangover, a fear of commitment or a sense of humour failure, we consider it an ailment that deserves a remedy.

But there's another difference too. Our medicines are not something you'll find at the chemist, but at the bookshop, in the library, or downloaded onto your electronic reading device. We are bibliotherapists, and the tools of our trade are books. Our apothecary contains Balzacian balms and Tolstoyan tourniquets, the salves of Saramago and the purges of Perec and Proust. To create it, we have trawled two thousand years of literature for the most brilliant minds and restorative reads, from Apuleius, second-century author of *The Golden Ass*, to the contemporary tonics of Ali Smith and Jonathan Franzen.

Bibliotherapy has been popular in the form of the nonfiction self-help book for several decades now. But lovers of literature have been using novels as salves – either consciously or subconsciously – for centuries. Next time you're feeling in need of a pick-me-up – or require assistance with an emotional tangle – reach for a novel. Our belief in the effectiveness of fiction as the purest and best form of bibliotherapy is based on our own experience with patients

bib•lio•ther•a•py

noun \ bi-blē-ə-'ther-a-pē, -'the-rə-py:

the prescribing of fiction for life's ailments (Berthoud and Elderkin, 2013) and bolstered by an avalanche of anecdotal evidence. Sometimes it's the story that charms; sometimes it's the rhythm of the prose that works on the psyche, stilling or stimulating. Sometimes it's an idea or an attitude suggested by a character in a similar quandary or jam. Either way, novels have the power to transport you into another existence, and see the world from a different point of view. When you're engrossed in a novel, unable to tear yourself from the page, you are seeing what a character sees, touching what a character touches, learning what a character learns. You may *think* you're sitting on the sofa in your living room, but the important parts of you – your thoughts, your senses, your spirit – are somewhere else entirely. 'To read a writer is for me not merely to get an idea of what he says, but to go off with him and travel in his company,' said André Gide. No-one comes back from such a journey quite the same.

Whatever your ailment, our prescriptions are simple: a novel (or two), to be read at regular intervals. Some treatments will lead to a complete cure. Others will simply offer solace, showing you that you are not alone. All will offer the temporary relief of your symptoms due to the power of literature to distract and transport. Sometimes the remedy is best taken as an audio book, or read aloud with a friend. As with all medicines, the full course of treatment should always be taken for best results. Along with the cures, we offer advice on particular reading issues, such as being too busy to read and what to read when you can't sleep; the ten best books to read in each decade of life; and the best literary accompaniments for important rites of passage, such as being on your gap year – or on your death bed.*

We wish you every delight in our fictional plasters and poultices. You will be healthier, happier and wiser for them.

---

* As PJ O'Rourke said, 'Always read something that will make you look good if you die in the middle of it'.

A–Z OF AILMENTS

'One sheds one's sicknesses in books — repeats and presents again one's emotions, to be master of them.'

DH Lawrence (*The Letters of DH Lawrence*)

A

abandonment

Plainsong
KENT HARUF

If inflicted early, the effects of physical or emotional aban-donment – whether you were left by too-busy parents to bring yourself up, told to take your tears and tantrums else-where, or off-loaded onto another set of parents completely (see: adoption) – can be hard to shrug. If you're not careful, you might spend the rest of your life expecting to be let down. As a first step to recovery, it is often helpful to real-ise that those who abandoned you were most likely aban-doned themselves. And rather than wishing they'd buck up and give you the support or attention you yearn for, put your energy into finding someone else to lean on, who's better equipped for the job.

Abandonment is rife in *Plainsong*, Kent Haruf's account of small-town life in Holt, Colorado. Local school teacher Guthrie has been abandoned by his depressed wife Ella, who feigns sleep when he tries to talk to her and looks at the door with 'outsized eyes' when he leaves. Their two young sons, Ike and Bobby, are left bewildered by her unexplained ab-sence from their lives. Old Mrs Stearns has been abandoned by her relatives, either through death or neglect. And Victo-ria, seventeen years old and four months pregnant, is aban-doned first by her boyfriend and then by her mother who, in a back-handed punishment to the man who'd abandoned them both many years before, tells her 'You got yourself into this, you can just get out of it,' and kicks her out of the house.

Gradually, and seemingly organically – though in fact Maggie Jones, a young woman with a gift for communication, orchestrates most of it – other people step into the breach, most astonishingly the McPheron brothers, a pair of 'crotchety and ignorant' cattle-farming bachelors who agree to take the pregnant Victoria in: 'They looked at her, regarding her as if she might be dangerous. Then they peered into the palms of their thick callused hands spread out before them on the kitchen table and lastly they looked out the window toward the leafless and stunted elm trees.' The next thing we know they are running around shopping for cribs – and the rush of love for the pair felt by both Victoria and the reader transforms them overnight. As we watch the community quicken to its role as extended family – frail Mrs Stearns teaching Ike and Bobby to make cookies, the McPherons watching over Victoria with all the tender, clumsy tenacity which they normally reserve for their cows – we see how support can come from very surprising places.

If you have been abandoned, don't be afraid to reach out to the wider community around you – however little you know its inhabitants as individuals (and if you need help turning your neighbours into friends, see our cure for: neighbours, having). They'll thank you for it one day.

accused, being

If you're accused of something and you know you're guilty, accept your punishment with good grace. If you're accused and you didn't do it, fight to clear your name. And if you're accused, and you know you did it, but you don't think what you did was wrong, what *then*?

Australia's Robin Hood, Ned Kelly – as portrayed by Peter Carey in *True History of the Kelly Gang* – commits his first crime at ten years old, when he kills a neighbour's heifer so his family can eat. The next thing he knows, he's been apprenticed (by his own mother) to the bushranger, Harry Power. When Harry robs the Buckland Coach, Ned is the 'nameless person' reported as having blocked the road with a tree and held the horses so 'Harry could go about his trade.' And thus Ned's fate is sealed: he's an outlaw for ever. He makes something glorious of it.

In his telling of the story – which he has written down in his own words for his baby daughter to read one day, knowing he won't be around to tell her himself – Ned seduces us completely with his rough-hewn, punctuation-free prose that bounds and dives over the page. But what really warms us to this Robin Hood of a boy/man is his strong sense of right and wrong – because Ned is guided at all times by a fierce loyalty and a set of principles that happen not to coincide with those of the law. When his ma needs gold, he brings her gold; when both his ma and his sister are deserted by their faithless men, he'll 'break the 6th Commandment' for their sakes. And even though Harry and his own uncles use him 'poorly', he never betrays them. How can we not love this murdering bushranger with his big heart? It is the world that's corrupt, not him; and so we cheer and whoop from the sidelines as pistols flash and his Enfield answers. And so the novel makes outlaws of its readers.

Ned Kelly is a valuable reminder that just because someone has fallen foul of society's laws it does not necessarily mean that they are bad. It's up to each one of us to decide for ourselves what's right and wrong in life. Draw up your personal constitution – then live by it. If you step out of line, be the first to give yourself a reprimand. Then see: guilt.

addiction to alcohol

SEE: **alcoholism**

addiction to coffee

SEE: **coffee, can't find a decent cup of**

addiction to drugs

SEE: **drugs, doing too many**

addiction to gambling

SEE: **gambling**

addiction to the internet

SEE: **internet addiction**

addiction to sex

SEE: **sex, too much**

addiction to shopping

SEE: **shopaholism**

addiction to tobacco

SEE: **smoking, giving up**

adolescence

The Catcher in the Rye
JD SALINGER

Who Will Run the Frog Hospital?
LORRIE MOORE

In Youth is Pleasure
DENTON WELCH

Hormones rage. Hair sprouts where previously all was smooth. Adam's apples bulge and voices crack. Acne erupts. Bosoms bloom. And heart – and loins – catch fire with the slightest provocation.

First, stop thinking you're the only one it's happened to. Whatever you're going through, Holden Caulfield got there first. If you think that everything's 'lousy'; if you can't be bothered to talk about it; if your parents would have 'two hemorrhages apiece' if they knew what you were doing right now; if you've ever been expelled from school; if you think all adults are phonies; if you drink/smoke/try to pick up people much older than you; if your so-called friends are always walking out on you; if your teachers tell you you're letting yourself down; if you protect yourself from the world with your swagger, your bad language, your seeming indifference to what happens to you next; if the only person who understands you is your ten-year-old sister, Phoebe – if one or more of those things is true for you, *The Catcher in the Rye* will carry you through.

Adolescence can't be cured, but there are ways to make the most of it. Lorrie Moore's *Who Will Run the Frog Hospital?* is full of the usual horrors – the narrator, Berie, is a late developer who hides her embarrassment by mocking her 'fried eggs' and 'tin cans run over by a car'; and she and her best friend Sils roll about laughing when they remember how Sils once tried to shave off her pimples with a razor. In fact, laughing is something they do a lot of together – and they do it 'violently, convulsively', with no sound coming out. They also sing songs together – anything from Christmas carols to TV theme tunes and Dionne Warwick. And we applaud that they do. Because if you don't sing loudly and badly with your friends when you're fourteen and fifteen, letting the music prepare your heart for 'something drenching and big' to come, when do you get to do it?

A teenage boy who makes no friends at all yet lives with incredible intensity is Orvil Pym in Denton Welch's *In Youth is Pleasure*. This beautifully observed novel published in 1945 takes place against the backdrop of an English country hotel over the course of one languid summer where Orvil, caught in a state of pubescent confusion, holidays with his father and brothers. Aloof and apart, he observes the flaws in those around him through a pitiless lens. He explores the countryside, guiltily tasting the communion wine in a deserted church, then falling off his bike and crying in despair for 'all the tortures and atrocities in the world'. He borrows a boat and rows down a river, glimpsing two boys whose bodies 'glinted like silk' in the evening light. New worlds beckon, just beyond his reach, as he hovers on the edge of revelation – and for a while he considers pretending to be mad, to avoid the horrors awaiting him back at school. Gradually, he realises that he cannot leap the next ten years – that he just has to survive this bewildering stage, and behave in 'the ordinary way', smiling and protecting his brothers' pecking order by hiding his wilder impulses.

Adolescence doesn't have to be hell. Remember that your peers are struggling to cross the chasm too and, if you can, share the struggles together. Friends or no friends, be sure to do the silly, crazy things that only adolescents do. If you don't get the chance while you're at school, then take a gap year while you're still in your teens (being sure to take the right books when you do). Then, when you're older, at least you'll be able to look back at these heady, high, hormonal times, and laugh.

 THE TEN BEST NOVELS TO READ ON YOUR GAP YEAR

Cult books, hip books, books that will define your life. You'll always have something to talk about with one of these in your backpack. They'll set the standard for your future relationships – and we're not talking just to books.

Purple Hibiscus CHIMAMANDA NGOZI ADICHIE
The Master and Margarita MIKHAIL BULGAKOV
On the Road JACK KEROUAC
Flowers for Algernon DANIEL KEYES
Lucy JAMAICA KINCAID
Dusty Answer ROSAMOND LEHMANN
One Hundred Years of Solitude GABRIEL GARCIA MÁRQUEZ
All the Pretty Horses CORMAC MCCARTHY
Moby Dick HERMAN MELVILLE
Cloud Atlas DAVID MITCHELL

SEE ALSO: **bed, inability to get out of** • **internet addiction** • **irritability** • **rails, going off the** • **risks, taking too many** • **teens, being in your**

adoption

Run
ANN PATCHETT

The Graveyard Book
NEIL GAIMAN

Children's literature is strewn with adoptees. Mary Lennox in *The Secret Garden* is a spoiled adoptee who learns to love in her new cold climate; Mowgli in *The Jungle Book* is brought up by wolves; Tarzan in the novels of Edgar Rice Burroughs is reared by apes. A romance seems to surround these lost and found – and indeed who, as a child, hasn't had a run-in with their parents and fantasised that they too were a foundling? Adoptees find their way into adult literature too: there's James in Grant Gillespie's *The Cuckoo Boy* – a novel with some disturbing views on adoption, but a riveting read nonetheless; Heathcliff in *Wuthering Heights* who upsets the delicate balance of his adoptive family; 'Wart' in *The Once and Future King* by TH White who is one of the rare success stories in this list – an adoptee who turns out to be Arthur, King of Camelot.

In reality, adoption is less romantic and can be hard for all concerned – for the natural parents who decide to give their child away; for the child who finds out in a non-ideal way (see: abandonment); for the child who blames their adoptive parents for their confusion, and who may seek out their natural parents only to be disappointed; and for the adoptive parents who have to decide when to tell their children that they are 'special' and not blood-related. The whole matter is fraught with pitfalls – but also with love, and it can bring an end to childless grief (see: children, not having) – and anyone involved would do well to explore its complexity via those who have been there before.

One of the loveliest modern novels featuring adoptees is Ann Patchett's *Run*. Doyle, the white ex-mayor of Boston has three sons, Sullivan, Teddy and Tip – one a white red-head, and two black, athletic and extremely tall. His fiery-haired wife Bernadette, Sullivan's mother, is dead. Teddy and Tip's real mother is 'the spy who came in from the cold' – she has watched her sons grow up from a distance, aware of their successes and failures, their friendships and rivalries, presiding over them like a guardian angel.

When eleven-year-old Kenya – the runner of the title – unexpectedly comes to live in the Doyle household, the complex family dynamics begin to move in new directions. Teddy and Tip seem to be successful, as a scientist and a would-be priest, but Doyle wishes they had followed him into politics. Their older brother Sullivan has been in Africa for some time trying to help in the battle against AIDS, running away from a terrible incident in his past. With the new issues raised by Kenya's presence in the house, the stories of the brothers' different origins gradually emerge – and it is Kenya's simple but overwhelming need to run, beautifully portrayed by Patchett ('she was a superhuman force that sat outside the fundamental law of nature. Gravity did not apply to her') that brings them all together. The overall message of the novel is clear, and delivered without sentimentality: blood matters, but love matters more.

Confirmation that even the most unconventional parents can make a good job of adopting a child is found within the pages of *The Graveyard Book* by Neil Gaiman. When a toddler goes exploring one night, he manages to evade death at the hands of 'the man Jack', who murders the rest of his family. Ending up in a nearby graveyard, he's adopted by a pair of ghosts. The dead Mr and Mrs Owens never had children of their own in life, and relish this unexpected chance to become parents. They name him 'Nobody', and refer to him as Bod. During his eccentric childhood, Bod picks up unusual skills such as 'Fading, Haunting, and Dream Walking' – which turn out to be very useful later on.

Bod's ghostly parents do an excellent job. 'You're alive, Bod. That means you have infinite potential. You can do anything, make anything, dream anything. If you can change the world, the world will change.' Their wisdom from the grave gives Bod the impetus to live his life to the full, despite the tragedy of his early years; and he certainly does.

Adoption is never a simple thing. Honesty on all sides is essential to allow those involved to come to terms with who they are, and what relationship they have to whom. Whatever part you play, these novels will show you you're not alone. Read them and then pass them round your family – however that family is defined. Encourage everyone to air their feelings. See: confrontation, fear of; and emotions, inability to express if this feels daunting; and empathy, lack of to ensure you're coming to the table with an open, compassionate mind.

SEE ALSO: **abandonment · outsider, being an**

adultery

The temptation to have an affair generally starts when one half of a pair feels dissatisfied with who they are – or who they feel themselves perceived to be – within their current relationship. If only they could be with someone new, they think, they would be a sparklier, wittier, sexier version of themselves. Perhaps they justify their betrayal by telling themselves that they married too young, when they were not fully grown into themselves; and now their real self wants its moment on the stage. And maybe they *will* be that sexier, shinier person – for a while. But affairs which break up long-term relationships usually go the same way in the end, as the old self and habits catch up, albeit within a slightly different dynamic. Often insecurities creep in too. Because if the relationship began as a clandestine affair for at least one of you, it's easy to become paranoid that infidelity will strike again.

For Emma Bovary, the temptation to stray comes almost immediately after tying the knot with doctor Charles, stuck as she is in her adolescent preconceptions of what a marriage should be. Instead of the calm existence she discovers, with a husband who adores her, she had expected love to be 'a great bird with rose-coloured wings' hanging in the sky. These absurd notions, we are slightly embarrassed to admit, were picked up from literature – Sir Walter Scott is named and shamed – for at the age of fifteen Emma swallowed down a great number of romantic novels, riddled with tormented young ladies 'fainting in lonely pavilions' and gentlemen 'weeping like fountains'.* When she meets the lustful, false Rodolphe, full of clichéd flattery and the desire to serenade her with daisies, she is putty in his hands. If you suspect you are harbouring similarly unrealistic ideas of romantic love and marriage, you need to dose yourself up with some contemporary realists: the works of Jonathan Franzen and Zadie Smith are a good place to start.

---

* Novels are not the only culprit, however: she knows by heart all the love songs 'of the last century', glories in the heady rites and rituals of the Catholic church; and likes the countryside only when it involves ruins – the responsibility for which we lay squarely at the foot of eighteenth-century art.

Anna Karenina is not actively looking for a way out of her marriage to the conservative Karenin, but she certainly finds the full expression of her vivacious self with Vronsky. When, on the way back to St Petersburg after having met the young officer on her visit to Moscow, she sees him on the platform, she is unable to stop the animation bubbling forth. And when she next sets eyes on her husband, she can't bear the customary 'ironical' smile with which he greets her (or, now she comes to think of it, his 'gristly' ears). More strongly than ever, she feels that she is pretending, that the emotion between them is false – and it's herself she feels dissatisfied with as a result. Now that she has seen herself around Vronsky, how can she go back to being the Anna she is with cold Karenin?

What Anna also finds, of course, is that loving Vronsky involves guilt. In fact (and this time we take pleasure in pointing it out), it is while she is reading a novel about a guilty baron that she first becomes aware that the emotion has hatched within herself. Guilt and self-hatred ultimately bring the stricken heroine crashing down: for she can never shake the principles and values that formed her, particularly with regards to the love she owes her son. Whatever the rights and wrongs of the situation, be aware that guilt is hard to live with. See: guilt for how to survive a stricken conscience and still come out standing the other end.

A more devious way of dealing with guilt is to ride in the slipstream of a partner who has been unfaithful first. In 1950's London, the eponymous heroine of *Patience* is a contentedly married woman, whose stuffy husband Edward expects little more from her than keeping house, cooking regular meals, and performing her duties in the bedroom, which she does while planning which vegetables to buy for tomorrow's lunch. The revelation that Edward is having an affair with the not-so-Catholic Molly leaves her feeling oddly relieved. Her sense of imminent liberation rapidly finds a focus in the form of Philip, a handsome, intriguing bachelor, who awakens her to what sex can be. Patience somehow brings about the end of her marriage and embarks on a new life with Philip in an almost painless way. Even her three young children remain unscathed. Her suggestion that Philip keep his bachelor flat going – where he works and where they sometimes have an assignation – seems to be particularly full of foresight. Perhaps a second home is the secret to an enduring second love.

Sadly, Edward doesn't come off so lightly: he is deeply thrown, his whole tidy world turned upside down, and is landed, somewhat unfairly we feel, with the blame for it all. There is a chance that adultery may free you from a loveless marriage and catapult you into a fine romance. But there's a chance it won't. You may simply take your problems with you, be capsized by religious or personal guilt, and leave at least one wreckage behind, apart from yourself. The fact is, unless you married late or were very lucky – or are one of the fortunate few whose parents raised you to be fully in your skin by age twenty – you probably will hit a time when you feel there is more to you than your marriage, at present, allows (see also: midlife crisis).

Having an affair does not always destroy a long-term partnership. If you're the aggrieved spouse who suspects or knows that your partner is having an affair, it's worth taking courage from Siri Hustvedt's *The Summer Without Men* – an intriguing take on the cliché of older man leaves wife of thirty years to try a younger version on for size. When her husband Boris announces he wants a 'pause' in their relationship, Mia feels all the things you'd expect, and which you may feel too: humiliated, betrayed and enraged. She ends up spending time in a psychiatric unit (see: anger; rage; and broken heart for help in dealing with this phase and thereby avoiding temporary madness yourself). But then she takes herself off to the backwater town in Minnesota where she grew up, and where her mother still lives in an old folks' home. Here, surrounded by various women who for one reason or another are living without men, she heals a vital part of herself. Sometimes, a relationship can be better for a dramatic 'pause' in which grievances are aired – by both parties. And if you don't want to return to a partner who has abandoned you, temporarily or otherwise, a summer without men (or women) may well give you the strength to forge ahead alone (see: divorce).

The breaking of trust causes deep wounds and, for many couples, recovery is just too hard. If your partner has been unfaithful, you have to be honest with each other and decide between you if your trust can be rebuilt (see: confrontation, fear of to get you started). If you're the one considering or having an affair, have a go at unleashing your unexpressed self within your marriage instead (see: stuck in a rut, to get some ideas.) You'll save everyone a lot of pain and trouble if you achieve it, and your partner may take the opportunity to become someone they like more, too.

SEE ALSO: **anger** · **dissatisfaction** · **divorce** · **guilt** · **jump ship, desire to** · **midlife crisis** · **regret** · **trust, loss of**

age gap between lovers

A Short History of Tractors in Ukrainian
MARINA LEWYCKA

May-to-December romances tend to worry those observing the relationship more than those actually having it. But the disapproval and suspicion of others can be undermining, and if you are on the verge of falling into the arms of someone significantly older or younger than yourself, it's worth asking whether your relationship will be strong enough to withstand the ingrained cultural prejudice against large age gaps that persists in the West.

The first thing to establish is what you're both in the relationship for – and whether either of you are in any sort of denial about your own or your partner's motivation. When Nadia's eighty-six-year-old father announces his engagement to Valentina, a thirty-six-old Ukrainian divorcée with 'superior breasts' and an ambition to escape her drab life in the East, she gets straight to the point: 'I can see why you want to marry her. But have you asked yourself why she wants to marry *you*?' Papa knows, of course, that it's a visa and a posh car in which to drive her fourteen-year-old son to school that she's after, but he sees no harm in rescuing her and Stanislav in return for a little youthly affection. She will cook and clean for him, and care for him in his old age too. That she'll also clean out his meagre life savings and bring them all to their knees with boil-in-the-bag cuisine is something he refuses to acknowledge, however. It takes a good deal of teamwork between Nadia and her estranged 'Big Sis' Vera to persuade him to open his rheumy eyes to the damage this 'fluffy pink hand-grenade' of a woman is doing to their family.

You'd have to be a bit mean-spirited to begrudge the elderly tractor expert the new lease of life that Valentina, for all her faults, gives him; and as long as both parties understand and accept one another's motivations, a relationship between people at opposite ends of the innocence-experience spectrum can be a wonderfully symbiotic thing. There needs to be openness on both sides, though, with no game-playing going on. If that's in place, you have our blessing. Fall away. Whatever the age of those arms.

ageing, horror of

Jitterbug Perfume
TOM ROBBINS

In an age where almost every person in the public eye has ironed away their wrinkles, botoxed their frowns and banished grey hair forever, we can understand King Alobar's need to flee the first signs of ageing like a hare from a fox. In fact, Alobar has more reason than most to escape the approach of senescence in his life – it is customary in his tribe to commit regicide with a poisoned egg at the first sign of their ruler's middle age. Here we distil the essence of *Jitterbug Perfume* in order to give you Alobar's recipe for eternal youth. For a fuller exposition, read the novel in its entirety.

Ingredients
1 eighth-century king on the brink of middle age
1 immortal, goaty god with a pronounced pong
1 vial of perfume that has the power to seduce whole cities
    when released
1 measure of Jamaican jasmine, which must be procured by
    the bee-keeper Bingo Pajama
1 most vital part of beetroot

Method

Fold ingredients earnestly inside a French perfumery until combined, adding at the last moment your beetroot's vital part. Breathe in a never-ending loop while you fold. Now ensure that the Bandaloop doctors preside over your potion while you take a hot bath. Then achieve orgasm with your sexual partner, drawing all the energy from this act up into your brain stem. Repeat daily for a thousand years.

If you have not by then achieved your aim, take Alobar's best advice of all: lighten up.

SEE ALSO: **baldness** • **birthday blues** • **old age, horror of**

ageing parents

The Corrections
JONATHAN FRANZEN

Family Matters
ROHINTON MISTRY

We wish this ailment on all of you. To have aged parents is something to celebrate, the alternative being to have faced their deaths before their time (see: death of a loved one). However, one can't deny that people can sometimes get annoying when they get old. They become crankier, more opinionated, less tolerant, more set in their ways. And on top of it all, they become physically incapacitated and need looking after, forcing a quite disconcerting reversal of the parent-child relationship. To that end, we address ageing parents as a condition requiring a salve as well as a celebration. We recommend two excellent novels with this theme at their heart, revealing the practical and psychological effects of ageing parents on the caring – or uncaring – children.

All three children veer heavily towards the latter in Jonathan Franzen's painfully funny *The Corrections* – though maybe Alfred and Enid Lambert had it coming. We first meet the Lambert parents in the final, most troubled stage of their lives. Alfred has Alzheimer's and dementia, and Enid joins the children in worrying about how to look after him (he has taken, amongst other things, to peeing in bottles in his den, because it's too far to get to the toilet). The driving force behind the narrative is Enid's desperation that all her children – and grandchildren – should come home for Christmas, as if this alone will reassure her that life is still worth living. But her eldest son, Gary, pretends that one of his children is ill in order to avoid the trip home. Daughter Denise has her own fish to fry with her new restaurant, Chip, the youngest, has fled about as far away as you can get – Lithuania – on the back of a highly dubious internet business.

As we move towards the inevitable Christmas showdown, we re-visit significant moments in the past of this seemingly conventional family: Alfred refusing – out of meanness – to sell a patent that could have made his fortune; Alfred dominating Enid in an increasingly worrisome fashion; and Enid taking out her misery on her children by feeding them the food of revenge (rutabaga and liver). Perhaps it's the memory of this meal that persuades these three grown children to put Alfred into a retirement home – which, never one to miss an opportunity for a joke, Franzen calls 'Deepmire'. It works well for everybody except Alfred. The terrorising experience of reading this novel will remind you that avoiding such poor parent-child relations in the first place is highly recommended.

Mistry's Bombay novel begins with a celebration: the seventy-ninth birthday of the patriarch of the Vakeel family, Nariman. Nariman is a Parsi, whose religion prevented him from marrying the woman he has loved for thirty years, and in fact lived with for many of these, until he gave in to his family's dogma and married a woman of his own faith. Now widowed and suffering from Parkinson's disease, he finds himself increasingly dependent on his two step-children, Jal and Coomy, who have always resented him because of his imperfect love for their mother. When one day on his daily excursion he breaks his leg, he's forced to put himself in their hands entirely. Soon he is lying in bed wishing that one of them would wash him, change his clothes, and play him some music – but is too worried about disturbing them to ask for help. When they hear him crying at night they realise he is depressed and, finding the management of his personal hygiene intolerable – loathing the details of bed-pans and bed-sores which they know come from their own neglect – they send him to live with his blood-daughter

Roxana in the far smaller flat which she shares with her husband and two sons.

Here Grandpa Nariman has to sleep on the settee with Jehangir, the nine-year-old, while Murad the older boy sleeps in an improvised tent on the balcony, which, luckily, he finds a wonderful adventure. Roxana and her husband do an infinitely better job, embracing Grandpa and his fastidiousness over his dentures with compassion. And years later, Jehangir remembers the time that his grandfather lived with them with fondness and affection.

Family Matters is a wonderful example of how to look after one's ageing parents with compassion – and how not to. And even though Nariman's stepchildren do a poor job, at least they take him in. In our Western world of dependence on care homes and hospitals, we would do well to take note of this example of a family caring for its elderly at home. Aged parents: don't be so objectionable that your children and spouse want to hole you up somewhere you can't embarrass them. Children of these parents: listen to their pleas for dignity and privacy, and do your utmost to help them retain these last vital assets. Both parties: try to forgive one another's different moralities and expectations. And, if possible, make it home for Christmas (see: Christmas to help you survive).

agoraphobia

The Woman in the Dunes
KOBO ABE

Agoraphobics experience great discomfort when they find themselves in new places. Surrounded by the unfamiliar, the fear that they could lose control can trigger a panic attack (see: panic attack). And so they prefer to stay at home – resulting in isolation, depression and loneliness. Kobo Abe's novel is the perfect antidote.

Jumpei Niki, an amateur entomologist, takes a trip to a coastal desert at the end of the railway line, on the hunt for a new species of insect. While he searches for invertebrates, he stumbles upon a village hidden among eternally shifting dunes. Here he finds a unique community who live in houses nestled at the bottom of holes fifty foot deep in the buff terrain. To prevent their homes from being submerged, the residents must dig bucketfuls of golden dirt every day, which they send up on ropes to the villagers above.

Their work takes place in the moonlight, as the sun makes their shafts unbearably hot. Jumpei is lured into one of the burrows for the night, where he helps a young widow in the endless battle against the fluid sand. In a twist of fate, Jumpei wakes the next morning to find the ladder that should have been his exit has been removed. His escape attempts are alternately heroic, sadistic and desperate. Slowly he accepts his fate as one who must work all day, sending buckets of sand up on ropes to helpers above – in between eating, sleeping and having sex with the widow. By the end of the novel you have shared Jumpei's humiliation – for the villagers above find his inadvertent life-change highly amusing – and his gradual acceptance of his bizarre new existence. And it's not all bad, for he does make a discovery under the sand.

Let Jumpei teach you to submit to the unexpected. And once you've experienced being hemmed in by imaginary walls of sand, you may be glad to take some tentative steps beyond your own, less imprisoning, walls.

SEE ALSO: **anxiety • loneliness • panic attack**

alcoholism

Alcoholics knock around in the pages of novels like ice cubes in gin. Why? Because alcohol loosens tongues. And because it's always the old soaks who collar us to tell a tale. When they're on the page, we can enjoy their ramblings without having to smell their beery breath. But let's agree to keep them on the page. Nobody wants a real one in their home; if you find yourself heading that way, we suggest you terrify yourself with a couple of graphic portrayals of bottle-induced ruin. Our cure is to be imbibed in three parts: two heady cocktails that will show you a glimpse of your potential fate to sober you up quick smart, followed by an enticing shot that will prompt you to put on your trainers and run yourself into a new, clean life.

Jack Torrance, the writer in Stephen King's spine-chilling *The Shining*, has been on the wagon for some years. Though his wife has stayed with him, he lost her trust when he broke his son Danny's arm in a drink-fuelled rage. By working through the winter as caretaker of the Overlook Hotel in the Colorado Rockies, he hopes he can reconnect with his wife and now five-year-old son, and get his career back on track by writing a new play.

The two big obstacles to Jack's happiness have been an excessive reliance on alcohol and an explosive temper – not a good combination to take to a vast, spooky hotel where you are likely to be cut off from the outside world for several weeks once the snow hits. Jack starts his work with the firm conviction that he will stay sober. But one of the Overlook's ghostly attributes – apart from architecture that re-designs itself regularly – is an ability to produce cocktails from out of nowhere.

At first these are merely imaginary, but soon Jack is confronted with a genuine gin served to him by the (deceased) bartender, Lloyd (see: haunted, being). Looking into the gin is 'like drowning' for Jack: the first drink he's held to his lips in years. In the company of increasingly malign spirits, the spectre of Jack's lurking alcoholism is delighted to break out and let rip. Observing Jack's disintegration will put the fear of the demon drink into you in more ways than one and will have you heading for the orange juice rather than the hooch.

Drunks tend to be either intoxicating or infuriating. Malcolm Lowry's *Under the Volcano*, set on the Day of the Dead in the Mexican town of Quauhnahuac, shows us both aspects of the psyche in dipsomaniac hero Geoffrey Firmin. The British Consul of this volcano-shadowed town, he spends the day juggling his drinking needs with the complicated reappearance of his estranged wife, Yvonne. This ought to be the most important day of his life, he suspects, but all he can do is drink, telling himself he's downing a beer 'for its vitamins' (he doesn't really bother with food), and dreading the arrival of guests who fail to bring fresh supplies of liquor.

The events cover just one day and take place largely inside the consul's head, but the scope of this enormously powerful novel attains to the epic. As the Day of the Dead celebrations build to their feverish climax, the consul plunges tragically and irredeemably towards self-destruction, his thoughts laced always with whisky and mescal. His musings are at times blackly funny, and references to Faust are frequent; Firmin is heading gleefully to hell, and his last words, 'Christ, what a dingy way to die' – foretold at the opening of the novel by Firmin's filmmaker friend Laruelle – echo with a ghastly reminder of what a horrible route this is to take in life.

Enough warnings! Those seeking to break such damaging habits need a glowing, inspirational model too – an alternative way to live. To this end, we urge you to read *Once a Runner* by John L Parker, Jr. An underground classic when the author self-published in 1978, it was taken up as a sort of novel-manual for competitive runners (bibliotherapy at work in the world). It tells the story of Quenton Cassidy, a member of Southeastern University's track team, training under Olympic Gold medal winner Bruce Denton to run the mile. Denton pushes him and his running cronies to limits they never even knew existed. Quenton revels in the countless laps that Denton forces him to run, pushing himself so much that he urinates blood and openly weeps, his 'mahogany hard legs' pounding the track all the while. At his peak, he is 'vital, so quick, so nearly immortal' that he knows that life will never be 'quite so poignant' as it is now.

Let *Once a Runner* inspire you to change your relationship with your body completely – to push it to the limits in a positive way, to put it to work, and see what it can do. While Firmin in Lowry's novel wishes away the minutes between drinks, Cassidy in John Parker's breathes space into every second, getting the very most he can out of each one. The pure joy – and pain – of running, the sweat and ruthless determination of the race, are as far a cry as you can get from the nihilism of the alcoholic. Buy yourself a pair of trainers and serve this novel up to yourself instead of after-dinner drinks. May it be a symbol of your commitment to ditching the booze.

SEE ALSO: **antisocial, being** • **cold turkey, going** • **hangover** • **hiccups** • **libido, loss of** • **rails, going off the** • **sweating**

alopecia

SEE: **baldness** • **stress**

ambition, too little

The Crimson Petal and the White
MICHEL FABER

If you find yourself watching everybody else's race but your own, or even that you're still standing on the starting line, you need a novel to galvanise you into setting some finishing posts, then pelting towards them. There's no better novel for the job than *The Crimson Petal and the White*.

Our young heroine starts life in a place most would say was so far from the possibility of even competing that she might as well give up before she starts. Sugar was forced into prostitution by her mother at the tender age of thirteen, and grows up believing she has no choice but to submit to the gentlemen who come to her bed 'to keep her warm'. But she yearns to rise above this base existence. Her way of going about it is to become the best in the brothel – and then the best in Britain. Soon she has not only acquired phenomenal accomplishments in the bedroom, but she knows how to make a man feel eloquent, witty, and full of vitality, simply by the way she listens and flirts. But underneath her charming exterior, she still finds her work grotesque and pours her disgust into a novel she writes in secret at her desk.

Her big break comes when she meets William Rackham of Rackham Perfumeries, who discovers her through the pages of the gentleman's magazine, *More Sprees in London*. Rackham is so smitten with Sugar that he arranges to keep her for his exclusive use. Eventually she becomes invaluable to him, not just for her charms and beauty, but for her brains, being more astute and more in touch with his customer's needs than he is himself. It's not long before Sugar is the guiding force behind his advertising campaigns and overall business strategy.

Faber portrays a Victorian world of social inequality and rigid convention in minute detail: 'Watch your step. Keep your wits about you. You will need them', he exhorts at the start of the novel. Follow Sugar (though not into prostitution), and rise wisely, determining your own fate rather than those of others. As Oscar Wilde put it: 'Our ambition should be to rule ourselves, the true kingdom for each one of us.'

SEE ALSO: **apathy • bed, inability to get out of • lethargy**

ambition, too much

Some of us have too little of it, others too much. According to the Taoist philosopher Lao Tzu, ambition – in its best ratio – has one heel nailed in well, 'though she stretch her fingers to touch the heavens'. When neither heel is nailed down firmly, and we overreach our innate talents and social limitations, we are in danger of losing our purchase completely.

This is what happens to Pip in *Great Expectations*. Orphaned Pip lives with his older sister, the harsh and unsympathetic Mrs Joe, whose face looks as if it has been 'scrubbed with a nutmeg grater' and who believes in bringing him up 'by Hand' (though she is tempered by her gentle husband Joe, who shows kindness to Pip throughout his turbulent life). When Pip meets Estella, the beautiful but ice-hearted ward of eccentric Miss Havisham, who is still wearing the wedding dress in which she was jilted at the altar forty years ago, Pip is encouraged by his sister to nurture a hope that this strange old lady has plans to groom him for Estella. The hope turns to a conviction, giving him the green light to behave 'like a gentleman' – not necessarily of the best sort – and look down on his origins, including his friend Biddy, who sees the way that Pip is going and doesn't like it.

Pip and his sister are proved horribly wrong. Though Pip does land a surprise inheritance, and outwardly this makes him a 'gentleman', worldly success is shown to be naught to success in love. Fortunes can be lost as easily as they are won. Pip would have saved a lot of time and heartache if he had never been 'raised up'. Let Pip's mistake stand as a warning. By all means look to the skies. But keep at least one foot on the terra firma of your origins.

SEE ALSO: **greed** • **selling your soul** • **social climber, being a** • **workaholism**

amputation

SEE: **limb, loss of**

anally retentive, being

The Life and Opinions of Tristram Shandy
LAURENCE
STERNE

If you're anally retentive, you'll know all about the importance of order, logic and neatness. A maker of lists, your life consists of accomplishing tasks that you can then tick off. Anything that comes between you and your task – an unexpected telephone call, a sun-lit field calling you to take a stroll, an uninvited guest dropping round for tea – is grossly unwelcome. Your single-track mind cannot wander from its course. Now is your moment to swap psyches with Tristram Shandy. After 480 pages of living inside the head of this loveable philosopher, and accompanying him on his remarkably prolix ramblings, you will be cured of your anal retentiveness forever.

Published in successive volumes from 1760 to 1767, *Tristram Shandy* is perhaps the first interactive novel, inviting the reader to take Sterne's proffered hand and join in the author's game. Like Italo Calvino's two hundred years later, the authorial voice intrudes often and merrily, asking the reader to consider the ways in which he has advanced their understanding of a character.

Shandy's determination to write his memoirs is unstinting, but it takes him until volume three to arrive at his birth. Because this memoir, and indeed his life, consists entirely of diversions from the point. While still a mere homunculus inside his mother's womb, the road to his existence is

amnesia, reading-associated

KEEP A READING JOURNAL

Sufferers of reading-associated amnesia have little or no recollection of the novels they have read. They come home from the bookshop, excited by the crisp new novel in their hands, only to be struck five or twenty pages in by a sense of déjà vu. They join a conversation about a classic novel they believe they've read, only to be posed a question they can't answer – usually what happened at the end.

What you need, blancmange-brained reader, is a reading journal. A small notebook to carry with you at all times – ideally one that's beautiful and pleasing to the touch. Dedicate one page to each book you read and on the day that you turn the last page, write down the book's title, author, the day's date and the place that you read it. You might like to sum up the story in one headline-grabbing line: MAN MURDERS PAWNBROKER, FEELS GUILTY FOR NEXT FIVE HUNDRED PAGES, for example. Or you might opine at length on the motivations of a character you found particularly intriguing. You may also want to make a note of how the book left you feeling – uplifted or downhearted? Like taking a walk on the windy moors, or emigrating to New Zealand? If words don't come easily, use images to summarise your feelings, or give it marks out of ten, or write a list of the words that you found in the book and liked.

This journal will be a record of your reading journey. Over the years you can flip back and recollect the highs and the lows. And if an author or title eludes you mid-conversation, make an excuse to go to the bathroom and look it up.

disturbed, at the very moment of procreation, by his mother asking his father if he had remembered to wind the clock. This interruption to the act of conception results, he believes, in his prenatal self falling prey to 'melancholy dreams and fancies' even before he came to fully exist. And when his name, which his father considered of enormous importance to his nature and fortunes, is accidentally mangled by the time it reaches the curate, and he is inadvertently christened Tristram – apparently the least auspicious of names – rather than Trismegistus, as intended, he believes himself to be even less blessed by the fates.

All of which, perhaps, explains why Sterne's prose is so unruly: a page left blank for the reader to draw their own version of Widow Wadman, the paramour of Uncle Toby; asterisks where the reader is invited to imagine what a character is thinking; and an entirely black page that supposedly 'mourns' the loss of Parson Yorick. There are even squiggly loops indicating the shape of the narrative digressions themselves.

One cannot help but come under the spell. 'Digressions, incontestably, are the sunshine. They are the life, the soul, of reading!' says Tristram at the start of the novel. And we wholeheartedly agree. Interrupt the reading of this book by opening *Tristram Shandy*. Go on, just for a chapter. Although after a few pages, perhaps, it'll be time for a cup of tea. And then a spontaneous excursion might take your fancy. You might forget you were reading this book in the first place. (That's OK; you can come back to it in the middle of some other task, some other day.) A digression a day keeps the doctor away – and so will *Tristram Shandy*.

SEE ALSO: **control freak, being a** • **give up halfway through, refusal to** • **humourlessness** • **organised, being too** • **reverence of books, excessive** • **single-mindedness**

anger

Because even after eighty-four consecutive days of going out in his boat without catching a single fish, the old man is cheerful and undefeated. And even when the other fishermen laugh at him, he is not angry. And even though he now has to fish alone – because the boy who has been with him since he was five, and whom he loves, and who loves him, has been forced by his family to try his luck with another boat – he holds no grudge in his heart. And because on the eighty-fifth day he goes out again, full of hope.

And even though when he does hook a big fish – the biggest fish that he or anyone else has ever caught – and it pulls on his line so fiercely that the skin on his hand is torn, he still lets the fish pull him further out. And though he wishes to God that the boy were with him, he is grateful that at least he has the porpoises that play and joke around his boat. And even when it's been a day and a night and another day stretches ahead, and it's only him and the fish and there's no-one to help, still he keeps his head. And even when he has been pushed further than he has ever been pushed in his life, and he begins to feel the edge of despair, he talks himself round, because he must think of what he has, and not what he does not have; and of what he can do with what there is. And though his hand becomes so stiff it is useless, and though he is hungry and thirsty and blinded by the sun, he still thinks of the lions he once saw on the beach in Africa, like some sort of heavenly vision. Because he knows that there is nothing greater, or more beautiful, or more noble than this fish that tugs him ever on. And even when it is dead, and the sharks come to feast – first one, then half a dozen – and the man loses his harpoon, and then his knife, in his attempts to fend them off; and even when he has ripped out the keel of his boat to use as a club; and even though he fails to save the flesh of the fish, and the ordeal leaves him so tired and weak he is nearly lost himself; and even though when he finally makes it to shore all that is left of the fish is a skeleton, he accepts what has happened, and is not broken, or angry, but goes, rather gratefully, to bed.

Because by immersing yourself in the simple, calming prose of this story, you too will rise above your emotions. You will join the old man in his boat, witness at first hand his love for the boy, for the sea, for the fish – and allow it to fill you with peace and a noble acceptance of what is, leaving no space for what was or what you would like to be. Sometimes we all go out too far, but it doesn't mean we can't come back. And just as the old man is made happy by his vision of lions on a beach, you too can have your vision – perhaps of the old man, and the way he talks himself round. And after you have read it, you will keep this novel on your shelf, somewhere you will see it whenever you feel angry. And you'll remember the old man, the sea, the fish, and you'll be calm.

SEE ALSO: **rage** · **road rage** · **turmoil** · **vengeance, seeking** · **violence, fear of**

angst, existential

Siddhartha
HERMANN HESSE

As anyone who has stood at the top of a cliff will tell you, alongside the fear of falling to your death is an equally strong and entirely conflicting emotion: the urge to jump. The knowledge that nothing is stopping you from making that leap, the leap into possibility – the realisation that you have absolute freedom of will, infinite power to create and to destroy – fills you with horror and dread. It is this horror, according to Soren Kierkegaard, that lies at the root of existential angst.

If you are unlucky enough to have been struck with this debilitating affliction, you will be in urgent need of spiritual refreshment. You need to pare back the possibilities, to renounce the world and join, at least for a while, the ascetics. You need *Siddhartha*.

Siddhartha, the young son of a fictional Brahmin in ancient India, brings joy and bliss to everyone – except himself. Leading a seemingly idyllic existence surrounded by a family who love him, he appears destined for great things. But despite his material and spiritual wealth, young Siddhartha feels that something is missing.

And so, as young men in ancient India were wont to do, he goes on a spiritual quest. First he joins the Samana, a band of self-flagellating ascetics who deny the flesh and seek enlightenment through renunciation. Fully flagellated, but still discontented, he encounters Gotama the Buddha, who teaches him the eightfold path that illuminates the way to the end of suffering. Not content with this knowledge alone, and wanting to reach his goal through his own understanding, he meets Vasudeva, a ferryman with an astonishing inner light, who seems content with his simple life. But this, too, fails to satisfy. Even after living a sensual and happy life for many years with the beautiful Kamala, still something is missing for Siddhartha. For a while he contemplates death by drowning. But then he remembers the astoundingly happy ferryman, Vasudeva, and learns that he must study the river.

Here he finds revelations to last a lifetime – including the true cycle of life and death, and what it is to be part of a timeless unity. And from that day on he radiates transcendent understanding, self-knowledge, and enlightenment. From all over the world, people come to him to seek wisdom and peace. People like you.

SEE ALSO: **anxiety** · **despair** · **dread, nameless** · **pointlessness**

angst, teenage

SEE: **adolescence** · **teens, being in your**

anorexia nervosa

SEE: **eating disorder**

antisocial, being

The Bone People
KERI HULME

So you'd rather stay home with a book? Well, of course we have no problem with that. But do you promise you're going to read and not feel sorry for yourself, because nobody seems to *get* you, and because everyone's having fun except for you?

Stay home and take *The Bone People* off your shelf. Meet the unapologetically antisocial Kerewin Holme, who lives by herself in a starkly-furnished six-floored tower, a crucifix in the hallway. Prickly, impatient, gruff, estranged from her family, odd in that way that sometimes people who spend too much time by themselves become odd (she talks to herself all the time), Kerewin is not everyone's cup of tea.

And neither is Simon everyone's ideal little boy. A strange urchin who breaks into Kerewin's tower, he is mute, stubborn, sullen, 'nasty', 'gnomish', and a 'smartass', Kerewin concludes when she first sets eyes on him, pinioned stiffly into a high slit window. 'Emotionally disturbed,' as the local telephone operator puts it. 'A right stubborn illnatured mess of a child.'

Then enter Joe Gillayley, Simon's father, a nice enough bloke, in fact, but an alcoholic who descends into rages and beats the boy – then tortures himself with the guilt. Not an attractive triumvirate, really. But Kerewin, because of her own strangeness, is able to accept Simon and Joe. The three of them slowly start to forge a bond, becoming an odd little family who share a warmth and companionship and ease that their antisocial tendencies had previously denied them.

Allow their friendship to make its mark on you. Being intrinsically antisocial doesn't bar you from having strong and wonderful bonds with other people. Next time there's a party, go. You might meet someone just as antisocial as yourself.

SEE ALSO: **cynicism** • **dinner parties, fear of** • **killjoy, being a** • **misanthropy** • **read instead of live, tendency to**

anxiety

The Portrait of a Lady
HENRY JAMES

To live with anxiety is to live with a leech that saps you of your energy, confidence and chutzpah. A constant feeling of unease or fearfulness – as opposed to the sense of frustration that characterises stress (see: stress) – anxiety is both a response to external circumstances and an approach to life. While the external circumstances cannot be controlled, the internal response can; laughter, or a big intake of oxygen (the former leading to the latter), usually relieves systems at least temporarily, as well as offering an encouragement to relax. The cause of the anxiety, however, determines whether laughter or breathing and relaxing is the appropriate cure. Luckily, our cure offers all three.

Of the fourteen causes of anxiety that we have identified,* the first chapter of *The Portrait of a Lady* by Henry James can be expected to ameliorate ten. Opening as it does with a description of the civilised and serene institution of afternoon tea in an English country garden – complete with 'mellow' late afternoon light, long shadows, tea cups held 'for a long time close to [the] chin', rugs, cushions and books strewn on the lawn in the shade of the trees – its indirect invitation to slow down and have a cup yourself (helpful for causes 2, 3, 4, 7, 10, 11, 12 and certain elements of 13) is re-enforced by James's unhurried, elegant prose, a balm for anxiety arising from all of the preceding causes, and also serving to begin the complete eradication of anxiety arising from cause number 8.

To say that James's prose spreads itself thickly, like butter, is not intended to suggest turgidness, but rather creaminess – and let us make that *salted* butter. For the pleasures of both prose and afternoon tea are made complete by James's dialogue, which contains both frankness and sharpness of wit (a curative for causes 1–4, and also excellent for cause 7). For the banter between the three men – the elderly chair-bound American banker, Mr Touchett, his 'ugly, sickly' but charming son Ralph, and the 'noticeably handsome' Lord Warburton with his quintessentially English face – is always aiming to trigger a chuckle, and the characters are not afraid of teasing (note Lord Warburton's markedly un-English reference to Mr Touchett's wealth). Freed of the chains of propriety

---

* 1) Trauma, including abuse, and death of a loved one; 2) Relationship problems, either at home or work; 3) Work/school; 4) Finances; 5) Natural disaster; 6) Lack of oxygen at high altitude; 7) Taking life too seriously; 8) Gnawing feeling that you should have read more of the classics; 9) Negative self-talk; 10) Poor health/hypochondria; 11) Taking too many drugs; 12) Being late/too busy; 13) Inadequate food, water, heat or comfort; 14) Threat of attack by wild animal/person.

and form that had been shackling dialogue on similar lawns three quarters of a century earlier, it is the sort of conversation which puts you at your ease (again, addressing causes 1–4 and 7, while also ameliorating causes 6, 9, and 10–12).

Once the little party are joined by Ralph's American cousin Isabel Archer, recently 'taken on' by Mrs Touchett, the conversation loses some of its ease but gains in spirit – for Isabel, at this stage in her life, has a lightness, a boldness and a confidence both in herself and others that cannot fail to rub off on the reader. Those suffering anxiety from cause 9 will find her presence in the story especially curative.

Indeed, we recommend this novel for all sufferers of anxiety except those made anxious by causes 5 and 14 (for the latter, in particular, a novel of any sort is unhelpful, except perhaps to use as a weapon), though readers suffering anxiety from causes 1 and 2 should be warned that the ending may backfire, and prompt their symptoms to get worse. In which case, they should immediately turn back to the beginning for another dose of afternoon tea.

SEE ALSO: **angst, existential · panic attack · stress · turmoil**

apathy

The Postman Always Rings Twice
JAMES M CAIN

Although it can manifest as physical sluggishness – like its heavy-limbed cousin, lethargy – apathy is essentially a mental condition, characterised by an attitude of indifference towards outcomes, both for oneself and the world at large. Its cure, however, is best tackled by addressing the physical sluggishness first, thus further distinguishing it from its other near relations, pessimism and existential angst, which require an overhaul of the mind. This is because apathy is also characterised by a suppression of positive emotions and to re-engage them, and re-kindle the desire for things to turn out well, one has to stir up the sediment at the bottom of the too-sedentary soul.

It's not that it all ends well for Frank Chambers, the itinerant chancer and jailbreaker in James M Cain's 1934 masterpiece *The Postman Always Rings Twice*. Indeed if one was to adopt his philosophy of life, you'd end up (as he does) with a price on your head and several angry women in hot pursuit. But the novel is written with such rattling exuberance that it's impossible to read without becoming physically buzzed. By the end, you'll be up and about with a bounce in your step, throwing caution to the wind in your determination to have a hand in fate, setting you on a more spontaneous and proactive – if slightly reckless – new tack.

From the moment Frank Chambers is thrown off the hay truck, the story is up and running. Within three pages he's swindled the honest owner of the Twin Oaks Tavern into fixing him a colossal breakfast (orange juice, cornflakes, fried eggs, bacon, enchilada, flapjacks and coffee, if you're interested), got himself hired as a mechanic, and set covetous won't-take-no-for-an-answer eyes on Cora, the tavern-owner's sullenly sexy wife. One thing leads to another – and then another – and Cain does a splendid job of keeping up with Frank, capturing his immoral inability to say no in short, snappy sentences laced with slang. The combination of story and style hits you like a triple espresso, and at only a little over a hundred pages, it's also a very quick fix. Rip through it in an afternoon, then jack your apathy onto your back and chuck it out on the street as you go. You'll be inspired by Frank's irrepressible interest in each new moment – even when things aren't going so well – and determined not to blow, as he does, the opportunities that arise.

SEE ALSO: **ambition, too little** • **bed, inability to get out of** • **lethargy** • **pessimism** • **pointlessness** • **zestlessness**

appendicitis

Madeline
LUDWIG BEMELMANS

If one day you're feeling fab
Then suddenly you sense a stab
Of searing pain in nameless parts
That never stops but comes in starts
Filling you with throbbing pain
Running down your abdomen
And you feel no end in sight as

Clearly you've appendicitis
The only cure we can advise
Is *Madeline*. So very wise
A book by Ludwig Bemelmans
Who's written rhymes that don't quite scan
But with his wry and charming tale
Leaves you feeling very hale.
For Madeline is tickled pink
She has a scar that will not shrink
To show to her eleven friends
After her appendix meets its ends
She's given flowers and sweets and toys.
The illustrations Lud deploys
Are very touching, and the book
Will keep your surgeon off the hook.

SEE ALSO: **hospital, being in • pain, being in**

appetite, loss of

The Leopard
**GIUSEPPE TOMASI
DI LAMPEDUSA**

Losing one's appetite is a terrible thing. For one's appetite for food is part and parcel of one's appetite for life. A result of various kinds of physical and emotional sickness (the latter including lovesickness, depression, heartbreak and bereavement), total loss of appetite can only lead in one direction. To bring it back, and solicit a re-engagement with life, whet and tempt with one of literature's most sensual novels.

The Leopard, Don Fabrizio Corbèra, Prince of Salina, feels as if he has been dying for years. But even now, in his old age, he is Appetite writ large. He still has the energy, at seventy-three, to go to brothels; and is still delighted to see his favourite dessert – a rum jelly in the shape of a fortress complete with bastions and battlements – on the dining table (it's rapidly demolished beneath the assault of his large, equally lusty family). There are ravishing descriptions of desire of many different kinds: the daily pursuit of a hare in the 'archaic and aromatic fields'; and the intense and overwhelming attraction of young Tancredi and Angelica as they chase each other around the palace, forever finding new rooms in which to yearn and dream, for 'These were the days when desire was always present, because always overcome'.

One cannot help but revel in the old patriarch's appreciation of the sensual world. This is a novel that will help you rediscover your appetite: for food, for love, for the countryside, for Sicily with all its history and rampant beauty; for a lost, unfair world before democracy; and most importantly for life itself.

arrogance

Pride and Prejudice
JANE AUSTEN

Angel
ELIZABETH TAYLOR

Mildred Pierce
JAMES M CAIN

Arrogance is one of the greatest crimes in literature. We know this because when Mr Darcy snubs Elizabeth Bennet at Bingley's ball – refusing to dance with her, dismissing her beauty as just 'tolerable' and generally turning sour on the inhabitants of Longbourn – he is immediately written off by everyone, even Mrs Bennet, as the 'proudest, most disagreeable man in the world'. And this is despite being much more handsome than the amiable Mr Bingley, despite his having a large estate in Derbyshire, and despite his being by far the most eligible man for a twenty-five-mile radius – which, as we know, means a great deal to Mrs Bennet with five daughters to marry off.

Luckily, the playful Elizabeth Bennet, Jane Austen's heroine of *Pride and Prejudice,* knows how to bring him down to size. She uses a combination of teasing ('I am perfectly convinced . . . that Mr Darcy has no defect,' said to his face) and blunt, hyperbolic rejection ('I had not known you a month before I felt that you were the last man in the world whom I could ever be prevailed on to marry') which not only corrects his flaws but displays the 'liveliness of [her] mind' to such a degree that he falls in love with her all over again, and properly this time. If you are inflicted with similar arrogance, learn from this novel how to spot intelligent teasing and courageous honesty – and welcome it. You should be so lucky to be turned into the perfect man/woman by someone like Elizabeth.

Sometimes, the arrogance is so deeply instilled, however, that nothing and no-one can shift it. The eponymous heroine of *Angel*, by Elizabeth Taylor – not the Hollywood actress but the mid twentieth-century British writer – is just fifteen years old when we meet her, and to say she thinks she's the bee's knees is an understatement. An incorrigible liar, this strange child is vain, bossy and utterly devoid of humour. She feels nothing but contempt for her classmates, is unmoved when one of them is taken to hospital with diphtheria, and fantasises about a future in which, dressed in emeralds and a chinchilla wrap, she'll be able to employ her own, tiresome mother as her maid. Naturally, her mother is pretty appalled by the daughter she's raised – just as Mildred is horrified by her similarly monstrous daughter Veda in James M Cain's *Mildred Pierce*. Veda drains the family coffers to support her extravagant lifestyle and steals her mother's new man. It's not hard to see why Mildred tries to kill the monster she's created.

Fascinatingly, Angel's uber-confidence carries her a long way – all the way to those emeralds, in fact. Veda, too, gets exactly what she wants. Neither discovers humility. Rejection – in Angel's case, from publishers and then critics; in Veda's by her own mother – has no sobering effect on either of them.

Do not be an Angel or a Veda. When you inspire rejection, question what you might have done to deserve it. Instead, be a Darcy. Though he's initially angered and mortified by Elizabeth's refusal of his proposal – and her accusations against his character – he knows the difference between right and wrong, and craves the good opinion of someone he admires. Be glad when someone pulls your leg – the chances are, they'll be improving you.

SEE ALSO: **confidence, too much** • **vanity**

attention, seeking

SEE: **neediness**

B

bad back

The Mystic Masseur
VS NAIPAUL

It have the wust pain in the world. You might as well go fetch a cutlass and cut your whole self up, push it right inside your heart, the pain so bad. It making you want to lie down and die like a pig. You go see the Mystic Masseur, Ganesh Pundit he call. He up Fuente Grove, he cure a boy of big Black Cloud that was sure going to dead he before Ganesh dead the Cloud. He have Powers, though some people call him Business Man of God, for he have a taxi run and a shop by his fine fine Hindu Temple. He have a way with words, for sure, he made that book, 'A Hundred and one Questions and Answers to the Hindu religion,' that Bissoon sold to us, was a smooth smooth book you mus' read before you lose all sensa values. Like Ramlogan when he so vex he turned into a little bird who told the whole of Trinidad that Ganesh he no Mystic, he a fake. But Ganesh, he cure the Woman Who Couldn't Eat because her food turned to needles in her mouth, and he cure the Lover Boy who made love to his bicycle. He can cure anything, he cure the spirit, not just the body. When it have Bad Back, you need to get off your bed and walk, and Ganesh Pundit, the Mystic Masseur, he your man for that.

SEE ALSO: **pain, being in**

bad blood

SEE: **anger** • **bitterness** • **hatred**

bad manners

SEE: **manners, bad**

bad taste

SEE: **taste, bad**

bad tempered, being

SEE: **grumpiness** • **irritability** • **killjoy, being a** • **querulousness**

baldness

Blow Fly
**PATRICIA
CORNWELL**

Sun Dog
MONIQUE ROFFEY

If you have a shiny, pink pate on which nothing grows – and you catch glimpses of its outward spread reflected in windows as you pass – you may feel dismay at the passing of your locks, and perhaps with them, a sense of virility (see: ageing, horror of). You envy the thick manes you see around you, and wish that some of their excess could be transferred to you. But think of the evolution of man from ape to nearly hairless human. You are the superior being, your high-domed forehead more evolved. It is the mop-headed brutes who should feel shifty in your presence and who would surely shave it all off if they had enough brains to think it through.

If these sentiments don't reassure you, Patricia Cornwell's seventeenth novel, *Blow Fly*, will. Jean-Baptiste Chandonne was born with a fine down of black hair – not just on his head but covering every inch of his body. As a child, he was treated as a worrying curiosity, hidden from the public by his embarrassed parents. As an adult he has assumed the role of monster, a 'wolfman' repellent to the eye – not merely because of his pelt, but because the condition brings with it a deformed body and a terrifyingly bestial face.

Hair hangs around this novel, clogging sinks, coming

out in tufts in people's hands, and left incriminatingly on dead bodies. Forensic science brings a magnifying lens to these hairs with medical examiner Kay Scarpetta on the case (and in fact she has met this hirsute beast before). As Scarpetta and Chandonne sharpen their claws on one another's armoury, you will be increasingly repelled by the sheer ickiness of all the hair, and will run your hand over your smooth scalp with untold relief.

And if you need further convincing that bald is best, read Monique Roffey's *Sun Dog*. Her protagonist, August, is a man who can change his bodily attributes with the seasons. In the autumn he has blood-orange hair that leaps from his head 'as if from a burning attic'. In winter he turns blue, and emits snowflakes. In spring, buds emerge from his armpits, nipples and ears. And in summer his hair comes off in swathes. It is then, at his baldest and most vulnerable, that August meets his true love. Luckily she has no interest in whether he's tufty or smooth; she loves him for himself.

SEE ALSO: **ageing, horror of**

beans, temptation to spill the

Tess of the d'Urbervilles
THOMAS HARDY

For reasons which medical science has never explained (although, naturally, we have our own hypothesis – see below), it's physically uncomfortable to keep a secret bottled up, and a great relief to let it out. And confessing – or spilling the beans – can bring not only immense relief, but also sometimes a sadistic pleasure. Because the look on someone's face during the moment of spillage can be both entertaining and gratifying (see: schadenfreude). But these positive emotions are usually short-lived, particularly if the spilling of the beans has caused pain or anguish in the spillee, or the beans were not yours to spill. Before such spillages are indulged in, therefore, the short-term gain (for you) of spilling must be weighed against the long-term consequences (for you and others). Because beans, once spilled, cannot be unspilled, and it may be better for everyone if you live with the discomfort of keeping them pent up inside instead.

If Tess Durbeyfield had lived with her beans – as her mother Joan advised her to – her marriage could have been saved and a happy ending secured. Tess's confession to her husband Angel Clare on their wedding night about her tarnished past with Alec d'Urberville is made after Angel owns up to a previous liaison of his own. She, understandably enough, sees this as the perfect moment for them both to clear their consciences. But Angel, to his great discredit, fails to forgive Tess as she has forgiven him. He rejects his sullied Tess, and heads off to Brazil in a serious sulk.

All might have been well if Tess had kept her beans inside her and waited until such time as Angel was man enough to see the situation for what it was – her as the victim, Alec as the assailant. By this time she would also have realised (as she eventually does) that the beans were not hers to feel guilty about in the first place – that they were in fact Alec d'Urberville's beans, and should have been his all along. Tess is an innocent victim of nineteenth-century patriarchy, of course, but the emotional truth still holds: she should have kept those beans inside.

A word of warning, though. If your secret is a guilty one through and through, and having weighed the pros and cons you've decided to keep the secret inside, be prepared that the discomfort may get worse over time – whether it indicts you or someone else. Bottled-up beans, like actual beans, give off a sort of gas that expands, producing flatulence and indigestion (see: flatulence) until they eventually erupt without warning, usually at the very worst possible moment. This is a situation worth avoiding at all costs, and indicates that your secret has more guilt attached than you may have realised. If you suspect that your beans might turn gaseous, find an intermediary on whom to off-load them, who can then spill them in a more considered and controlled fashion – or help you to. See: guilt for an example of an intermediary at work in this way.

SEE ALSO: **goody-goody, being a** · **guilt** · **regret**

bed, inability to get out of

Bed
DAVID
WHITEHOUSE

Perhaps you have a headache or a hangover (see: headache; hangover). Perhaps you hate your job and have declared a Duvet Day (in which case see: PMT for our list of The Ten Best Novels for Duvet Days). Perhaps your central-heating is on the blink, and you can't get warm. Perhaps everything seems pointless (see: pointlessness) or you're depressed (see: depression, general). Whatever the reason, if you know that sometimes staying in bed seems a much better idea than emerging into your day, keep this volume under your pillow (so you don't have far to stretch). Read it once, and then during subsequent attacks of the condition you will need only a brief dip to send you leaping out from under your duvet and thence into anything other than the small suburban bedroom and freakshow of a life depicted within its pages.

Malcolm Ede has stayed in bed for so long that his skin is as 'white as an institution'. He is deprived of sunlight, and drained of life. Weighing in at 102 stone, an 'umbrella of fat' pins him to his bed. After deciding for complex reasons on his twenty-sixth birthday to simply never get out of bed again, he's been there ever since. Cared for and fed by his hopelessly devoted mother, his dreamy dad and his broken brother, he is the planet around which they orbit. A great big hot-air balloon of a planet.

Malcolm escapes his carapace of flesh in the end. But unless you want to be living in your parents' bedroom aged forty-three, unless you want blisters and sores on parts of your body that you can't even see, unless you fancy being unable to even meet your hands together to pray for escape, read this then get up, out of bed, right now.*

SEE ALSO: **ambition, too little** • **depression, general** •
lethargy • **read instead of live, tendency to**

---

* And that means *now*.

bereavement

SEE: **broken heart** • **death of a loved one** • **widowed, being** • **yearning, general**

biological clock ticking

SEE: **children, not having** • **children, under pressure to have** • **shelf, fear of being left on the**

birthday blues

*Midnight's
Children*
SALMAN RUSHDIE

So you're about to be one year older, and you don't like it at all. You may fear the loss of your looks (see: vanity; baldness). You may fear the loss of your health and marbles (see: senile, going.) Well, you're not the only one (see: ageing, horror of). In fact, at this very moment, one million, seventy-six thousand, two hundred and eighty* other people on this planet are also experiencing the birthday blues. Just like Saleem Sinai, the hero of *Midnight's Children*, who shares his birthday (midnight on August 15th, 1947) with the birth of a newly independent India and one thousand others, so you too took your first breath on the same day in the same year as an awful lot of other people around the world.

You don't have to believe in astrology – or magical realism – to see that you have a special connection to these people. Just as Saleem's life is yoked to the history of his country, and to the other 'children of midnight' with whom he shares a strange telepathy and magical gifts. Think of it this way: it's already an uncanny coincidence to be alive on this planet with anyone else at all, given how long the universe has been in existence and how long it is likely to remain so into the future. To think that there are other people born the *very same day, the very same year* – well, they're practically your siblings! Doesn't it make you want to rush out into the world and wish them all Happy Birthday?

On the eve of your big day, tuck in to *Midnight's Children*

---

* Give or take a few.

along with all the other birthday boys and girls your age. Raise your glass to your extended family. Experience, simultaneously, the vibrancy and colour of this delightful novel, chuckle in tandem at its goofy humour and attention to the craziness of life. As you laugh, you will feel young again, together. Keep reading all night, as you used to do years ago. It's a long novel. From over the top of the page, watch those blues turn pink with the dawn.

SEE ALSO: **ageing, horror of** • **dissatisfaction** • **old age, horror of**

bitterness

Oroonoko
APHRA BEHN

If you feel you have been dealt an unfair hand, and deserve better, that everybody else has it easy but you; if you are outraged when things do not go your way, you may have succumbed to the scourge of bitterness. It may well be true that you were dealt a bad hand. But life is what we make it and nobody said it would be fair. Besides, people tend to shun bitter characters – in life as well as literature – as they exude anger and ill will. Unless you want to make your life even harder, we urge you to take a lesson from the magnificent Prince Oroonoko, hero of a tale of betrayal, true love and stoicism published in 1688.

Prince Oroonoko, tall, proud and strikingly regal, loves Imoinda. She loves him too – and marries him – but she is so beautiful that the King of Coramantien (present-day Ghana) falls in love with her as well, and forces her to join his harem. She and Prince Oroonoko manage to escape together, but are caught and sold into slavery. Miraculously, they find each other – in Surinam – and even conceive a child, but their plea to return to their homeland is ignored. Abandoned and betrayed, they tackle the political forces that keep them enslaved head on, and things go from bad to worse – and then to even worse still.

No-one has greater reason to be bitter than Oroonoko. Not only is his wife taken from him, but he is caught up in the terrible injustice of slavery. Right at the end, when all is

lost, Oroonoko faces a final, horrific ordeal – the dismember-
ment of his limbs, one by one. But having recently discovered the consolation of the tobacco pipe, he bears the torture
by calmly smoking, sanguine and pensive. We don't recommend that you take up smoking. But we do recommend that
you emulate Oroonoko's ability to rise above life's unfair-
ness and live life without a grudge.

SEE ALSO: **anger** • **cynicism** • **hatred** • **jealousy** • **regret** • **scars,
emotional** • **schadenfreude**

blocked, being

SEE: **constipation** • **writer's block**

blushing

*Lady: My Life as
a Bitch*
MELVIN BURGESS

Blushing is something we dread. Occurring when adrena-
lin generated by a rush of embarrassment makes the blood
vessels just under the surface of the skin expand, it turns
the visage a bright, unnatural crimson that nobody can fail
to notice. We all suffer the horror of blushing as teenagers;
and it can happen occasionally as adults (see: shyness). But
a few continue to suffer from it chronically through adulthood, to the point where it becomes a vicious circle – fearing the blush so much that the fear creates it.* The truth is
that blushing is something we respond to warmly: recent
research has shown that those who blush are seen in a positive light by their peers. But if you feel that your blushing is
a hindrance to your enjoyment of social situations, we prescribe one of Melvin Burgess's unashamedly dirty teenage
novels, *Lady: My Life as a Bitch*.

Sandra Francy is a girl of seventeen who is seriously
hot for boys. She's been hanging around with a lot of them
recently, loving every minute. But two pages in, she loses
her feminine charms in a rather shocking way. It happens
by accident. An 'alchie' in the street whom she annoys by

---

* The technical name for this is 'erythrophobia'.

knocking over his beer calls her a 'bitch'. Suddenly she's down on all fours, baring her teeth at him – and when she runs away, she's delighted by her unaccustomed speed. She has lived up to his accusation – not that she realises it for a while. Wondering why her family keep shouting at the mad dog that seems to be just behind her, she finally sees a mongrel in her bedroom mirror – and realises it's her.

Burgess handles the weirdness of the situation with consummate skill. Sandra tries to speak to her parents, and they can half hear her trying to form words. She does her best to walk on her hind legs to show them she's really human, and while they begin to believe her, they are still creeped out by the freak before them. Soon she finds herself out on the street.

And so Sandra discovers the joys of canine fun. 'Life at the edge tastes so sweet! It's steal or starve, life or death . . . Glorious days!' She fluctuates between doggy hilarity, hunting cats in clever half-human ways, and trying to find a way back to humanity. When she sees the picture of her human self on a 'MISSING' poster, she remembers her past and longs for home. But might she in fact be better off as a dog?

Certainly a constant blusher might. Immerse yourself in the uninhibitedness of this novel. Get hairy. Lose that self-consciousness that is unique to humanity. Run with the pack, clatter through deserted streets, take no heed of human laws. Dash until your pads bleed, then lick them dry. Discover your doggy nature, and your roseate cheeks will no longer concern you.

boredom

Room
EMMA DONOGHUE

Ma and I live in Room. There is one window, which is Skylight. You have to stand on Table to see through it, and then you can see Sky. There is also Bed, Wardrobe, Shelf, TV, Table, Door and Clothes Horse. Ma was all sad til I happened in her tummy. Now I am Mr Five because it's my birthday. My birthday present was a picture drawn with a

book-buyer, being a compulsive

INVEST IN AN E-READER AND/OR CREATE A CURRENT READING SHELF

We know your type. You love the look and feel of books so much that you yearn to possess them. Just walking into a bookshop turns you on. Your greatest pleasure in life is bringing the new books home and slipping them onto your immaculate shelves. You stand back to admire them, wonder what it will be like to have read them – then you go off and do something else instead.

Invest in an e-reader. By reducing a book to its words – no elegant cover, no fashionable or esoteric author name for others to notice – you will soon discover if you really want to read the book, or if you just want to own it. If it passes the test, wait until you're actually ready to read it before you press 'download' (keeping it on a wish-list in the meantime). If, and only if, you love it when you read it on your e-reader, then you may allow yourself a beautiful hard copy to keep on your shelves, to read and re-read, to love and touch and drool over, to show off to your friends, and just *have*.

If an e-reader's not for you, designate one shelf in your house a Current Reading shelf. This should be near your bed, or wherever you like to read most, and contain the half dozen books next-up on your 'to read' list. Keep the turnover on this shelf brisk. Because rule number one is that you can only buy a new book when one of the other books on your Current Reading shelf has been read and returned to its place on your general shelves. Rule number two is that you must read the books on this shelf in the order in which they arrive there, more or less. And rule number three is that if any of the books are leap-frogged more than once, or stay on the shelf for more than four months, they go to a friend or a charity shop.

No cheating! You'll be cured of your habit within the year.

pencil. It was of me with eyes shut. We pin it in Wardrobe so Old Nick can't see. Sometimes he comes in Room, after nine. Afterwards, the air is different.

Before I came Ma left TV on all day and got turned into a zombie because TV rots your brains. Now after we watch Dora the Explorer we switch it off so that the brain cells can multiply again. We have thousands of things to do every morning in Room, like Trampoline on Bed, and Simon Says, then Orchestra, where we run round and see what noises we can bang out of things. Today we cut a strip from the cereal box that's as big as her foot. Then we use it to measure Room. Sometimes we stand on Table and do Scream, and I crash the pan lids like cymbals. After, I play Telephone with toilet rolls. Sometimes Ma says she wants to hit something but she doesn't because she doesn't want to break anything. Then she says actually I'd really like to break something, I'd like to break everything. I don't like her like this. It's like when she's on and I'm off. But worse.

Today we make a birthday cake with three eggs. We keep the eggshells under Bed for making things. While the cake is in the hot stove we sit in front and breathe in the lovely air. Ma says that if people in Outside are bored, they should come and live here in Room. They'd be amazed at all the things there are to do.

SEE ALSO: **apathy** • **dissatisfaction** • **lethargy** • **mundanity, oppressed by** • **stagnation, mental**

boring, being

SEE: **anally retentive, being** • **humourlessness** • **organised, being too** • **risks, not taking enough** • **sci-fi, stuck on** • **teetotaller, being a**

bossiness

SEE: **bully, being a** • **control freak, being a** • **dictator, being a**

brainy, being exceptionally

'I don't know what good it is to know so much and be smart as whips and all if it doesn't make you happy.' So says Mrs Glass in JD Salinger's novella *Franny and Zooey* – and she should know. Mother of seven precocious prodigies who have all featured as panellists on the popular radio show 'It's a Wise Child', she has since lost her eldest (Seymour) to suicide, and is now watching her youngest (Franny) have a suspected nervous breakdown on the living room couch.

Being brainier than everyone else should, in theory, be a positive thing. But there's nothing mediocre people hate more than having their mediocrity exposed. Unfortunately this sentences the exceptionally brainy child to a lifetime of alienation. The Glass children find themselves branded either 'a bunch of insufferably "superior" little bastards that should have been drowned or gassed at birth' or the kinder but distrustful 'bona-fide underage wits and savants'. And if the exceptionally brainy are not pushed away by others, they often end up pushing others away. Clever people are easily bored and disappointed by their peers. Franny's apparent breakdown is triggered by a weekend date with her college *beau* Lane, during which she finds herself criticising him relentlessly. 'I simply could *not* keep a single opinion to myself,' she laments to her brother Zooey. 'It was just horrible. Almost from the very second he met me at the station, I started picking and picking and picking at all his opinions and values and – just *everything*.' It makes her hate herself.

In life, it's usually the Lanes of this world who get the sympathy – those 'normal' people on the receiving end of 'abnormal' behaviour. But literature likes to side with the freaks, and the exceptionally brainy will find great relief in Franny's description of her torment. Luckily, readers adore characters like the Glass siblings for the very traits for which their peers dislike them; and the exceptionally brainy should take some comfort from this.

If, like Franny and Zooey, your cleverness has cut you off from the world, it's vital not to hate the world for it (see: bitterness). Franny and Zooey eventually find a way out of their disaffection via an epiphany that allows them to see God in everyone. You may prefer to leave God out of it; the invocation really is just to love others. This charming novella will fill you with a sense of solidarity and replenish your tank of love whenever it threatens to run dry.

SEE ALSO: **different, being**

breaking up

High Fidelity
NICK HORNBY

As the songs say, breaking up is hard to do – and whether you're the dumper or the dumped, one should never go through it alone. Ideally you need your hand held by a friend who has been battered and bruised by relationship bust-ups themselves, and knows how it feels (for more of which, see: broken heart). We offer you the hand of Rob, the music-mad hero of Nick Hornby's paean to pop, *High Fidelity*. In our list of all-time best break-up novels (see below), this holds the number-one spot. For though the vinyl may have dated, the experience, the emotions, the lessons and the truths have not.

In order to make sense of his latest break-up – with live-in girlfriend Laura – Rob revisits his all-time top five most memorable splits, from the 'first chuck' inflicted by twelve-year-old Angela Ashworth who, for reasons that remain as unfathomable as they were then, decided to snog Kevin Bannister after school instead of him, to the humiliation of Charlie Nicholson upgrading to someone called Marco. Every page jangles with bells of recognition; who hasn't experienced the initial wave of tentative optimism – part liberation, part nervous excitement – that washes over you in the immediate aftermath of a break-up, only to have it wiped out by a crushing sense of loss the minute it hits you that she or he is not coming back? And who hasn't wondered which comes first, the music or the misery, as they've played out their heartache to the accompaniment of 'Love Hurts' or 'Walk on By'?

One of the hard truths Rob learns is that break-ups do not get easier the more we go through. 'It would be nice to think that as I've got older times have changed, relationships have become more sophisticated, females less cruel, skins thicker, reactions sharper, instincts more developed . . .' bemoans thirty-five-year-old Rob. And yet, with some help from Hornby, one can try to do it a bit better than the time before. The main lesson for Rob is one of commitment (see: commitment, fear of), but as you watch him pick through the shards of his broken loves, you'll soon know which lessons are meant expressly for you. Are you the sort, like the twenty-something Rob, to react to your bust-ups by flunking college and going to work in a record shop (or today's equivalent)? Do you beat yourself up, like the older Rob, for being a rejection magnet – when, in fact, you've left your own fair share of broken hearts in your wake? The wisdom of this novel may be from a decidedly masculine point of view, but there are patterns here that will map onto almost any breakup and which you can use to help you recognise the part you played. Girls will do well to remind themselves that boys cry into their pillows too. And the spurned may get a kick from the forty-something woman who tries to flog her husband's priceless record collection for fifty pounds because he's run off to Spain with a twenty-three-year-old friend of her daughter's. (Before you get any similar ideas, note Rob's impressively disciplined response and see: vengeance, seeking.)

Read *High Fidelity* and allow your heart to absorb the lessons from Rob's – and your own – past mistakes. Are you going for the wrong sort of guys/girls? Are you failing to be the solid rock that your partner needs? Or are you living your love life to the wrong soundtrack? Get it right, and this break-up will be your last.

 THE TEN BEST BREAK-UP NOVELS

SEE ALSO: **appetite, loss of** • **bed, inability to get out of** •
broken heart • **cry, in need of a good** • **lovesickness** •
sadness • **shelf, fear of being left on the** • **single, being** •
tired and emotional, being

broke, being

So you're skint. That's half the problem. Maybe you're out
of work (see: unemployment; and depression, economic) or
maybe you're spending more than you earn (see: extravagance). Either way, you're convinced that if only you had
a bit more money in the bank, all your problems would be
solved. That's the other half of the problem. We'll deal with
that half first.

James Gatz – aka Jay Gatsby – had the same stupid idea:
that money would bring him what he most longed for, in
this case, Daisy Buchanan. In ill-begotten ways, he amassed
a fortune, bought the flashiest house on West Egg, then
hurled his hundreds on stupendously extravagant parties to
lure the lovely Daisy back into his arms, like a moth to an
enchanted flame.

Gatsby is one of literature's most powerful dreamers
(hence the 'great'), and his passion and longing for Daisy
is as gorgeous to behold as the little green light at the end
of her dock. But the fact is, having more money than we
need to cover the essentials in life (food, clothes, shelter
and, of course, books) causes more problems than it solves.
Not only does it fail to bring Gatsby lasting happiness with
Daisy, but the making of it causes him to abandon and
defile his true self. What does he think he's doing calling
everyone 'old sport' in a fake English accent, owning more
shirts than he can possibly wear, and holding parties that he
doesn't enjoy? And what did he expect Daisy to do when she

discovers how he earned it all? When the flame sputters, and Gatsby goes out, he has no-one to blame but himself.

As for being broke, our cure comes in three parts. First, read *Money* by Martin Amis to remind yourself of the horrible ways in which money can taint and corrupt. Then read *Young Hearts Crying* by Richard Yates to see how an inherited fortune can obscure the path to a life of purpose and a sense of self-worth. Finally, return to *The Great Gatsby* and do what James Gatz should have done: inhabit and accept your impoverished self and find someone who loves you as you are. Then quit wasting money on lottery tickets, downsize, and learn to budget. If your job still doesn't bring in enough for the basics, get another one. If it does, stop whingeing and get on with living happily ever after within your modest means.

SEE ALSO: **tax return, fear of doing**

broken china

Utz
BRUCE CHATWIN

The percussive smash of china hitting the floor is a shock of a sound that is always impressive. Unfortunately the satisfaction it brings doesn't last long, and is quickly superseded by dismay. Broken china is strangely symbolic of the human heart – one minute so robust and whole, and the next so irreparably damaged. Luckily, unlike a broken heart, broken china can often be Araldite-ed back together.

But if your broken Davenport sugar-bowl, handed down through the generations, is beyond repair, read *Utz*. Kaspar Utz is a Czechoslovakian connoisseur of Meissen porcelain with compulsive collecting habits who becomes a prisoner to his own pieces. Jewish, he risks his life by staying in Russia under Stalin, because he cannot take his priceless artefacts with him. Such is the danger and tyranny of beautiful possessions.

But when Utz dies, having left his collection to the Rudolfine Museum in Prague, his china is nowhere to be found. Various theories are offered as to where it has vanished, and we will not spoil the ending by giving away the one that proves correct. Suffice to say, Professor Utz was finally liberated of his obsession. If, through Utz, you can learn to accept the essentially transitory nature of both lives and material possessions, you will be liberated of your upset too.

broken dreams

Requiem for a Dream
HUBERT SELBY JR

To witness the destruction of a loved one's dreams – or resign yourself to the loss of your own – is a terrible thing to go through. And it's much more common than you'd think. Because having a dream is easy, but finding the right way to make it come true is much harder – and success or failure can make or break you. If you've given up on your dreams, ask yourself if you ever really gave them a chance. As this hard-hitting novel shows, it's possible that you chose the wrong way to achieve them.

Everyone has a dream in this novel. Harry and Marion dream of having their own little business, a café with art for sale on the walls, including Marion's own. Harry's best friend Tyrone simply wants to escape the ghetto. And Sara, Harry's mother, has hopes for the mystic realms of live television, in the beam of which she spends most of her waking life.

The dreams are innocent enough; it's the way they go about realising them that's the problem. Because the key to escaping their bottom-rung lives in New York, so Harry and Marion believe, is a particularly potent type of heroin which they plan to sell at a massive profit. They test the heroin for quality, and before they know it, they're hooked. Tyrone too. Meanwhile Sara sits on her daybed, simultaneously eating chocolate and popping slimming pills, convinced she will make it onto the weight-loss show she's glued to. She never gets there.

Instead of achieving their dreams they each descend into a living hell. Read this devastating, shocking novel. It's too late for Harry, Marion, Tyrone and Sara – but it's not too late for you. Think of a practical, realistic way to achieve your dreams – one that doesn't involve the sale of Class A drugs (see: drugs, doing too many). Keep your eyes on the dream, but also on each rung of the ladder.

SEE ALSO: **disenchantment** • **hope, loss of** • **broken friendship**

broken friendship

SEE: **friend, falling out with your best**

broken heart

As It Is in Heaven
NIALL WILLIAMS

Jane Eyre
CHARLOTTE BRONTË

Rare is the person who goes through life with their heart intact. Once the arrow has flown from Cupid's bow and struck its target, quivering with a mischievous thrill, there begins a chemical reaction that despatches its victim on a journey filled with some of life's most sublime pleasures but also its most tormented pitfalls (see: love, doomed; love, unrequited; lovesickness; falling out of love with love; and, frankly, most of the other ailments in this book). Nine times out of ten,* romance is dashed on the rocks and it all ends in tears.

Why so cynical? Because literature bursts with heartbreak like so many aortic aneurisms. You can barely pick up a novel that does not secrete the grief of a failed romance, or the loss of a loved one through death, betrayal or some-such unforeseen disaster. Heartbreak doesn't just afflict those on the outward journey; it can strike even when you thought you were safely stowed (see also: adultery; divorce; and death of a loved one). Those afflicted have no choice, at least initially, but to sit down with a big box of tissues, another of chocolates, and a novel that will open up the tear ducts and allow you to cry yourself a river. Heart-rending music could accompany your read; some would say this is crucial, especially if you have a tendency to keep your emotions under tight control (see: emotions, inability to express).

It works for the father and son in Niall Williams' seriously hanky-drenching *As It Is in Heaven*, both still broken hearted and stunned by the deaths in a car crash of Philip's

---

* Studies have shown that accurate numbers aren't any more useful than the ones you make up.

wife Anne and their ten-year-old daughter some years before. Both being cut from the same cloth, retired tailor Philip and his shy, history teacher son Stephen have retreated into their separate, solitary worlds, shutting their hearts to one another and everyone else. Indeed Philip can think of little else but giving his money away to the poor and joining his wife as quickly as possible, aided and abetted by the cancer he's been diagnosed with.

But once a month, when they meet to play chess, they are enveloped by the music of Puccini. And as we meet the other inhabitants of Ennis, the small town in Ireland where they live, we watch how Stephen finds himself compelled to go to a concert despite driving his car into a ditch on the way – and everything changes overnight. For at the concert he hears Italian violinist Gabriella Costoldi, causing 'pools' of 'clear black sadness' to fill inside him, and he begins to let out his grief at last. When a thirst for the music becomes a thirst for the musician herself, Stephen's father Philip plays a pivotal role – because romantic love was the most powerful motivation in his life too. Now his greatest desire is to help Stephen find happiness with Gabriella. And as the symphony builds to its uplifting conclusion, we see how Stephen's healing brings healing to his father too. Let yourself be swept along for the ride. As this novel shows, the passage of time – and love – does heal.

Broken hearts can be redeemed – and for those refusing to give up on their lost love, we prescribe *Jane Eyre*. When Jane and Rochester's marriage ceremony is interrupted by the announcement that the owner of Thornfield Hall has a wife already, Jane is too shocked to cry – 'I seemed to have laid me down in the dried-up bed of a great river,' she says – although later the 'full heavy swing' of the torrent comes. Bereft, she forgives Rochester in an instant when he shows that he still loves her as much as ever. But the better part of her knows that there is neither 'room nor claim' for her, and despite the 'cracking' of her heartstrings, she tells him she must go. At which point it's Mr Rochester's turn to be heartbroken: 'Jane! . . . Jane, do you mean to go one way in the world, and to let me go another?' Was there ever a more heart-rending spelling-out of the pain of parting?[†]

All is not lost, however, as Jane gets her dark hero in the end – but on her own terms and with her self-respect intact. Mr Rochester, true, is a charred ruin of his former self by this time, but it doesn't seem to matter. Jane has a fortune of her own now, which enables them to meet as equals, and she never gets tired of reading out loud to him. Follow Jane's example: on no account must you attempt to mend your broken heart by compromising your integrity. Better to suffer with dignity than to self-placate in shame. And you never know who might notice and love you all the more for your strength of character and ability to endure.

It's vital to grieve when love is lost. Drop out for a while to do it. (See: cry, in need of a good, for our ten best weepies.) Don't compromise unwisely in an attempt to make yourself feel better. Cupid will strike again, either with new love or the same love, in new circumstances. And if you decide that you're better off on your own, there are plenty of solitary pleasures to be had in this book.

SEE ALSO: **appetite, loss of** • **cry, in need of a good** • **despair** • **divorce** • **falling out of love with love** • **hope, loss of** • **lovesickness** • **sadness** • **turmoil** • **yearning, general**

broken leg

Cleave
NIKKI GEMMELL

Being able to move – to walk, to run, by extension to run away – is overrated. There's much more sense in staying put. But if you've broken your leg and are wondering how you will stay sane lying in one place or hobbling around on crutches for the next few weeks, turn to *Cleave* by Australian novelist Nikki Gemmell. The title of Gemmell's debut – written in crisp, inventive prose ever aware of its sounds and contours – is an antagonym, a word that, by a freakish accident of linguistic evolution, also means its own opposite. Muse as you read on the relationship of cleave ('to split') to

---

† If there was, send it to us on a postcard, damp with tears.

cleave ('to stick fast to'). It will help you visualise the cleft nature of your bone and therefore speed up its new cleaving.

Snip, 'thin and bitten from too much life on the run', had her first taste of being on the move when her father took her from her mother twenty-five years ago. He cut her hair (hence, Snip) to make her look like a boy so no-one would find her. Now thirty, Snip has made sure that the men in her life have always had the feeling she'll be out the door any minute, so that while they're with her they're hooked. Then when she decides it's over, out the door she goes. 'No number. No forwarding address. A new town, another rupture.'

That is, until she meets Dave, a city boy who answers her ad for a companion to drive her and her Holden Ute from Sydney to Alice. Snip is quick to dismiss him as not her type. His face is 'too open', too untroubled. He 'blares' good health. He shows all the signs of having been loved very much in his life, like a rock that's been sitting in the sun. She runs away again, of course, but headlong into an experience that forces her to re-evaluate her habit.

Don't be a Snip. Be a Dave. Lie in that hospital bed with the expanse of the Australian desert unfolding in your mind (you'll particularly appreciate, no doubt, the image of 'the great stretch of blue arching above . . .[with] the shin-bone beauty of a lone ghost gum against a reddened hill beneath') and be like a rock emanating heat to those that come to your bedside. Not only will you get lots of attention, but you'll end up with new friends to go and see once you're up and about again. As the reader you invest a lot in Dave and ardently hope for Snip to find a way to cleave to him – a desire that will manifest itself in the reknitting of your bones.

SEE ALSO: **hospital, being in** • **pain, being in**

broken promise

SEE: **trust, loss of**

broken spirit

I am David
ANNE HOLM

Those broken in spirit need gentle handling. For this reason our cure is a novel for children, simple and short but with immense power. Read it to renew hope and re-build resilience when your very sense of self seems lost.

Incarcerated in an Eastern European concentration camp from the age of one, twelve-year-old David has never known what it is to be cherished by loving parents, or that there is a world outside with beauty in it. When he escapes and begins a perilous journey across Italy and northern Europe, knowing only that he must find Denmark, he has to learn how to be a person with his own will, his own rights, his own needs. 'I am David,' he says out loud one day, by way of introduction to God.

This declaration of existence and identity, of his right to be himself, becomes a sort of mantra. He repeats it throughout the book, and the phrase gains beauty and strength each time. 'Someone's broken his spirit,' one character observes. 'No', says another. 'A boy's spirit is not so easily broken.' Who is right?

Follow David's example and assert your identity to yourself and others each day. And as you watch David forge a sense of self out of nothing, decide for yourself how resilient the human spirit is. Your conclusion will herald your cure.

SEE ALSO: **hope, loss of** • **identity crisis**

bulimia

SEE: **eating disorder**

bullied, being

Cat's Eye
**MARGARET
ATWOOD**

Bullying comes in many forms. Among boys it tends to be aggressive and physical. Among girls, spiteful and verbal. And although we tend to think of it as a childhood phenomenon, it happens just as much among adults – in the workplace and at home. Both our cures are about bullying amongst young people, but they capture a common ingredient: that of the shame or bewilderment of the victim which, at least initially, prevents them from seeing the situation for what it is, and getting help. If you suspect you are being bullied, these novels will give you some perspective. You'll recognise the techniques the bullies use to assert their authority. And, depending whether you're the sort to crumble or fight back, you'll recognise one or other response.

When middle-aged Elaine returns to Toronto for a retrospective of her paintings in Margaret Atwood's chilling *Cat's Eye*, she wonders if she'll bump into her old friend Cordelia, and if so, what she will say. Cordelia was the most powerful and alluring of a trio of girls at school (the others being Carol and Grace) to whom she became joined at the hip – the one Elaine most wanted to please. Whenever Cordelia had a 'friend day', putting her arm through Elaine's and singing and laughing together, Elaine would feel gratitude – and anxiety. Because sooner or later she knew Cordelia would turn from friend to foe and, as the ringleader of the group, encourage Carol and Grace to do the same. When, in Toronto, Elaine finds a marble like a cat's eye, given to her at the time by her brother Stephen, it brings to the surface a traumatic memory she's long blanked out.

Anyone who has ever been bullied will recognise Elaine's emotional numbness, and won't be surprised at her failure to remove herself from the damaging trio. Victims of bullying often don't realise they're being bullied at first, and in what can seem a strange act of complicity, the bullied is drawn to the bully, craving their acceptance while dreading their rejection and scorn. Like Elaine, they can become so browbeaten that they lack the strength and belief in themselves to overcome their abusers (see: self-esteem, low if this applies to you). Only when things finally go too far does Elaine wake up and discover the power to walk away, if she wants to: 'It's like stepping off a cliff, believing the air will hold you up. And it does.' If you find you can map yourself onto the dynamics of this group, learn to walk away before the numbness occurs.

No such crumbling goes on between Tom and his bully

Flashman in Thomas Hughes's *Tom Brown's School Days*. No sooner has Tom arrived at Rugby school than the appalling Flashman does his best to make Tom's life a misery. Flashman threatens and physically attacks Tom, and it all comes to a head when the older boy instigates a 'burning' of Tom in front of an open fire. It is at this point that Tom decides to do something about the injustices he and his fellows experience at the hands of all the school bullies. It helps that Tom has become strong and feisty, and crucially, that he has earned the respect of older boys, one of whom comes to his aid in bringing Flashman down.

Tom's triumph over his oppressors will leave you elated and inspired; but it is Hughes's acknowledgement of the lasting damage inflicted on Tom that you may find most cathartic. Who knows how long the emotional scars will remain (see: scars, emotional)? For Elaine in *Cat's Eye* they last into middle age, but by revisiting the scene of her childhood trauma, she achieves redemption. Take heart from these two literary victims. They may have struggled with the effects of bullying for a long time, but they come out stronger in the end.

SEE ALSO: **anxiety** • **left out, feeling** • **nightmares** • **self-esteem, low** • **superhero, wishing you were a**

bully, being a

A Death in the Family
JAMES AGEE

You may not think of yourself as a bully. But if you ever purposefully inflict pain on someone more vulnerable than you in a routine, unthinking way – perhaps verbally, rather than physically – you may well be guilty of this shameful practice. If you know, deep down, that you do, we ask you to read *A Death in the Family*, winner of the Pulitzer Prize in 1958 and one of the most moving accounts of bullying that we know.

Rufus lives on a 'mixed sort of block' in Knoxville, Tennessee. It's a place where supper's at six and over by half past, at which point the children go out to play while the mothers clean the kitchen and the fathers hose down the lawns. Rufus, not yet old enough for school himself, likes to watch the older children going back and forth from school. First he watches them from the front window, then from the front yard and then from the sidewalk outside his house. Finally he dares to stand on the street corner where he can see them coming from three directions. He admires the different boxes they carry for lunches and pencils, and the way the boys swing their books in the brown canvas straps – until, that is, they start swinging them at his head. The bullying quickly builds to daily mockery and humiliation. Desperate to believe that they can be trusted – that their pretence of friendship is for real – Rufus walks into the traps they set for him again and again, much to the bullies' mounting hilarity. He is younger than all of them, and their violation of his guileless trust is exquisitely painful to witness.

Agee was a poet first and foremost and his agile prose delves into emotional crevices previously unexplored. When Rufus suffers a tragedy he is too young to fully comprehend – and the bullies make no amends – the reader's heartbreak is complete.

If you're guilty of exploiting another's weakness – whether in the playground, the home or at work – and have never paused to think about the effect of your behaviour on your victim, we defy you to read this novel and remain a bully thereafter. If you know you were a bully in your youth, see: guilt, and then move on. Sadly, you may know only too well what it's like to be bullied – as many bullies were bullied themselves initially. If you belong in this camp, switching sides is not the answer. See our cure for bullied, being, above.

SEE ALSO: **dictator, being a**

burning the dinner

The Belly of Paris
ÉMILE ZOLA

Domestically speaking, there are few things more catastrophic than burning the dinner. Whether you have slaved for hours over a *daube de boeuf*, or rustled up a *crêpe suzette*, a scorched, acrid offering fit only to be flung out on the garden path to be eaten by scavenging animals will leave you not just hungry, but ill-humoured. On such occasions, grab *The Belly of Paris*, the third novel to be published in Zola's multi-generational Rougon-Macquart saga.

It tells the story of Florent Quenu who returns to his native Paris to live with his family in an apartment on the edge of the newly rebuilt Les Halles food market. As you wander with him here, you will find meat, vegetables, fruit and cheese, all laid out before you with mouthwatering voluptuousness. Take your pick from stuffed Strasbourg tongues, 'red and looking as if they had been varnished', pâtés, casseroles, pickling jars of sauces and stocks, preserved truffles, salmon 'gleaming like well buffed silver', and peaches with 'clear, soft skin like northern girls'. Soon you'll be dribbling with desire and rushing to your nearest farmer's market for more.

Even if you hadn't burnt it, your dinner would not have been as tasty as the delicacies offered up to us by Zola. Tell this to your guests; convince them by reading from this novel aloud. And next time you go shopping, stock up on glorious fruits, and fish, and cheeses – which you can serve up without needing to turn the oven on.

burning with desire

SEE: **lust**

busy, being too

The Thirty-Nine Steps
JOHN BUCHAN

You've got a company to run (see: dictator, being a), a book shelf to assemble (see: DIY), dinner to cook for twenty (see: burning the dinner) and your best friend is in hospital (see: hospital, being in). So you're too busy to read this prescription, let alone the novel we're prescribing. But just for a minute, enter the life of Richard Hannay, and you might find an antidote.

Hannay, at the very start of Buchan's novel, is at a loose end. Just back from war in Rhodesia, with all his faculties thankfully intact, he's decided he will give the Old Country one more day to prove it's not as 'flat as soda water that's been left standing in the sun'. If it is, he'll head back for the

Veld. Then, to his rather shameful delight, he finds a dead man in his room. He's not dead in the conventional sense; the dead man proceeds to tell Hannay a very gripping tale about how he is not here at all, but is actually lying in his pyjamas, on his bed, with his jaw shot off, in another apartment in the same building.

From this moment, and for the next nine short and snappy chapters in this phenomenally pacy novel, Hannay is a fugitive. And so you will be too – from your busy-ness. So hooked will you be by his flight from the sinister man with the hooded eyes that you will have to find ways to escape your errands and grab a moment to sit down and read. You're probably someone who can multi-task, in which case read this while you run between meetings. Hannay can multi-task too. He solves a vital code while on the train to Scotland, all the while pretending to be a thickly accented farmer. He walks into the heart of a British governmental secret meeting, and works out which one of them is the German spy. Finally, he captures the infamous 'Black Stone', a ring of spies, by using his keen intuition. After spending twenty-one days in a row in constant flight from top international killers, Hannay saves the day – and the world.

Your world, on the other hand, is unlikely to combust if you don't get your jobs done. In fact, this novel will make you question whether you have taken on enough. Surely you could fit in a bit of code-solving? Farmer impersonating? Can't you get out and save the world? Until you meet Hannay, you didn't really know what *true* busyness was.

SEE ALSO: **busy to read, being too** • **children requiring attention, too many** • **exhaustion** • **live instead of read, tendency to** • **stress**

busy to read, being too

LISTEN TO AUDIO BOOKS

Your life is one big to-do list, and living is about ticking things off. You don't have time to phone your best friend – let alone to sit down with a book. But one thing we know you can do is multi-task. So we suggest you learn to inhale a book on the hoof. Kit yourself out with a supply of audio books (see: noise, too much for our list of The Ten Best Audio Books to get you started). Order a set of comfortable headphones. And next time you're busy doing something with your body which is not taxing to your mind – ironing, gardening, washing the dishes, pounding the running machine, or walking to work – listen to a novel while you're at it. You'll find that you use a different part of your brain to take in the story than you need for whatever task is at hand – and suddenly, the menial, workaday aspect of your life will be transformed. You'll soon be on the lookout for more chores to tackle. Any task will do, just as long as it earns you another half hour – and then another – with your audio book.

cancer, caring for someone with

When someone you love is diagnosed with cancer, and you suddenly find yourself in the role of carer, it can be a tremendously difficult time. Not only will you need to give your loved one emotional support, absorbing their distress as well as managing your own, but you may need to acquire the practical skills of a nurse, as well as a cook, cleaner, accountant, social secretary – indeed all the domestic duties which they cannot manage at this time. You will find you are called upon to help your loved one make choices about their treatment, to engage with doctors and play the go-between with concerned relatives and friends. You may have to deflect or encourage visits depending on how well your loved one is. And you may find it difficult to tell others when you need a break. Because who is going to support you, while you're doing all this work, giving all this care and shouldering all these worries?

It helps enormously at times of stress to read about other people who are going through similar things; watching how other people cope or fail to cope will make you feel less alone and give you strength. To this end, here are three excellent novels that explore the impact of cancer on the lives of those nearest to the patient.

The Spare Room by Helen Garner deals with both the agonising and the humorous (albeit dark) sides of caring for someone with cancer. When the narrator, Hel, hears that her old friend Nicola is coming to Melbourne to undergo alternative treatment for her end-stage bone and liver cancer, she prepares her spare room. It is very quickly apparent to Hel that Nicola is dying – and in denial about it. Hel is furious with the 'quack' Theobold Clinic for taking Nicola's money so freely and giving her false hope. She begins to feel that she must tell her friend what the therapists there, with their bogus Vitamin C treatment, are not. As her increasing duties as carer start to take over her life, her rage escalates and she battles against self-hatred – reaching the stage where she is desperate for Nicola to get on with her dying somewhere else. Garner shows immense understanding and compassion for her characters, but it is the bitter humour alongside the horror of the situation that makes this such a gripping read. This is a novel for those inclined to beat themselves up when they struggle to care for their patient 24/7. However much you want to help, you still need to function. It's also a reminder that, however serious things are, it helps to laugh.

Bodies have few secrets these days, and in the light of our ever-increasing ability to detect and predict the course of an illness, the question of honesty, and how much information is too much, is pressing. Surgeon Dr Andrés in Alberto Barrera Tyszka's *The Sickness* is in the unusual position of diagnosing his own father's cancer. The x-rays show that, without a shadow of doubt, his father Javier has a stage IV spinocellular carcinoma and there is nothing that can be done. Having spent years informing his patients that they have a terminal illness – quite brutally, he now realises – he simply cannot find the right moment to tell his father, and begins to question the whole notion of knowledge. Is it, in fact, better for the patient not to know? His relationship with his beloved father has always been good; now, for the first time, it becomes strained.

He decides to take his father on a week-long holiday to the Isla Margarita, where his father took him when his mother died. There he will calmly tell his father the news. But when it comes out, it comes at a moment of high emotion. Javier is horrified that Andrés has been keeping it from him and by the burden his illness will place on others.

Anguished and distressed, the old man's health deteriorates almost immediately, and he wishes it could all be over swiftly. The shattering of the father-son relationship is painful to watch, and serves as a reminder of how much of a strain a serious diagnosis can place on a bond, however loving. The message to take away is, perhaps, to try and maintain a sense of 'business as usual' in your relationship with your loved one – particularly if that relationship is good. The cancer brings with it enough change as it is.

The question of how to help and protect children when someone in the family is diagnosed with cancer is a fraught one. When and what should they be told? And how will the child be affected outside the home? In *A Monster Calls*, Conor O'Malley's mother is diagnosed with cancer soon after his father has left the family to live in America with a new partner. When his mother's hair falls out following chemotherapy, Conor starts being bullied at school – about her bald head, and about his increasingly odd behaviour. When his peers at school realise his mother is dying, they avoid him completely.

One night Conor is visited by a monster in the form of an ancient walking-talking yew tree. The looming tree insists that Conor must call upon his own inner reserves of strength in order to face the months ahead, telling him stories – parables which teach him ways to deal with the school bullies, and also with his grandmother who is helping, badly, to look after him. The monster acts as a catalyst, bringing Conor's confrontation with the bullies to a head, instigating the violent destruction of his grandmother's sitting-room and, ultimately, helping him find a way to accept his mother's death. Incredibly moving, this novel is not for the fainthearted. It has the power to force you to face mortality – and will hold your hand as it does so.

Looking after someone with cancer is difficult, both practically and emotionally. For a start, isolate the emotion you battle with most – see: grumpiness for instance, or guilt; empathy, lack of; anxiety; sadness; and stress. Then move on to these novels, which will help you to stand back from your particular experience and see that others have been there too. They'll take you on a cathartic journey from which you'll return with greater resilience and the understanding that to be gentle on yourself as well as your loved one is crucial to the wellbeing of you both.

SEE ALSO: **busy, being too** • **cope, inability to** • **empathy, lack of** • **tired and emotional, being** • **waiting room, being in a**

cancer, having

When you're sitting through chemo, when you're feeling weak, when your brain refuses to work, when you haven't the strength for company . . . what you need is a short and perfectly formed piece of prose.

 THE TEN BEST NOVELLAS

To the Wedding JOHN BERGER
Breakfast at Tiffany's TRUMAN CAPOTE
Do Androids Dream of Electric Sheep? PHILIP K DICK
The Good Soldier FORD MADOX FORD
The Children's Bach HELEN GARNER
Train Dreams DENIS JOHNSON
An Imaginary Life DAVID MALOUF
I was Amelia Earhart JANE MENDELSOHN
Flush VIRGINIA WOOLF
Chess Story STEFAN ZWEIG

SEE ALSO: **hospital, being in** • **pain, being in** • **waiting room, being in a**

career, being in the wrong

The Sisters Brothers
PATRICK DEWITT

It's no small thing to change career when you suspect you're in the wrong one. For a start you're probably too exhausted from doing your current job to have much time to figure out what you could be doing instead. And the thought of all those years of training and experience going down the drain makes you feel faint. As does kissing that nice silver Audi goodbye. As does the thought of the expression on your partner's face when you let drop that you've had enough of your lucrative career and fancy opening a hat shop instead.

It would spoil one of the many delightful sentences in this unputdownable novel to divulge the exact line of work the brothers Charlie and Eli Sisters are engaged in. But suffice to say, it is not an easy one to get out of alive. Set during the crazed days of the Californian goldrush, younger brother Eli starts to admit to himself that he is ill-suited to his profession after passing through a doorway around which a hairless old crone with blackened teeth has hung a string of beads – the sure sign of a hex. The beads may or may not have anything to do with it, but from that point on, Eli finds himself increasingly ashamed of who he is and what he does, and develops a tendency to make decisions which surprise his unsentimental elder brother (see: sibling rivalry). When Providence offers him a fine, strong black horse, he rejects it in order to remain loyal to his trusty Tub, a dangerously slow ride and blind in one eye. Soon he is giving his money away to strangers, newly aware of its power to corrupt.

When he comes into contact with Hermann Kermit Warm, a man who has allowed his own interests and ingenuity – plus a desire for honest friendship – to lead him to work he is passionate about, he is filled with admiration and envy. As he watches Hermann reap the benefits, both monetary and spiritual, of his labours, Eli has his Damascan moment. Initiating a shift in the balance of power between himself and his domineering elder brother, he persuades Charlie that they should join forces with Hermann, and experiences a moment of ecstatic happiness, partly because the physical nature of the work is so pleasant (standing in a river in dappled sun, with a warm wind 'pushing down from the valley'), and partly because he is being himself, a self he likes.

Stand with Eli in that river and take inspiration from Hermann Warm. If you, too, could find a way of earning money that brought you spiritual as well as financial rewards – and involved you spending your days in a way that brought you joy – what would it be?

SEE ALSO: **dissatisfaction** • **Monday morning feeling** • **seize the day, failure to** • **stuck in a rut**

carelessness

The Little Prince
**ANTOINE DE
SAINT-EXUPÉRY**

If you lived on a planet as small as the Little Prince's planet, Asteroid B-612 – so small that if you took a herd of elephants there you'd have to pile them on top of one another; that you'd have to take great care, after you'd finished washing and dressing each morning, to dig out any baobab shoots that had appeared overnight lest they take over your planet; and that one day you watched the sunset forty-four times, just by moving your chair; you'd be living a simple life that would inculcate in you the habit of carefulness. You would water the one flower that grew on your planet every day, and never forget. You would take the trouble, before you went away on a trip, to rake out your volcanoes, even the extinct one. Because you would know that it's the time and care you spend on things that makes them important. And that if you didn't take this care, you'd wake up one day to find yourself surrounded by things that were sad, feeling their unimportance themselves.

Whatever the size of your planet when you begin reading *The Little Prince*, we guarantee it will have shrunk and become much more like Asteroid B-612 by the end. And that afterwards you will live your life with more care.

SEE ALSO: **risks, taking too many • selfishness**

carnivorousness

Under the Skin
MICHEL FABER

When you pass by those fields in the springtime, do you see frolicking lambs or do you see so many Sunday roasts? Or an uncomfortable collision of the two? Whatever your take on the consumption of animal protein – whatever your religious, political or ethical stance – this novel will shatter any veneer you might have conveniently placed between yourself and the slab of meat on your plate.

To reveal exactly why Michel Faber's genre-defying novel is a cure for eating meat would be to spoil the delicious pleasure of savouring it. But we can hint. The unforgiving beauty of the Scottish landscape with its 'glimpses of rain two or three mountains away', is the only uplifting feature in the deeply disturbing events that unfold. Isserley is an attractive but strange woman who spends her days driving around the countryside. Her job is mysterious, but seems to involve picking up hitchhikers, and her car has been specially adapted for her duties. Disconcertingly, Isserley herself seems uncomfortable in her car seat and travels with the heat turned incredibly high. And the people she lives with seem afraid of her.

Essential reading for anyone debating the ethics of the food they eat; for those considering shacking up with a vegetarian and wishing to avoid culinary conflict; and for those who suffer spasms of guilt whenever they bite into what was once a cute, fluffy, innocent creature, *Under the Skin* will continue to live with you long after you finish the final page, and long after you have learnt to love tofu.

carsickness

If you suffer from carsickness, hop out and take the train instead. Train journeys offer unparalleled opportunities for immersing yourself in a book. When else does one have a guilt-free few hours to do nothing but read in the anonymous company of other readers and with an ever-changing view out the window? Trains are beloved of writers too, it seems, whisking characters off as they do to unknown futures. And there's always the chance of an unexpected liaison en route ...

 THE TEN BEST NOVELS TO READ ON A TRAIN

Possession **AS BYATT**
Murder on the Orient Express **AGATHA CHRISTIE**
Stamboul Train **GRAHAM GREENE**
Love on a Branch Line **JOHN HADFIELD**
Strangers on a Train **PATRICIA HIGHSMITH**
Mr Norris Changes Trains **CHRISTOPHER ISHERWOOD**
Leaving the Atocha Station **BEN LERNER**
The Railway Children **EDITH NESBIT**
The Train **GEORGES SIMENON**
The Wheel Spins **ETHEL LINA WHITE**

SEE ALSO: **nausea**

change, resistance to

Some of us sit like a boulder on a hill, unmoving since time began. Perhaps we have gathered some lichen over the years. Comfortable, safe, confident with who we are, the last thing we want is to change. Then along comes a fluctuation in the climate. Or maybe a passing troll. Before we know it, we are cracked, our composure spoiled and our well-made plans awry. Suddenly we find ourselves rolling down the mountain, to land who knows where, and with what emerging from our cracks?

It is understandable to be nervous of change – we get used to our comfortable crannies and the idea of climbing out of them is frightening. To deviate or question our perceived norms makes us feel vertiginous, and we wonder who we are, provoking a crisis of identity (see: identity crisis). But change is essential for growth and development and fear of change is no reason to resist it. For exhilarating proof of the essential mutability of life, we offer you the joyous *Monkey*, written by a Ming Dynasty Chinese hermit and poet in the sixteenth century.

It too begins with a rock. Since the creation of the world, the rock has absorbed the pure essences of Heaven, the 'vigour of sunshine and the grace of moonlight'. Then it becomes pregnant and gives birth to a stone egg and out of the egg comes Monkey. Monkey is an irreverent, powerful beast, with a delight in life that has him soon fearlessly embracing the seventy-two polymorphic transformations taught him by a Taoist Immortal. One day he learns to 'cloud trapeze' – hitching a ride on a cloud from one end of the world to another, and even into the Heavens themselves – and the next, he learns to turn the hairs of his body into other things, from armies to paint-brushes. He acquires a magical staff that he can tuck behind his ear, the size of a needle, or growing if he commands it to the size of the Milky Way. Indeed, Monkey's adaptability and ability to create at whim poses such a challenge to the Heavens that the Buddha decides to lock him into a mountain for 500 years to teach him some humility. Monkey's final transformation is to embrace this monkish wisdom and learn moderation. But he is still always happy to take on a new role, aiding the young monk Tripitaka on his own spiritual quest.

Stop sitting pretty in your inflexible sameness. Burst open like the boulder on the mountain, and discover the exhilaration of change and reinvention of self. You too have wisdom to attain, perhaps a pilgrim to assist, a kingdom to run. You might even find out how to use clouds as vaults which will launch you to the heavens.

SEE ALSO: **control freak, being a** • **single-mindedness**

cheating

SEE: **adultery**

childbirth

The Birth of Love
JOANNA
KAVENNA

If you're facing the great unknown of childbirth for the first time, you're probably keen to prepare yourself mentally, and may have the urge to ask anyone who looks like a mother what it entails, how it feels, and what tips they can pass on for how to get through it with minimum pain and maximum joy. But anyone who has given birth knows that it is almost impossible to convey the experience as it is, by definition, unique every time. For a less didactic approach than the latest pregnancy manual, women on the verge of delivering are encouraged to turn to fiction to find out what it's all about. Besides, it's a great time to rest on the sofa with a good novel (see also: pregnancy).

The Birth of Love by Joanna Kavenna tackles the challenge of capturing childbirth in its varied forms head on, with four interweaving stories. In the present, Brigid is going through her second labour. As we accompany her through ever agonising contractions all the way to an eventual C-section, we watch her dream of a home birth shatter. In the past is real-life scientist Ignaz Semmelweis, struggling to hold on to his sanity in a Viennese asylum after coming to the horrifying realisation that the high rate of 'childbed fever' fatalities could have been stemmed if only the doctors had washed their hands before examining their patients. Michael Stone, a novelist telling Semmelweis's story, goes through his own version of birthing pangs as he watches his first novel, *The Moon*, go out into the world to stand or fall on its own merits. And in a laboratory of the future, Darwin C, where people are kept and bred in cells, their wombs closed off and their eggs harvested at the age of eighteen, a female escapee successfully manages to bear a child in the natural way.

Giving birth – or watching a partner give birth – is perhaps the closest any of us will get to witnessing a miracle. Read this novel to prepare you for the intensity of the experience; but also to make you glad to be doing it amid the high hygiene standards of today. While Semmelweis tosses and turns, swamped in nightmares of oceans of blood – the death of thousands of women and babies on his hands; and while the parents in Darwin C, known only as 'Sperm Donor' and 'Egg Donor' are unable to touch their offspring, you can indulge in the joy of skin-to-skin contact. Brigid's story does not spare the squeamish, taking us graphically through the emotional rollercoaster and physical pain of birth. But reading it will fill you with respect for the medical staff who help her – as well as the mother herself. It'll also remind you how, the minute the baby has arrived, you'll be so swept away on a tidal wave of love that you'll forget the pain at once. Giving birth is a physical, messy, joyous and agonising thing, and whether you read this novel before, after – or, God help you, during – it will help you live the experience to the full.

SEE ALSO: **hospital, being in** • **motherhood** • **pain, being in** • **pregnancy**

children, having

children, not having

Waterland
GRAHAM SWIFT

She
**H RIDER
HAGGARD**

Pondering the positives of not having children is easy for those who are already encumbered. Acres of limitless time to read novels. Sleeping in on Sunday mornings. No plasticine or mashed banana in your hair. The simple luxury of having an uninterrupted thought, let alone a bath.

But when you have that negative space in your life, the luxury of doing what you want with your time may not have the same appeal. And for those who would have liked to have had children but, whether for practical or medical reasons, have not been able to, the absence of a child can bring acute feelings of loss and grief. Certainly it does for Mary, the wife of history teacher Tom Crick in Graham Swift's masterful *Waterland*, whose botched abortion by the hands of a reputed witch when she is just sixteen leads to her subsequent infertility. For years the couple seem to get along well in their childless state, but at the age of fifty-three Mary leaves everyone gobsmacked when she kidnaps a baby left in its pram by the turnstiles at the supermarket.

Swift's whimsical novel meanders eel-like through several generations of Cricks and Atkinsons on the watery Fens of eastern England, making as it goes a magnificent case for people being so moulded by the landscape from which they come that their destinies are written in its mud. Because this is a place of 'unrelieved and monotonous' flatness where, like the silted rivers, spirits are so 'sluggish' with phlegm, 'despite the quantities of it they spat out', that melancholia and its accompaniments – suicide, drinking, madness, acts of violence – are inevitable. Mary, it seems, cannot escape her beginnings. As Tom Crick asks his students on the eve of his enforced retirement following his wife's shameful arrest, 'How do you acquire, in a flat country, the tonic of elevated feelings?'

Of course one can't change the past. But one can change one's vision of the present and the future. The message to take from this novel is that, unlike Mary, we can choose to let go of what we imagined our lives to be. If things haven't turned out the way you thought they would, do not, like Mary, dwell on your preconceptions. That way lies insanity. Start afresh. Be someone else. (See: change, resistance to).

To that end, we offer you a thrillingly positive outlook on childlessness in the form of H Rider Haggard's *She*, the fantastical nineteenth-century tale of a white queen ruling over a lost kingdom in an undiscovered realm of Africa. She, or Ayesha to her friends, uses her child-free years to become a goddess among men. Not only does she *not* lose her looks, but she manages to stay alive for 2,000 years. With that much time to put into her career, she does become something of a megalomaniac, it's true. Known as She-who-must-be-obeyed, Ayesha makes the most of her thirst for knowledge, and eventually holds the enigmas of the universe at her fingertips.

She and its companion piece *Ayesha: The Return of She* are royal adventures and rollicking reads – all the better enjoyed for not having constant interruptions from any progeny. Let these spirited novels show you how to glory in your child-free life and use your time and energy to develop other qualities – wisdom, worldly success, and never-ending desirability, for a start. What else will you add to the list?

SEE ALSO: **children, under pressure to have** • **empty-nest syndrome** • **fatherhood, avoiding it** • **yearning, general**

children, trapped by

SEE: **trapped by children**

children requiring attention, too many

DESIGNATE A READING HOUR

If you are like the old lady who lived in a shoe, with an excess of children at your feet requiring love, food and cleansing, the only real option is to do as the Victorians did and declare a quiet hour after lunch when everybody reads a book. If the mites are too young to read by themselves, settle them down to an audio book. During reading (or listening) hour, no-one is allowed to make a noise, except to giggle or weep in response to the written (or spoken) word. Once it's over, they can demand your attention once more – and you can enjoy telling each other about what you have read (or heard). You might be surprised by how much they come to enjoy it. If your children struggle to last an hour, try reading aloud together. Sharing a book you love with your children, particularly if it's around a fire, is probably the most idyllic way to spend restful time together that we know.

children, under pressure to have

We Need to Talk About Kevin
LIONEL SHRIVER

If you are sick of justifying your childlessness; if you are happy with your life as it is and don't want to spoil things; if you think that the world is populated enough already; if you know that you'd make a useless parent; if you like your nights uninterrupted, and your cream sofa without fingerprints, then the next time someone asks you when they're going to hear the patter of tiny feet in your house, send them this novel for Christmas. They won't ask you about it again.

SEE ALSO: **children, not having** • **thirty-something, being**

Christmas

A Christmas Carol
CHARLES DICKENS

Christmas can be a time when all your afflictions seem to come at once. If you have a big family, you'll be stuck under one roof with an extended bunch of relatives (see: family, coping with), which may include a number of over-excited children (see: motherhood; fatherhood; trapped by children). You will probably spend as much in one month as you normally spend in three (see: broke, being; tax return, fear of doing); you'll certainly eat too much (see: gluttony; obesity) and get wind (see: flatulence), and maybe even diarrhoea (see: diarrhoea) or the opposite (see: constipation), and end up paying the penalty from an excess of drink (see: hangover; or, if you're a veteran of many punishing Christmases: alcoholism). If you're married or have a partner, one of you will no doubt have a few run-ins with the in-laws (see: mother-in-law, having a) which may result in a run-in with one another (see: married, being). If you have a boyfriend/girlfriend, you will probably be forced to answer personal questions about this relationship (see: coming out; children, under pressure to have). And if you are single, you will be asked why (see: single, being) which may make you wish you weren't (see: shelf, fear of being left on the) and leave you feeling unbearably lonely (see: loneliness). If you don't have a large family, or are spending Christmas with just the dog, you may indeed feel lonely (again, see: loneliness) or be missing your family (see: family, coping without). All in all, Christmas is an experience very likely to lead to loss of faith (see: faith, loss of) and a desire to lock yourself in a dark cupboard all alone (see: misanthropy).

In these pages you will find cures for all of the above. As preventative medicine, read them slowly, over the course of the year, to steel yourself for the big day. And when it comes, announce to your family, partner, Granny or potted plant that instead of a film on Christmas Day you will be reading aloud to them, around the fire, mulled wine and roasted chestnuts to hand, the multi-generationally appealing *A Christmas Carol* by Charles Dickens.

It is a brilliant ghost story. Ebenezer Scrooge: lonely, old, covetous, mean. Bob Cratchit: a beaten, ground down, humble employee, though cheerful. Tiny Tim: adorable, at death's door, son of Cratchit, and pathetic. Jacob Marley: solicitous, vengeful, deceased, alarmist, and a colleague of Scrooge's. They combine to tell a tale that has all the comfort and charm of a children's classic while also being satisfying for adults. Revel in those ghostly apparitions. Gasp with dismay at Scrooge's pointless greed and the endless postponement of his marriage. Cry tears of pity for Tiny Tim. Jubilate with all at the end. 'I am as light as a feather, I am as happy as an angel, I am as merry as a schoolboy. I am as giddy as a drunken man,' trills Scrooge. It was Dickens who perpetrated the myth that we should expect a white Christmas; who first exhorted us to 'Keep Christmas Well', to make merry and to give what we can to others. In other words, he is largely responsible for making it what it is now. So make Dickens an annual tradition. A lovely sense of warmth will pervade your heart – and the hearts of your rellies – as you read. Indeed, you may well find that even more come next year. And if you are on your own at Christmas, offer yourself as a reader to a nearby family. Put on your best Dickensian voice. By diluting the family dynamic you may be doing them more of a favour than you know.

city fatigue

The City and the City
CHINA MIÉVILLE

Life in the city can grind you down. The commuting, the hoards, the rush, the anonymity. The drab dreariness of unending concrete, the flashing billboards, the litter, the crime. If your city is making you sick, we implore you not to step foot outside your door again without first medicating yourself with *The City and the City* by China Miéville. Quite simply the best novel about living in a city we know, Miéville's deeply unsettling, yet wholly familiar tale will put a 3D lens on what you had only before seen in 2D.

Because when you walk down the streets of the fictional city Beszel you must 'unsee' those people who are walking next to you on the street, but are in a different city – a second city, called Ul Quoma, which occupies the same geographical space. To inhabit these overlapping cities successfully, you must study the architectural quirks, the clothing and even the gait and mannerisms of those living in your city, and how they differ from those living in the parallel city. If you cross from one city to another, you are 'in breach'; if you commit breach, you disappear.

Inspector Tyador Borlú has been called to investigate the murder of a female student named Mahalia, which takes place in the city of Beszel. A thoughtful and intelligent man, he soon realises that the murder breaches all the rules of living in either city. An academic named Bowden – who once claimed there was a third, unseen city called Orciny between Beszel and Ul Quoma – is summoned. Mahalia seems to have stumbled upon this third city and was conducting her own investigations into its existence, as a curious academic who got sucked into a dangerous underworld.

The brilliance of this gripping novel – part detective story, part conceptual thriller – rests on the chilling familiarity to us of a subconscious state of 'unnoticing'. How many times have we, too, ignored people in our own city because to interact with them may be unsafe? Miéville messes with your brain so immeasurably that you will never be able to look at your own urban sprawl in the same way again. The metropolis you thought you knew will take on a completely new sense of space, reality and possibility. And you might find yourself seeing a lot of people that you somehow missed before.

claustrophobia

Little House on the Prairie
**LAURA INGALLS
WILDER**

If you've a tendency to suffer from claustrophobia, never enter an enclosed space without *Little House on the Prairie*, second of the nine novels in the much-loved series of settler life by frontierswoman Laura Ingalls Wilder. In an instant, you'll be taking up the reins on the high seat of the covered wagon and riding over the enormous, open Kansas prairies, grasses 'blowing in waves of light and shadow', and a great blue sky overhead. There you'll find Pa – crystallised for ever in our minds with the helmet of thick black curls on actor Michael Landon's head – splitting logs with swings of his axe, while Ma sits in the shade of the cabin stitching a patchwork quilt and Laura and her sisters hunt for birds' nests in the long grass, their sunbonnets bouncing against their backs. Before long, you'll be so plumb tuckered out you'll be needing a scrub in the tin wash basin, with fresh water brought from the creek. Then you'll sit down to an open-air supper of cornmeal mush and prairie-hen gravy while the notes of Pa's fiddle wind up into the huge starry sky.

And you'll have forgotten you are crammed into an immobile elevator with fifteen other people, your nose pressed into someone else's armpit and no EXIT sign or ventilation duct in sight.

SEE ALSO: **anxiety • panic attack**

coffee, can't find a decent cup of

The Coffee Story
PETER SALMON

Many of us are familiar with the rage that descends when in dire need of a decent cup of coffee. The very suggestion that such crimes against nature as 'instant' coffee or 'camp' coffee could be a reasonable substitute are enough to send the coffee addict into a paroxysm of gut-clenching withdrawal (see: cold turkey, going). Can literature help at such times? We suggest holing up with some gentle encouragement to steer clear of the rocket fuel – or at least cut down – because if it's a choice between bad coffee or none, you might as well abstain. The following novel offers you a lot of reasons for not drinking Java, but it can't help but sing a paean to the bean at the same time. So you will be consoled by this cure, as well as encouraged to hold back.

Theodore T Everett lies propped up on his deathbed, sipping a coffee 'so weak you could read a book through it'. He is determined to tell us the tempestuous story of his life – a life that contained 'a wife here and a wife there', dreams of Africa, Africa itself, an awful memory of bullets hitting flesh, a broken coffee-table, a dead child. Amongst it all, the one constant is coffee, the drink that made it possible to keep going. Teddy is the last in a line of white coffee moguls who built their wealth on the back of the aromatic bean.

Everett's intimate knowledge of what coffee does to us physiologically is horribly fascinating. How coffee neutralises the neural inhibitor, adenosine, throughout the body, so that the consumer experiences a rise in nervous activity. So far, so good, thinks the coffee lover. But also how the body reacts by creating additional adenosine, in the expectation that this will be neutralised by more coffee. If more coffee does not come, then the coffee lover begins to experience light-headedness, nausea and flushing. All of which gives a jolt to the gut not unlike the first hit of coffee of the day. On top of that, we learn of the rotten roots of the coffee trade.

Everett's story is a grim one, admitting and revelling in addiction while scorning and deriding it too. It will work on you like a sobering draft of cold water. At the very least, you'll be reminded to make sure your coffee is from a non-exploitative source. And it may well plant the bean of the idea that alternative beverages would be better for your spiritual and physical health.

Now, let that percolate through your system.

SEE ALSO: **cold turkey, going** • **concentrate, inability to** • **constipation** • **cope, inability to** • **headache** • **irritability** • **lethargy**

cold, common

There is no cure for the common cold. But it is an excellent excuse to wrap up with a blanket, a hot water bottle and a comforting, restorative read.

THE TEN BEST NOVELS FOR WHEN YOU'VE GOT A COLD

A Study in Scarlet ARTHUR CONAN DOYLE
Memoirs of a Geisha ARTHUR GOLDEN
The Princess Bride WILLIAM GOLDMAN
Journey to the River Sea EVA IBBOTSON
The Secret Life of Bees SUE MONK KIDD
Comet in Moominland TOVE JANSSON
Jamaica Inn DAPHNE DU MAURIER
The Lost Art of Keeping Secrets EVA RICE
The Devil Wears Prada LAUREN WEISBERGER
The Age of Innocence EDITH WHARTON

SEE ALSO: **man flu**

cold turkey, going

To combat the physical and emotional agony of weaning yourself off an addiction, you need books that hook, compel, and force you to search your weather-beaten soul. Full immersion is recommended, as is the option of aural administration.

THE TEN BEST NOVELS FOR GOING COLD TURKEY

Journey to the End of the Night LOUIS-FERDINAND CÉLINE
Stuck Rubber Baby HOWARD CRUSE
The Neverending Story MICHAEL ENDE
Ask the Dust JOHN FANTE
Neverwhere NEIL GAIMAN
Oblomov IVAN GONCHAROV
Blood Meridian CORMAC MCCARTHY
King Rat CHINA MIÉVILLE
Nausea JEAN-PAUL SARTRE
The Chrysalids JOHN WYNDHAM

SEE ALSO: **anxiety • appetite, loss of • concentrate, inability to • headache • insomnia • nausea • paranoia • sweating**

coming out

If you're lesbian, gay, bisexual or transgender, coming out – first to yourself and then to other people – can take years, and sometimes a lifetime. Indeed it may never happen at all. But however hard it is, it can't be harder than for Jeanette in Jeanette Winterson's heavily-drawn-from-life novel, *Oranges Are Not the Only Fruit*. Adopted for the express purpose of being raised as a 'servant of God' by her fundamentalist Christian mother, Jeanette is forced to undergo an exorcism by the church to which she and her mother belong when they discover her preference for girls.

Jeanette does not want to shock her mother, or push her away. And when she tries to tell her mother what it is she feels for Melanie, her difficulty in getting the words out will ring bells for many readers – for her mother, 'very quiet, nodding her head from time to time', clearly just does not want to know. She has erected an impenetrable wall between herself and her daughter; and as soon as Jeanette stops speaking, her mother says 'Go to bed now,' and picks up her Bible as if it were a literal manifestation of this wall. In a way it is, for when, eventually, she turns her daughter out of the house, leaving her with no home, no money and no friends (if this is familiar, see: abandonment), it is the church that she evokes as her justification. Mrs Winterson's response is so clearly absurd, so clearly lacking in empathy, that it will strengthen your resolve to assert who you are to the world. If they can't handle it, that's their problem, not yours.

Thankfully, there are more positive coming-out tales to latch on to in literature – and one of our favourites is the delightful, rich gay epic that spans the Fifties to the Eighties, *Like People in History* by Felice Picano. The coming-out experiences of its two male protagonists are almost entirely celebratory, occurring as they do within the context of the newly emerging gay rights scene in Sixties America, and part and parcel of the hedonistic, drug-drenched party culture.

Cousins Roger and Alistair first meet at the age of nine, when Alistair is precociously cool and camp – already at ease with his burgeoning sexuality – while the baseball-playing Roger has yet to recognise his own. Alistair comes out to his family when caught rather marvellously *in flagrante* with the Italian gardener. For both men, stepping into their homosexuality is associated with joy, compassion and tenderness – wishful thinking for some, maybe, but certainly an inspiration. And with a confident character like Alistair, who does not care what others think of him, one can start to see how, by leading the way and being blasé and untroubled by the fact of homosexuality oneself, one might plant the idea of a nonchalant acceptance into the minds of those you are telling.

Though Roger lives for a while in Alistair's shadow, he eventually falls for an Adonis – a macho Navy veteran with a damaged leg who writes poetry (does it get any better?) *and* loves him back (yes it does!). Their relationship hits complications after a while but their deep love lasts a lifetime and must be one of the best examples of enduring love in literature, gay or straight. Every would-be out-and-proud gay man or woman fearful of announcing themselves to the world – and of finding and holding on to true love in the smaller homosexual pool – should commit this vital, exultant novel to heart.

SEE ALSO: **homophobia**

coming too soon

Pamela
SAMUEL
RICHARDSON

Our dear Reader,

Our hearts bleed for your distress. This is the most terrible of Maladies. For if your shame be to ejaculate without ado when you experience contact with your esteemed Spouse (for of course you would not countenance the taking advantage of a Boldfaced Jade such as Pamela, that serving girl who is lowly and base despite her verified prettiness), then we hereby offer your Cure. You must without delay read this most powerful of volumes, *Pamela*, penned by the right

admirable Samuel Richardson, which is so very command-
ing in its intrigue. Indeed it has come to our attention that
in one village this tome was read aloud by the Blacksmith
at weekly meetings by the well, and such was the jubilation
at the justified conclusion of the story that the bells of the
church were rung for all to hear!

Reader, let your wife lie with you and if the urge to yield
to the violence of your passion is overwhelming, you must
meditate upon the vicissitudes of Mr B, who was so drawn
to his Sauce-box maid that he attempted to ravish her in the
summer house on more than one occasion. Naughty as she
then knew him to be, the pert creature resisted him for several hundred pages during which you, the reader, will be on
tenterhooks of desire, desperate for the climax of the novel.
This payoff is so long coming that you will train your Will,
and your Organ, to withstand the temptation of arriving at
too early a fruition.

Written in letter form from this Jade to her parents and
back again, we hear tell of Pamela's sore trials at the hands of
Mr B, who locked her up and attempted her ravishment several times. However, her great piety and intelligence meant
that at last she had him by the short and curlies and, Reader
– she married him!

We regret that we have hereby revealed the happy consummation of the novel. But in truth, dear reader, we are not
very good at holding in that which excites us ourselves. And
since this is a long and saucy read, well worth the undertak-
ing, your Virtue if you keep going to the end will be Reward-
ed. This will improve your habits. And when you reach the
end, you will verily swoon with joy at the Coming you will
have at the Ripe and Proper time.

Your ever faithful bibliotherapists,
Berthoud and Elderkin

SEE ALSO: **dissatisfaction**

commitment, fear of

Blindness
JOSÉ SARAMAGO

When you begin a sentence by the Portuguese writer José Saramago, you are making a commitment to follow it wherever it goes, because this ingenious writer does not follow the normal rules of grammar, but uses commas in unexpected ways, ways that will have your inner grammarian's jaw dropping open and your outer one reaching for his or her red pen, surely that was a clause, and this is another, shouldn't there be a full stop in between or at the very least a semicolon, and your inner and outer grammarians are right, of course, but Saramago is right as well, he knows exactly what he's doing, and by the end of the first two paragraphs he will have you hopelessly ensnared by these sentences which flow from one to the other with an unstoppability that mimics the silent and terrifying epidemic of blindness which gives this novel its title and the cause of which nobody can explain.

Because in an unnamed city at an unspecified moment in history, the inhabitants begin to go blind, quite suddenly, one by one. And as the narrative moves between one unnamed character and the next, from the young prostitute with the dark glasses to the car thief to the ophthalmologist and his wife, so we submit to the surreal and powerful accumulation of sentences, and any resistance to Saramago's unconventional style that we might have felt at the start is soon forgotten.

Because the rewards of commitment – whether to a sentence, a novel, a relationship, or indeed to anything you believe may have value and which you decide to believe in – are great, as is about to be demonstrated within the story of *Blindness* itself. For in the mental asylum where the blind are quarantined in an attempt to stem the epidemic, and where armed guards stand at the gates ready to shoot should anyone try to escape, conditions quickly descend into squalor and disrule as the helpless inmates fight over the limited rations of food. And in the midst of all this, the wife of the ophthalmologist looks after her husband, tenderly, carefully, devotedly. In a moment of great foresight which shines out from all the horror, the eye doctor's wife, her vision mysteriously intact, has managed to inveigle her way into the asylum with him, pretending to be blind herself so that she can stay by her husband's side. When he has been to the toilet, she washes him. When he needs to move, she guides him. She realises that if anyone discovers she is sighted, they might use her to their own ends, and so she takes great care to continue to act as if blind – not just to protect herself but also so that she can continue to look after her husband.

The invisible actions of the wife are the actions of a woman for whom loyalty, love and commitment come first, and are not questioned. From the moment the blindness strikes her husband, the doctor's wife is fighting first for him and then the others who share their ward, because by dint of being the first to go blind, this group which includes the ophthalmologist and the prostitute form a familial bond, one that is maintained and strengthened by acts of kindness and support, and by finding humour and hope in amongst the hell. It leaves us in no doubt that if they survive it will be because of their commitment to one another. It is also what enables them to keep their humanity, while everyone around is losing theirs.

Whether it is to a novel, a relationship, a job or a dog you struggle to commit, let Saramago and the doctor's wife be your teachers. You can practice with this novel. When you begin the first sentence, commit to all the others. When you put it down, commit to Saramago's oeuvre (this won't be hard: once hooked by *Blindness*, you'll want to read all the rest). And after reading Saramago, when your transformation from commitment-phobe to one willing – nay, eager – to jump with two feet into anything, in life or in literature, however unfamiliar the prose style, however seemingly hard the ideas, however daunted you are by the prospect, we offer you the ultimate test: Proust. You will never be better prepared.

SEE ALSO: **coward, being a · give up halfway through, tendency to · starting, fear of**

common sense, lack of

Common sense is the ability to make sound decisions about the everyday matters of life. Such as cleaning the floor with a mop rather than a toothbrush. Or going through the empty field rather than the one with the bull. If you lack common sense, you may find that you lead a rather inconvenient – not to say frightening – life. To cure this lamentable lack, read Stella Gibbons's much-loved Gothic spoof, *Cold Comfort Farm*, which parodies the novels of the era (1930s), and will introduce you to an unforgettable character from whom you have a lot to learn.

Nineteen-year-old Flora Poste is full of practical, good common sense which she is determined to inflict upon her less sensible relatives. Finding herself an orphan (see: abandonment), she feels a need to sort out stray members of her family, and thus writes to all her living relatives to ask if she can come and live with them. (If you find yourself in a similar state, see: homelessness.) The most intriguing – and not just for the address – are those at Cold Comfort Farm, in the village of Howling, Sussex, who claim that 'there have always been Starkadders at Cold Comfort', and that because these Starkadders did some nameless wrong to her father, they would be pleased to give her a home and redress it. Flora had averred that she would not go if she had any cousins at the farm called Seth and Reuben, because 'highly-sexed young men living on farms are always called Seth and Reuben, and it would be such a nuisance', but in the end she doesn't have a chance to find out their names in advance. Off Flora goes, carrying, as she always does, a copy of *The Higher Common Sense* by Abbé Fausse-Maigre under her arm, sending a telegram to her friend on arrival: 'Worst fears realised darling Seth and Reuben too send gumboots.'

What she finds is that Aunt Ada Doom has been lurking in the attic at Cold Comfort ever since, as a small child, she 'saw something nasty in the woodshed'. Running the farm with an iron rod from this safe haven, she frankly has rather a good life up there, being brought three meals a day and not having to do any work. Flora conquers her fear of Ada, and cleverly uses a copy of *Vogue* as a means of luring her out into the world. With her breezy, optimistic, common sense solutions, she goes on to sort out pretty well everyone, herself included, and we forgive her for being shallow, bossy and opinionated.

Flora really does leave her relatives a lot better off than she found them and you too will be far less likely to get yourself foolishly impregnated, left to run a farm that you have no interest in, living out the rest of your days in an attic (see: agoraphobia), or muttering darkly about family secrets after reading this hilarious, bracing tome. Give it to all your unsensible friends and relations, and if anyone gives it to you, you'll know exactly what they think of you.

SEE ALSO: **risks, taking too many**

confidence, too little

SEE: **bullied, being** • **confrontation, fear of** • **coward, being a** • **neediness** • **pessimism** • **risks, not taking enough** • **seize the day, failure to** • **seduction skills, lack of** • **self-esteem, low** • **shyness**

confidence, too much

The Golden Ass
APULEIUS

So you reckon you're something. A mover-shaker. You can deal with anything life throws at you. You know how to do it all, don't need any help, thanks very much. You are the King of Karaoke, the Queen of Comedy, and frankly, you can do it on your head with aplomb.

We applaud you. Confidence can be self-fulfilling and infectious, after all. But being over-confident can easily stray into the realms of arrogance (see: arrogance). It is not quite the same thing, though, because the over-confident tend to do what they do with a grin rather than with a smirk. They are delighted with themselves, rather than pleased they are better than everyone else. Which makes them much more likeable. But what do your friends, O over-confident one, say about you behind your back? Do they think you are

concentrate, inability to

GO OFF-GRID

When so many ways of bamboozling our brains are available to us, from the constant visual stimuli of the internet to the audio assault of podcasts, the tactile temptations of tablets, and the compulsion of social networks – all offering tasty nuggets that can be gulped rather than savoured – it is out of step with the zeitgeist to focus on a book. What's worse, many of us seem to have lost the skill of concentrating on one thing for long stretches at a time. We are so accustomed to leaping from one brightly coloured flower to another, moving on as soon as we feel the smallest twinge of boredom or mental exertion, that sitting down with a book – which may take some time before it offers up its precious nectar – is uncomfortable and hard.

Don't let your brain fragment. Declare an afternoon a week to go off-grid. Two hours minimum, no upper limit. Switch off phones and disconnect from all possible sources of distraction. Then go somewhere else entirely, with a good book. It doesn't matter where you go (though a reading nook is recommended – see: household chores, distracted by) – the key is to have guaranteed hours of interruption-free thought. Slowly, your brain will piece itself back together, and continuity and calm will return.

a bit cocky? If so, rein yourself in with the help of Lucius Apuleius's *The Golden Ass*.

Written in the second century AD, this adaptation of an earlier Greek fable is the only Latin novel to survive in its entirety. According to Pliny the Younger, historian and philosopher of this period, storytellers would preface their street-corner entertainments with a shout of 'Give me a copper and I'll tell you a golden story'. This, then, is a golden story, designed to be engrossing, full of extravagant language, and containing a moral at the end.

Its hero, also named Lucius, is waylaid while on business to Thessaly by a desire for a magical experience. He has always been curious about the arts of personal transformation, and when he meets an attractive slave-girl named Fotis, he begins a sexually athletic affair with her, not just because he likes her, but because he has heard that she may have access to ointments and spells that could transform him into an owl. Desperate to try his hand at metamorphosing himself, Lucius persuades Fotis to obtain some of her mistress's powerful ointment. He rubs this onto his skin, saying the magic words – and seconds later he can only communicate his fury to Fotis by rolling his huge, watery, donkey eyes. It turns out that she muddled her ointments. But she reassures him that all he needs to do is find some roses to eat, and they will bring him back to human form.

As it transpires, Lucius spends twelve months in the ass's skin, roaming in search of the restorative flower from one rose season to the next. And though he delights in the unaccustomed enormity of his masculine organ, and enjoys his hirsute state (he was going bald when a man*), he is constantly thwarted in any opportunities he might have for fun. His inner voice is wry and self-deprecating, always humorous but vividly descriptive of his strange and troubling state. His adventures as an ass, under almost constant threat of death from bandits, cruel masters and from the fruits of his own foolhardy escapades, bring him closer and closer to true humility.

---

* If this chimes a chord with you, see our cure for baldness.

Luckily his transformation doesn't last forever. And as a symbol of having renounced his vain affectations, he decides that he will now wear his human baldness with pride. By the end of this frequently hilarious and constantly entertaining novel, you will feel as though you too have worn the ears of the ass for long enough to have attained the humility that Lucius gains himself. The moral of the tale for both the Romans and for you is that the over-confident will indeed be brought low.

SEE ALSO: **arrogance** • **optimism** • **risks, taking too many**

confrontation, fear of

My Name is Asher Lev
CHAIM POTOK

We who fear confrontation are the natural peace-makers – or, to put it less kindly, the pushovers, the oh-let's-just-do-it-your-way types. We give in at the slightest sign of disagreement. Yes, we do! Well, if you say so, we don't. But our greatest fear is an argument. And we will do anything to avoid one. We will eat our words, smile through our rage, mutter self-deprecatingly and let the other party take all. Then we are left seething internally, the unresolved conflict festering until it either erupts more violently another day (see: rage), or simmers for several decades, causing intangible but real pain.

Overcoming your fear of confrontation is essential if you have any hope of dealing with conflicts as and when they arise, which they inevitably will. We suggest you study the eponymous hero of Chaim Potok's *My Name is Asher Lev*. Asher finds himself in conflict with his parents from a very young age because of his prodigious talent for painting. Being Hasidic Jews, his parents don't think art is an honourable thing to do. But Asher is unable to control his own talent. He draws constantly, sometimes subconsciously. One day at school, a face appears in fountain pen on an inside page of his Chumash. Fellow pupils are outraged at this desecration of the holy book, and Lev's parents feel personally attacked. But Asher's habit of repressing his artistic ability is already so advanced that he has no memory of even drawing the picture.

The conflict within the family is painful to behold, as Asher's parents strive to understand their complicated son. His mother, Rivkeh, is damaged by the loss of her dead brother and is terrified that Asher will also disappear; and he does not help this by staying out late at the museum drawing without letting her know where he is. She is forever torn between her husband and her son. Asher's father Aryeh is permanently disappointed with Asher's choices and things are often explosive when the two do spend time together. The leader of the Ladover Hasidic community has a profound influence over all of them. A wise and powerful man, he speaks to Asher in ways that make him listen and take note, gently reminding the young man where his loyalties should lie. 'They tell me the world will hear of you one day as an artist,' he says. 'I pray to the Master of the Universe that the world will one day also hear of you as a Jew. Do you understand my words?' The rebbe does not disapprove of Asher's artistic ability, but he desires that the young man should be as committed a Jew as he is an artist. Asher's way of dealing with all these conflicts of interests is to pretend they don't exist for as long as possible – and as a result is left tormented for years.

Whether your conflict is born of differing beliefs, ambitions, approaches to living or simply domestic issues, face it before it escalates into estrangement or worse.

SEE ALSO: **violence, fear of**

constipation

Shantaram
**GREGORY DAVID
ROBERTS**

Some novels make you want to keep it all in; others make you want to let it all come out. This sprawling, voluminous novel set in the poverty-stricken slums of Bombay written by Australian ex-bankrobber Gregory David Roberts will have you unblocked in no time at all. Read it for its narrator's great warmth, its embracing of all that is spirited and lawless inside. Read it for the ease with which the words tumble out, raising up this city of twenty million with its choking heat and dirty mirages and the acre upon acre of shanty town made of reclaimed junk in which people go about their lives: eating, smoking, arguing, copulating, haggling, singing, shaving, birthing, playing, cooking and dying, all in full view of one another. Read it for its lovely list of soft fruits which may loosen your small intestines like a lexical laxative: paw paw, papaya, custard apples, *mosambi* (sweet lime), grapes, watermelon, banana, *santra* (orange), mango. And, above all, read it for Prabaker's description of the male slum-dwellers' morning 'motions', which occur en masse from the side of a jetty, young men and boys squatting with their buttocks to the ocean in convivial harmony, able to spectate at will on one another's progress, or lack of it. 'Oh yes!' says Prabaker, the narrator's friend, urging him to come to the jetty, as he knows other people are waiting for them. 'They are a fascinating for you. You are like a movie hero for them. They are dying to see how you will make your motions.'

With this image of bare buttock cheeks doing their business in public engraved on your memory, you will be forever grateful for your own private toilet, and eager to make use it. And if, when you get there, the long-awaited 'motions' fail to motate, this doorstopper of a novel will keep you marvellously entertained while you wait.

SEE ALSO: **irritability**

control, out of

SEE: **adolescence** • **alcoholism** • **carelessness** • **drugs, doing too many** • **rails, going off the** • **risks, taking too many**

control freak, being a

The Teahouse of the August Moon
VERN SNEIDER

You know the way you like things. So you like to keep things that way. And you like to tell everyone around you the way you like things, so that they can keep things that way too. Why should you listen to anybody else when you already have things under control?

We'll tell you why. Because you're a control freak and nobody likes you. Because being a control freak is hard, endless work which rarely yields good results. And because there's another, better way to be, and no book shows this more cleverly, or more charmingly, than *The Teahouse of the August Moon*.

Captain Fisby has nothing under control. As an American official in post World War II occupied Japan, he is tasked with implementing Plan B in the village of Tobiki. Plan B dictates that the thatched village schools be pulled down and replaced with brick, pentagon-shaped schools; and for every village to have a Women's League, with lectures on democracy and chicken aspic on the menu for luncheon (Plan B having originated with Mrs Purdy and her Tuesday Club back in Pottawattamie, Indiana).

Not surprisingly, the Japanese inhabitants of Fisby's sleepy village are not that fired up by chicken aspic. They'd rather stay in bed than build schools. Fisby's office becomes overrun with goats and geisha girls, and no-one listens to a word he says. But Fisby's inability to control the villagers conceals a greater strength. Through the geishas, the villagers gradually find their own motivation to work, and Fisby becomes that rare and valuable thing: a facilitator.

Read *The Teahouse of the August Moon* and, just for a day, relinquish control and be like Fisby. Listen to other people and let them do things their way. Everyone else will be happier and more productive, and you'll have more time on your hands. Time to sit still, have a cup of tea, and listen to the wind in the pines – as Fisby does. Or time to watch how badly everyone else is screwing things up and tell them how much better you would do it . . .

Oh, sod it. There's no curing you.

SEE ALSO: **anally retentive, being** • **dictator, being a** • **give up halfway through, refusal to** • **organised, being too** • **reverence of books, excessive** • **workaholism**

cope, inability to

There are variations in the intensity of one's inability to cope. At one end of the spectrum, there's not being able to deal with the confusion of one particular moment: the laundry, the cat poo, the baby. And at the other end, our coping mechanism – perhaps depleted further by hormones, exhaustion, insomnia or some sort of physical sickness – is so compromised by the volume of demands that it seizes up completely. Here we prescribe for the mild form of the ailment – somewhere between spilt milk and spilt blood. But if your inability to cope is more extreme, see: stress; and depression, general. And if you suffer just from being too busy, but are in fact juggling it all rather well, stop complaining and get on with whatever it is you've got to do (and, while you're at it, see: busy, being too).

Colette, in Gerard Woodward's excellent debut novel, *August,* is at a particularly trying time of her life. A 'funny, interesting wife' to Aldous, she's also a mother of four with a quirky, blithe spirit. They live together in a bohemian North London home, camping in the same field in Wales each August – a holiday which becomes the symbolic centre of their lives. When we first meet Colette she seems imperturbable, delighted by all that surrounds her – her children, her clothes, her ability to move 'like a ballet dancer' in her job as a bus conductress. But it all starts going downhill when she discovers a new means of mental escape: glue-sniffing.

Colette's glue-induced hallucinations are described in thrilling, tempting terms. On holiday, she watches the top of a nearby Welsh hill from her tent, normally a 'blend of moss greens and lime greens', but this afternoon becoming 'slowly, a brilliant fluorescent orange, as though a spoonful of syrup had been tipped over it.' But by the time they get back to London, things have become more disturbing, and Colette is scrabbling around her living-room floor trying to catch miniature sheep.

Set in the Seventies, when substance abuse was more or less unheard of, Colette's family are completely out of their depths. It's not long before her children start to show signs that they too are failing to cope. But even while Colette's family disintegrate around her, there's warmth and love here too. For those hanging over the precipice, the pellucid prose of this sympathetic novel will help clear the clamour of your mind – because at least you have your mental faculties intact. Use them to re-group and set some priorities: deal with what's important first (feeding the baby), and leave what isn't (pretty much everything else) till later on. It won't be hard to feel more in control than Colette. Before you know it you'll be looking up control freak, being a; and organised, being too, instead.

SEE ALSO: **busy, being too** • **Christmas** • **cry, in need of a good** • **exhaustion** • **fatherhood** • **motherhood** • **single parent, being a** • **stress**

coward, being a

To Kill a Mockingbird
HARPER LEE

Gunnar's Daughter
SIGRID UNDSET

It's impossible to live a good life and be a coward. How can you aspire to do the right thing by others – or even by yourself – if your first impulse when things get sticky is to run off and hide your knocking knees?

We don't mean you have to be fearless. It's OK to be afraid. But you have to feel the fear and do it anyway, as the self-help books put it. If you know that you tend to bottle out, be a wimp or let others take the rap – or if you need a shot in the arm to step up to an occasion that requires you to be especially brave – inspire yourself with the feats undertaken by the gutsiest characters in literature.

Our favourite – and oh, how we love him for it – is Atticus Finch in *To Kill a Mockingbird*. This single father of Jem and Scout (and if you're in this predicament, see: single parent, being a) reveals his bravery in the face of physical danger when he quietly picks off a rabid dog in the main street of Maycomb, Alabama, with just one shot. It wins him the immediate, startled respect of his children, who have up until now written him off as feeble and half-blind, being older than the other local fathers. Atticus teaches his children that there is nothing brave about tormenting the neighbourhood recluse, Boo Radley, and that it sometimes takes more courage to walk away from a fight when someone's taunting you ('Scout's a coward!') than to hit back. But it's his courage in defending Tom Robinson, a black man accused of raping a white woman in a community where racist attitudes are taken for granted, that teaches them – and us – the biggest lesson. Brave enough to hold firm even when his children get bullied at school for their father's moral stance, brave enough to confront – single-handedly – an aggressive mob determined to lynch Robinson at the local jail, Atticus is made of the sort of stuff that sets a man apart.

To Kill a Mockingbird remains one of the most scathing condemnations of racial prejudice in literature and Harper Lee's own courage – a white woman writing about the people she grew up amongst – should not be overlooked. Lee published the novel in 1960 – before the American civil rights movement had reached its peak – and her decision to speak out in this way puts her on a par with her own creation.

If Atticus's quiet, lawyer's approach is not your style, take a leaf from Vigdis, the tough-as-a-bloodied-axe Viking heroine of Sigrid Undset's extraordinary 1909 novel, *Gunnar's Daughter*. Written in the style of a Norse Saga from the twelfth century, Undset tells the story of the young and beautiful Vigdis, daughter of the respected Viking Gunnar. When we meet her, Vigdis is on the threshold of womanhood: quintessentially feminine, she cuts a striking figure with her jewels and cascade of blonde hair reaching down to her knees. One day she meets the mysterious Ljot with his dark-blue eyes and heavy fringe, and there is an immediate chemistry between them.

But the lustful Ljot takes Vigdis against her will – leaving her pregnant and her reputation soiled – and her Viking blood boils over with fury and a thirst for revenge. As life becomes increasingly tough, we watch her rise to meet each challenge, somehow acquiring the strength she needs. Her flight on skis through a dark, snow-bound forest full of howling wolves, a frightened two-year-old strapped to her back and the most violent men in history making chase, is one of the most galvanising scenes in literature. And at the end of it she utters not a squeak when three of her frost-bitten fingers are chopped off – at her own request.

Vigdis's courage is not merely physical. A woman in a man's world, she wins great admiration for her tough-but-fair negotiations with kings, outlaws and suitors. She rebuilds her family home and cunningly manages to acquire two father figures to make a manly man of her son, Ulvar. Yet it turns out that even this 'most mettlesome of women', as Ulvar calls her, was feeling fearful all the time. Even as she slit the throat of the man who killed her father, her legs were trembling; years later she admits to having been 'afraid of every man who has wooed me' since that first disastrous introduction to carnal love.

Don't allow being afraid to make you a coward. Whatever it is you have to do, take your fear with you. With Atticus, Vigdis and Harper Lee as your mentors, step boldly into the shoes of a modern-day hero.

SEE ALSO: **confrontation, fear of • risks, not taking enough • seize the day, failure to • superhero, wishing you were a**

cry, in need of a good

Sometimes you just need to let the misery out, whether it's a broken heart, a broken heirloom or your hormones are out of control. Take these novels with tissues and brandy.

 THE TEN BEST NOVELS TO MAKE YOU WEEP

A Lesson Before Dying ERNEST J GAINES
The Fault in Our Stars JOHN GREEN
Tess of the d'Urbervilles THOMAS HARDY
One Day DAVID NICHOLLS
Doctor Zhivago BORIS PASTERNAK
Kiss of the Spider Woman MANUEL PUIG
The Notebook NICHOLAS SPARKS
Sophie's Choice WILLIAM STYRON
The Story of Lucy Gault WILLIAM TREVOR
My Dear, I Wanted to Tell You LOUISA YOUNG

SEE ALSO: **tired and emotional, being**

cult, being in a

Amity and Sorrow
PEGGY RILEY

'Join us, wear strange clothes, get castrated and then drink poison.' This was the message, if not the slogan, of the American cult Heaven's Gate whose members were brainwashed into believing that by committing mass suicide they would escape the imminent 'recycling' of planet Earth and transport themselves to a waiting alien space craft.

Being in a cult, it seems, may not give you the best chance of long-term happiness, or indeed survival. Should you ever find yourself receiving an unnervingly enthusiastic welcome by a previously unheard-of community with a single, charismatic leader; if your previous culture, community or habits are roundly criticised and rejected by them; and if you are encouraged to break ties with family and friends and give all your resources away, a cult will have just made you one of its members. If it's already happened, we're too late. If it hasn't, vaccinate yourself immediately with this luminous account of the trap – and lure – of life in a cult (in this case, a fundamentalist, polygamous community in the far north of Idaho). One injection should be enough, but if you are particularly vulnerable we recommend a booster every five to ten years.

SEE ALSO: **bullied, being** • **family, coping with** • **family, coping without** • **outsider, being an** • **self-esteem, low**

cynicism

The Darling Buds of May
HE BATES

If you're a cynic of the twenty-first century variety,* your attitude could be deemed a realistic one. But when cynicism makes a turn towards the mass rejection of society and all its values, we feel the need to administer a stern lecture on the importance of social responsibility (for which, see the second half of our cure for: depression, economic) followed by regular draughts of something truly and deeply

---

* The original Cynics of Ancient Greece espoused the rejection of materialism in favour of a virtuous, simple life lived in harmony with nature. One of them, Diogenes of Sinope, famously lived in a tub on the streets.

restorative. For this we prescribe repeated immersions in HE Bates's highly efficacious *The Darling Buds of May* and its four sequels. These effervescent novels will spritz your dried-up faith in the powers of love and goodness, while offering your inner cynic an option to save face by re-styling itself along Greek lines.

The Larkins live as many of us would like to live 'if only we had the guts and nerve to flout the conventions', as Bates put it when he explained his reasons for writing the series. Pop Larkin is a farmer and dealer in whatever he can make money out of, who refuses to pay his taxes, drinks as a matter of course, and kisses any attractive women that come his way (while remaining loyal and adoring to the generously sized 'Ma' Larkin). The couple and their six children live together in an idyllic country nook down a long lane in Kent, where they believe that no-one can find them. That is, until the tax inspector calls.

But Cedric Charlton proves no match for the Larkins's charms. He is instantly captivated by eldest daughter Mariette and, steeped though he is in the necessities of filling in forms, estimating incomes and distrusting his senses, he is little by little seduced into their bucolic world. Plied with whisky, strawberries and goose eggs, games of crib and carpets of bluebells, his conditioned cynicism recedes into the background. It's not long before Cedric has become Charley and Pop's habit of drinking Red Bull cocktails in the Rolls has caught on.

Let Pop's sheer exuberance, and his refusal to be blighted by killjoys, infect you too. Life is 'perfick' if you choose to see it so.

SEE ALSO: **antisocial, being** • **bitterness** • **killjoy, being a** • **misanthropy** • **pessimism**

D

Daddy's girl, being a

Emma
JANE AUSTEN

Being a Daddy's girl never did anyone any favours. It's fine when you're the doted-upon darling who can't put a foot wrong. But when you grow up and discover that the rest of the world doesn't find your foibles as adorable as Daddy does, it will come as a bit of a shock. The new boyfriend won't be amused to discover he's barred from the number one spot in your heart. But maybe it doesn't matter, because he won't last very long anyway. Nobody's good enough for a Daddy's girl, and Daddy will make sure he knows it.

Twenty-one-year-old Emma, the eponymous heroine of Jane Austen's satire of nineteenth-century marriage, is the ultimate Daddy's girl. To her nervous, frail and foolish father – whose chief obsession in life is to protect himself from draughts and persuade his friends to eat a nourishing boiled egg – the beautiful, clever Emma is a model of good-ness who deserves to have everything her way. It doesn't help Emma's skewed vision of herself that her parental trian-gle is completed by an absent (dead) mother and an overly devoted governess.

And so her hapless, hopeless father sends Emma, at twenty-one, out into the world with an overly high opinion of herself and a self-centredness that can only bring her grief. When she competes in love with the equally accomplished yet impoverished Jane Fairfax, and points out to Miss Bates, Jane's aunt, what a chatterbox she is, Emma is not only being unkind but is breaking unspoken rules of social propriety regarding the treatment of one's social inferiors. For a while she risks losing the respect of everyone in her community – a calamity for someone in her position. And we blame her silly old dad. Because who better to correct a child of their faults than a parent who loves them regardless? Imagine the fairer, stronger person Emma might have become if she had been affectionately teased through the years.

Heed this cautionary tale. Daddies: don't do it to your daughters. And daughters, beware of having a doting Mr Woodhouse for a dad. If you do, your best option is to stop playing the game and show him what a bad girl you can be. See: rails, going off the, for some inspiration.

death, fear of

White Noise
DON DELILLO

One Hundred Years of Solitude
GABRIEL GARCÍA MÁRQUEZ

Do you ever wonder how anybody manages to function knowing they may be wiped out at any moment? Do you ever wake in the night in a cold sweat, pinned to your bed by the terrible knowledge that a looming eternity of non-existence awaits you?

You're not alone. An awareness of death is what sets us apart from animals. And how we choose to deal with it – whether we opt to believe in God and an afterlife, reconcile ourselves to non-existence, or simply repress all thoughts of it – is something that sets us apart from one another.

Jack Gladney, chair of Hitler Studies in a Midwestern college, suffers constantly from an acute fear of death. Jack obsesses about when he will die, about whether he or his wife Babette will die first (he secretly hopes that she will), and about the size of 'holes, abysses and gaps'. One day he discovers that Babette fears death as much as he does. Until then, his blonde and ample wife had stood between him and his fear, representing 'daylight and dense life'. The discovery shakes his soul – and the foundations of their otherwise happy marriage.

Jack explores all manner of arguments and philosophies to overcome his fear of death, from placing himself within the protective realm of a crowd, to reincarnation. ('How do you plan to spend your resurrection?' asks a friendly Jehovah's Witness, as though asking about a long weekend.) His most successful method for soothing (and distracting) himself is to sit and watch his children sleep, an activity which makes him feel 'devout, part of a spiritual system'. For those lucky enough to have sleeping children at hand, this is a balm we heartily condone not just for fear of death, but fears of all kinds.

Maybe one of Jack's mental arguments will work for you. If not, at least *White Noise* will give you an association between thoughts of death and laughter. DeLillo is a funny writer, and his description of Jack attempting to pronounce German words gets our vote for one of the funniest passages in literature. Reach for it in the night when your death terror hits, and witness the metamorphosis of fear into laughter.

The other cure to keep by your bed is *One Hundred Years of Solitude*. This novel about the Buendía family of Macondo can be read over and over, as the events occur in a sort of eternal cycle, and it's so densely written that you'll find new gems and revelations every time. Spanning a century as it does, death occurs often and matter-of-factly and the characters accept their part in the natural order of things – an attitude which, in time, may rub off on you.

If it doesn't, keep reading. Over and over again. And one night, perhaps, as you wearily reach the last page and begin again, you'll start to see the need for all good things to, eventually, come to an end.

SEE ALSO: **angst, existential**

death of a loved one

After You'd Gone
MAGGIE O'FARRELL

Incendiary
CHRIS CLEAVE

Of all the challenges we may be faced with in life none, perhaps, is harder than this.

Whether it is a parent, spouse, sibling or child we have lost, a life-long friend, or someone we only knew for a short while, the death of a loved one brings with it a bewildering slew of emotional states, all of which can be bracketed under the general heading of grief. It has

D

108

helped many people to think of their grief in terms of the five stages as identified by Elisabeth Kübler-Ross in the late Sixties in relation to those facing their own mortality: denial, anger, bargaining, depression and acceptance. Not all mourners go through these five stages, and those that do don't necessarily experience them distinctly or in this order. But we hope that by borrowing these categories we might more clearly direct mourners to the novel most likely to offer them solace and comfort when they need it.

If you suspect you are in denial about your loss – which many see as the body's way of moderating the onslaught of grief, stalling its flood with numbness and shock – we offer Maggie O'Farrell's *After You'd Gone*. When we first meet Alice, she is on her way to visit her sisters in Edinburgh. But in the ladies' loo at the station she sees something so terrible, so unrepeatable, that she cannot process it – and immediately takes the train back to London. That night, her state of shock is made absolute when she is hit by a car, sustaining a head injury that puts her into a coma. It is from this dream-like state of the heroine's coma that we explore her life up to this point, and discover a lurking and unprocessed grief. Let this novel give you permission to exist for a while in your own cocoon of shock. Don't worry if you can't seem to persuade yourself to come out of it; your body will shed the cocoon when it's ready.

If anger dominates, you need to let it out. There is no better model for this than *Incendiary*, Chris Cleave's heart-rending cry of anguish and fury from a woman who has lost both her husband and small son in a fictional terrorist attack on Wembley Stadium. Written in the form of a letter to Osama bin Laden – who is thought to be behind the attack – the narrator hopes to make Osama understand and love her boy so that he won't ever kill again. 'I'm going to write to you about the emptiness that was left when you took my boy away . . . so you can look into my empty life and see what a human boy really is from the shape of the hole he leaves behind,' she writes. Her voice is as unforgettable as its message, for the rawness of her delivery – ungrammatical, full of crude colloquialisms and tabloid headline shorthands – shows a woman past caring about things that don't matter. Words 'don't come natural for me', she tells Osama – but oh, do they pack a punch.

Fearless and increasingly maddened by imagining her lost boy shouting for his mummy, she vents until she cracks – but we know, by the end, that this venting was deeply necessary. Your anger may feel endless, and so it should, for it is the transmutation of your love. But it can only dissipate if you let it out. Again, this stage cannot be rushed. Mourners experiencing grief in this way should also see: rage.

It is not uncommon when suffering from acute grief for us to enter into a negotiation with ourselves, or fate. If only we can find the right answer to x or y, we believe, the pain will go away. Children are particularly prone to this – as illustrated by the search over New York undertaken by nine-year-old Oskar Schell in *Extremely Loud and Incredibly Close*. After his father Thomas is killed in the 9/11 terrorist attack, Oskar finds a little key in an envelope at the bottom of a vase in his father's closet. The envelope has the word 'Black' written on it. Oskar decides that if he can find the lock the key opens, he will understand something about what has happened to his father, and he embarks on a mission to visit all the Blacks in the telephone directory.

The search turns out to be a wild goose chase – but what Oskar finds in the process is more precious: an understanding of suffering and loss from the lives of his grandparents before he was born and, in a touch that will help to re-warm your heart, the desire for a grief-stricken but loving mother to help her son recover from his enormous loss.

The stage which everyone dreads the most, perhaps, is depression. There is no getting round it: some things cannot be made better, and it is vital that we allow ourselves, and others, to exist in this bleak, dark stage, where attempts to cheer up are inappropriate and unhelpful, for as long as we need to. Siri Hustvedt's novel, *What I Loved*, is an unflinching exploration of this place. Leo Hertzberg, the narrator, and his friend Bill Wechsler are both in mourning. The lives of both men were once so full of promise, but now they are disintegrating – and both also mourn the past, their intellectual life in New York which they had somehow thought would last all their lives.

Hustvedt's characters, including the children, are an intelligent, thoughtful crew. What she shows is that our intelligence cannot save us from pain; sometimes, it actually makes it harder for us to find our way through. Pain is an unavoidable part of life, and experiencing yours in the company of these characters will help you inhabit its darkest corners – perhaps the most vital part of the process of grieving if you have any hope of moving on.

Some people find their way to acceptance more easily than others. When the narrator of John Berger's *Here is Where We Meet* encounters his mother – dead for many years – in a park in Lisbon, it's her walk he recognises first. In the conversation that follows, he finds himself watching familiar, endearing gestures – licking her lower lip, as she always used to after applying lipstick – and being irritated, as he was as a child, by an outward show of sureness which, to his eyes, seemed to conceal a complete lack of sureness underneath.

Berger's narrator – or perhaps it is Berger himself – travels from city to city, finding evidence of his dead. In Kraków he re-encounters his mentor Ken and, as they observe a chess game together, he 'suffers his death' as if for the first time – reminding us that grief is often experienced in waves, and at random, unpredictable moments throughout our lives. In Islington, London, he re-meets his friend Hubert who is overwhelmed by the problem of sorting out the drawerfuls of sketches created by his dead wife Gwen. 'What am I to do?' he cries. 'I keep on putting it off. And if I do nothing, they'll all be thrown out.'

Walking in these places offers the narrator a way of remembering, and the conversations with the dead a way of assimilating his love of those he has lost. 'I've learnt a lot since my death', the narrator's mother tells him, referring afterwards to 'the eternal conundrum of making something out of nothing' – for she knows, finally, that this is what it is about. The narrator considers the question of what to leave at a graveside (one of his leather gloves perhaps?) and notices how his dead take on new elements to their character – his mother, for instance, has a cheeky new impertinence about her, 'sure now that she is beyond reach', and his father claims to prefer swordfish now rather than salmon. Thus Berger allows the dead to change and develop as the living do. Give your relationships with your dead the same new lease of life – you will find it more rewarding than leaving them locked and static.

So it is that, further along in our mourning process (though the process never ends), we come to see the lost loved one as they really were, the good and the bad together. We can settle accounts; and we can also gather together the wonderful things about them, the things that we miss and, perhaps, find a way to incorporate them into our lives in a different, magical way. Take a trip, with Berger, to the places where you spent time with your loved one, do the things you used to do together, and relish and celebrate all that they gave you while they were alive – and continue to give you now.

SEE ALSO: **anger** • **appetite, loss of** • **broken heart** • **guilt** • **insomnia** • **loneliness** • **nightmares** • **sadness** • **turmoil** • **widowed, being** • **yearning, general**

demons, facing your

Beyond Black
HILARY
MANTEL

We've all got a few demons on our backs. Some of us live with them so successfully that we're able to forget all about them until, one day, we catch sight of one in the mirror, and there's hell to pay. Some of us, however, live with our demons in plain sight, rolling their eyeballs like marbles as they follow us down the street. Luckily our friends can't always see them. We maintain that all demons should be faced and vanquished, sent back to the hell from which they crawled out. To help you purge, we prescribe the scourge of *Beyond Black* by Hilary Mantel.

Alison lives off her demons, unwillingly. A charming, friendly psychic, she indulges in a vast amount of comfort food to keep her complex past safely smothered (for more on psychological battles with weight, see: obesity). After a demanding performance in front of an audience of hundreds on the outer edges of the M25, she wakes up in the early hours of the morning craving sandwiches, doughnuts, pizza. Alison's assistant, Colette, tries to put her boss on a diet. But this turns out to be as doomed as Alison's efforts to find out what really happened to her when the men that she still finds sprawled semi-clad around her living room – having now 'passed into spirit' – first took her to the shed to 'teach her a lesson' as a little girl. To bring this traumatic memory to the surface, Alison must quite literally confront them, led by her spirit guide, Morris. Was her father one of these men? she wonders. And if so, which one?

Alison first discovered her ability to communicate with 'spirit' when, also as a girl, she was befriended by a little pink lady named Mrs McGibbet in the attic – who faded back into the space behind the wall whenever her mother's heavy tread came up the stairs. Her powers don't come without pain. 'When I work with the tarot, I generally feel as if the top of my head has been taken off with a tin opener,' she tells us. But little by little, we begin to understand the references to what the dogs ate in the woodshed, and to what happened to the invisible Gloria to whom Alison's mother speaks continually. The almost constant prickle of fear only disappears when the psychic meets her monsters head on. Alison's final epiphany is an act of supreme psychic redemption. Take heart from her triumph, shake that demon off your back, and look it in the eye at last. The process may not be painless, but you will, like Alison, find it less terrifying than you think.

SEE ALSO: **haunted, being** • **scars, emotional**

dependency

SEE: **alcoholism** • **coffee, can't find a decent cup of** • **cold turkey, going** • **drugs, doing too many** • **gambling** • **internet addiction** • **neediness** • **shopaholism** • **smoking, giving up**

depletion of library through lending

LABEL YOUR BOOKS

Yes, you want to tell everyone about the book you've just read, and you want everyone you love to share the experience too. This is how news of a good book gets about, and we are all for spreading the word. But what about the lurking anxiety that you won't get the book back? The gradual depletion of a library of its most beloved tomes is a woeful thing. To protect your treasured books, design your own 'ex libris' label to stick inside each book as you lend it out – complete with careful instructions as to how to return the book once read and a warning about the consequences of late or non-return. (Be imaginative about this. We find the threat of a curse to be effective.)

For extreme cases – if your books have a tendency to fly off your shelves faster than you can buy new ones – we recommend keeping a library-style catalogue. Check books out, and then in, and set up an alarm on your digital calendar to alert you to overdues. Then see: control freak, being a; and friend, falling out with your best.

depression, economic

The Adventures of Augie March
SAUL BELLOW

South Riding
WINIFRED HOLTBY

In these times of austerity, when money-making opportunities are thin on the ground and a flexible approach to one's métier is called for, what better companion to have at one's side than Augie March, an Everyman struggling to make good in his own hard times of the American Great Depression. Raised on the rough west side of Chicago, Augie is a man who lives by 'luck and pluck', going at things 'freestyle'. Never quite managing to get himself a formal education, Augie moves from job to job – and girl to girl – as he searches for what he was meant to be.

The litany of lives he tries on for size makes for an eclectic list of job ideas and as such is an excellent resource for anyone in search of a novel way to spin a dime. For your convenience, we list them here: distributor of handbills at a movie theatre; newspaper boy; stock unpacker at Woolworth's; Christmas elf; funeral wreath-maker for a flowershop with a gangster clientele; butler, secretary, deputy, agent, companion, right-hand-man (plus arms and legs) to a wheelchair-bound real-estate dealer; assistant manager to a heavyweight boxer; robber; salesman of shoes, hunting gear and paint; driver of illegal immigrants over the border; pampered dog trainer, washer and manicurist; book racketeer; house surveyor; trade union organiser; hunter (with trained eagle); researcher for wannabe author; merchant marine.

If you're out of work and have plenty of time, read this charming, picaresque novel and stumble on the jobs yourself. You'll see that a life that takes in so many different roles – not all of them entirely honest – ends up a somewhat shapeless thing, to which Saul Bellow's baggy narrative testifies. But its go-with-the-flow opportunism, its eye for a laugh, its shrug, its easy-going all-American swagger, are precious commodities in these highly competitive, pared-down days, and Augie's winding trajectory will help free you up when mapping your own path.

Apart from forcing us all to tighten our belts (which for some might be no bad thing – see: extravagance), one of the first casualties of economic depression is the funding of public services – health, education – and the arts. For a sobering reminder of the hard-won advances we are in danger of seeing slip away, read Winifred Holtby's *South Riding*, set in the north of England just before the formation of the welfare state. It tells the story of local schoolmistress, Sarah, a feisty redhead swimming with ideals who falls in love with tortured, married landowner, Robert Carne, whose wife is mentally ill. Part socialist-idealist meets conservative-traditionalist, the tale shows how the members of a rural community work with and against one another with varying degrees of selflessness. One of the characters, Joe Astell, knows he is dying of TB, but becomes an alderman – an elected member of the local council – in the hope of rescuing the town from being the 'waste-paper basket of the South Riding'. Perhaps Holtby modelled him on herself, for she, too, was dying as she wrote this fervently political book.

As public funding dwindles, values and individuals are trampled underfoot. Let Holtby remind you that in times of austerity, we must strive not just for ourselves but for the collective good.

SEE ALSO: **broke, being • job, losing your • unemployment**

depression, general

The Unbearable Lightness of Being
MILAN KUNDERA

The Bell Jar
SYLVIA PLATH

Mr Chartwell
REBECCA HUNT

Depression is a sliding scale. At the mild end, where most of us dip in a toe from time to time, are those days or periods when nothing goes right, it seems as if we don't have any friends, and we feel plunged into a state of gloom (see: failure, feeling like a; left out, feeling; sadness; grumpiness; pointlessness). At these times, we need a novel that shifts our perception of the world, reminding us that it can be a place of sun and laughter too. See our list of The Ten Best Novels to Cheer You Up below for a positive pick-me-up read that will open the window and let in a blast of fresh air.

But at the other end of the scale, sufferers experience a heavy black cloud that descends without warning, for no particular reason, and from which they can't see any way out. This is clinical depression, a severe form of mental illness which is hard to treat and can recur. If you are unlucky enough to be prone to this kind of depression, your spirits are unlikely to be lifted by a light and breezy read. Such a novel may well make you feel worse – guilty that you can't muster a chuckle, irritated by anything that strikes you as naïvely optimistic, and hating yourself even more. It sounds counter-intuitive at first, but at such times a novel that tells it like it is – with characters who feel as depressed as you do, or with an uncompromisingly bleak view of the world – is likely to hit home, encourage you to be gentler with your-self, and support you in a more appropriate way; a novel which can accompany you into your dark melancholic place, acknowledging and articulating it, so that you realise that others have been there too, and that you are not, after all, so different, or so dreadfully alone.

The mental torment and nightmares experienced by Tereza in Milan Kundera's novel *The Unbearable Light-ness of Being* may help in this regard. Tereza's anguish is triggered by her lover Tomas's inveterate womanising; having cut himself off from his failed marriage and young son, Tomas has chosen to embrace the life of a libertarian bachelor. But from the start Tereza is portrayed as someone weighed down by life: the heaviness to Tomas and his mis-tress Sabina's lightness. Because Kundera divides people into two camps: those who understand that life is mean-ingless, and therefore skim its surface, living in and for the moment; and those who cannot bear the idea that existence should come and go without meaning, and insist on read-ing significance into everything. When Tereza meets Tomas she knows that she has no choice but to love him forever; and when she turns up in Prague to see him again, with her worldly goods in a suitcase, she also brings a copy of *Anna Karenina* – a novel that perhaps sums up more than any other the suffering that results when meaning breaks down. Much as he loves her, Tomas knows she will be a heavy pres-ence in his life. When she is pushed to the brink of insanity by Tomas's refusal to give up other women, Tereza berates herself for her weakness at wanting Tomas to change. At her lowest ebb she tries to take an overdose. Whenever you have sunk to such depths that it seems impossible for anyone else to reach you, pick up this novel and let Tereza keep you company down there. She, too, wants to live and rise above her sadness, and she finds a way to do so in the end.

A disproportionate number of writers suffer from depression. Some say creative types are more vulnerable to it, others that writing about one's illness is carthatic. The American novelist Richard Yates would spend hours staring blankly at the wall in a state of catatonic depression. Ernest Hemingway too was increasingly plagued by depressive episodes, and drank heavily (and if this is your choice of escape too, see: alcoholism). He lost his battle with depression in the end, as did Virginia Woolf, and Sylvia Plath, but not without leaving the invaluable gift of their experience behind. These gifts – novels about the experience of mental illness – are there for us to make use of, so that we can find solace where these writers did not.

Plath suffered from bipolar disorder, and in her powerful autobiographical novel *The Bell Jar*, she documents through her young heroine Esther Greenwood the bewildering mood swings that caused her to be searingly happy one moment, 'lungs inflating' in a rush of delight to be alive, and unable to rise to any emotional reaction at all – 'blank and stopped as a dead baby' – the next. Esther's voice is a great comfort for depressives: what makes this novel so readable is the lightness of Plath's prose, and the way that even in the most disturbing passages of the novel Esther's humanity and youthful zest shine through. Remember this when you can't imagine ever feeling happy – or even just plain 'normal' – again. Others can see the potential for lightness in you, even when you can't.

Learning to perceive your depression as something separate from you – such as a big, black smelly dog – may seem a bizarre notion, but it can be a useful way of distancing yourself from your illness so that it doesn't define who you are. Rebecca Hunt's bold first novel, *Mr Chartwell*, will take you through the process. Mr Chartwell is the manifestation of Winston Churchill's 'black dog' – the depression that haunted the august politician for much of his life – and which also moves in with his temporary secretary, Esther Hammerhans. Visible only to his victims, Black Pat (as the dog is called) arrives on the second anniversary of Esther's husband's death by suicide, ostensibly answering her advertisement for a lodger. Soon he is making free with her house, crunching bones outside her bedroom door, and even doing his best to join her in bed. Black Pat may have revolting habits, but as only sufferers of depression will understand, he has a peculiar charm that is hard to resist and Esther receives him with a mixture of despair and fascination.

She is not the first of his victims. Because not only has Black Pat been visiting Churchill, but Esther deduces that he's lived in her own house before, unperceived by her. As she begins to understand more about her husband's illness, and therefore her own, her relationship with the shaggy mutt heads towards its resolution. You'll have to read the novel to find out if she overcomes her depression; we all know that Churchill managed to hold down a job through it all. And when Esther and her elderly mentor first realise that they can both see the dog, but are afraid to mention it – such is the taboo surrounding mental illness – Churchill's tactful circling around the giant black creature's malodorous presence and his rousing encouragement to Esther to 'stand firm' is touching and reassuring to Esther and reader alike.

In serious cases of depression, bibliotherapy is very unlikely to be enough. But we urge sufferers to make full and imaginative use of fiction as an accompaniment to medical treatment. Whether you require a novel to take you out of your funk, or one which joins you in it, novels can often reach sufferers in a way that little else can, offering solace and companionship in a time of desperate need. Stand firm with Churchill, the two Esthers and Tereza. Take reassurance from the fact that they – and the authors who created them – know something of what it's like to live with depression; and if their experience doesn't overlap with yours, maybe one of the others on our list of The Ten Best Novels for the Very Blue will (see below). You might not be able to see a gap in the clouds, but the knowledge that you're not the first to lose your way beneath them will keep you going as you wait for them to pass.

THE TEN BEST NOVELS TO CHEER YOU UP

When the Green Woods Laugh HE BATES
Auntie Mame PATRICK DENNIS
Fried Green Tomatoes at the Whistle Stop Café FANNIE FLAGG
Cold Comfort Farm STELLA GIBBONS
All Creatures Great and Small JAMES HERRIOT
Fever Pitch NICK HORNBY
Man and Boy TONY PARSONS
Major Pettigrew's Last Stand HELEN SIMONSON
I Capture the Castle DODIE SMITH
Miss Pettigrew Lives for a Day WINIFRED WATSON

 THE TEN BEST NOVELS FOR THE VERY BLUE

Herzog SAUL BELLOW
Betty Blue PHILIPPE DJIAN
The Unbearable Lightness of Being MILAN KUNDERA
The Bluest Eye TONI MORRISON
The Bell Jar SYLVIA PLATH
Last Exit to Brooklyn HUBERT SELBY JR
Some Hope EDWARD ST AUBYN
By Grand Central Station I Sat Down and Wept ELIZABETH SMART
To the Lighthouse VIRGINIA WOOLF
Revolutionary Road RICHARD YATES

SEE ALSO: **antisocial, being • anxiety • appetite, loss of • despair • exhaustion • hope, loss of • indecision • insomnia • irritability • lethargy • libido, loss of • nightmares • paranoia • pessimism • pointlessness • sadness • self-esteem, low • tired and emotional, being • turmoil**

despair

Alone in Berlin
HANS FALLADA

One would never choose to live without hope (see: hope, loss of). But sometimes one has no choice. Despair is to be found at the place where all hope is lost, and those in its grim grip need a cure that acknowledges what it is like to exist in this place. The author of *Alone in Berlin* understands it all too well, and so do the characters that populate this sobering novel about life under the Third Reich. Let them be your companions as you acquaint yourself with your despair. Watch them and learn from them. As you will see, there are cracks of light to be found even in the darkest of places.

Berlin is a city in thrall to the Führer and his henchmen. Opponents of the regime – which include anyone failing to inform on anyone else deemed disloyal to the Führer – face violent intimidation and arrest, followed by summary execution or internment in one of the notorious concentration camps. When their only son is killed on the front line, uneducated factory-worker Otto Quangel and his wife Anna begin their own, unique form of resistance: leaving postcards around Berlin urging their fellow citizens to stand up to the Nazis and fight back.

Unfortunately, the postcards backfire. Far from encouraging anti-Nazi sentiment, their postcards succeed only in engendering more fear and paranoia among the already cowed citizens of the city. This realisation, when it comes, risks sending them deeper into despair. But the act of resisting has already saved them. It has given them the moral victory, and when they face their persecutors, it is the Quangels who have access to hope, light, and even joy. Their persecutors do not.

The Quangels are not the only ones who rescue themselves from despair in this way. Dr Reichhardt, Otto's cellmate, does it by continuing to live as he's always lived: taking a walk each day (back and forth in his cell) and extending kindness and love to everyone he meets, good or bad. Eva Kluge, the ex-postwoman, does it by leaving the Nazi Party when she discovers that her adored son Karlemann has been photographed swinging a three-year-old Jewish boy by the leg and smashing his head against a car. Dr Reichhardt and Eva Kluge put their lives at risk by these actions but keep their self-respect intact. As Eva says, this 'will have been her attainment in life, keeping her self-respect.'

It sounds a small thing, but it is not. Our lives are nothing without it. And with it, our lives become notable, rich, meaningful. Despair cannot co-exist with these things; certainly they bar the descent to depression. There may not be hope, but *Alone in Berlin* teaches us that sticking tenacious-ly, proudly, defiantly, to our sense of what is right and true is enough – and the only fail-safe cure for despair that there is.

SEE ALSO: **broken spirit · depression, general · hope, loss of**

determinedly chasing after a woman even when she's a nun

In the Skin of a Lion
MICHAEL ONDAATJE

If you are in the unfortunate position of having fallen in love with a nun,* Michael Ondaatje's *In the Skin of a Lion* is the novel for you.

First, because it features the best chance meeting be-tween a man and a woman in literature, and if you're in a love with a nun, you'll need to engineer a good chance meeting. He, Nicolas Temelcoff, is a migrant manual labourer who happens to be dangling in a harness from a viaduct under construction in central Toronto. She is one of five nuns who have mistakenly walked onto the unfinished viaduct at night, and are scattered by a sudden gust of wind. When she is blown over the edge, Temelcoff, hanging in mid-air, sees her fall, and reaches out an arm. The jolt of catching her rips his arm from its socket. Terrified and in shock, she stares at him, eyes wide. He, in excruciating pain and barely able to breathe, asks her, politely, to scream.

This unparalleled meeting (inspired by a real-life topple from a real-life viaduct) is especially serendipitous because it begins the process by which Temelcoff's nun decides she wants to kick the habit – which obviously, at some point you'll need your nun to do too. Before the night is over, Temelcoff's nun has whipped off her wimple for him to use as a sling, allowed brandy to pass her lips for the first time, imagined what it's like to have a man run his hand over her hair, and re-named herself Alice, after a parrot. If your chance meeting does not have such a transformative

---

* While we assume that most readers will not question our categorisation of this predicament as an ailment, we would like to suggest that those who do turn instead to common sense, lack of; and love, unrequited. Only then, and if, the predicament still persists, should they return to this cure.

effect, however, don't despair. Read on. Because *In the Skin of a Lion* features another man (Patrick Lewis) who is so in love with another woman (Clara, an actress) that even after a number of blunt rejections, even after she tries to pass him off onto her best friend Alice (the ex-nun, in fact), and even after her boyfriend Ambrose Small sets him on fire with a Molotov cocktail, he still wants to sleep with her. And sleep with her he does.

In fact, Patrick Lewis ends up with the nun, but again that's beside the point. (If you're thinking this is a complicated novel, you're right.) Reading this novel will teach you determination. You'll get your nun. And when you do, you'll be able to read to her passages from what is, in our view, one of the most lyrical and ingeniously constructed novels of the past half-century.

SEE ALSO: **common sense, lack of • love, unrequited • Mr/Mrs Right, holding out for**

determinedly chasing after a woman even when she's married

The English Patient
MICHAEL
ONDAATJE

If you are in the unfortunate position of having fallen in love with a woman who is already married,* Michael Ondaatje is once again your man. (Ondaatje likes a challenge when it comes to love.)

The determined chaser is the English patient himself, who turns out not to be English at all but a Hungarian count named Almásy, although he is definitely a patient. When we meet him, he is lying in a ruined villa in Tuscany, burned beyond recognition after his plane crashed in the North African desert. It's the aftermath of the second world war, and there are people dying from war-related injuries all around him; but it gradually transpires that the English patient's plane did not crash as a result of being gunned down by

---

* If you do not see why this predicament is unfortunate, please turn first to adultery; and love, unrequited.

enemy fire, but as a result of . . . you've guessed it, him having fallen hopelessly in love with a married woman.

It is her voice he falls for, at first, reciting poetry around a campfire in the desert, with Almásy himself sitting just outside the fire's halo. 'If a man leaned back a few inches he would disappear into darkness,' Ondaatje tells us in prose that succeeds in inhabiting the metaphysical spaces of poetry. Before long Almásy and the freshly married Katharine Clifton are consumed by the sort of passion that hovers on the edge of violence.

We're not the sort to moralise, and Ondaatje isn't either. But sometimes literature finds it hard to resist. And one could argue that the price this pair of lovers pay for their adultery is their due comeuppance. But then again, maybe there is no moral message here, and Almásy and Katharine were just the random victims of Ondaatje's cruel pen. Go ahead and chase your married woman. Get her, for all we care. But think, now and then, about the cold, dark emptiness at your back, and the dangers of getting on the wrong side of husbands, especially very jealous ones with planes.

SEE ALSO: **common sense, lack of** • **love, unrequited** • **Mr/Mrs Right, holding out for**

diarrhoea

Waste no sedentary moment. Select a novel from our list below, all of which are made up of fragments, vignettes, or very short chapters that won't suffer from being read in short snatches. Make a special shelf for them in the smallest room of the house.

 THE TEN BEST NOVELS TO READ ON THE LOO

Company **SAMUEL BECKETT**
Women in a River Landscape **HEINRICH BÖLL**
Invisible Cities **ITALO CALVINO**
The Big Sleep **RAYMOND CHANDLER**
Diary of a Bad Year **JM COETZEE**
Nowhere Man **ALEKSANDAR HEMON**

dictator, being a

Your average dictator is more likely to sit down of an evening with a manual on how to rule the world and avoid being superseded than with a good novel. Which is a shame because given the right prescription of fiction, he or she might improve their human rights record considerably. Instead we address this ailment to the mini-tyrants who micro-manage their companies and their households in a despotic manner. These more parochial dictators spend their time amassing fortunes instead of weapons, and tend to fire those who disappoint them, rather than make them disappear. But their method of domination using fear and coercion as their tools is exactly the same and can cause plenty of misery in the little empire over which they rule. Look in the mirror. If you find one such tyrant staring back, make these novels your bed-time reading and prepare for a re-shuffle of your realm.

The Successor, by the Albanian writer Ismail Kadare – himself an inhabitant of an erstwhile repressive regime – will show you why you don't have any close friends. The story opens with the sudden death of the nominated successor to a communist-style dictator in the Land of the Eagles (Albania). The death is not altogether surprising as an alarming number of 'suicides' seem to happen in this dictator's vicinity. People who get too close to him don't tend to live for very long. Chillingly, Kadare reveals the constant state of paranoia in which the dictator's friends and family live, as we glimpse the thoughts of those characters most at risk. Fear, paranoia and a dream-like sense of doom run rife – infecting, of course, none more the dictator himself. Those of you who have a tendency to act as a dictator in the sphere of the domestic, take note: no-one wants to live in a house that's more about hubris than home. Whether through envy or anger, an uprising will most likely bring about your downfall in the end.

And when that happens, there's no getting round it, dictator wannabes: a horrible death awaits. Nowhere is this inevitability more apparent than in Patrick McGuinness's novel, *The Last Hundred Days*. Enjoyably depressing, it describes the deposing of the real-life tyrant Nicolae Ceausescu in Romania. While an unnamed young Englishman observes the events leading up to Ceausescu's execution, his friend Leo obsessively records the overnight disappearances of Bucharest's streets and buildings. Leo's book, *The City of Lost Walks*, was originally conceived as a guide to the city, but fast becomes a book of yearning for places lost at the hands of the police state. The horrible denouement is brilliantly and powerfully drawn.

Despots large and small, read this and rue the day you chose to strike terror into the hearts of those around you, destroying your relationships, and instilling paranoia and distrust in your intimates. Whether you run a war-torn state,* an international corporation or a semi-detached house inhabited by a family of five, you will surely see reason, abdicate in a hurry, and invite a democracy to be installed in your place.

SEE ALSO: **bully, being a** • **control freak, being a**

different, being

Jonathan Livingston Seagull
RICHARD BACH

Generally speaking, human beings can be divided into two categories. There are those who fit in, and those that don't. As everyone knows, life is infinitely easier for those who fit in. You're accepted; you get to be one of the gang. If you don't fit in, at best you're misunderstood and feel left out. At worst, you're cast out entirely (see: bullied, being; unpopular, being). If you have always felt that you're different, your life will be much more successful if you can learn to see your differentness as a plus.

Jonathan Livingston Seagull is a short piece of fiction that's embraced by some† as an inspirational story about

---

* Yes, we're still hoping to net some real dictators.
† Generally, people who fit in.

what it is to be different, and rejected by others[‡] as a poorly concealed religious tract not worthy of lovers of true literature. Wherever you sit on this continuum JLS remains a fast and effective cure for anyone who is miserable because they feel themselves to be different.[§]

Jonathan Livingston Seagull is different from the other gulls in the Flock. While they spend their days screeching and squabbling over anchovies, the finding of food their sole purpose in life, JLS is concentrating on greater things: learning how to fly. Not just any old flying, but the sort of high-speed nose-dives and aerobatics usually associated with birds of prey. Pushing himself harder and harder, he achieves feats no seagull has ever achieved before: full power vertical dives from 5,000 feet, a top speed of 214mph, loop-the-loops, rolls, spins and pinwheels. He even flies in the dark. When, somewhat out of control but exhilarated beyond measure, he cannonballs through the Breakfast Flock at 212mph, he naïvely expects to be praised for his difference. Instead he is shamed and rejected: a seagull who is different cannot be a member of the Flock. JLS tries to be ordinary again, but how can he flap gracelessly at 100 feet now that he knows what it's like to fly streamlined just above the surface of the water?

To all those who are different, the message of *Jonathan Livingston Seagull* is clear. Don't apologise for your difference. Don't try to hide it. And never, ever wish it away. If you know that you're different, you do yourself a great disservice unless you explore that which makes you different to the full. If this means, like JLS, that you are ostracised from the group, so be it. At least you'll have more time to practice and perfect whatever it is that you know you can do which other people can't.

SEE ALSO: **foreign, being • hype, put off by • left out, feeling • outsider, being an**

[‡] Generally, people who feel that they are different.

[§] By recommending JLS to lovers of literature, we are aware that we are putting ourselves out on a limb and being different from those who also consider themselves to be different. But having re-read JLS recently and been reminded of its efficacy as a cure for being different, we don't care.

dinner parties, fear of

There but for the
ALI SMITH

Cold sweat. Strange new rash. Sudden sickness. Facial tics. Inability to find anything clean to wear. Discovery of vital work to be done for tomorrow. Urge to sit and talk to the babysitter for an hour. These are the symptoms of the dinner party avoider. Partner of avoider, meanwhile, grits teeth and cajoles. They're about to leave at last when shrinking violet announces urgent need to go to the loo and locks themselves in the bathroom. At which point, exasperated partner slips *There but for the* under the door . . .

Our cure for a chronic fear of dinner parties tells the story of Miles, who leaves a dinner party (having first purloined a salt cellar) and locks himself in a spare room upstairs. He stays there for several weeks. Word spreads, and while the world observes him through a window from Greenwich Park, setting up camps to encourage his 'protest', he becomes a minor celebrity.

At first the appalled hosts try to ignore what has happened. Then they begrudgingly slide flat packs of wafer-thin ham under Miles's door. Nine-year-old Brooke, however, the precocious daughter of some neighbours and chief observer in the local community, is the one to demonstrate what Miles should have done when struggling with the social event that started this off: learn to be curious and ask your fellow guests questions about themselves. And, if all else fails, fall asleep at the table.

Emulate Brooke. You'll have a much better time at the party and get home again sooner, too.

SEE ALSO: **antisocial, being** • **misanthropy** • **shyness**

disenchantment

*Le Grand
Meaulnes*
ALAIN-FOURNIER

The malady of disenchantment comes with being a grown-up. It's not surprising, really. We spend our childhoods dreaming of great adventures, our teens whipping them into intense, romantic fantasies, and our twenties (if we're lucky) making bold steps towards these new horizons. And then responsibility hits: work, mortgage, a routine. And suddenly we find that the world has gone from an enchanted place, where anything could happen, to a place of humdrum mundanity where only predictable things happen (see: mundanity, oppressed by). Where, we can't help wondering, have all the dreams gone?

To answer this question, re-acquaint yourself with the character in whom the romance and hopes of adolescence find their most intense expression: Le Grand Meaulnes. The mysterious seventeen-year-old arrives one Sunday in November at the schoolhouse home of the narrator François in Sainte-Agathe. François has heard his footsteps in advance in the attic: a step 'very sure of itself'. A moment later, Meaulnes impresses Francois by setting off fireworks on his doorstep. Two 'great bouquets' of red and white stars shoot up with a hiss and, for a wondrous moment, Francois's mother opens the door to see her son and the tall stranger hand in hand, captured in the glow of this fantastical light.

To François and the other schoolboys at Saint-Agathe, Meaulnes is everything they find compelling: fearless, a dreamer of impossible dreams, an adventurer who always has one eye on a distant horizon. He is bold in the way that only the young are bold, before doubt and cynicism and the possibility of failure set in (if this is you, see: cynicism; and failure, feeling like a). They christen him, with canny accuracy, Le Grand Meaulnes. Translators the world over have struggled to do justice to that seemingly simple word *grand*, capturing as it does both the literal, physical meaning (big, tall, even great) but expanding as the story progresses into something loftier, and more fabulous.

Le Grand Meaulnes will take you back to the world of heightened senses in which everything is more enigmatic, more lovely and more intoxicating. Where in the background one can detect the faint strain of music; where children, left in charge, transform themselves by dressing up; and where a moment of peace and serenity becomes prophetic of a future happiness. Meaulnes's tragedy is that when he finds happiness he can't embrace it. His sense of identity is too firmly bound up with yearning, and he needs the dream to remain a dream. But we can live differently. Let Meaulnes remind you how to live a life of enchantment – then bring this enchantment into your every day.

SEE ALSO: **cynicism • innocence, loss of • mundanity, oppressed by • zestlessness**

dishonesty

SEE: **lying**

dissatisfaction

Cannery Row
JOHN STEINBECK

Many of us live to the accompaniment of a perpetual sense of dissatisfaction – a gnawing feeling that we have not quite achieved enough, or don't quite have enough to show for our time of life. For some it's not enough things, and from our teens onwards we think that if we could just afford that new gadget or gold lamé swimsuit, we'd be satisfied. For others it's not enough time – an endless sense of scurrying through to-do lists before we finally achieve the space to think and breathe (see: busy, being too). And for still others it's a sense of being emotionally, intellectually or spiritually incomplete, not quite full up – and we yearn for the better relationship (see: Mr/Mrs Wrong, ending up with) or better job (see: career, being in the wrong) or better lifestyle (see: broke, being; and taste, bad) that would make us feel we had finally arrived and could, at last, begin our lives for real.

We hate to break it to you, but if you keep looking for the answers outside yourself, the dissatisfaction will stay. Clichéd it may be, but the answer lies within. And often the only way to see this is to stop chasing those butterflies and stand still for a while and take stock.

Mack and the boys know how to do this. In *Cannery Row*, John Steinbeck's ode to the ambition-free life of the bum, we meet them sitting on the discarded rusty pipes from the sardine canneries in a vacant lot: Mack, Eddie, Hazel, Hughie and Jones, men who have three things in common:

no families, no money and no ambitions beyond food, drink and contentment.

In fact, this isn't entirely true. Their non-blood-related family is one another – plus Doc, the loveable owner of Western Biological Laboratory who lives among his jars of marine specimens. Doc understands his fatherly role in this family, and he exposes all those that enter his home to improving blasts of Scarlatti or Monteverdi, or a reading from the Chinese poet Li Po. And then there's Dora, the madam who runs the whorehouse with her flaming orange hair and Nile-green evening dresses. And Lee Chong, their grocer-come-banker who sells them cheap whisky and extends credit with flashes of his gold tooth. And they do have an ambition of sorts in that they make a home – an old fish-meal store loaned by Lee Chong which they christen the Palace Flophouse Grill and which they decorate lovingly with bits of old carpet, chairs 'with and without seats', and the 'glory and heart and centre', a silver-scrolled monster of a stove that it takes two of them three days to carry home.

To many they are no-goods, thieves and bums. But to Doc, they are life's success stories – healthy, 'clean' men who are able to spend their days doing what they want. They live a hand-to-mouth existence, living on the cash earnings of whatever jobs they can get, but they are happy this way. While others race through life striving to achieve and accumulate and keep up in their endless search for more, forever falling short of their targets, Mack and the boys approach contentment 'casually, quietly', and absorb it gently. 'What can it profit a man to gain the whole world and to come to his property with a gastric ulcer, a blown prostate, and bifocals?' Steinbeck asks.

You might think this side of America with its scattered iron and rust, chipped pavements and weedy lots, its honky-tonks and flophouses, doesn't exist any more. But it does if you know where to look. Take a day out of your life to steep yourself in this tender, loving, idle world of men who are happy with little, who make a hopeless mess of it when they try to 'do something nice' for Doc, but whose hearts are in the right place – a place of non-striving and accept-ance. Then apply this casual, quiet approach with its whiff of sardines to your own life. With practice, you'll soon sit back and watch the dissatisfaction – like the water in the rock pools where Doc and Hazel collect starfish – ebb softly away.

SEE ALSO: **boredom** • **grumpiness** • **happiness, searching for** • **mundanity, oppressed by** • **querulousness**

divorce

Divorce may be common these days, but it's still one of the most traumatic experiences a person can go through – par-ticularly if there are children involved – and if there's any chance of avoiding it, we urge you to take it. All marriages go through peaks and troughs and even if you've been in a trough for a number of years, your problems may very well be more easily surmountable than you realise – see our cure for married, being. If your marriage is on the rocks because either you or your partner are suffering from one of the sit-uational predicaments in this book – such as being out of work (see: job, losing your; and unemployment) or because you're under financial strain (see: broke, being) – we urge you to treat the problem at its root, rather than cast off your marriage prematurely. Life after separation may have less conflict, but it will be harder in other ways (see: loneliness; and, if you've got children, single parent, being a). If there's another person involved, see: adultery. Perhaps there is a lack of kindness and understanding between you (see: em-pathy, lack of; and judgemental, being), or one of you strug-gles with change or demons (see: change, resistance to; rut, stuck in a; and demons, facing your). Perhaps the demands of children have got in the way of your sex life (see: orgasms, not enough; sex, too little), or you find yourselves wanting to spend your spare time in different ways (see: non-read-ing partner, having a.) Or perhaps your spouse's bodged attempt to fix the dishwasher has brought calamity to your kitchen (see: DIY).

Whatever the cause, conflict or unhappiness at home will inevitably make you vulnerable to a host of additional ailments (for which, see this book) – and we therefore urge you not to exist in a state of turbulence or angst for too long. Our cure begins with two novels for those on the brink: be sure to read them before any knots are severed. And to those for whom divorce is a *fait accompli* – or who need encouragement to see it through – we offer a one-in-a million novel of hope and inspiration about a woman who gets it right the third time round.

Intimacy is the raw, and at times uncomfortably honest, first-person account of Jay, a man who has decided to leave his partner of six years, Susan, in the morning. As he puts his two little boys to bed and sits down to a supper *a deux*, he is aware that this is the last night they will all spend as 'an innocent, complete, ideal family'. Inevitably, there's a tumult of conflicting emotions in his head – all of which will be horribly familiar to anyone who has ever come close to packing their bags. Jay feels guilt, confusion and terror at the damage he's about to inflict on the children; and also a desperate need to 'live' again, to close the door on unhappiness and move on. When Susan, a successful publisher, comes home from work, we get a glimpse of what has gone wrong. As she casts him an infuriated gaze, he feels his body 'shrink and contract'. Clearly there has been a communication break-down – for the presence of anger and hurt in this moment remains unacknowledged between them. And in the monologue that ensues, we never get a sense that their problems have really been aired and shared, or that Jay has attempted to find out what Susan thinks is wrong. Read this as your wake-up call. If, like Jay, you haven't fully disclosed your negative feelings about the marriage to your partner, you may be giving up too easily too. Take some responsibility for the failure. Initiate the conversation. Don't give up until you both understand – and agree – where you went wrong, and have at least attempted to fix things. Chances are that the return of honest communication will bring you closer again. See: confrontation, fear of, to help you reach this point.

Certainly a mutual acceptance of what is happening will make life as a divorced couple easier – and if you have children, you will need to continue a relationship as parents together for many years. Two years on from his divorce, Frank Bascombe – the sportswriter of Richard Ford's *The Sportswriter* – is beginning to be conscious that if he were to live his life again, he might not choose to get divorced. He and X, as he calls his ex, still live near one another in the suburb of Haddam, New Jersey, so that their two kids Paul and Clarissa can move between both homes. They talk at least twice a week on the phone and often bump into each other. It was X who initiated the divorce, but Frank is reconciled to it – living alone has helped him to know himself better – and this seems to be the case for X too, for she is finally making 'a go of it' with the promising golf career she gave up when she married. And maybe Frank will get back to that unfinished novel he put in a drawer when he became a sportswriter instead. As he has discovered from his own experience – and from the other men at the Divorced Men's Club in Haddam – life as a divorcé isn't all about sex and liberation.

What, in fact, sets Frank and X apart as a divorced couple is that they are not only bound together by Paul and Clarissa, but by a third child who died. Frank denies that the boy's death was the cause of the breakup, but nevertheless there is a lassitude, a lack of conviction in Frank's voice and worldview that seems closely affiliated to grief. And though he and X's shared grief makes them kinder to each other than they might otherwise be, a sense of exhaustion and failure hangs heavily over the novel. For people, like Frank, who lack faith in life in the first place (and if that's you too, see: disenchantment; dissatisfaction; faith, loss of), the dismantling of the structure of marriage, with all its solidity and support, can leave one floundering even more. Take note of this realistic, unromantic view of life on the other side of the divorce proceedings.

If you have genuinely tried to make your relationship work and it feels like hitting your head against a brick wall, it may be time to admit defeat. Maybe getting hitched was a mistake, and you both need to set yourselves free. Certainly turning her back on a rushed marriage to dull local farmer Logan Killicks turns out to be a good thing for Janie in Zora Neale Hurston's tale of love in the deep American south, *Their Eyes Were Watching God*. Brought up by her grandma, an ex-slave who is determined that Janie will marry well and not be left for men to go 'usin' yo' body to wipe his foots on', she is eager to marry her off as soon as she notices Janie taking an interest in men. There's little joy to be had with Logan, though, who she can't bring herself to love, and when Jody Starks, an energetic and entrepreneurial man with a plan comes through, his hat set at an angle, Janie doesn't think twice. They elope and settle in an emerging all-black town in Florida and live a comfortable, respectable life for many years.

It's not a marriage made in heaven, though – Jody is old-fashioned and increasingly critical, and the ever-feisty Janie feels stifled. As luck would have it, she gets a third bite of the apple, and this time it's the real thing. If you think your romantic life is over, take note of Janie – a woman who, at forty, still swaggers down a street with her true love, Tea Cake. For this is a life-affirming novel of the most beautiful kind: poetic, profound and wise, with dialogue lively and true. Stay open-hearted. Give your marriage every chance it's got, but if it's well and truly over, be kind and generous to your ex. Then move on with a lighter step. Know, like Janie, that the world is made new every day. Something, or someone, amazing may yet come your way.

SEE ALSO: **anger • breaking up • broken heart • falling out of love with love • murderous thoughts • sadness • single, being • single parent, being a • turmoil**

DIY

Caribou Island
DAVID VANN

You are balancing on a stool with a screwdriver between your teeth, a bespoke light bulb in one hand, a fistful of ill-matched screws in the other, and a hammer under your arm. It is imperative that you mend this light fixture today, as tonight you're having a much-anticipated dinner party. As you accidentally touch two wires together with your screwdriver, you are thrown across the room by a compelling force. And no, it's not your partner's rage.

In the UK, six hundred people are injured every day in their own homes. Invariably, the cause is DIY. Fingers are severed, roofs cave in and shelves come tumbling down with hapless DIY-ers sprawled beneath them. Under the glare of DIY disasters, marriages melt like fuses.

If you are feeling an irresistible urge to build that lean-to, customise your IKEA unit or sandblast your patio, make sure a copy of *Caribou Island* is sitting just inside your toolkit, ideally between you and the drill. After you read this, the absolute folly of attempting DIY will become indisputable. We are not only saving you hours of pain, but also your marriage or partnership, all your other intimate relationships, and quite possibly even your life.

In this magnificently grim novel, Irene observes her husband Gary make one last, superhuman effort to either save or destroy their marriage by building a log cabin on the other side of Skilak Lake. They already live in the wilderness of Alaska, but Gary has always dreamed of a haven for their retirement which is more remote still. Even before it gets underway it is clear that the project is doomed. 'They were going to build their cabin from scratch. No foundation, no plans, no permits, or advice; no previous experience.' Gary wants to pit himself against the elements unaided by friend or written aid. (If only he had *The Novel Cure* to hand.)

We watch Gary as the rain 'drives into his eyeballs like pin-pricks' and he puts the door of the cabin on the wrong way round. He leaves vital implements at home across the soon-to-be-frozen lake. Irene half-heartedly attempts to help, realising more and more profoundly that Gary's dream of his log cabin never actually involved her. While he rages against the rain in Anglo-Saxon: *'Bitre Beostcare, hu ic oft throwade!'* (Bitter heartcare, how I often suffered!), feeling abandoned by all humanity, she huddles in a tent, longing for home.

And then, a part of her she never knew existed is awakened: her inner Diana, huntress to whom mere dwellings are irrelevant. As this civilised woman is taken over, Irene becomes magnificent, irresistible, a force more impressive than the elements. The superb conclusion of this novel will have you rushing straight to the Yellow Pages for a handyman.

SEE ALSO: **divorce** • **pain, being in**

dizziness

My Ántonia
WILLA CATHER

Whether it is a physical dizziness from which you suffer – seeing stars before folding, puppet-jointed, to the floor – or an emotional giddiness in which you lurch from pillar to post, you'll need to stop the world spinning by holding on to something solid and firm. Perhaps you're pregnant (see: pregnancy) or in pain (see: pain, being in), jetlagged or sleep-deprived (see: exhaustion), or coming down with something (see: cold, common; man flu). Or perhaps you suffer from an emotional lightheadedness which makes you flaky and indecisive (see: common sense, lack of; and indecision). After tending to these specific ailments individually, we suggest a no-nonsense dose of *My Ántonia*.

Ten-year-old Jimmy Burden first hears of Ántonia when, after losing both his parents in the space of a year – enough to make even the steadiest child lose his footing – he is sent to live with his grandparents in Nebraska. The most striking thing about Nebraska is that after a day on the railroad train it 'was still, all day long, Nebraska'. When he reaches the end of the line, he and the immigrant Bohemian family who will become his closest neighbours are driven by wagon through the night. At one point Jimmy peeps out from under the buffalo hide and sees nothing – 'no fences, no creeks or trees, no hills or fields . . . nothing but land.' He has the feeling that they have left the world behind and as the wagon jolts on, he allows himself to submit to its rhythm, to offer himself up to destiny. While in Nebraska he teaches Ántonia, the daughter of the immigrant family, to speak English and in return learns about the importance of grit and hard work in order to survive. Their friendship turns out to be one of the most instructive in his life.

It is Jimmy's submission to fate and his connection to the grounded Ántonia that you need to emulate. If your body is loose, and you submit to what will be, you won't hurt yourself if you fall. And if, in your emotional dizziness, you focus on an image of solid, uncomplicated land, you will find something for your heart to hold on to. Read *My Ántonia* and inhale its waft of smelling salts. And, like Jim in later years, return to this landscape whenever you need to, to the pale, cold light of winter which does not beautify but is instead 'like the light of truth itself', and says: 'This is reality, whether you like it or not.'

dread, nameless

Something Wicked This Way Comes
RAY BRADBURY

You slide the CD into the car stereo, with, well, considerable dread. With a title like that, how could you not? Besides, rods of October rain are coming down hard against the windscreen, heavier by the minute, and you have a long drive ahead.

Five hours later, you are still pummelling through rain down the motorway, wipers flashing back and forth across your vision. But inside your head you are crouched behind a bookstack in the library of Greentown, Illinois. Beside you are Will and Jim – both just turned thirteen – and the 'Illustrated Man' is drawing inexorably closer. He knows exactly who he is looking for, for the boys' faces are tattooed on the palms of his hands. He wants them for his sinister circus.

As this predator from the Pandemonium Show makes his way along the bookstacks, muttering to himself –'B for Boys? A for Adventure? H for Hidden . . . T for Terrified?' – your windscreen suddenly fogs up.

No matter how much you wipe the windows from the inside, it doesn't seem to make any difference. Your breathing comes hard and fast. It is as if your eyes are being sewn shut by the witch in the novel who travels with the circus, cruising in a black balloon muttering spells at anyone who thwarts the circus's progress: 'darning-needle dragonfly, sew up those eyes so they cannot see!' You pull over and turn the audio book off, pale and shaking.

But it is too late: you are hooked. You have to *know*. You wind down the windows to let in the air, not caring about the rain and, cautiously, you press play. After a while you resume the journey, windows wide open.

It's a close thing. You are almost swallowed up by mist, feeling yourself beginning to turn to wax as Will and Jim so nearly do, but when a powerful secret in the novel is divulged, your dread, quite suddenly, disappears. And it does not come back.

By the time you arrive at your destination you are cackling with glee. And as you pull up outside the house, you notice that it is the sort of house that would previously have filled you with a nameless dread . . . But this time you are armed.

SEE ALSO: **angst, existential** • **anxiety**

dread, of Monday morning

SEE: **Monday morning feeling**

dreams, bad

SEE: **nightmares**

dreams, broken

SEE: **broken dreams**

drugs, doing too many

Brave New World
ALDOUS HUXLEY

Less Than Zero
BRET EASTON ELLIS

For Sherlock Holmes, the use of cocaine three times a day in a seven per cent solution was 'transcendently stimulating and clarifying to the mind'. But Watson was appalled by Holmes's habit, noting his punctured forearm with dismay. Sir Arthur Conan Doyle was ahead of his times in realising there might be an addictive and dangerous side to the use of laudanum,* heroin† and cocaine‡. In any era there are substances that creep up on us with their addictive qualities (prozac; caffeine; nicotine; barbiturates and morphine, perhaps, in ours) whose negative properties were not at first understood. And there are the drugs we might consider 'recreational', until they become, for some, more than just an occasional diversion. What are the signs that an experimental or occasional habit is becoming something more sinister and life-threatening? When dabbling becomes depending? Read the following to help identify your symptoms and cut your supplies off before it's too late.

A far cry from Baker Street, where the syringe came in a leather-bound case and the user lay back on a velvet armchair, are the users and abusers of *Trainspotting*, Irvine Welsh's Scottish journey into modern-day heroin hell. Here the highs and the horrors of heroin addiction are spelled out blow by blow, from the death of baby Dawn who asphyxiates while her parents are out cold, to the amputation of a needle-infected leg, and the disintegration of friendships, family and, seemingly, the entire run-down district of Edinburgh in which the novel is set. 'It's all okay, it's all beautiful; but ah fear that this internal sea is gaunnae subside soon, leaving this poisonous shite washed up, stranded up in ma body,' reports Sick Boy, predicting the horror after the high. Because even while he shoots up, he knows that it is a 'short-term sea', and a 'long-term poison'. Welsh's novel makes for gruesome reading and offers a compelling case for going cold turkey – or steering well clear in the first place.

The alarm bells truly ring out when we become so addicted that we can't recognise the need for help. In Huxley's dystopian *Brave New World*, the entire framework of society is dependent upon Soma – a drug described as 'like Christianity without the tears' by the 'science monitors' who legislate this world in which babies are made in

---

* Used as a teething balm for babies.
† A popular cough suppressant.
‡ Known for its benefits in dental surgery.

hatcheries, and raised in factories. Because taking Soma – a mild hallucinogenic that leaves the taker on a blissed-out high – is mandatory: two grams on weekdays, six on Saturdays. When Lenina and Bernard, two products of this society, meet John, the 'Savage' who lives on a reservation where Soma is unknown, their dependence on the drug appals him. He urges them to throw away their 'poison' and be freed. But they are too far gone to hear him. Be chilled by this example of the point of no return.

For many of us, drugs feature – or have featured in our youth – in a more recreational sense, but it's easy to become complacent. Easton Ellis's *Less Than Zero* reveals the pivotal role of drugs on a generation characterised by a generally nihilistic popular culture. Clay is the dispassionate and deadpan observer of his classmates, all in their late teens, who have turned to hedonism, drugs, and meaningless sexual encounters to spice up their lives. Ignored by their parents, dropping out of their colleges, they lack direction and belief. 'You have everything,' Clay says to a friend heading down the road to self-destruction. 'No I don't,' replies Rip. 'I don't have anything to lose', and with that he returns to the immediate distraction of sex with a barely conscious eleven-year-old girl. Could a scene like this do anything other than drive that last nail in the coffin for those tending towards excess.

SEE ALSO: **broken dreams** • **cold turkey, going** • **concentrate, inability to** • **insomnia** • **irritability** • **nightmares** • **paranoia** • **rails, going off the**

dumped, getting

SEE: **anger** • **appetite, loss of** • **breaking up** • **broken heart** • **cry, in need of a good** • **insomnia** • **lovesickness** • **murderous thoughts** • **sadness**

dying

Pearl
THE GAWAIN POET

Metamorphoses
OVID

Death cannot be deferred forever, and when the time comes, we need to be ready. In the West we have a tendency to avoid thoughts of death, and to more or less obliterate the fact of death in our everyday lives. Gone are the days of the memento mori, a daily reminder that we must die. It is however essential both to live in the presence of death – and so be sure we are always fully alive – and to prepare ourselves with appropriate literary companions. So that when the time comes we do not arrive at a deathbed – our own or another's – without due armoury. Whether it is you that is dying, or whether you find yourself at the bedside of a loved one as they release their grip, some literature that consoles and stills, while gently encouraging acceptance, is an inestimable boon. You will be glad to have prepared yourself with these two works of timeless serenity and great beauty – either to read to yourself, if you are able, or to read aloud or have read to you.

At such heightened moments in life, one needs language that can rise above the ordinary. *Pearl* is one of the most exquisite poems in the English language written, so people believe, by the same person who penned 'Sir Gawain and the Greene Knight', the gripping and evocative fourteenth-century Christmas 'aventure'. *Pearl* describes the loss of a 'pearl of great price', which many critics believe to represent the two-year-old daughter of the poet; others maintain that the pearl is entirely allegorical, representing the loss of the soul and deliberately allowing ambiguity in the many interpretations of what the pearl means. So little is known about the poet's life that no-one can be sure of the biographical details of his supposed bereavement; it is inferred from the poem, but this in turn is so thick with layer upon layer of allegory, that certainty of interpretation is impossible. But this very ambiguity is also what makes the poem so rich and irresistible. The agony of loss expressed, the purity of love felt, the beauty of the pearl described, are all wrought intricately into a poem that is remarkably complex in structure. Don't be alarmed by the *olde* English – you will soon get your tongue around it, and you can read it in a modern translation if you prefer. Composed of 101 stanzas of twelve lines each, link words cleverly tie verse to verse, and thematic links create a connection between the two ends of the poem that produces a structure that is itself circular – much like the cycle of life and death.

We mention all this because the poem is so beautiful – as neat and satisfying as a pearl tucked into the palm of your hand. If you interpret the poem literally, the 'pearl of great price' represents the thing, or person, you love most in the world (and which the dying should, if possible, have with them at this crucial time). And if you are a believer reading this, you will feel ready to pass into the hands of God – for the Christian message is overt, the pearl appearing as a maid telling the poet that he must put himself at God's mercy in order to cross the stream and enter her realm.

Both believers and non-believers can take comfort from the concept of transformation at these times. For even if we believe that death is the end, there is a sense in which we merely change in form. To help you feel part of the eternal wheel of life, read Ovid – for his great work, *Metamorphoses,* is about how one thing becomes another, ad infinitum.

There is all of life within these pages, from the myths of creation to the lives of the philosophers, from Chaos to Eros, from the coming of the gods, to the trials of Hercules and Prometheus. But Ovid's central theme is love – the power that transforms all things. Because of his desire, Zeus transforms himself into a swan, a bull, a shower of light. By his attempts on their honour, his victims become trees, water nymphs, birds or beasts. Diana turns Actaeon into a stag because he fatally spied her naked. Narcissus metamorphoses into a flower out of his own self-love. And Echo lives forever as a repetitive sound, having pined away from lovesickness (see: lovesickness, if it's not too late). Arachne is turned into a spider because she loved to weave so much. Everything is mutable, nothing remains static, and all beings pass from one state into another – not dying, but becoming.

And so Ovid's verse holds us mesmerised, for he writes of myth and legend, love and loss, showing how we abide in wild flowers, olive trees and streams, our lives flowing from one form to another in never-ceasing metamorphoses.

D

eating disorder

Eating disorders come in many forms. Self-starvation (anorexia nervosa) and bingeing and purging (bulimia) are the most common; while there are also lesser known but no less damaging disorders such as orthorexia nervosa (an obsession with ingesting only the purest foods), and pica (an obsession with chewing and eating non-food items). The jury's out on what causes these obsessive behaviours. Some can perhaps be traced back to a root cause of abuse, neglect or trauma. And, of course, many people point the finger at the persuasive media culture of toothpick-thin catwalk models. A need to feel in control is likely another major cause. Whatever the trigger, literature has solace, comfort and wisdom for both the victim and those with the painful, frightening task of watching, and trying to help, from the side-lines.

Leslie, the talented fourteen-year-old in Deborah Hautzig's *Second Star to the Right* has a happy home life in New York with a mother who loves her 'to the moon and back' and seemingly everything going for her. But she begins to diet because she feels too fat – and then becomes addicted to the thrill of losing weight. Set within the context of her whole adolescence, we follow her desire to reach her goal weight of seventy-five pounds amid a tangible teen world of boyfriends, clothes and uncomprehending grown-ups – and a loyal and intelligent best friend, Cavett, who supports her unquestioningly throughout her illness. The title is borrowed from Peter Pan, who directs Wendy to Neverland, with the instruction, 'Second to the right and straight on till morning'. But it resonates on a more complex, shocking level too. For it refers also to Leslie's mother's cousin, Margolee, who died as a teenager in Auschwitz along with her own mother. Given the choice of going 'to the right' and living, or 'to the left' to die in the gas chamber along with her mother, she chose to go 'to the left'. The tragedies of their deaths echo through the novel and provide a profoundly moving backdrop to what's going on.

Despite the seemingly selfish soliloquy of the anorexic, the question of whether Leslie chooses to go to the right or left herself – for it is, in the end, a choice – captures our sympathy absolutely. *Second Star to the Right* is a great novel for a sufferer of an eating disorder to read, exploring as it does the immense psychological complexities of anorexia with clarity and compassion – and may offer hope for a way out.

Our second cure, *Life Size*, is meant for friends and caregivers, taking as it does a character even further down the road of self-harm. In this disturbing novel, a young woman named Josie – described as a 'starving organism' – does almost nothing but lie supine, occupying space. In the final stages of anorexia, she manoeuvres her skeletal frame out of bed when nobody's looking and runs on the spot in a frantic attempt to burn calories. She feels that her brain is 'closer to the surface' now, that she's able to see colours and experience smells more vividly than when everything was coated in 'a thick aspic of fat'- as if she has attained 'the self in its minimal form'. As she rages against the hospital 'despots' who try to make her eat, recites the number of calories in everything from a piece of bubble gum to a slice of cucumber, and reveals her obsessive fascination with food through the imaginary recipes and menus she concocts, we become aware of the extraordinary cost for her of triumphing over her appetite. When a new path opens up for Josie, a genuine hope is planted in the reader. A gruelling but important read, you'll glean new insights into the powerful psychologies at play in eating disorders, and come away reassured that there is light at the end of the tunnel even in the most serious cases.

SEE ALSO: **appetite, loss of** • **hunger** • **self-esteem, low**

egg on your face

SEE: **blushing** • **idiot, feeling like an** • **regret** • **shame**

egg on your tie

Restoration
ROSE TREMAIN

For once, you're on time. You've got your best suit on and your notes in your hands. You climb the podium, and look down to adjust the microphone. As you do, you notice a dribble of bright yellow egg yolk snaking down your shirt.

Sound familiar? If so, make the acquaintance of Robert Merivel, the hero of Rose Tremain's *Restoration*, set in the debauched court of King Charles II. Merivel is a glutton for the bawdy pleasures of seventeenth-century life. He's generally to be found with his stockings around his ankles enjoying a tumble with a juicy wench, or laughing so hard he sends a mouthful of raisin pudding across the table at a banquet. When Merivel is given a rare audience with the king, he messes it up so atrociously that it seems he has squandered his one opportunity for bettering himself. But then he gets a second chance. And it's on this occasion, just as he'd being offered the illustrious position of Court Physician to his Majesty's dogs, that Merivel notices the egg stain on his breeches.

It matters not a bit. The king is delighted by Merivel, by his appetite for life and his ability to fart on demand, and goes on to bestow a string of favours on his feckless new friend. It doesn't last forever, but the message remains: the tendency to spill food on your clothes can be an advantage. You just have to choose your context.

SEE ALSO: **failure, feeling like a** • **idiot, feeling like an**

egotism

SEE: **arrogance** • **confidence, too much** • **dictator, being a** • **misanthropy** • **selfishness** • **vanity**

eighty-something, being

 THE TEN BEST NOVELS FOR EIGHTY-SOMETHINGS

Cruising in your Eighties MIKE BEFELER
The House in Paris ELIZABETH BOWEN
Lord Jim JOSEPH CONRAD
World's Fair EL DOCTOROW
Parade's End FORD MADOX FORD
Across the River and Into the Trees ERNEST HEMINGWAY
Call It a Gift VALERIE HOBBS
The Master of Go YASUNARI KAWABATA
Sanctuary Line JANE URQUHART
The Camomile Lawn MARY WESLEY

embarrassment

SEE: **egg on your tie** • **idiot, feeling like an** • **regret** • **shame** • **shame, reading-associated**

emotions, inability to express

Like Water for Chocolate
LAURA ESQUIVEL

As I Lay Dying
WILLIAM FAULKNER

Those who find it difficult to express their emotions – or who share their life with someone who does – should bear in mind that a) an inability to express emotion doesn't necessarily mean that emotions are absent, and b) that there are alternative forms of expression not involving words or gestures which may be (and may be being) used instead.

In Laura Esquivel's popular novel *Like Water for Chocolate*, Tita is forbidden from marrying her childhood sweetheart Pedro because tradition requires her, as the youngest daughter, to remain single and devote herself to looking after her tyrannical mother instead. And so Tita pours the love she's not supposed to feel for Pedro into the sumptuous food she prepares. Into the cake for Pedro's wedding – for Pedro marries Tita's sister Rosaura in order to stay close to Tita – she whisks martyrdom and bitterness. Into the meringue icing goes her longing. And in the way we have come to expect from the Latin American magical realists, the guests digest the emotions along with the wedding cake and are all overcome by grief for the lost loves of their pasts. Tita's quail in rose petal sauce, infused as it is with her sensuous passion for Pedro, turns her virginal sister Gertrudis into such a frenzy of sexual excitement that she strips off her clothes and runs naked through the streets – to be duly carried off on the back of a horse by an equally horny rebel soldier. If you, too, find it difficult to say 'I love you', try saying it with food. And partners who don't get to hear those words, look out for the sentiment expressed in other ways.

You may have to look quite hard. Of the five Bundren siblings watching their mother Addie die in William Faulkner's *As I Lay Dying*, Darl is the most articulate, Jewel the most demonstrative, and Cash – though the eldest – the one who struggles most to express his love for his mother. He does it by building her a coffin, right under her window. His brother, Jewel, watches his meticulous, careful sawing of 'the long hot sad yellow days' into planks and puts his act of intense and complex devotion into words for him: 'See. See what a good one I am making for you.'

And the coffin *is* good. Cash makes it in the shape of a grandfather clock 'with every joint and seam bevelled and scrubbed with the plane, tight as a drum and neat as a sewing basket' so that they can lay her in it without crushing her dress. The young man funnels all his grief and desire to please into the making of this coffin, and his inarticulacy is deeply touching – especially in the chapter that consists of a list of reasons for making the coffin 'on the bevel'. Embrace your – or your loved one's – inability to express in conventional ways. Employ – and allow – a wider repertoire.

SEE ALSO: **stiff upper lip, having a**

empathy, lack of

Johnny Got His Gun
DALTON TRUMBO

The first thing he realises is that he is deaf. Not just a little bit deaf. Not halfway deaf. But stone deaf. He can't even hear the beat of his own heart.

And then he realises his left arm isn't there. He thinks he can feel the heel of his hand, but it's up high, where his shoulder is. They've cut his left arm off. And then he realises it's not just his left arm that's missing. His right is too. They've cut off both his arms.

The thing is, this is only the start of it. The horror of being Joe Bonham as he emerges into flickering consciousness in an unknown hospital in an unknown town is beyond the realms of anything even Edgar Allan Poe dreamt up. For Joe Bonham is an ordinary boy from Shale City, Colorado, caught up in World War I, a war that was none of his business. In fact he never really knew what the fight was all about anyway.

Johnny Got His Gun is the ultimate anti-war novel and pacifist's tract, a story of deep suffering like no other. Take the most unempathetic heart you know, even one that has lived its life in a freezer. Then give it this novel, this achingly beautiful, devastating novel, and watch the heart take its first steps towards compassion.

SEE ALSO: **emotions, inability to express • selfishness**

empty-nest syndrome

The Woman Who Went to Bed for a Year
SUE TOWNSEND

It can be embarrassing to admit to, but many women feel lost when their children leave home. What on Earth are they to do with themselves without all those packed lunches to make, dirty rugby shirts to load into the washing machine, and teenagers to chauffeur on Friday nights? Get a life, of course – except it's not so easy when you're out of the habit. Now, thankfully, it's a 'syndrome' – and you can diagnose yourself with it, as Eva Beaver does in Sue Townsend's novel on the subject after hearing about it on Woman's Hour. And, with this typically Townsendian cure, you can have a laugh at the funny side, for there's no better way to take the air out of a syndrome than to, affectionately, mock it.

To anyone familiar with the seemingly endless chores that go with being a mother and housewife (see: cope, inability to; housewife, being a; and motherhood) going to bed for a year seems a completely sensible – and enviable – reaction. But Eva is not only tired; she doesn't know who she is anymore. After twenty-five years of seeing to the needs of others and making, as she now sees it, a 'pig's ear' out of bringing her children up, she retreats from the world in order to relearn how to be in it. Kicking her husband Brian out of the bedroom, she looks back over her marriage and the things she gave up when her twins Brian Junior and Brianne were born (reading, among them) and feels a crushing sense of disappointment. When Brian moves into the shed with his long-term mistress, Tatiana, and Brian Junior and Brianne learn how to live away from home, Eva starts to make friends with various passers by – including the handyman – while she gets to the bottom of her grief.

As a strategy for recovering and recharging – and opening the doors to new friends, new careers and new domestic arrangements – we recommend it heartily, though we think a year is a tad too long. If you start to test the patience of your loved ones, see: bed, inability to get out of for a counter-cure.

SEE ALSO: **children, not having** • **loneliness** • **yearning, general**

English, being very

SEE: **stiff upper lip, having a**

envy

SEE: **jealousy**

exhaustion

Physical exhaustion can be a fantastic feeling, if brought on by arduous exercise – the swimming of lakes, the scaling of peaks, riding a galloping horse along a beach. But when brought on by standing on your feet for ten hours, plucking chickens, or digging a ditch in the rain, there's little pleasure in the pain. Mental exhaustion can be even more depleting still, causing stress (see: stress) and an ill-functioning brain (see: memory loss). And exhaustion through lack of sleep is a particularly miserable sort of feeling, which can only be remedied by an uninterrupted eight hours in bed. Truth be told, sleep is a pretty good cure for exhaustion all round; but if you're exhausted and want to find a way to keep going, read on.

Meet Zorba, a man of many soups and stories, with bright, piercing eyes, a weather-beaten face, and a gift for expressing himself through dance. Zorba uses dance to tell stories, to define who he is, to explain the world, and as a way to revitalise his spirits when they flag. Our narrator is a young Greek intellectual, interested in Buddhism and books. But when he meets Zorba, with his irrepressible lust for life, he knows he's met a man with a spiritual secret. When the nimble-footed wanderer accepts his offer to become foreman of the lignite mine he has recently acquired on the island of Crete, he's delighted and the two take to drinking wine late into the night, discussing philosophy, with frequent musical accompaniment by Zorba's *santuri*. During these sessions Zorba often laments that if only he could express his friend's philosophical conundrums in dance, they could take the conversations even further.

And one day, Zorba really does teach his young friend to dance – impetuously, defiantly, ecstatically. Soon they are both telling tales with their gravity-defying bodies. Zorba, we realise, is a man of great wisdom through natural understanding, who can reach spiritual heights which take others years to attain in 'one bound'. What we love most about this archetype of energy is his apparently limitless ability to throw himself wholeheartedly into the next project, frequently picking himself up off the floor (when by all rights he should sleep for a week) and dancing himself back to life.

Become a student of Zorba yourself. When exhaustion hits, don't flop. Take to your feet, play some music, and find a dance within you. Wouldn't you rather say, with Zorba, in years to come: 'I've done heaps and heaps of things in my life, but I still did not do enough. Men like me ought to live for a thousand years!'?

SEE ALSO: **bed, inability to get out of** • **busy, being too** • **busy to read, being too** • **libido, loss of** • **tired and emotional, being**

existential angst

SEE: **angst, existential**

extravagance

*Kingfishers
Catch Fire*
RUMER GODDEN

Extravagance – as in spending money on things you can't afford and don't really need – is a habit borne in times of abundance and profligacy. In times of austerity (see: depression, economic), it needs to be stemmed. If not, you'll find yourself working round the clock to pay off your credit card debts (see: workaholism), broke (see: broke, being; and tax return, fear of doing), and tempted to live your life in unprincipled and character-defiling ways (see: rails, going off the). 'He that is extravagant will soon become poor, and poverty will enforce dependence, and invite corruption,' as Samuel Johnson has already beaten us to saying.

Extravagant people tend to be dreamers and romantics. One way to curb an extravagant nature is to decide to romanticise frugality. This is very much what single-mother-of-two Sophie does in Rumer Godden's *Kingfishers Catch Fire*. An expat wife estranged from her husband Denzil, Sophie has until now been someone who spent money 'extravagantly, carelessly . . . selfishly'. Yet the deeply flawed Sophie falls in love with the beauty and simplicity she sees around her in rural Kashmir where the women fetch water, pound grain, and spin their own flax and wool. For the peasants themselves who have no choice, it's a tough existence. But to Sophie it's picturesque and charming. She too wants to '[pick her] toothbrushes off a tree' and, much to the anguish of her daughter Teresa who longs to put down roots and live in a 'proper' house back in England, she moves them into Dilkhush, a semi-ruin with no electricity. 'We shall be poor and frugal,' she tells her children. 'We shall toil'. And toil she does. She also gives up cigarettes, alcohol and coffee and works so hard that she almost dies from pneumonia. But she doesn't give up.

It helps, of course, that by opting to be poor amongst people who are even poorer than she is, Sophie makes herself, by comparison, rich. But whether or not she embarks on her frugal life with realistic eyes, Sophie does discover the pleasures of it, and so do her children. Teresa and little Moo spend their days climbing trees, sailing walnut-shell boats in a stream, and tending to their animals, while Sophie, with only a few books to entertain her in the long, lonely evenings, soon finds she is reading in a new way. 'Every word impressed her, and what she read in the evening she pondered over the next day. She felt her mind stretch and deepen, grow rich; sometimes an evening had passed before she had noticed.'

In fact, Sophie doesn't manage to kick her extravagance habit completely. She buys too many flowers from the flower-boats, keeps animals for pets rather than food and cannot resist buying a Persian rug with money she does not have, so entranced is she by its exquisite rose design. Sophie believes that sometimes, particularly when one is afraid, one should do something rash in order to reinforce one's sense of self – in her case, as a lover of fine things.

Clearly, extravagance on a daily basis is a disaster. Spend what you have wisely to make it go further, and paint alluring visions of monkish austerity if it helps. But if the joy begins to go out of life, indulge in one rash purchase. Buy the rug with the roses on it, and when you are hungry, the extravagance of colour will feed your soul.

SEE ALSO: **book-buyer, being a compulsive** • **broke, being** • **common sense, lack of** • **greed** • **shopaholism**

F

failure, feeling like a

*The History of
Mr Polly*
HG WELLS
....

So you feel like a failure. Perhaps your past is littered with abandoned enterprises. Perhaps you feel that everything you touch turns to lead. Your very anticipation of failure is self-fulfilling – although your fear of failure means that sometimes you don't even begin. You walk with your head hung low, your shoulders slumping. You're the embodiment of non-success. If we've just painted a picture of you, it's time to meet HG Wells's most charming creation, the unsuccessful Mr Polly.

When we first meet Mr Polly, he's sitting on a stile near his home in fictional Fishbourne, Kent, complaining that he is stuck in an 'Ole!' – a 'Beastly Silly Wheeze of a Hole'. Prone to mixing up his words ('See? I'm going to absquatulate, see? Hey Presto right away') which is part of his charm, Mr Polly lives in a permanent state of indigestion caused as much by his negative self-image as by his dubious diet. Having succumbed to the 'zealacious commerciality' of keeping a drapery shop for the past fifteen years, he has grown fat, balding and forty. Realising that he has spent his life so far 'in apathetic and feebly hostile and critical company, ugly in detail and mean in scope' – and that company includes his wife – he is disconsolate enough to set up a life insurance policy that will ensure his wife is comfortably catered for. Then he plans to kill himself (see: midlife crisis).

As luck would have it, his suicide attempt goes so splendidly wrong that he finds himself feeling – no, not a failure (though you would) – more alive than ever before. Realising that Fishbourne is not, after all, 'the world', he sets off onto the open road, heading vaguely towards the sea. Walking for eight or nine hours a day, sleeping in countryside inns and the occasional moonlit field, Mr Polly comes at last to Potwell Inn. Nestling under the trees at a bend in the river and surrounded by hollyhocks, a picnic table out front and a buttercup meadow behind, the inn appears as a vision of perfection. All the more so because it's inhabited by the Plump Lady, so wondrously 'firm and pink and wholesome' that she seems filled with infinite confidence and kindliness. The two realise almost at once that they are 'each other's sort'. And so Mr Polly finds his kingdom – or would have, if it weren't for one obstacle in his way.

Read the novel and find out if Mr Polly completes his transformation from failure to success story. Our guess is that, by the end, your sense of the inevitability of failure, for yourself and for Mr Polly, will have absquatulated into thin air. Align yourself to Mr Polly. Turn your supposed failures on their head. Stand tall. Then stride off in search of your own Potwell Inn.*

SEE ALSO: **give up halfway through, tendency to · self-esteem, low**

failure to seize the day

SEE: **seize the day, failure to**

faith, loss of

Salmon Fishing
in the Yemen
PAUL TORDAY

The Exorcist
**WILLIAM PETER
BLATTY**

For some people, having faith means believing in God; for others it means believing there's a point to life (see: pointlessness) and for others still it means having faith that there's goodness in the world. Whatever faith means for you,

---

* Do not, however, align yourself with Mr Polly so much as to attempt your own suicide and insurance scam. Mr Polly only survived by chance, and such eventualities are unlikely to happen more than once, both in fiction and reality.

to lose it can mean that the light goes out of your life. At such times, we need novels that return us to the tenets we need to uphold if we are to go forwards with joy and confidence. Our cures cover three different approaches to faith; take the one best suited to you.

If you see faith as the triumph of personal conviction over science, then make *Salmon Fishing in the Yemen* your bible. When Fred Jones, a civil servant in charge of the National Centre for Fisheries Excellence, receives a letter asking for his help in introducing salmon, and salmon fishing, into the Yemen, he does what any self-respecting scientist would do – he says no. It is 'nonsensical' – 'risible' – to attempt to defy the laws of nature for the whim of a sheikh with too much money and no education. But that is before he has met Sheikh Muhammad and discovered the power of one man's determination. Because Sheikh Muhammad is a visionary and, as Dr Jones soon realises, this is not so much about fly-fishing, as about faith. This feel-good novel will restore your belief in the power of faith to move mountains.

If your belief in God has been shaken, *The Exorcist* will send a powerful shiver up your spine that might just have you reconsidering. In this chilling novel – perhaps the most terrifying we know – we witness a mother's dawning realisation that her daughter, Regan, is possessed. In desperation, she calls in Father Karras. Karras is himself currently questioning his belief in God, but the palpably hellish horror that he witnesses in Regan so clearly testifies to the existence of the Devil that it brings his belief in the ultimate presence of Good and Evil in the world rushing back. It may have the same effect on you.

If you've lost a sense of the point of it all – and whether it matters if you're good or bad – we have a much gentler cure. Harold Fry is a dispirited, grey retiree, who barely exchanges formalities with his wife and has lost touch with his grown-up son. When he receives a letter from his old friend Queenie telling him she's dying of cancer, he writes her a postcard and sets off immediately to post it. On the way a chance conversation with a petrol pump attendant (the 'garage-girl') lodges in his mind, and when he gets to the postbox, instead of posting his letter, he keeps on walking – all the way from Devon to Berwick-on-Tweed, in fact, where Queenie lives, beset with an increasing conviction that, while he walks to Queenie, she will stay alive.

Harold's conviction is tested many times on his journey. But he places his trust in providence, never taking more than he needs, sleeping in the open air rather than in people's homes, and becoming more and more like a pilgrim from another age. Eventually the press hear of him, and he is soon being referred to as 'that pilgrim', someone who everyone wants to touch and be touched by. The spread of faith, it seems, is infectious. His wife Maureen begins to fall back in love with him from afar; and Queenie . . . well, you'll just have to read it and find out.

At times of bleakness, when you've lost faith in life, God, love, someone else, or yourself, use these novels to bring you back to some fundamental truths. Because the garage-girl is right: 'If you have faith, you can do anything.'

SEE ALSO: **hope, loss of** • **pointlessness**

falling head over heels in love

SEE: **appetite, loss of** • **concentrate, inability to** • **dizziness** • **infatuation** • **insomnia** • **lovesickness** • **lust** • **obsession** • **optimism** • **romantic, hopeless**

falling out of love with love

1Q84
HARUKI
MURAKAMI

True Love. Moonlight. Roses. Eternal devotion. *The one.*

Get real, we hear you say.

Some of us reach the end of the road with love. We feel that our capacity to love has been used up; that our ability to inspire love has faded. That the time for romance in our lives is over.

We have no time for such jaded attitudes. We hereby pledge to pluck you from scepticism and re-awaken you to the never-ending ability of love to return, again and again. The novel with which we'll do it is Murakami's epic *1Q84.*

To say that *1Q84* is a complex novel is an understatement. It is remarkably long, and takes place in two different worlds. But it is deeply, fundamentally romantic. The kernel of the romance rests in the pasts of the two main characters. When they were both eleven years old, they held hands for one very long moment in their classroom at school. The moment – silent, charged with meaning, quite unexpected for Tengo, planned but inexplicable at the time to Aomame – has continued to haunt them both ever since. Aomame knew that she was leaving, and Tengo had always been kind to her. She imprinted her essence on the palm of his hand, and his soul was altered forever.

Now, more than twenty years later, we follow Tengo and Aomame as they lead their separate, solitary lives. Neither has developed a grown-up relationship. Tengo now teaches at a maths 'cram school' and is writing a novel; Aomame lives a disciplined life teaching self-defence while moonlighting as a kind of hit woman. But then they both become embroiled with a religious cult, Sagigake, which soon has them on the run, separately, becoming slowly aware of each other's continued relevance to their lives.

One of the novel's preoccupations is with the idea of becoming irretrievably lost – whether this is morally, or between two parallel worlds, or simply lost to love. While Tengo visits his dying father in a home, he reads him a story about the 'Cat Town', a place where people can become irretrievably lost beyond the reaches of love. Tengo thinks about the Cat Town a lot, seeing it as a place of ultimate lovelessness. And when, in contrast, things start happening that reach beyond realism – a tangible but inexplicable pregnancy, two people finding each other against all odds, love coming to those who gave up on it long ago – it seems that the power of love has been shown to triumph over all else. Take this epic journey with Tengo. Fall with him back in love with love.*

SEE ALSO: **disenchantment** • **hope, loss of** • **Mr/Mrs Wrong, ending up with**

---

* But don't fall *too* hard. If you do, see: romantic, hopeless.

falling out of the window

SEE: **alcoholism • bad back • DIY • drugs, doing too many • hospital, being in**

falling out with your best friend

SEE: **friend, falling out with your best**

family, coping with

A Suitable Boy
VIKRAM SETH

When we are with our families we have the best of times and the worst of times, if we may misquote Dickens. Certainly it's within the family unit that we seem to have our biggest conflicts – be they out in the open or swept under the carpet. Whoever it is that gets your goat the most – your tyrannical toddler, your squabbling siblings, your pressurising parents, your critical in-laws, your adolescent outlaws, your crepuscular cat, or the one particular member of the family who consistently fails to do their share of the washing up – we offer you a hefty tome that explores the jockeying for power that goes on in families, Vikram Seth's *A Suitable Boy*.

It tells a familiar story: Mrs Rupa Mehra wants to choose the man that her youngest daughter Lata will marry, but Lata has other ideas. 'I do know what is best,' Mrs Mehra tells Lata, and 'I am doing it all for you.' We don't need to be Indian to have heard these words before. (Imagine that, instead of a husband, Mrs Mehra is talking about an item of clothing, a hairstyle, or a suitable time to get up.) For nearly 1,500 pages Lata ricochets between Haresh, the 'suitable boy' of her mother's choosing, 'solid as a pair of Goodyear Welted shoes'; Kabir, the fellow amateur actor she falls in love with; and Amit, the friendly dilettante poet pushed forward by his sisters.

Lata is surrounded by people seeking to influence her. But whose life is she living anyway? She knows that ultimately she must make the choice herself – not as an act of rebellion or to win approval, but freely. The length of the novel testifies to the difficulty of her task.

The choice Lata makes shows that although we may fight our families for the freedom to be ourselves, we are also part and parcel of them – steeped in their culture, traditions and values. We may turn our backs on them, but they have made us what we are. Battle it out with your family, but know that ultimately you are battling it out with yourself.

SEE ALSO: **ageing parents • Christmas • mother-in-law, having a • sibling rivalry**

family, coping without

I am Legend
RICHARD MATHESON

Far away from your family, physically or emotionally, you feel conflicting emotions. On the one hand relieved and freed, on the other, lonely and bereft. Whether your distance is self-imposed or involuntary, keep this novel in your backpack to remind you that you can cope on your own – as long as you're not the last man on Earth.

Matheson's genre-creating vampire novel begins with an unforgettable scene. Robert Neville sits in his barricaded house, drinking beer and listening to a symphony called *The Year of the Plague* on his record player. This is, partly, to drown out the eerie calls of 'Neville! Neville!' coming from outside his house.

We soon realise that his wife and daughter have both been lost to vampirism. Neville goes outside during the daylight hours only, grimly attempting to kill his predators as they sleep in their daytime comas. Not that this is a gore fest; we see little of the vampires and their unpleasant deaths at Neville's hands. Instead it's Neville's solitude that comes to the fore, his efforts to understand the new world order, and his increasingly desperate attempts to find an ally. His sincere endeavour to befriend a dog apparently unaffected by the virus is one of the most tragic moments in the story. A likeable chap to whom driving stakes through hearts has become routine, his metamorphosis into a creature of nightmare goes completely unnoticed by the reader – and herein lies the genius of the novel.

Neville's resilience is impressive. Staying alive in this

vampire-infested world depends on keeping the generator going and foraging for tinned goods from ghostly supermarkets. Keeping his spirits up by listening to Schoenberg and attempting to find a cure for the disease that wants to claim him, he does his best to live in the moment, and cling to glimmers of hope for a different future.

If living far from your family leaves you feeling lost and alone, this book will give you solace. At least you're not forced to go around killing off vampires on a daily basis, or strewing garlic necklaces and mirrors around your house to keep them out. Instead you'll be so gripped by this story that you'll forget your isolation – or discover that yours isn't nearly as bad. And if you become *too* comfortable without your family, the final revelation will sort you out.

SEE ALSO: **empty-nest syndrome • loneliness**

fatherhood

The Road
CORMAC MCCARTHY

I'm the King of the Castle
SUSAN HILL

At its best, being a dad is a chance to be a kid all over again – while precipitating you into a new phase of maturity, both as a father and as a partner. It gives you the opportunity to pass on your passions and all that you've learned. But it brings with it enormous responsibilities and can change your relationship with your partner in ways you don't like – and sometimes this resentment gets let out on the child. If the mantle of fatherhood does not sit on your shoulders easily, or you wish to strengthen a father-child bond that has perhaps been blemished by this sort of emotional transferal, we offer you the fictional equivalent of a father-son how-to manual, Cormac McCarthy's harrowing, but astonishing, *The Road*.

Its premise is grimmer than the reality of any of our lives – we hope – will ever be. Following a cataclysmic event, the exact nature of which the survivors can only guess at, America – and perhaps the wider world – has been devastated. Ash blocks out the sun. The cities have burned, and trees have died. Through this 'barren, silent, godless' land, a man and his son (known to us only as 'the man' and 'the boy', as befits a world without colour and with scant humanity) follow the road south where they hope to find warmth and increase their chances of survival. Along the way they try to sleep through nights that are long and dark and 'cold beyond anything they'd yet encountered', scavenge what food they can – from wild mushrooms to occasional cans – and are under constant threat from the 'bad guys', filthy, terrifying men who travel in packs wearing masks and hazard suits, carrying clubs and lengths of pipe, plundering and killing like animals.

It's as shorn of beauty as a world can get. The boy is frequently so sick with fear that he can't run when his father commands it. He's half-starved, he yearns for his mother, and the possibility of playmates, let alone any of the normal pleasures of childhood – toys, sports, green grass, cake – are unknown to him. At one point, the father finds a can of Coca Cola in a soft drinks machine that's been opened with a crowbar and tells the boy to drink it all, and slowly. 'It's because I won't ever get to drink another one, isn't it?' says the boy. And so, through a can of Coca Cola, we feel the full thud of the loss of a world that will never return.

But in emotional terms, it's rich. For here, with everything else taken away, is revealed in its purest, most primal form, the extraordinary love that exists between a father and a son, where the only thing that matters is making sure the boy is 'all right'. If the boy dies, the man knows that he will want to die too. For what is the essence of fatherhood if not the hope for the next generation?

The novel leaves us on a note of hope; an essential ingredient for living (see: hope, loss of). Celebrate your fatherhood, then, and along the way, pick up the habit of absolute honesty that exists between these two. Observe the trust between them, the son's need to see that his father will never break a promise, never leave him, will always tell him the truth if he asks – except, perhaps, if they're dying. His need for reassurance that they're the 'good guys', that they 'carry the fire'. If honesty is there, and love, a firm set of moral principles and a dependable presence, you can't go wrong.

And if you do – well, you can't go as horribly wrong as Joseph Hooper does when he brings Helena Kingshaw and her son Charles to live in his house. We smell a parenting rat straight away, as Joseph never loved the ugly house he inherited from his own father, along with the collection of moths that made the old man a celebrity in his dusty field. And he clearly has not earned the respect of his son, Edmund, either. If only he were older, Joseph muses, and he could blame adolescence for the boy's recalcitrance – but he had left all the child-rearing up to his late wife. It is a mark of his desperation that he has asked Helena Kingshaw to come to live with them as housekeeper. Her son Charles is almost the same age as Edmund, and both adults assume the boys will grow up to love one another as brothers.

They do not count on the deep-rooted dagger of ice that has already established itself in Edmund's chest. From the moment 'Kingshaw' steps foot in his house, Edmund does his absolute best to cow him, scaring him with ghost stories, and undermining him in every way he can. When the boys spend a night lost together in the woods, the tables seem to turn, as Kingshaw is more at home in the natural element – able to light a fire and reassure Edmund when he is scared of the dark. Edmund seems appreciative of this undeserved consideration, but the moment they are rescued, he reverts to type. 'It was Kingshaw, it was Kingshaw, he pushed me in the water,' he accuses. Kingshaw defends himself, but his mother takes her host's side; she has marital designs on Mr Hooper and doesn't want to jeopardise things by suggesting his son's a liar.

Mrs Kingshaw, unforgivably, lacks motherly intuition and indeed wisdom of any sort – failing even to notice when her son is locked in a concrete shed for several hours. But we lay the ultimate blame for the chilling events that follow at Joseph's door. By neglecting his son after the death of his wife, he has created the monster that Edmund, by sheer lack of love and attention, has become; and we hereby hold Joseph Hooper up as one of the worst fathers in literature. Anyone unfortunate enough to be in possession of such a father – or indeed a mother like Mrs Kingshaw – should see the cure for abandonment as a matter of urgency.

As this agonising novel speeds towards its terrible finale, let it teach you not to be too hard on yourself. The path of parenthood is already strewn with guilt: don't let self-criticism trip you up in addition. Women are often reassured that there's 'perfect' and 'good enough' – and 'good enough' is often preferable. It's time men heard the message too. Even if you occasionally burn the beans, forget the gym kit, or catch your child experimenting with the contents of the bathroom cabinet, allow yourself a pat on the back every so often for not being a Mr Hooper, and remember that how-to manual, *The Road*. Keep it simple: love and honest communication are all you need.

SEE ALSO: **children requiring attention, too many** • **single parent, being a** • **trapped by children**

fatherhood, avoiding it

Birdsong
SEBASTIAN FAULKS

No more late night drinking. No more lazy Sundays with newspapers and coffee till noon. No more undivided devotion of girlfriend/wife/partner/dog/mother. No more being able to say, without guilt, 'Just off for a weekend with the boys. See you on Sunday night.'

It's easier for women. As soon as they're pregnant, they start to be changed not just physically but emotionally by the new life that's growing inside them. This is what happens to Isabelle in *Birdsong*, Sebastian Faulks's tear-jerking World War I epic. She realises she is carrying Stephen's child soon after they run away together from Isabelle's unhappy marriage and, almost immediately, she discovers a hitherto unnoticed 'starving' desire for a child. But in her (perhaps hormonal) confusion, she decides not only not to tell Stephen about it, but she abandons him and runs to her sister Jeanne instead.

The next time we see Stephen – emotionally shut down and not having touched a woman for seven years – he is in charge of a platoon in the trenches of the Somme. As they struggle to cope with unimaginable daily horrors, and the possibility of death at any moment, the men send and receive letters from home. We become very aware of which of them has children and which do not as, rightly or wrongly, Faulks uses the existence of children in these men's lives to elicit our greater sympathy. There is Wilkinson, newly married and with a baby on the way, who dies a horrible frontline death. And there is the good-humoured Jack Firebrace who gets word from his wife that his son John is in hospital dangerously ill with diphtheria, and he asks his lieutenant – who, at that moment, is considering whether or not to have Jack shot for falling asleep on duty – whether he has children himself. That lieutenant is Stephen. 'No,' comes the reply. But we, of course, know that he probably does.

We may or may not approve of Faulks differentiating between one man and another in this way, but nevertheless a world opens up in this novel in which those with children differ from those without – and we cannot help feeling that Stephen, a father without knowing it, loses out by his ignorance of his and Isabelle's child. If he were aware of being a father, how might he be different? He does not have Jack shot, but neither is he given hope in the dark days of war by the existence of his child in the way that others are. The novel ends with a birth, and it is one which brings the father concerned such a burst of unexpected joy that he rushes outside and hurls conkers into the air.

If you're an expectant father feeling nothing but bewilderment and a vague sense of dread at the apocalypse lying ahead, this novel's for you. If you're stepping crab-like around the issue of commitment and marriage, this one's for you too. We know of many male partners who have not a jot of fatherly feeling for the embryo they've sired while it's still in the womb, only to fall hopelessly in love the moment it's born. Journey with Stephen and decide for yourself: a narrow escape, or a lost chance to experience an extra dimension to life?

SEE ALSO: **commitment, fear of**

fear of being left on the shelf

SEE: shelf, fear of being left on the

fear of commitment

SEE: commitment, fear of

fear of confrontation

SEE: confrontation, fear of

fear of dinner parties

SEE: dinner parties, fear of

fear of death

SEE: death, fear of

fear of doing tax return

SEE: tax return, fear of doing

fear of finishing

SEE: finishing, fear of

fear of flying

SEE: flying, fear of

fear of sci-fi

SEE: sci-fi, fear of

fear of starting

SEE: starting, fear of

fear of violence

SEE: **violence, fear of**

fifty-something, being

 THE TEN BEST NOVELS FOR FIFTY-SOMETHINGS

White Lightning **JUSTIN CARTWRIGHT**
Disgrace **JM COETZEE**
Spending **MARY GORDON**
The Diaries of Jane Somers **DORIS LESSING**
The Invisible Bridge **JULIE ORRINGER**
The Tenderness of Wolves **STEF PENNEY**
The Satanic Verses **SALMAN RUSHDIE**
The Stone Diaries **CAROL SHIELDS**
Dinner at the Homesick Restaurant **ANNE TYLER**
Young Hearts Crying **RICHARD YATES**

flatulence

*A Confederacy
of Dunces*
**JOHN KENNEDY
TOOLE**

If you have a tendency to suffer from excessive gas leading to belching or flatulence – or, heaven help us, both – you will no doubt feel a great sense of camaraderie and solidarity with the highly educated but seriously slobbish thirty-year-old Ignatius J Reilly. The hero of John Kennedy Toole's posthumously published novel, *A Confederacy of Dunces*, is beset by such calamitous gastro-intestinal problems that he is forever swelling to gargantuan proportions and bouncing, supine, on his bed in order to try and release his 'pyloric valve'* – and thus the pockets of air that tear through his stomach in 'great gaseous rages'. When his mother, with whom he still lives (and who, incidentally, is something of a belcher herself) complains about the terrible stink in his room, Ignatius claims that he finds the smell of his own emissions 'comforting'. 'Schiller needed the scent of apples rotting in his desk in order to write,' he points out. 'I, too, have my needs.'

---

* The ring of muscle which lets food pass from the stomach to the duodenum.

find one of your books, inability to

CREATE A LIBRARY

There are few more frustrating things in life than being possessed by the urge to read or refer to a particular book and then not being able to find it. You know you own it. You can picture it – the colour of the spine, where you last spotted it on your shelves. But it's not there any more. And what is the point of owning books if you can never find the one you want?

We aren't going to *insist* that you alphabetise.* Some people keep their books in a totally random arrangement and are still able to hone in on the required volume with the accuracy of a guided missile. Others use a system that is discernible only to themselves. In her lovely book, *Ex Libris: Confessions of a Common Reader*, Anne Fadiman makes a convincing case for sorting English literature chronologically (the better to 'watch the broad sweep' of six centuries of literature play out) while arranging American literature alphabetically.

It doesn't matter what system you choose; just have a system. Take inspiration from Borges and designate one room in your house the library. If rooms are scarce, hallways, landings, staircases and downstairs loos work well. Build shelves from floor to ceiling. Invest in a small stool on wheels or, even better, a ladder. Every so often, collect stray books and return them to their rightful place (wearing glasses perched on the end of your nose as you do so). Keep a lending diary. Consider a catalogue or an app that stores your books on digital shelves. By giving books a respectful place and space in your house, you enable them to remind you of their presence, breathe their wisdom, and offer themselves up to you, like a long-lost lover, at exactly the right moment in your life.

---

* This is the system of organising books we espouse, although Susan Sontag's insistence that to have Pynchon next to Plato 'would set her teeth on edge' has definitely given us pause for thought. We also arrange according to geography on occasion.

According to Ignatius, the gas has several causes: his mother's erratic driving, the absence of a 'proper geometry and theology' in the modern world, and lying in bed in the morning 'contemplating the unfortunate turn that events had taken since the Reformation.' (Unsurprisingly, his mother, in despair at his slothful lifestyle, is constantly urging him to get a job.) According to his girlfriend Myrna Minkoff (a mouthy wench from the Bronx whom he met at college) it's lying around in his room and feeling like a failure that's the problem (if this sounds familiar, see also: bed, inability to get out of; lethargy; and failure, feeling like a). 'The valve closes because it thinks it is living in a dead organism,' she tells him. 'Open your heart, Ignatius, and you will open your valve.'

It's impossible – unless you're Ignatius – to ignore the role of diet in generating all this gas. Ignatius is partial to a fizzy drink called Dr Nut, and also hotdogs: he works for a while as a hotdog seller and eats far more than he sells. At one point he emits 'the gas of a dozen brownies'.

We suggest that fellow-sufferers allow themselves to cohort with Ignatius only for the duration of the novel. After that, they should avoid processed and fatty foods, quit lying around and go and find a decent job – *not* as a hotdog seller.

SEE ALSO: **accused, being** • **blushing**

flight, missing your

The Stars in the Bright Sky
ALAN WARNER

Och! It's a total disaster. You've missed yer bloody flight. And you've already blown all yer cash on it, money which wasn't yer ain in the first place, but borrowed on your Da's credit card. Yer really ought to be making some phone calls, to yer wee sonny and yer Da, but, aye, have a wee doocht instead. Grab yerself a Guinness Extra Cold to get into the right frame of mind, hog an armchair in Garfunkles in the airport Retail Village, plonk yer arse down and grab *The Stars in the Bright Sky*, and you'll really miss yerself. You'll soon be away with the six perishing characters meandering

find one of your books, inability to

CREATE A LIBRARY

There are few more frustrating things in life than being possessed by the urge to read or refer to a particular book and then not being able to find it. You know you own it. You can picture it – the colour of the spine, where you last spotted it on your shelves. But it's not there any more. And what is the point of owning books if you can never find the one you want?

We aren't going to *insist* that you alphabetise.* Some people keep their books in a totally random arrangement and are still able to hone in on the required volume with the accuracy of a guided missile. Others use a system that is discernible only to themselves. In her lovely book, *Ex Libris: Confessions of a Common Reader*, Anne Fadiman makes a convincing case for sorting English literature chronologically (the better to 'watch the broad sweep' of six centuries of literature play out) while arranging American literature alphabetically.

It doesn't matter what system you choose; just have a system. Take inspiration from Borges and designate one room in your house the library. If rooms are scarce, hallways, landings, staircases and downstairs loos work well. Build shelves from floor to ceiling. Invest in a small stool on wheels or, even better, a ladder. Every so often, collect stray books and return them to their rightful place (wearing glasses perched on the end of your nose as you do so). Keep a lending diary. Consider a catalogue or an app that stores your books on digital shelves. By giving books a respectful place and space in your house, you enable them to remind you of their presence, breathe their wisdom, and offer themselves up to you, like a long-lost lover, at exactly the right moment in your life.

around the airport, while you drunkenly consider yer next move. By the time yer've read twenty pages, yer'll most likely hole up in the airport fra few days, and forget about getting on a plane at all.

The novel takes off, unlike you, with five girls from Warner's previous novel, *The Sopranos*, a group of Scottish teenagers from Our Lady of Perpetual Succour who were on their way to a singing competition from their remote Highland village but bunked off to drink and explore their sexuality instead. Now in their early twenties, they are minus one of their group, who has died from cancer in the unrecorded period between the two novels. She is replaced by Ava, beautiful, rich and complicated, who adds a frisson of stately-home entitlement to the gang with her free-handed purchasing of champagne and largesse with other substances. But the group is dominated by Manda, a large single mother prone to excesses of Guinness and vodka, touchingly vulnerable and oddly appealing despite the many scenes of degradation she incites – puking copiously into a hotel ice machine, cutting up her own turd with a hotel spoon that she then uses to stir everyone's tea, and sliding down a hill at Hever Castle on her ample bottom. Whether it's Bacardi Breezers or Red Bull and vodka, Warner lists their consumption in fascinated, forensic detail during their five days in Gatwick Airport. Yes, that's right, with one brief excursion, they end up spending their holiday at the airport.

Which is what we suggest you do too. It's a pretty disastrous week for them, but for you it'll be a hell of a lot of fun. Whether it's Gatwick or LAX, you'll have a far better time reading this novel than you would have had traipsing around some far-away place where you don't know anyone and where you have no reason to be (see: wanderlust). This group of girls will soon have you guffawing with laughter, spitting with disgust and quite possibly throwing up in the big squishy chairs of the lounge as you eavesdrop on their banter about bikini-lines, threesomes, ghosts and VIP lounges. It'll be the time of yer life.

SEE ALSO: **waiting room, being in a**

flu

The Murder of
Roger Ackroyd
AGATHA CHRISTIE

Something that no medical doctor or scientific researcher has yet noticed, or even studied, is the following strange coincidence: the moment a flu patient begins to read an Agatha Christie novel (and our favourite is *The Murder of Roger Ackroyd*, the Poirot mystery that confirmed Christie's genius as a writer of detective fiction) marks the commencement of their recovery.

If the correlation is more than mere coincidence, we can only speculate as to what is, medically speaking, going on. Perhaps, like fish who cannot refuse the bait, our innate curiosity to find out whodunnit is stronger than the urge to wallow in our fluey misery.* Aches, chills, fever, sore throat, runny nose – all these are as nothing compared to the determination to work out the guilty party *before* Poirot.[†] Perhaps the degree of brain-power required to follow and attempt to solve an Agatha Christie is just the right amount to rally your sick grey cells without actually taxing them unduly – as if you had given them a light, healing massage as opposed to sending them out on a five-mile run.

Whatever the reasons, we prescribe it. Prop yourself up on your pillows. The master work of Poirot – that 'detestable, bombastic, tiresome, egocentric little creep' (Christie's words) – has begun.[‡]

SEE ALSO: **appetite, loss of** • **cold, common** • **exhaustion** •
headache • **man flu** • **nausea** • **pain, being in** • **sweating**

---

* Unless you have the much more serious strain known as man flu, in which case it's the other way round. See: man flu.
† Forget it. You never do.
‡ If this cure works, it proves that you didn't actually have flu in the first place but just a bad cold. See: cold, common. The search for a literary cure for Flu goes on.

flying, fear of

Night Flight
ANTOINE DE
SAINT-EXUPÉRY

Our unconventional cure for this debilitating modern affliction is to slip into your carry-on luggage an account of
a pilot struggling to wrest control of a flimsy two-seater
aircraft caught in a cyclone on its way from Patagonia to
Buenos Aires with the Europe-bound mail: Antoine de Saint-
Exupéry's hair-raising *Night Flight*.

F

173

Fabien, the pilot of the mail-plane, has only been married
three weeks. As his wife gets up in the darkness of the small
hours to kiss him goodbye, she admires him in his flying
leathers, and sees someone almost godlike: here is a man
capable of waging war with the very elements. By the time
ground control spots the storm heading off the Atlantic, it is
too late. Somewhere over the Andes, Fabien is surrounded
and can't turn back. With visibility reduced to nil, he has no
choice but to tough it out from his tiny cockpit, the aircraft
rolling and floundering in its vast sea of pitch. It takes all his
strength to hold the controls steady so that the cables don't
snap. Behind him, the radio operator gets electric shocks in
his fingers when he attempts to tap out a message. No-one
can hear them, no-one can see them. The peaks of the Andes
loom up like towering waves trying to pluck them to their
deaths. Any slackening of will-power, any weakening of his
grip, and Fabien knows they are lost.

You, meanwhile – yes, you, reading *Night Flight* in the air-
conditioned fuselage of your Boeing 747 with a blanket on
your knee, your G&T neatly stowed on your pull-down table
and smiling air hostesses tripping down the aisle beside you,
the mellow voice of the captain calmly announcing that you're
levelling out at 35,000 feet, lifting the blind with your finger to
admire the low orb of the sun ... Terrified, did you say? *Terrified?* Really? How Fabien would smile at the thought!

If your heart insists on pounding, let it pound for Fabien
and his radio controller, for the stricken wife waiting by her
phone, for Fabien's boss, Rivière, holding his terrible vigil on
the tarmac. Or, for that matter, let it pound for Saint-Exupéry
himself, who disappeared while flying over North Africa
in 1943. Peer out your window again. See anyone trying to

shoot you down? Hmm. Don't think so. Get back to your novel, chuck back that G&T, and pull yourself up by your cosy inflight socks.

 THE TEN BEST NOVELS TO READ ON PLANE JOURNEYS

So gripping you'll forget you're 35,000 feet up in the air.

I'm Not Scared NICCOLÒ AMMANITI
The Count of Monte Cristo ALEXANDRE DUMAS
The Magus JOHN FOWLES
Carter Beats the Devil GLEN DAVID GOLD
The Woman in Black SUSAN HILL
The Girl with the Dragon Tattoo STIEG LARSSON
Labyrinth KATE MOSSE
Gaudy Night DOROTHY L SAYERS
The Lovely Bones ALICE SEBOLD
The Shadow of the Wind CARLOS RUIZ ZAFÓN

SEE ALSO: **anxiety • claustrophobia • panic attack**

foreign, being

*Everything is
Illuminated*
**JONATHAN
SAFRAN FOER**

If people dub you a foreigner and you do not dig this appellation very much, and it spleens you that they think you have shit between your brains just because you come from a different part of the globe, we suggest you make a feature of it, like Alex, the noncompetent narrator of *Everything is Illuminated*. Then, even if you're not a particularly premium sort of person and not many girls want to be carnal with you, you can parrot him and at least make people dig you. Alex insures his father, the owner of Heritage Touring, that he is fluid in English, and so he's despatched to be a translator and guide for the novel's hero Jonathan Safran Foer (we are meaning the character here, not the author, though you are right to be confusing as they share many qualities, all of them premium) and together with Alex's weeping grandfather, once a farmer but now retarded, and a mentally deranged dog called Sammy Davis Junior, Junior (which we agree is not very flaccid to utter) they promenade in quest of a small Ukrainian shtetl dubbed Trachimbrod in the hope of dishing up the woman who may have salvaged Jonathan's grandfather from the Nazis. The history of Trachimbrod, told by Jonathan in interminable chapters, is an electrical one. But it's Alex's abnormal and memorisable voice – a potent result of him referencing a thesaurus rather than a dictionary – that is winning us. We suggest that if you are anticipating being foreign in the near future or when you are less miniature, you go forth and disseminate some currency on a thesaurus or equivalent (we are cocksure that a cookery book or an automotive manual would deliver you) in the language in which you are incompletely fluid and you will not only illuminate yourself but make yourself very charming and oppressive in the process.

SEE ALSO: **different, beinghome** • **sickness** • **left out, feeling** • **outsider, being an** • **words, lost for**

forty-something, being

 THE TEN BEST NOVELS FOR FORTY-SOMETHINGS

The Kindness of Women JG BALLARD
Seize the Day SAUL BELLOW
The Debut ANITA BROOKNER
The Good Earth PEARL S BUCK
Daniel Deronda GEORGE ELIOT
Daisy Fay and the Miracle Man FANNIE FLAGG
May We Be Forgiven AM HOMES
A Heart so White JAVIER MARÍAS
In Praise of Older Women STEPHEN VIZINCZEY
A Handful of Dust EVELYN WAUGH

friend, falling out with your best

So Long, See You Tomorrow WILLIAM MAXWELL

We hear a lot about the pain of a failed romantic relationship, but what about the loss of a best friend of many years standing when, for whatever reason, you fall out irredeemably? Friends are meant to be forever, after all, and the pain of losing the one person in your life who has known you (perhaps) from your youth, seen you at your worst and understands you inside out, is truly gutting. Not only must you face a future without them, but you will find yourself questioning whether you are, in fact, a good friend to others and, in turn, a good person.

This sorry state of affairs is captured in all its poignancy by William Maxwell in his exquisitely written novella, *So Long, See You Tomorrow*. Clarence Smith and Lloyd Wilson are tenant farmers on adjacent properties in rural Illinois. Marooned on the vast grasslands, the only lights that can be seen from one house are the lights of the other. And over the years the two men come to depend on each other: when Lloyd has a sick calf, he calls Clarence before calling the vet. And when the blades of Clarence's mower jam, Lloyd hears the sputtering engine from a quarter of a mile away and if it doesn't start up again immediately, he goes straight over. They are the only friend each other has.

Fifty years on, the novel's elderly narrator – a man who grew up nearby and has an equally moving story of his own, which we won't go into here – looks back at the painful journey of Smith and Wilson and its tragic endgame. There is no judgement of either the betrayer or the betrayed – for both Smith and Wilson have their sides of the story, and Maxwell shows compassion for both points of view. What is left is a weight of sadness that the narrator still finds difficult to bear. Maxwell's slow, elegiac prose, rising up like mist from the page, takes you beyond simplistic he-saids/she-saids to a place concerned with the ineffability of grief, the terrible fact of shattered lives.

If it's not too late, do whatever you can to mend your friendship: new friends are hard to come by the older you get and you can never replace all that shared history. If the hurt or resentment feels too great, or you cannot win your friend's forgiveness, Maxwell's deeply understanding novel will help you feel your loss and grieve – and ensure that you'll never again treat a friend in a way you'll regret.

SEE ALSO: **loneliness** • **regret** • **sadness**

friends, in need of

SEE: **left out, feeling** • **loneliness** • **outsider, being an** •
unpopular, being

G

gambling

The Dice Man
LUKE RHINEHART

Take a dice. Write down six actions you could take today. Think sublime. Think ridiculous. For example:

1. Shave off all your body hair
2. Invite to dinner the next person that walks past you, regardless of age, sex or species
3. Stick a pin in a world map and go wherever it lands
4. Send this book to your boss, highlighting all the ailments from which he or she suffers
5. Take a bucket and spade and walk all the way to the sea
6. Read *The Dice Man* by Luke Rhinehart, to cure you of your addiction to gambling

Make a solemn promise that you will do whatever the dice tells you.

Now, you know what to do.

SEE ALSO: **broke, being** • **risks, taking too many**

gas, excessive

SEE: **flatulence**

genius, being a

SEE: **brainy, being exceptionally**

give up halfway through, refusal to

ADOPT THE FIFTY-PAGE RULE

Some readers cannot bear to leave a novel unfinished. They'll plough on doggedly, joylessly, until they've reached the bitter end, either so that they can say, 'I've read it' without blushing, or so that they aren't left with an unfinished story, however dull or irksome, dangling in their over-dutiful head.

Life is too short. Read the first fifty pages of every novel you start, preferably in a maximum of two sittings. If, after that time, the book has failed to infiltrate your solar plexus, abandon it. As a reader it's important you learn to trust your judgement and your knowledge of your own literary taste; every book you read or try to read helps to hone and direct your future reading path (and if you need help with this, see: identity, unsure of your reading). Don't bludgeon yourself into taking paths that are not fruitful or enjoyable to you. Give every book you don't finish to someone who may like it better. This is both a gesture of respect to the book and the effort that went into writing it, and an insurance against ending up with a houseful of unfinished books staring at you balefully every time you walk past.

give up halfway through, tendency to

READ IN LONGER STRETCHES

It may be that you are reading a terribly slow book – as although some have momentum from the very first line, and others gain it more slowly but reach full speed by the midway point, some are defiantly, or obliviously, slow for the duration. But if you notice a recurring tendency to launch in with great enthusiasm but to slow to a dawdle before finally grinding to a halt, if your books are studded with telltale bookmarks forever at the halfway point, the chances are that the problem is not the book, but you.

The most likely diagnosis is that you don't give books a chance. You read in very short snatches – perhaps only five or ten minutes at a time – and therefore never get into the book. This is not fair to either book or author. Stories worth telling take time to tell: characters, like houses, must be built on firm foundations and we need to care about them before we can be moved by what happens to them.

Do not attempt to begin a new book until you can devote at least forty-five minutes to the first and second sittings. Hopefully, by then, the book will have wound itself around your innards and will keep you coming back for more. But if you're an inveterate giver-upper, try not to read for less than forty-five minutes *every* time you read. And if that still doesn't work, you've no option but to take a day off work, tie one of your limbs to the leg of your chair and not release yourself until you've reached the end.

giving birth

SEE: **childbirth**

giving up

SEE: **give up halfway through, tendency to** • **hope, loss of** • **smoking, giving up**

gluttony

The Debt to Pleasure
JOHN LANCHESTER

The word gluttony, derived from the Latin *gluttire*, means to gulp down or swallow. This translates in modern parlance into over-indulgence in and over-consumption of food, drink, or other consumables to the point of extravagance or waste. In other words, being a greedy pig. If gluttony is your malady, indulge in this juicy novel before you sit down to eat. (If it's a friend that's the pig, leave this novel on their plate and serve the supper up late.)

The cure it affects will be served to you in three courses, as follows.

For Starters: this book is impossible to gulp down quickly, and will delay the eating of your dinner, perhaps indefinitely. Tarquin, the narrator, expresses his thoughts so precisely, with such relish for the words themselves, that you'll want to read every paragraph twice then copy it out in your reading journal to chew over as you would a morsel of calf's liver. Read not just before eating, but between courses too, to slow a meal down. You might even get up from the table to try out one of the recipes it contains (blinis, omelette, and salt marsh lamb, to name a few). For this novel, as with this part of your cure, is an almost eternal digression, using recipes as an excuse to reminisce, philosophise and hint at where we are really going with this meandering yarn.

For your Main course: the lingering delight that Tarquin takes in each ingredient will teach you how to savour, rather than scoff. Each edible you come across divulges a surprise. Peaches, for instance, remind Tarquin of his brother, Bartholemew – not just because they spent a summer gorging on this furry fruit in boyish delight but because as a six-year-old, our culinary enthusiast could not resist an early experiment in jam-making, peach kernels and all, accidentally releasing the cyanide in the kernel that caused a near-fatal case of poisoning.

And for Dessert: there is none, after all. Sorry. Because by now you will have the disconcerting sense that there is something sinister going on – and that you need to watch your waistline (or see: obesity).

This novel will teach you to relish more, but eat less – and get to know the exact origin of every ingredient before it makes its way to your stomach.

SEE ALSO: **flatulence • obesity • toothache**

goody-goody, being a

The Master and Margarita
MIKHAIL BULGAKOV

When the devil appears in a Moscow park one fine spring evening in the 1930s, he inserts himself between two bookish types deep in discussion on a bench. One is Berlioz, the bald, portly editor of a literary magazine. The other is Bezdomny, a young poet. The devil has no trouble seizing control of the conversation – which is about the existence or otherwise of Jesus Christ. For the devil, expensively dressed in a grey suit, 'foreign' shoes, a grey beret cocked jauntily over one eye, has more charisma than both men put together. 'Oh, how delightful!' he exclaims when his two new friends confirm they are atheists. The devil has an unpredictable, childlike mind, easily bored and always on the lookout for a joke – ideally at someone else's expense. One minute he's bursting into peals of laughter loud enough to 'startle the sparrows out of the tree', the next he is cruelly predicting Berlioz's death by decapitation under a tram (it comes true). And when Berlioz asks him where he's going to stay while in Moscow, he winks and says, 'In your flat.'

The devil has edge, he has wit. As in *Paradise Lost*, he has all the good lines and keeps everyone on their toes. When Bezdomny feels an urge for a cigarette, the devil – or Professor Woland, as it says on his calling card – reads his mind and whips out an impressive, gold cigarette case with just the right brand inside. He and his bizarre retinue – which includes a large, crude, vodka-swigging cat called Behemoth – astonish the audience at the theatre by causing a collection of Parisian *haute couture* (hats, dresses, handbags, lipsticks) to materialise on stage and inviting all the ladies to strip and re-dress.

And, of course, the devil holds the best parties. Moscow has never seen the likes of it before or since: a midnight, full-moon ball at which the guest of honour (Margarita) is washed in blood and roses. There's champagne in the fountains, scarlet-breasted parrots screeching 'Ecstasy! Ecstasy!', and an orchestra conducted by Johann Strauss. This is the devil, though, and it's not all innocent fun and games. Apart from Margarita, the guests at the ball arrive in various states of decomposition, having come straight from hell.

We're not suggesting you renounce goodness and turn to evil. We're just saying liven up, get an edge. Don't go twisting off heads like Behemoth, but do throw scandalous parties. Keep a glint of mischief in your eye, a shard of wickedness up your sleeve. It will make you a lot more fun.

SEE ALSO: **beans, temptation to spill the** • **organised, being too** • **risks, not taking enough** • **teetotaller, being a**

greed

The Pearl
JOHN STEINBECK

The Colour
ROSE TREMAIN

The desire to have more than you actually need – more money, more possessions, more power – is a strange predilection. Because to what purpose do we acquire, collect, amass? If you don't need it, how will you use it? An excess of possessions can sit as heavily as excess weight; and having more money in the bank than you know what to do with will spoil the pleasure of working and saving towards a hard-won treat. Besides, when is enough enough? Because greed knows no end, and when our greed becomes insatiable – leading to hoarding, stealing and deceiving – we know we have become lost in its meaningless pursuit.

Steinbeck demonstrates the power of greed to destroy a

simple family in his allegorical tale, *The Pearl*. Kino and Juana
have what he portrays as the perfect life: they live in a shack
by the sea, where Kino makes his living by diving for pearls.
One day their infant son, Coyotito, is bitten by a scorpion and
becomes dangerously ill. Unable to pay for medical treatment,
Juana prays that Kino will find a pearl of great value so that
their son can live. Miraculously, Kino finds exactly the pearl
of their prayers. Not only can they now afford a doctor for
Coyotito, but they can give him an education. But no sooner
is the pearl in Kino's possession, than their world begins to
unravel. Other people hear about the pearl, and want it for
themselves. Soon, Kino will do anything to protect the pearl.
His wife immediately sees the potential for trouble and tries
to persuade Kino to hurl the pearl back into the sea. But he
won't let his dream of wealth go. Before long they are forced
to leave their village, and will soon lose more than they know.

It's not the lure of gold that brings Joseph Blackstone to
New Zealand in Rose Tremain's *The Colour*. His motivation
for upping sticks from his Norfolk origins and buying land
in the New World for a pound an acre is to start a clean state.
But when the settler finds flecks of gold in the creek on his
farm, his innocent dreams alchemise into something more.
The modest rewards of farming suddenly seem small and
petty compared to the wealth that gold would bring him and
he turns his attention fully to the search for 'the Colour'.

Tremain vividly conveys the desperate lengths that men
will go to in order to satiate their lust for gold – up to their
necks in mud, sleeping in rat-infested tents, walking for days
over treacherous terrain to find the longed-for virgin seam.
When Joseph's wife Harriet turns up at the digging site,
Joseph is horrified, viewing her as a potential thief of his
meagre findings. His awakened greed becomes the unholy
twin of the evil deed that caused him to run away from England. But Harriet's reasons for joining him are nothing to do
with greed at all – she has come looking for her husband's
love.

Let Harriet and Juana be your mentors, representing the
more grounded approach to the possibility of unexpected
wealth. If you allow greed to take root inside you, it will take

over your life. No good comes of avarice – but plenty comes from taking the moral high ground.

SEE ALSO: **extravagance** • **gluttony** • **selfishness** • **selling your soul**

grief

SEE: **broken heart** • **death of a loved one** • **sadness** • **widowed, being** • **yearning, general**

grumpiness

The Island of Doctor Moreau
HG WELLS

If you are as grumpy as Doctor Moreau in HG Wells's anti-vivisection polemic of 1896, beware of the effect you are having on friends, colleagues and cohabitants. Peevish demeanours are infectious – so much so that you'll soon find yourself surrounded by other truculent, ornery people, when they were previously sunny and light.

Moreau, in the privacy of his island in the Pacific, is attempting to turn various four-legged animals – hogs, hyenas, dogs and leopards – into human beings, using a mixture of surgery and behavioural conditioning. Witness to his experiments is Edward Prendick – a shipwrecked Englishman who is rescued by Moreau only to find himself being held captive. At first Prendick gets the wrong end of the stick, believing Moreau's intention is to turn humans into beasts, and fears for his life. Then he realises it's the other way round. Moreau is only partially successful; his semi-human creations have a tendency to revert to their bestial natures, going down on all fours and chasing rabbits – hence his bad mood. And in the end, Prendick has nothing to fear from the Beast Folk. But by the time he has spent many months on this island, he's as crabby as Moreau, having been exposed for far too long to the scientist's grumps.

Don't bring everyone down with you. See our cures for: irritability and misanthropy; then consider a change of career (see: career, being in the wrong).

SEE ALSO: **dissatisfaction** • **querulousness**

guilt

Crime and Punishment
FYODOR DOSTOYEVSKY

Have you compromised your own standards of conduct, or violated a moral code? Or does your guilt spring from something that you should have done, but didn't?

Some people have an inability to feel guilt, and they should be avoided (psychopaths, babies). For the rest of us, guilt and its little sister shame (see: shame) should perhaps be embraced, as some psychologists argue these emotions are essential to the collective morality that binds society together. As with any negative emotion, left to fester guilt can be destructive to oneself and others – easily turning into passive or not-so-passive aggression, a desire to control (see: control freak, being a), or into anger that eats you away from the inside out (see: anger). We advise that you feel your guilt, then immediately read our cure. Duly acknowledged, it can be rooted out, analysed and then – once any appropriate apologies have been made or accusations levelled – you are free to move on.

Our cure is the most radical and profound exploration of guilt in literature: Dostoyevsky's *Crime and Punishment*. Written when Dostoyevsky himself was near destitution and deeply in debt, many autobiographical elements have crept in, and one can't help thinking that Dostoyevsky felt many of the same emotions as his hero. Rodion Romanovich Raskolnikov is a former student in need of a job, living in a tiny garret on the top floor of a run-down apartment building in St Petersburg. Bilious, dressed in tatters, and broke, he has an unnerving tendency to talk to himself, but he is good-looking, proud, and intelligent. One would think he had prospects, therefore, but it's clear from the start that he is contemplating something desperate and dreadful – and indeed he has resolved to murder an old woman for her money, having persuaded himself that, being a pawnbroker, she is morally moribund, and therefore her death justifiable. Unfortunately, he's caught in the act by the old woman's half-sister, and, in the heat of the moment, Raskolnikov murders her too.

He steals from the old woman, and hides his bounty

guilt, reading-associated

You have bought the latest talked-about novel. It winks at you seductively from the shelf next to your bed. You absolutely intend to read it. All your friends are reading it. But somehow you never seem to . . . actually . . . read it. Sometimes it's a problem of over-ambition. You decide on a whim it's time to tackle *Infinite Jest*. Or to read all the winners of the Booker Prize since its inception. Unsurprisingly, you never begin.

The key is to schedule regular reading times into your week. Designate one lunchtime per week to reading – even if it's only half an hour in a café near your place of work. Block-book one evening a week as your reading evening; and announce it to whoever you live with. Fence off a part of the weekend – just an hour to start with, then two when your reading muscles are toned. Slowly, you will find yourself developing a good reading habit. And before long you'll have swapped your reading guilt for all sorts of other kinds of guilt: housework guilt, failure-to-walk-the-dog guilt, DIY guilt . . . We would go on, but it's time for us to go and read.

under a rock. But almost immediately he is overcome with appalling remorse. A terrible liar, he wanders around St Petersburg, wracked with fever and raving. Meanwhile, another man confesses to the murders and – were it not for his conscience, and the friendship of the wise Sonya who understands how life cannot resume without a confession – it's clear that Raskolnikov could get away with his crime if he chose to.

Dostoyevsky's portrayal of his young hero's torment is fascinating and painful to witness. It is mostly down to Sonya that Raskolnikov survives. If you don't have a Sonia in your life, borrow Raskolnikov's. Confess, pay your penance, expunge your guilt. Only then will you deserve the Sonias – and their equivalents – of this world.

SEE ALSO: **guilt, reading-associated** • **regret**

H

haemorrhoids

Downriver
IAIN SINCLAIR

If you suffer from piles, it's unremitting agony. And we all know about those medical cures. Tie an elastic band round them till they drop off. Freeze them off, have them amputated. Stuff them back into your arse. Ignore them. Walk around wanting to shove a cactus up your bum. Have colonic irrigation.

A more gentle (and potentially permanent) cure is to read Iain Sinclair's novel, *Downriver*. In twelve interwoven tales, stretching from the tragic sinking in the Thames of the Princess Alice in 1878 when 640 people drowned, to a near future in which the Thatcherite-style government policies of the 'Widow' have inexorably destroyed life along London's river, Sinclair's enigmatic narrator takes us on a waterside tour. He travels mainly by foot – for Sinclair is the 'walking author' renowned, like Dickens, for his London perambulations – and in the company of a motley collection of friends: actors, second-hand book dealers, tour-guides. We visit a world of rare and second-hand bookshops, criminals and vagrants obsessed with the occult – a London that most of us were unaware existed. His prose is dense and witty, sending your imagination ahead of your feet. Play as an audio book and walk as you listen. You'll be so well entertained that your mind will be taken off your bottom.

hangover

The Little White Car
DANUTA DE RHODES

Your forehead is a stage, thudding with the beat of thirty drummers. Your tongue is a piece of cooked bacon that's been sitting in the fridge for a week. And your mind is a washing machine on a fast spin cycle, with shreds of the events of last night whapping against the sides, revealing their colours for a brief, ghastly moment before sinking back into the foamy suds.

Yes, you have a hangover.

You get out of bed, or off the sofa, or wherever it was you passed out. You stumble towards the sink and fill a glass with cold water. You tip back your head (ouch!) and begin to gulp, the lovely cool liquid bringing back to life the . . . oh god. Because that's when you remember. Worse than the pounding head. Worse than the confusion. The memory. Of what. Exactly. It was. You did. Last night.

At this point, reach for *The Little White Car* by Danuta de Rhodes. Because whatever it was you did, it wasn't as bad as what Veronique did, the spoilt twenty-two-year-old Parisian girl who emerged from her hangover to realise, with a plunge into a new Ice Age . . . well, you'll have to read it and see.

Call in sick, then go back to bed. There you will read – in big fat type that won't challenge your eyes, and straightforward prose that won't befuddle your head – a lesson in how much worse it *could* have been. Go on, indulge.*

SEE ALSO: **anxiety** • **bed, inability to get out of** • **headache** • **lethargy** • **nausea** • **pain, being in** • **paranoia** • **sweating**

---

* British author Dan Rhodes did – although he hid his shame at having used such a tasteless premise for this delightful trifle of a novel by passing it off as the work of one Danuta de Rhodes, an authoress several years his junior who works 'in the fashion industry'.

happiness, searching for

Fahrenheit 451
RAY BRADBURY

Happiness: life's ultimate goal. Or is it?

Many of us in the West spend our lives searching for this transient state: in love, in work, in travel, in the decoration of our homes. That it beckons to us from advertisements and lifestyle television is a modern malaise. But it's important to remember that people did not think of happiness as a given right until the twentieth century – and in many Eastern cultures, still do not. For many, life is something to be endured and learnt from, rather than a source of expected pleasure. To have food, a roof over your head and the freedom to pursue your religious beliefs – these things are enough. Start thinking that you *ought* to be happy and you open yourself up to all kinds of disappointment.

We're with the East on this: the relentless pursuit of happiness is an ailment, and must be cured. Ray Bradbury knew this too. His prescient *Fahrenheit 451*, first published in 1953, came very close to showing us life as we now know it. In his dystopian future, nobody reads novels any more. At first this is because people want their fiction in smaller and smaller doses, not having the attention span or patience to read a whole book (sound familiar? See: give up halfway through, tendency to). Then they start to think that books are their enemy, irresponsibly presenting different views and states of mind. Surely they'd all be happier living in an emotionless no-man's-land with no strong feelings at all?

To counteract their emotional void, deprived of culture and deep thought as they are, they begin to live faster and faster, racing around the city at break-neck speeds (in Bradbury's future, Beetles are the super-cars of the highway) – and killing whatever gets in their way. They almost never see their children, who go to school nine days out of ten. Having kids is a waste of time anyway, they opine; the women prefer to stay at home watching an endless interactive soap called *The Family* – the fate of which becomes more important to them than their own. (Brilliant as he was, Bradbury didn't quite make the leap into a time when women might want to work too.) Doped by these sagas, they go to bed with 'shells' in their ears transmitting junky newsfeeds and more meaningless dramas all night long. Sleeping pills are popped like candy. Suicide is common, and attracts little remark.

When Montag, a Fireman whose job it is to burn illegal books – and sometimes the people reading them too – meets a teenage girl who takes the time to look at the stars, smell the grass and question the dandelions about love, he realises that he is not as happy in his emotionally neutered state as he thought he was. He begins to wake up to a world of beauty and feeling, and wonders what the books that he burns might contain. One night he reads Matthew Arnold's poem 'Dover Beach' to his wife's guests, interrupting an episode of *The Family* to do so, and the result of his reading is uncontrollable weeping and heartbreak: 'Poetry and tears, poetry and suicide and awful feelings, poetry and sickness; all that mush!' one distraught listener cries. Montag is forced to burn his own books – and his house with them – but he holds onto the belief that a future without the wisdom of books is an unbearable one. He would rather feel and suffer than live the comatose life that 'civilisation' considers the route to happiness.

Fahrenheit 451 will teach you that life is made of a rich variety of experiences. Live to the full not by seeking happiness, but by embracing knowledge, literature, truth and feelings of every sort. And in case Bradbury's vision becomes a reality, consider learning a novel by heart, as Montag does. You never know when you might need to pass it on to the rest of humanity.

SEE ALSO: **dissatisfaction** • **Mr/Mrs Right, looking for**

hatred

The River
Between
NGŨGĨ WA
THIONG'O

Nineteen
Eighty-Four
GEORGE ORWELL

Hate is like a poisonous plant. Allow it to take root in your being and it will gradually consume you from within, contaminating everything you touch. Whether you hate another person, other drivers, semolina, hipster bloggers or reality TV, it doesn't make much difference. Neither does it make it any better if the hate is justified and understandable, such as hating someone who has done you a grievous harm. The fact that you are nurturing this violent emotion in your heart will ultimately be a violence against yourself.*

In *The River Between*, Ngũgĩ wa Thiong'o shows very clearly how hatred can set in between two factions with opposed religious, political or philosophical beliefs. Those consumed by hate would do well to read this fable-like retelling of *Romeo and Juliet* and ask themselves whether they too might be guilty of clinging too rigidly to a set of beliefs.

On either side of the river Honia (meaning 'cure'), lie two ridges. On one is the village of Kameno, and on the other Makuyu. Here the Gikuyu people of Kenya live undisturbed – until the white man arrives with his 'clothes like butterflies', new ways and new religion. Joshua, an elder of Kameno, is the first convert to Christianity. Soon he has the villagers turning away from their tribal customs. Trouble hits when his daughter Muthoni decides that she wants to be initiated into womanhood in the traditional, 'beautiful' way – circumcision – and dies following the procedure. She rapidly becomes a symbol for everything deemed barbaric and pagan about the old Gikuyu ways. The two villages pit themselves against each

H

193

---

* Because of this, neuroscientists have worked hard to investigate the neurobiology of hate. A few years ago they announced that they'd pinpointed the specific areas of our brains responsible for the venomous emotion. These areas included the middle front gyrus, the right putamen, the premotor cortex and the frontal pole. We tell you this mostly because we wanted a reason to write 'middle front gyrus' and 'right putamen', but also because we find it amusing to point out that some of these areas of the brain – the putamen for example – had previously been named by neuroscientists investigating the neurobiology of love and claiming to have pinpointed the specific areas of our brains responsible for the feeling of love. Which either goes to show that love and hate are closely related, or it shows nothing at all. Luckily, we have literature as a back-up to neuroscience.

other, the old ways against the new. And when Waiyuku from Makuyu, with his beautiful 'kinking' hair and eyes that 'blaze', falls in love with Nyamburu, Joshua's remaining daughter, the people are given a focus for their hate. This shared, group hate gains momentum in the same way as a herd of bullocks running downhill gains speed; and in the way of things that have lost control, it heads to mayhem and destruction.

Don't let yourself get swept up mindlessly by hate in this way. Instead, allow yourself to be lulled by Thiong'o's poetic, expansive prose, the importance he places on the land, and the concept of love as a guiding principle. Don't be a zealot. Be a moderate. See things from another's point of view. Be open to compromise and the fact that others may not wish to live as you do. This way you can turn your hate into love.

If letting go of your hatred is just too hard, read George Orwell's *Nineteen Eighty-Four* and study what happens in 'Hate Week' – seven days dedicated to rousing processions, speeches, banners and films intended to whip the masses into a frenzy of hatred directed at the state's number-one enemy, Eurasia. By day six, the crowd is in such a maddened delirium of hatred that had they got their hands on individual Eurasians they'd have torn them to pieces. But then, suddenly, the object of hatred is switched. Word goes round that the enemy is no longer Eurasia. It's Eastasia. Hurriedly, posters are ripped off walls, banners are trampled underfoot. The crowd barely misses a beat. Within a few moments, the 'feral roars of rage' have been redirected to the Eastasians instead.

The apparent ease of this redirection certainly gives one pause for thought. Does the feeling of hate have anything to do with the object of hate at all? Does it not perhaps have more to do with a determination to *find* an object on which to unleash one's hatred? Take a break from your hating, and take a long, hard look within yourself. If this moment in *Nineteen Eighty-Four* doesn't make you reconsider, you're too serious a case for the gentle reaches of our cures. Possibly you're a psychopath, and we refer you to a psychiatrist instead.

SEE ALSO: **anger** · **bitterness** · **judgemental, being** ·
murderous thoughts · **rage**

haunted, being

If you count yourself among the haunted, one of the problems can be getting others to take your tales of the haunting seriously. If this is the case, give them *The Woman in Black* by Susan Hill. Set in Eel Marsh House, a lonely abode that is cut off by the tide twice a day, it tells of the haunting by an extremely bitter ghost of Arthur Kipps, the solicitor called in to clear up the estate of the house's mistress, recently deceased. It's a novel that cannot fail to send multiple chills down the spine, and while doing nothing to cure you of your own haunting, will persuade your friend to listen to your story, wide-eyed.

For you, we prescribe Toni Morrison's Pulitzer Prize-winning novel *Beloved*. Sethe is an ex-slave living with her teenage daughter Denver, and the ghost of her dead baby. They have grown used to the presence of the spiteful spirit, which shatters mirrors, makes baby handprints in the icing of birthday cakes, and creates puddles of red misery in the doorway that visitors must wade through to come inside. Indeed most people give the house and its occupants a wide berth. But when Sethe's old friend Paul D reappears after eighteen years, the ghost seems to go quiet. Until, that is, it returns in human form.

Beloved walks out of the river as a fully clothed adult. She spends a few days summoning up the energy to open her eyelids, while her dress dries and her perfectly unlined skin grows accustomed to the sun. Her voice is peculiarly low, she is eternally thirsty, and she seems to possess superhuman strength, able to pick up her older sister with one hand. But Beloved is not a positive force: she drinks in her mother's love like the milk she never had enough of. She pushes Paul away from Sethe while forcing him, against his better judgement and desire, to 'touch her on the inside part'. She gorges on life like a blowfly. We know this cannot last. Sethe has within her the means to placate Beloved – but first she has a difficult truth to acknowledge to herself.

Hauntees take heart. Whatever haunts you can not only be faced, but spoken to, negotiated with, even loved. If your ghost wants to come and live with you for a while, spend all your money and drive your loved ones away, so be it. Once it's got over itself, you can send it back to where it belongs.

SEE ALSO: **demons, facing your**

hayfever

20,000 Leagues Under the Sea **JULES VERNE**

Hayfever can ruin entire summers. When the itchy eyes, streaming nose, tight chest and difficulty in breathing gets too bad, you long to plunge into a cool, clear pool – somewhere no pollen can reach you. Or, even better, to hitch a ride in a submarine and go and live at the bottom of the ocean. Perhaps it was hayfever that drew Captain Nemo, the mysterious nautical traveller of the most famous of Verne's novels, to his peculiar underwater existence. The misanthropic Captain shrugged off 'that intolerable earthly yoke', and took to living in a 'sea unicorn of colossal dimensions' (which naval observers at first took to be a giant narwhal), shunning everyone and everything apart from the sea creatures that he studies (see also: misanthropy). His ship, *Nautilus*, travels at incredible speeds and is capable of scientific wonders far beyond the technological know-how reached on land, since Nemo is both explorer and inventor. He dines off sea cucumber preserves that he believes even a Malaysian would declare to be unrivalled, sugar from the North Sea fucus plants and marmalade of sea anemone. Nemo is not shy about his success as an underwater despot, calling himself 'the Man of the Waters, the Spirit of the Seas', recognising no superiors, and confident that he could pay off the ten-billion-franc national debt using the treasures he has found beneath the waves.

Whenever those pesky pollen motes threaten to invade your head, grab Jules Verne and escape to the airlessness of Captain Nemo's underwater kingdom. You never know, it might inspire you to design your own *Nautilus*, or strap an oxygen tank to your back and take to the depths yourself.

headache

. Snow falls; flame-hair Snow steps light through air.
Bed of ice. Resting blind.
Mind pure. .

SEE ALSO: **pain, being in**

hiccups

Nobody knows what causes them, but we all have our own favourite method of curing them. John, the narrator of Philip Hensher's *The Fit* (in which a hiccup is designated by an '!') has the hiccups for an entire month – starting the morning his wife Janet unexpectedly walks out. He tries a litany of cures, from the classics (drinking a glass of water backwards, holding his breath, drinking champagne) to the not-so-classic (smoking a cigarette, being tickled, kissing, and snorting cocaine). Several shocks occur, quite by chance – including a German man with three rucksacks who turns up on his doorstep and announces he's in love with him. None of it works.

But then, finally, something does. You'll have to read to the end to find out what – but suffice to say that, as with most literary afflictions, psychology has a lot to do with both cause and cure. It certainly won't hurt to join John on his journey of self-discovery, either to trigger one of your own, or simply for the empathetic company of a fellow sufferer. One doesn't want to wrestle with a spasming diaphragm all alone. And if they're still there after *The Fit* (and be warned, as John discovers in his *Guinness Book of Records*, one unfortunate hiccupper had them for seventeen years), we suggest you administer a short, sharp literary shock, the best of which are waiting to jump out at you from the pages of the novels below.

Guaranteed to deliver an ice-cube down your back, these novels either accumulate shock as they go or pack a punch on a particular page. We're not telling which.

Señor Vivo and the Coca Lord LOUIS DE BERNIÈRES
The Hunger Games SUZANNE COLLINS
Gone Girl GILLIAN FLYNN
A Prayer for Owen Meany JOHN IRVING
Schindler's Ark THOMAS KENEALLY
The Painted Bird JERZY KOSIŃSKI
Beside the Sea VÉRONIQUE OLMI
The White Hotel DM THOMAS
Anna Karenina LEO TOLSTOY
Legend of a Suicide DAVID VANN

high blood pressure

Known to reduce anxiety, reading is a great habit to acquire if you've got high blood pressure; especially if you do it with a small furry animal curled up on your knee. Be careful what you choose though, something too racy, or nail-biting, and you'll be pumping the blood even harder than before. To slow you down, reduce anxiety, and encourage you to live in the moment, take your pick from our list of calming reads: novels that do not rush towards their resolutions, but luxuriate in non-event and the virtues of the placid life. What they lack in pace they more than make up for in beauty and their ability to promote thought.

THE TEN BEST NOVELS TO LOWER YOUR BLOOD PRESSURE

The Mezzanine NICHOLSON BAKER
Villette CHARLOTTE BRONTË
A Closed Eye ANITA BROOKNER
The City of Your Final Destination PETER CAMERON
Your Presence is Requested at Suvanto MAILE CHAPMAN
The Hours MICHAEL CUNNINGHAM
The Heart is a Lonely Hunter CARSON MCCULLERS

homelessness

If you're a vagabond at heart – or in reality – homelessness may have had an initial appeal. Without being tied down to one particular place, you're free to go where the wind blows you; without rent or bills to pay, you can spend your time in non-labouring ways. But whatever its cause, the state of homelessness becomes exhausting after a while. Whether you are constantly on the road, living in a makeshift tepee exposed to the elements, or endeavouring to adapt to the habits of other people kind enough to take you in, the need for privacy, independence and rootedness becomes impossible to ignore in the end.

For twelve-year-old Anne in Mona Simpson's spirited novel *Anywhere But Here*, homelessness brings with it a constant state of anxiety. After three short years of marriage, her mother Adele decides it's time to move on, and drives them both from Wisconsin to California on her abandoned husband's credit card – ostensibly so that Anne can 'be a child star while [she is] still a child', but actually because being on the move is all Adele knows how to do. While they're waiting for their car to be fixed in Scottsdale, Arizona, Adele asks a real-estate agent to show them round a house – and for a moment, Anne allows herself to believe her mother is serious, that this is a place she might, at last, make her home. She starts 'to breathe slower' again. But once they've eaten all they can eat at the restaurant the agent takes them to afterwards, they're back on the road again.

Anne understands more than her mother ever will that to develop and explore in normal adolescent ways, she needs stability and routine. If you spend all your energy looking for somewhere to sleep every night, how can you have energy for anything else?

Perhaps the answer is to build yourself a house. If you've

holiday, not knowing what novels to take on

PLAN AHEAD TO AVOID PANIC PURCHASES

Don't make the mistake so many of us do of thinking you'll find the perfect novel to take on holiday with you at the airport bookshop. You'll be in a rush, and you'll have a limited selection to choose from – and you'll probably end up grabbing the nearest heavily promoted bestseller. Don't waste your precious holiday on pulp. It's the perfect opportunity to tuck into something that transports you to another era. Hang out with something eminently readable and gorgeously, hedonistically historical.

 THE TEN BEST NOVELS TO READ IN A HAMMOCK

Island Beneath the Sea ISABEL ALLENDE
Jack Maggs PETER CAREY
Shōgun JAMES CLAVELL
Skios MICHAEL FRAYN
The Island VICTORIA HISLOP
Small Island ANDREA LEVY
Dissolution CJ SANSOM
Snow Flower and the Secret Fan LISA SEE
Tipping the Velvet SARAH WATERS
Forever Amber KATHLEEN WINSOR

got a big enough book collection you could steal an idea from Carlos María Domínguez's novel *The Paper House*. This delightful book about books begins at the scene of an accident: the narrator's friend Bluma has been hit by a car while engrossed in a volume of Emily Dickinson's poems. While debate rages as to whether Bluma was killed by a car or by a poem, the narrator receives a mysterious parcel meant for Bluma. Inside is a book encased in cement. It turns out to be a Conrad novel from the collection of an obsessive bibliophile named Carlos Brauer who has lost his mind in the interstices between reality and fiction. (Beware his fate, readers – see: read instead of live, tendency to.) Obsessed with the preservation of his 20,000-strong collection, he decides to encase them in cement and build a book-house. Which all goes well – until he needs to find one of his books.*

If you don't have enough books for such DIY measures, acquire *A House for Mr Biswas* by VS Naipaul instead. Set in the rich cultural melting pot of 1940s Trinidad, the story follows the young Mohun Biswas from cradle to grave as he searches for a place of his own. Biswas comes from a 'family of nobodies', with no reason to hope for anything better than a life as an odd-job man. Awkward and ineffectual, he nevertheless wants to move with the times. When, more by accident than design, he finds himself marrying into the vast and successful Hindi Tulsis family, he's guaranteed a roof over his head for the rest of his life. But in return, he has to contend with an entire extended network of in-laws at Hanuman House. Too sensitive to hold his own, he finds himself yearning for privacy and solitude.

Mr Biswas gets his house in the end. His chequered journey will give you courage, and faith, that you too can find a roof of your own.

homesickness

The Arrival
SHAUN TAN

Whether you're a student living away from home for the first time, or an immigrant who has left their country, perhaps

---

* If you do the same, leave *The Novel Cure* out of it.

forever, homesickness can become an overpowering longing that colours all your days. Made up of nostalgia, yearning, the desire for parents, friends, and whatever home means to us – a view of rolling hills, a fog-bound city, a desert, the smell of the sea – we all experience homesickness from time to time.

Shaun Tan's graphic novel, *The Arrival*, captures the melancholy of homesickness perfectly. Tan's illustrations – meticulous line drawings with an astonishing degree of detail – are painted in sepia, grey and gold, the colours of nostalgia. There are no words at all in this novel – and you'll find you don't miss them; the illustrations are so revealing, so intricate and multi-layered, that there seems to be nothing that words could add.

The story drawn is an old one: a man leaves home to find work in another city. His search is successful. He misses his family. But he also begins to acclimatise. Surrounded by extraordinary architecture, loveable hybrid creatures and familiar urban realities, our hero communicates with his family via origami aeroplanes that magically cross continents to find them.

Just as in a novel of words, the meaning of each frame is not always immediately obvious, and requires returning to again and again – like a new territory we are getting to know. As we discover previously unnoticed elements, and bring different feelings to them every time, we are united with the man who is learning the contours of his new location. And so *The Arrival* incorporates the loss of the old into the experience of the new and shows us how to make the best of our unfamiliar surroundings. Gradually, we transpose and recreate what home is, building a new home where we are.

SEE ALSO: **family, coping without** • **foreign, being** • **loneliness** • **lost, being** • **yearning, general**

homophobia

Maurice
EM FORSTER

Once – and it wasn't so very long ago – society sought to 'cure' homosexual men of their sexual persuasion, seeing it

as an aberration, a perversion, a sickness (while either oblivious, or content to turn a blind eye, more or less, to gay
women). Thankfully, in recent years homophobia is replacing homosexuality as the unacceptable element in society.
But it very much still exists, and our contribution to curing
those still harbouring sexual prejudice – whether openly or
in the dark recesses of their heart – is an invocation to read
or reread *Maurice*, arguably the first homosexual novel of
modern times.

It is impossible not to be moved by this story of male-
to-male love, from the first stirrings in Maurice's heart when
he meets Clive Durham at Cambridge, to his initial refusal
– both to himself and to Clive – of that love, despite their
tender connection and the gentle eroticism of their touch, to
the moment when he finally turns from inward self-loathing
to outward fury at a world which won't allow him, and his
deepest emotions, to be 'normal'. There is hardly a single example of enlightened attitudes in *Maurice* outside Maurice
himself. Clive, the one who first enabled his love, becomes
the worst oppressor of them all.

Read it and be stirred (for yes, the early moments between Maurice and Clive have an erotic charge for hetero-
sexual men and women too). Share Maurice's sad joy at
overcoming his own hypocrisy having already denied and
humiliated Clive. Burn with Maurice's rage at the society in
which he has to live with 'the wrong words on his lips and the
wrong desires in his heart'. Ache with Maurice at the devastating loneliness which descends when Clive finally rejects
him with disgust. And be thankful that we no longer live at
a time (1913) when an author of Forster's stature thought it
necessary to wait until after his own death to publish a novel
of which he was proud, knowing that its depiction of genuine love flouted a scandalous law.

SEE ALSO: **hatred** • **judgemental, being**

honest, being too

SEE: **beans, temptation to spill the**

hope, loss of

Of Mice and Men
JOHN STEINBECK

Never underestimate the importance of hope. To live without hope is to live without cheer or comfort (see: despair). We can cope with almost anything – imprisonment, a serious illness, enforced exile – if we have hope that, one day, we will be released and find our way home.

If you don't believe this, you've clearly never read *Of Mice and Men*. George and Lennie are itinerant farmhands. They arrive at a new ranch, 'work up a stake', then go to town and blow it all. With no family, no home, nothing more to look forward to in life, they consider their kind to be the 'loneliest guys in the world'.

Except that they are different – as George keeps telling the big, slow, mentally-challenged Lennie to keep his child-like spirits up, and to comfort himself too. For on top of it all, George has Lennie to look after, and Lennie, who likes soft things to pet and doesn't know his own strength, brings trouble wherever they go. One day George and Lennie will hit the jackpot and have enough money to buy themselves a little house and a few acres on which to keep a cow and some chickens and 'live off the fatta the lan' '. When it rains they'll sit around the fire and listen to the rain on the roof. And they'll have rabbits, which Lennie will get to tend – and pet.

When George no longer believes in the possibility of this future, everything becomes flat and sad – because their shared dream has been keeping them going. We all have a Lennie inside us who needs to hear someone else 'tell about the rabbits' from time to time. And we can all take our turns being George and tell about the rabbits to cheer someone else.

SEE ALSO: **broken dreams** • **despair**

hormonal, being

SEE: **adolescence** • **cry, in need of a good** • **menopause** •
     PMT • **pregnancy** • **teens, being in your** • **tired and**
     emotional, being

hospital, being in

When we're in hospital we desire the tender ministrations of angels – and an escape to somewhere wild and woolly. Take your pick from our choice of 'angels' or 'adventures'.

 THE TEN BEST NOVELS TO READ IN HOSPITAL

Angels

Skellig DAVID ALMOND
Good Omens NEIL GAIMAN AND TERRY PRATCHETT
The Vintner's Luck ELIZABETH KNOX
Mr Pye MERVYN PEAKE
Gabriel's Angel MARK RADCLIFFE

Adventures

The War of Don Emmanuel's Nether Parts LOUIS DE BERNIÈRES
The African Queen CS FORESTER
The Woman and the Ape PETER HØEG
The Bean Trees BARBARA KINGSOLVER
The Call of the Wild JACK LONDON

SEE ALSO: **boredom** • **pain, being in**

housewife, being a

Are your cleaning products shelved in alphabetical order? Do you devise husband-welcoming strategies for the end of the day, dressed in seductive outfits? Do you have unnaturally gleaming grapefruit spoons? On the surface, you're the perfect wife and mother – content to stay at home and look after your spouse and children. But underneath, all is not well. You perhaps find you need to self-medicate with a shot of vodka before you pick up the kids in the afternoon. And that you are just a bit too obsessed with plumping your scatter cushions. If so, you are suffering from being a housewife in the clinical sense and you require one of our hat-trick of cures to wrench you away from the kitchen sink.

Rose, the heroine of Winifred Peck's 1942 novel *House-Bound*, set in Edinburgh, has 'never washed a vegetable' in her life. But the war has caused a national shortage of

household chores, distracted by

If there isn't a meal to cook, there's hoovering to be done. And if the hoovering's done, there's the bathroom to clean. If the bathroom is clean, there's the fridge to sort. And if the fridge has been sorted, it's probably time you went shopping. And when you come back, they'll be the laundry, the beds, the car-cleaning, the garden, the recycling, the rubbish, and all the other myriad tasks that living in a house demands. What hope for one dreaming of a precious hour tucked away with a book?

Create a cosy reading nook – a dedicated space where you go to read. This should be in a small and enclosed corner of your house or garden – an alcove, a tepee, a study, or behind the curtains in a large bay window, where you are hidden but have a view. The important thing is that when you are nestled inside it, you cannot see anything that needs your attention.

Make your nook deliciously warm and inviting. If you like to curl up on the floor, fill it with cushions and a furry rug. If you prefer to stretch out, treat yourself to an elegant chaise longue. You'll need good lighting in your nook, a soft blanket, socks or slippers, and a flat surface on which to put some books, your reading journal, a pencil and a cup of tea. Keep ear plugs in there, and a set of headphones for audio books. Hang a sign at the entrance to your nook gently dissuading others from visiting – unless they too want to crawl inside and read. Once in your nook, forget about the chores. Take your hour with your book. With luck, someone might see you in there, and do the chores instead.

servants, and Rose decides that she must learn to run the house herself. Chaos ensues. As she becomes increasingly enslaved by domestic duties – and every housewife will surely smile at her mounting alarm at how much there is to do – Rose comes to realise that we are all housebound, not just within our four walls, but 'tethered inexorably to a collection of all the extinct memories like bits of mental furniture, inspected and dusted daily'. She has visions of freedom that hint at bolder ways of living, ways that do not revolve so completely around the domestic. This middle-aged housewife gradually overcomes her sense of inadequacy, and though this novel is primarily about the battle within the house, it is far from being a mere domestic farce. This was a time when mothers were losing their sons, and tragedy does not leave this family unscathed. Rose is liberated from her house by dramatic means in the end. You might appreciate the freedom, if not the means, too.

The more modern and sassy *Diary of a Mad Housewife* (published in 1968) describes the mental meltdown of Bettina (Tina) Balser, a thirty-six-year-old mother of two living a Manhattan life that looks pretty hunky-dory to us. She has a maid, a handsome husband, and if she likes she can float around drinking cocktails all day. But she is dissatisfied, and has taken to writing in her diary as a way of staying sane. 'What I really am and have been since midsummer is paralysed,' she writes.

To fill the emptiness, Bettina begins an affair with the appalling George, an A-list celebrity. Meanwhile husband Jonathan is having a fling of his own, and things at his work are going down the tube. Like the cockroaches trapped inside the clock face in Bettina's kitchen, squeezed between the two hands, the couple seem doomed to a slow, suffocating marital death. Luckily, they realise what is happening in time.

Breaking free of the husband as well as the house is the only answer for the female inhabitants of *The Stepford Wives*. Ira Levin's 1972 novel is a terrifying exploration of what could happen if all the men in a small American town were to conspire to transform their spouses into their idea of the perfect wife. By chance, they have the necessary technical and practical expertise at their disposal to do just this, as one of them is a retired Disney cartoonist, one a robotics engineer, and another has a PhD in plastics. We all know what happens next – but it still makes for thrilling reading.

Joanna Eberhart, a motivated mother who earns a small income from her photography, and her broker husband Walter move to Stepford from New York in search of a calmer, suburban life. At first the women Joanna meets are interesting and engaging. But when her two new best friends rapidly turn from bohemian intellectuals into trolley-pushing dolls who live to wax their wooden floors, she suspects the activities of the Men's Association. But is it too late for her?

Let these three novels act as a warning, and a goad. If you feel you're spending too much time with your marigolds on, remember that these are all stories from past decades – being enslaved in your own home is no longer a woman's inevitable lot. You may be perfectly happy keeping the home fires burning, but sometimes it's good to get out and meet other people, take a job, and see the world, too. And if you'd like to escape your domestic chains but suspect that your husband is complicit in the arrangement, put these novels in a hot oven and serve them up dripping with gravy for his tea.

SEE ALSO: **boredom** · **dissatisfaction** · **household chores, distracted by** · **loneliness** · **stagnation, mental**

humility, lack of

SEE: **arrogance**

humourlessness

Everybody's funny-bone requires a different trigger. Use this list to find what sets you off.

SEE ALSO: **grumpiness** · **killjoy, being a** · **querulousness**

hunger

Hunger
KNUT HAMSUN

In those days when you wander about hungry in a strange city that no-one leaves before it sets its mark on him; when you consider, by force of habit, if you have anything to look forward to today; and when you realise you have not a single *krone* in your pocket, you must seek out Knut Hamsun and you will find yourself so energised by this novel that you will be able to see everything in sharp and perfect detail, and have no question that the mere appetite of your body is necessary to satisfy but that the nobility of your mind is incalculably more important. If only you might sit down and write a treatise on philosophy, a three-part article that you can sell to the paper for probably ten *krone*; if only you will sit and write it now on a park bench in the sun, then you will have the money to buy a decent meal. Or, alternatively, pawn your jacket, your waistcoat, for one *krone* fifty *øre*. Just make sure you don't leave your pencil in the pocket, like the unnamed hero of Hamsun's novel did, as then you will never be able to write your article which will not only earn you money but will help the youth of the city to live in a better way. You're only pawning it, of course, because it is getting a bit tight for you, and you will pick it up again in a few days time, when your article is published. Then you can give a few *krone* to the man on the street with the bundle in his hands who hasn't eaten for many, many days, and who made you cry because you could not give him a five *krone* piece. Of course you haven't eaten either, and your stomach will not hold down ordinary food any more as it has been empty for too long. Though don't forget that you gave that ten *krone* note that you felt was wrongly yours to the cake seller, you thrust it into her hands and she had no idea why, and perhaps you can go to her stall and demand some cakes that were paid for on account, so to speak. The police might pick you up as you are out in the early hours of the morning, lacking a place to stay – but then how could you wish for anything more than an excellent clean, dry cell? The police believe of course that you are really a man of good character and principles, who has merely been locked out of his house, and has plenty of money at home. You can use this experience and write all about it in your next article that you can sell to the paper, and it may even make fifteen *krone*; and of course, there is your play, the one you just need to clinch that elusive last act of, and if this is published, you will never have to worry about money again. Before this, you will arrive at the joyful insanity hunger brings, and be empty and free of pain.

hypochondria

*The Secret
Garden*
**FRANCES
HODGSON
BURNETT**

Reading *The Secret Garden* serves as a polite reminder that many of our ailments are, in fact, fictional.

Young Colin, confined to his bedroom since birth, is convinced there is a lump on his back that will, eventually, grow into a hunch and lead to an early demise. Of course, there is no lump, unless you count the vertebrae of his spine. His caregivers have encouraged him to believe he is deformed, doomed never to grow to adulthood, and that fresh air is poison to his blood. Mary, his spoilt cousin, just as capable of throwing tantrums and ordering others around as he is, will have none of it. The only person brave enough to tell Colin that there's nothing wrong with him, she matches his rage at his presumed fate with her own fury at his inertia. Only a fierce little girl hell-bent on bringing her secret garden to

hype, put off by

TEAR A STRIP OFF THE BOOK

Sometimes a book generates so much buzz in the press – perhaps it has won a major award, or the author is particularly young or good-looking – that you are bored of it by the time you get round to reading it. You've read so many reviews that you feel you know the book already. And you're too sullied by everyone else's opinion to have any hope of forming your own.

The best way to give such a book a chance, is to store it in your garden shed, greenhouse, garage, or outdoor loo. You might also like to re-cover it in a piece of leftover wallpaper, some Christmas wrapping paper, a brown paper bag or silver foil. And when taking a break from watering the tomatoes one day, pick it up and start to read. The unexpected, un-bookish surroundings will bring an air of humility to the book, counteracting the hype, and encourage you to come to it with a more generous and open mind.

life can pierce the bubble of Colin's terror and show him the truth.

Mary's passion for the garden lures Colin out of his sick-chamber into the world of buds and birds – a world also inhabited by freckled, irresistible Dickon, the quintessence of health. Let this novel lure you from your bed to find your own secret garden, maybe even your own Dickon, and a lusty return to tip-top health.

SEE ALSO: **anxiety** · **cold, common** · **dying** · **man flu**

I

identity crisis

Who are you, reader? A parent, a professional, a student, a child? Are you always yourself, or do you have two selves – one that you show only to certain people, one you show to everyone else? Or do you feel that the 'real' you has never seen the light of day at all?

Literature is stuffed to the gills with people having identity crises – whether it be through memory loss, psychiatric breakdown or some other, more inexplicable, process. The narrator of *I'm Not Stiller* by the Swiss writer of the post-war years, Max Frisch, persistently denies accusations that he is the missing sculptor Anatol Stiller. And indeed, according to his passport, his name is James (or Jim) White. But friends, acquaintances and even his wife repeatedly identify him as Stiller – a conundrum that confounds us as much as White (or should we say Stiller). As the truth gradually emerges, we are given a rare glimpse into the fragility of our relationship to ourselves. We don't want to give too much away, but those who feel their identity is up for grabs should make sure they trust whomever they ask to help them pin it down, themselves included.

One thing's for sure, you might want to carry more than a passport and a name tag on your jacket to identify yourself as you go through life. When a man is found clubbed to near-death in Trieste during the Second World War, the Finnish name tag on his clothes proclaims him to be Sampo

Karjalainen. But when the man regains consciousness, he has no memory of who he is – and no language. This is the intriguing opening premise for *The New Finnish Grammar* by Diego Marani. A Finnish doctor is among those on board the hospital ship where the man ends up, and he begins to re-wire Finnish into the man's brain, complete with its fiendishly complicated grammar and consonant-rich words. But what if this man wasn't really Finnish in the first place? What will he become in a different language? What is it that makes him himself? In the end it's the new relationships that he forges on the boat that seem to reveal him to himself. Read it and your relationship to the novel may show you new things about what it means to be you.

But if you are ever unlucky enough to lose your identity completely, the best cure you can get your pincers round in fact is *Metamorphosis* by Franz Kafka. Travelling salesman Gregor Samsa wakes up one morning to discover he has turned into a cockroach – a giant one. He is disgusting not only to himself but to his entire family; and though Gregor tries to continue life as it was before, it becomes increasingly difficult. Eating is challenging, communication impossible, basic hygiene ever more compromised; and Gregor slowly sinks into an empty but peaceful, ruminative state as he starves to death.

Count your blessings that even if you don't know who you are, you are at least human. Admire your fingers, toes and the tip of your nose. Revel in the use of your limbs. Read the last paragraph of Kafka's masterpiece aloud. Enjoy the fact that your voice is not the terrifying rasping of an insect. Celebrate your humanity – whoever's it may be.

SEE ALSO: **identity, unsure of your reading**

idiot, feeling like an

The Idiot
FYODOR
DOSTOYEVSKY

The room goes quiet, and you find yourself the focus of a sea of faces. It dawns on you that you're the only one who doesn't understand what's wrong with what you've just said. Then someone starts to laugh, and one by one the others

identity, unsure of your reading

CREATE A FAVOURITES SHELF

If you feel you have forgotten – or perhaps that you have never known – what sort of books are *your* sort of books, and as a result find yourself unable to choose what to read next, we suggest that you keep a Favourites shelf. Select ten books that fill you with warmth, nostalgia, and a flutter of nervous excitement. If some of these are favourites from your childhood, all the better. Make these that beckon you your standard. Put them on a special shelf in the room in which you tend to do your reading or where you will pass them every day. If possible, re-read them (or at least parts of them). They will remind you of what you love most in literature, and – if your reading life has been rich – of who you are. Next time you feel unsure of what to read next, use your Favourites shelf as a guide and gentle nudge to your literary soul. It will tell you the answers to questions you didn't even know you had.

join in. You feel a hot flush take over your face (see: blushing), followed by a blood-draining sense of shame (see: shame). They're not laughing with you, but *at* you.

We've all been there. Feeling like an idiot is almost as inevitable as falling in love. In fact, being an idiot is not necessarily a bad thing.* The gentle prince Lev Myshkin in Dostoyevsky's *The Idiot* is an idiot in a social rather than an intellectual sense, standing outside society because he has no comprehension of its mechanisms: money, status, small talk and the subtle intricacies of daily life are all obscure to him. But when we readers think about Prince Lev it is not with any sense of disparagement, but with absolute fondness and love. Indeed, everyone who encounters the prince in the novel is both exasperated by him and deeply enamoured of his profound understanding of a version of reality that most of us do not see.

Next time the room falls silent around you, remember the prince. Look everyone back in the eye, and anticipate affection instead. You'll probably get it.

SEE ALSO: **failure, feeling like a**

ignorance

SEE: **homophobia** • **idiot, feeling like an** • **racism** • **xenophobia**

indecision

Indecision
**BENJAMIN
KUNKEL**

If you're inclined to get yourself tied up in knots whenever you are called upon to make a decision; if you are the kind of person who sees things from everybody else's point of view except your own; if you drive yourself and your friends crazy as you bounce between a plethora of paths, unable to choose or commit to any one of them, then you are suffering from the quintessential ailment of our age: indecisiveness. Because never before has there been more choice – and yet never have we been more paralysed.

* While falling in love, with the wrong person at least, frequently is. See: love, unrequited; and love, doomed.

Dwight Wilmerding, the twenty-eight-year-old slacker hero of Ben Kunkel's novel *Indecision* finds that he can't 'think of the future until [he's] arrived there' – a quality shared by many indecisive types. Underemployed, half-hearted about his girlfriend Vaneetha, he makes decisions on whether or not to accept invitations out by flipping a coin – the only way to ensure that his 'whole easy nature' doesn't end up seeing him doing everybody else's bidding. Meanwhile, decisions continue to be made for him: his employers at the pharmaceutical company where he works give him the boot, and when his old schoolfriend Natasha invites him – in a suggestive sort of way – to join her in Ecuador, he goes. And, unsurprisingly, when his friend Dan offers him a new drug being trialled for the market called Abulinix that promises to cure him of his indecision, he embraces the gem-like blue-capsuled medicament. Only after gleefully ingesting it is he told that it has some interesting side effects: 'satyriasis', or an excessive desire in the male of the species to copulate, and potentiating alcohol, meaning that once in the bloodstream, one drink becomes two.

Perhaps because of the Abulinix, and perhaps not, things take an exciting turn in Ecuador. Because, even better than Natasha, he finds the beautiful and highly politicised Brigid, who speaks in alluringly foreign tones. Whether it is the Abulinix, or the psyche-altering hallucinogenic they take in the jungle – or, in fact, a fundamental shift of consciousness – Dwight begins to make proactive choices for the first time in his life.

Take this novel with you, go find your Abulinix, and/or your Brigid and/or your jungle-drug equivalent, and be prepared to wake up to a newly decisive life. Or, on the other hand, don't.

SEE ALSO: **holiday, not knowing what novels to take on** • **starting, fear of**

indifference

SEE: **apathy**

infatuation

Les Enfants Terribles
JEAN COCTEAU

There is nothing so heady, so sweet, or so intoxicating as being in the throes of a serious crush. Whoever your love-object, to be lost in the admiration of a fellow being is one of the most absorbing and deliriously pleasurable ways to lose great chunks of your life. But for all the pleasure of this state, there is a price to pay. The love-object may well not feel the same way; and, by its very nature, infatuation is blind to practicalities. It is an unreasoned, extravagant love, feeding off itself more than off the returned affections of the love-recipient (see also: love, unrequited). And though not as dangerous as obsession, it can be a precursor to this state, rendering the sufferer incapable of seeing their own folly and the inadequacies of their object.

Cocteau's enigmatic little novel is a paradigm of intoxication. It illustrates a perfectly puzzling love maze, in which a brother and sister score points by transferring their infatuation with each other to other young men and women, then back again. Paul and Elisabeth nurse their mother in a Parisian apartment with one huge room, so that it's rather like a stage. Eventually, they are left alone there, with their imaginations and neuroses, to grow like hot-house flowers. At school, Paul had been infatuated with Dargelos, a beautiful boy who threw a snowball at him with a stone inside it. This sends the delicate Paul to bed for several weeks, where as an invalid enjoying the 'sweet delights of sickness', he learns to love his sister a little too much. On recovery he meets Agathe (who closely resembles Dargelos) and Paul transfers his infatuation to her. But meanwhile Paul and Elisabeth have perfected 'the Game', a means of deepening their relationship by wounding each other in a series of circling conversational attacks. As their mutual infatuation becomes more extreme, they withdraw from the world into a make-believe existence where all that matters is 'the Game'.

It cannot but end badly – it is all too heady, too intense and prismatically refractive. And it's only a matter of time before we hear the shatter. If you are in the throes of a similarly intense infatuation, switch the object of your fascination from life to the page. Cocteau was known in the artistic circles of his time (whose members included Picasso, Modigliani, Proust and Gide) as the 'frivolous prince', and inspired infatuation many times himself. His sensual prose and mercurial imagination are equally ravishing. *Les Enfants Terribles* was written during a period of withdrawal from opium, and you can feel the call of his blood for the drug in each heightened sentence. 'The world owes its enchantment to ... curious creatures and their fancies,' he muses. 'Thistledown spirits, tragic, heartrending in their evanescence, they must go blowing headlong to perdition.'

Don't let yourself be blown to perdition by currents of whimsical desire. The pleasure to be found in aesthetic heights will last forever; your mortal crush will not.

SEE ALSO: **lovesickness** • **lust** • **obsession**

innocence, loss of

The Greengage Summer
RUMER GODDEN

Get used to it, readers: innocence, once lost, can never be regained. This is not a cure, therefore, but a balm – to be administered during those times when you miss the simplicity, the naïveté, of those far-off times.

Thirteen-year-old Cecil, the narrator of *The Greengage Summer*, is on the verge of losing it. Years later, she recalls the summer that she 'became a woman', when she and her siblings were left to fend for themselves in the seemingly exotic world of a French hotel. Here, they gorge themselves on greengages, guiltily, being still 'at the age when they thought that being greedy was a childish fault'. Unfettered in the arcadia of a deserted orchard, they eat so many of these fruits with their pale blue bloom, that they make themselves ill. It seems inevitable that a snake must lurk in the grass.

The snake is charismatic Mr Eliot, the beau of Madame Zizi who runs the hotel. He works his serpentine alchemy on each of the five children in turn, using his charm, money and intrigue. Sixteen-year-old Joss, 'a twig erupting with flowers' in her younger sister's eyes, is his chief target. Transforming from a stick-thin girl to a beautiful young woman in the space of just two weeks as she lies on her hotel room sickbed, she emerges anew one day to dazzle Eliot and the other guests. Cecil, meanwhile, becomes aware of having started 'Eve's Curse' the same night she obtains a 'proper kiss' from Eliot while he was diverted briefly from his pursuit of Joss. Their younger brother, Willmouse, spends most of his time dressing up his dolls in homemade bras and *haute couture*. His untroubled play with these miniature mannequins is an example of the untramelled pleasure these children are about to lose.

Each of the children take a different attitude to their fall. Cecil welcomes hers with exultation, Joss with strangely resolute trepidation, and Willmouse, resignedly, with a pair of doll's false bosoms in his hands. He is the one who is almost broken by his fall; witness to Eliot's epic deception of the whole crew, it nearly costs him more than just his innocence.

If you're advancing towards this heady rite of passage yourself, Cecil is an excellent best friend to hold your hand. And if you're watching someone else go through it, Godden's nostalgia will take you back to your own prelapsarian state, awakening blood memories of the tangle of emotions that accompanies the first sip of champagne, the first dance, the first touch, helping you to sympathise with tenderness and understanding from the sidelines.

SEE ALSO: **disenchantment**

insanity

SEE: **madness**

insomnia

The House of Sleep
JONATHAN COE

The Book of Disquiet
FERNANDO PESSOA

Everyone suffers from it occasionally. But if you suffer from it nightly, it can wreak havoc with your relationship, your career and your ability to get through the day. If you're afflicted with this sort of insomnia you probably feel trapped in a vicious circle. Because as your level of exasperation rises with your accumulating fatigue, the problem feeds on itself: nothing is more likely to stop you sleeping than the anxiety that you might not be able to sleep.

Insomniacs often turn to reading as a way to endure those lonely, wee hours. We heartily agree that there is no better way to spend this otherwise wasted time – as long as you're not disturbing anyone else as you turn the pages – but it has to be the right novel.* For instance, Jonathan Coe's novel *The House of Sleep* is an invaluable tool for exploring your sleeplessness but it should not be read at night unless you are prepared to accept that you will be up until dawn – despite its title, the novel is far from peaceful in its contents. Pick it up during the day when you are wide awake and prepared for a thorough analysis of why the hell you can't get to sleep.

The novel is divided into six parts, each representing the various stages of sleep, and follows four loosely connected characters who each have a different issue with sleep. Sarah is a narcoleptic whose dreams are so vivid that she can't tell the difference between them and real life. Terry, a budding film critic, sleeps a minimum of fourteen hours a day because he is addicted to dreams of such 'near-paradisal loveliness'. Gregory, Sarah's boyfriend, becomes a psychiatrist at a sleep clinic and begins self-experimenting with sleeplessness for scientific purposes, believing it to be a disease that must be conquered. Robert is – seemingly – the most normal of the four, but he becomes so obsessed with Sarah that he puts himself through a dramatic transformation in order to inveigle his way into her life, and bed.

Full of lustrous technical detail which will fascinate the sleep-deprived, this novel will trigger an analysis of your own hypnagogic hallucinations and entice you to look curiously into your mirrored narcoleptic eyes – as well as suggesting a litany of practical cures, amongst which you may find one that works for you. But we repeat: do not read it at

---

* Of course, if someone is sharing your bed, they may be the culprit in the first place – whether by the resonance of their airways (see: snoring), or perhaps by something they said to you before they went to sleep (see: adultery; guilt; irritability; grumpiness).

night. It's so good you'll force your eyes to stay open rather than put it down.

Instead the novel to reach for in those restless hours is *The Book of Disquiet* – a novel without a plot, and which, while not sending you to sleep exactly (though it may; we'll come to that) allows you to reside in that heavy, pre-sleep state which you need to inhabit before gaining entry to full slumber. *The Book of Disquiet* is the journal of Soares, assistant-accountant at Vasques & Co on the Rua dos Douradores – a job which is 'about as demanding as an afternoon nap'. Soares both despairs and celebrates the monotony of his humdrum life because he recognises that everything he thinks and feels exists only as a 'negation of and flight from' his job. And what thoughts and feelings they are! Because Soares, a man in possession of a face so bland that it causes him terrible dismay when he sees it in an office photograph, is a dreamer, his attention always divided by what is actually going on and the flights of fancy in his head.

For his disappointment in himself, his dreaminess, his constantly breaking heart, it's impossible not to fall in love with Soares. Quiet, unobtrusive, plaintive; a man who is constantly drowsy; who, though prone to nostalgia and bouts of desolation, is not immune to joy; he is the perfect night-time companion. Soares will sit up with you hour after hour to ponder whether, for instance, life is in fact 'the waking insomnia of [our] dreams' and sleep our real existence. Because Soares thinks a lot about sleep. In fact, he barely discriminates between the states of sleeping and wakefulness because he dreams while he lives *and* while he sleeps, and sleep is, as he points out, still living.

And besides all this, nowhere in literature are the rhythms of prose more attuned to the lovely, lumbering gait of the sleepless hours. If your eyelids start to droop as you read, no matter. Soares won't mind. You can pick up the conversation with him tomorrow night, wherever you left off. He'll be waiting, ready to pose the next existential question.

SEE ALSO: **depression, general** • **exhaustion** • **irritability** •
stress • **tired and emotional, being**

internet addiction

What have we become? We are a race that sits, by our millions, for hours and days and years on end, gazing in solitary rapture at our screens, lost to a netherworld of negligible reality. Even though we may get up from time to time to eat, sleep, make love or a cup of coffee, our computers and smart phones call to us like sirens to come back, interact, update, reload. Like moths drawn to brightness and warmth, we seem unable to resist – even though our eyes are strained, our backs are sore (see: back, bad), and our ability to focus is shorn (see: concentrate, inability to). Sometimes it can seem as if life is more compelling on our screens than off them.

I

223

Our cure for this most deplorable of modern ailments is one which will require you to turn your back on life for a few hours more – the delightfully eccentric John Cowper Powys's mystical 1929 novel, *Wolf Solent*. Set in a West country already familiar to fans of Thomas Hardy (and indeed the two have much in common), it is a densely written tome – but it's worth it. Because once you discover JCP, as we shall call him, you'll chuck your monitor into the nearest skip and go and live out the rest of your days among the birds and the bees.

Wolf Solent opens with the eponymous hero – an unprepossessing thirty-five-year-old with 'goblinish' features – making an escape from London, where he's been chained to a dull teaching job for ten years. He's returning to the town of his childhood, where he will reconnect with his own 'furtive inner life.' Because at Wolf's core is what he calls his 'personal mythology', a sort of mystical place he goes to connect with nature, and from the moment he catches his first whiff, from the train, of the smells of a Dorset spring morning – fresh green shoots, muddy ditches, primroses on a grassy bank – his 'real life' begins again. He experiences what he describes as an 'intoxicating enlargement of personality' that draws its power from nature itself.

It's heady stuff – and becomes more so. Soon after Wolf arrives and takes up his new job as researcher for the malicious squire Urquhart, he falls in love with two women at once – the 'maddeningly desirable' Gerda who can imitate the song of a blackbird, and Christie, who shares his passion for books. As Wolf struggles to find a way to love them both, and chases after the bodily sensations that make him feel alive, it's impossible to resist his raw, ecstatic response to the natural world. Through his eyes you will come to see the animal energy in other people. As a way of rediscovering how to live in the world again – sensually, sexually, with the full engagement of mind and body – it can't be beaten. And perhaps, like Wolf, being surrounded by all that vegetable efflorescence will soothe your eyes, strengthen your back and, most crucially, return your fractured brain to full capacity.

SEE ALSO: **antisocial, being** • **concentrate, inability to**

irritability

The Blackwater Lightship
COLM TÓIBÍN

Where someone is being irritable, you can be sure there's another, unexpressed emotion lurking, iceberg-like, beneath the surface. Often irritability is a sign that issues are being avoided (see: confrontation, fear of). Left unchecked, the verbal snap can become a reflexive habit you're hardly aware of.

There are no unexpressed emotions behind the narrator Helen's husband Hugh's benign exterior in *The Blackwater Lightship*. He is 'easygoing', 'consistent', 'modest', with 'nothing secret, nothing held inside'. Helen, on the other hand, is 'unsettled and untrusting' – full of icebergs which she only half understands. In this novel Colm Tóibín dissects the bitterness and hurt that has set in between three generations of Helen's family – grandmother Mrs Devereux, mother Lily and daughter Helen – since Helen and Declan's father died many years ago.

When Helen hears that her brother Declan is dying of AIDS, she has to break the news to their estranged mother Lily – the mother she didn't invite to her wedding seven years ago, and who has never met her husband or two sons. And when they decide to take Declan to their Grandmother's house in Blackwater – where she and Declan came when their father took ill, disappearing to Dublin with their mother 'for tests', never to return – she is thrust back into a world she had hoped not to have to revisit.

The knives are out between Lily and Helen before they've even arrived. 'And you never told me?' cries Lily when Helen says she's known Declan was gay for ten years. 'I've never told you anything,' Helen snaps back. Once they are all shut up in the small house with its uncomfortable sheets and stuffiness, the barbed comments really start flying. 'I don't know how he puts up with you,' says Lily of Helen's husband Hugh – the one, you will remember, she's never met. Helen gets her own back by blatantly changing the subject when Lily asks a question. The grandmother Mrs Devereux is no better, offending everyone then letting herself off the hook with: 'I'm old and I can say what I like.'

As the light from the lighthouse washes over the house at regular intervals – it too an area of troubled water – Declan lies dying in their midst, the catalyst of all the arguments, yet the only one not drawn in. Luckily Declan's two loyal friends are present – the talkative Larry, the coolly direct Paul – who take the women aside, one by one, and encourage them to vent their feelings. The icebergs soon come into view, and by the end of the novel, Helen, her mother and her grandmother have a much clearer understanding of one another's grievances. Don't wait for a crisis to force your irritability to the surface. If you – or someone you know – is prone to irritation, invite a couple of loquacious friends into the mix and talk your icebergs out of the water.

SEE ALSO: **anger** • **dissatisfaction** • **grumpiness** • **querulousness**

irritable bowel syndrome

SEE: **constipation** • **diarrhoea** • **flatulence** • **nausea** • **pain, being in**

itchy feet

The Odyssey
HOMER

The urge to be constantly on the move is both a virtue and a blunder. While we may gain insight and maturity from constant change and new experiences, we risk polluting our fragile environment (see: wanderlust) and becoming a stone that gathers no moss. For how do we build a life in multiple places? One needs to commit to a destination in order to put down roots (see: commitment, fear of), fertilise relationships, and come into flower. To soothe and still your itchy feet, therefore, we recommend a chapter of *The Odyssey* every morning, taken after your shower and before your breakfast. It will invigorate your circulation and satiate your desire for travel.

Odysseus himself is an inveterate sufferer of itchy feet. King of Ithaca, he left his island home ten years before the action begins in order to fight the Trojan War. Now, he sets off back to Penelope, his wife, and his small but significant sovereignty. But it'll be another decade before he feels the soil of Ithaca under his well-worn sandals – and frankly, the gods alone cannot be blamed for all his meanderings. Many of his diversions are self-induced.

Fair enough, he is held captive for some of these years by the sea-nymph, Calypso. And the Cyclops Polyphemus keeps him in a cave, along with his men and ovine herd, for some time before Odysseus cunningly blinds his gaoler. He is regularly at the mercy of an enraged Poseidon, who sends storms that wash him and his crew up on the island of Circe, where they are all turned temporarily into pigs. But it was foolish of Odysseus to shout his name to Polyphemus, triggering Poseidon's pursuit of him in the first place. Had he kept quiet, he would have saved himself, his wife and his citizens several turbulent years.

In the end, after twenty years of tardiness, he only just returns in time to save his wife from an enforced re-marriage. Don't make the same mistake and let your life go by in your absence. By the time you finish reading this ancient novel, meandering in its adventures but introspective in nature, you will have had enough vicarious travels to last a lifetime. Now get on with life in the place where you are.

SEE ALSO: **dissatisfaction** • **happiness, searching for** • **jump ship, desire to** • **wanderlust**

itchy teeth

Henderson the Rain King
SAUL BELLOW

If you've never even heard of this ailment, you've clearly never met the long-suffering hero of Saul Bellow's *Henderson the Rain King*. But if you have heard of it – and/or suffer from it – you probably have. Because Gene Henderson – a fifty-five-year-old millionaire with big, 'blustering' ways, a large nose and more children than he can remember the names of – has had itchy teeth all his life. In fact all his pain, physical and emotional (and there's a lot of it), congregates in his teeth. When he's angry, his gums ache. When he's faced with heartbreaking beauty, his teeth itch. And when his wives, his girls, his children, his farm, his animals, his habits, his money, his violin lessons, his drunkenness, his brutality, his haemorrhoids, his fainting fits, his face, his soul and – yes – his teeth, all start giving him grief at once, he decides to gatecrash his friend Charlie's honeymoon in Africa, and from there go 'in country', to find himself.

I

227

It doesn't work. What he finds is the same blustering fifty-five-year-old millionaire he left behind. And what's more he breaks the bridge at the side of his mouth while he's away, ruining many dollars-worth of complicated dentistry and leaving him spitting fragments of artificial molar into his hand.

Itchy teeth is a rare complaint, but it does exist – and not just in Bellow novels. Those afflicted experience almost unbearable torment. The only thing that can drive a person madder than the itch of the teeth themselves is not being believed when they tell other people about it. Now sufferers of this complaint can give doubters this uproarious battering-ram of a novel and elicit sympathy for their affliction at last.

J

jam, being in a

Jams come in many flavours, hues and consistencies, but they do not get any stickier than that of Pi Patel, who finds himself stranded on a lifeboat at sea with a zebra, a hyena, an orang-utan and a three-year-old Bengal tiger. The young hero of Yann Martel's Booker Prize-winning novel *Life of Pi* is under no delusions about how dangerous the tiger is (for soon it's just him and the tiger, the laws of natural selection swiftly despatching the other three). And when he and the tiger first confront each other, the tiger with its eyes blazing, its ears 'laid tight to its head', and its weapons drawn, Pi's response is to throw himself back overboard and sweat it out in the sea.

Which is the correct response. As is building a raft alongside the lifeboat so that he and the 450-pound carnivore can occupy separate quarters. But it's what he does next that wins our admiration. Spotting the tiger's weakness – seasickness – he draws on the training skills he acquired by osmosis in his father's zoo, and wages a battle of minds with the tiger that reduces the magnificent creature to a state of begrudging obedience. The face-off that clinches the boy's authority is the best staring contest in literature. Keep this novel at hand whenever you are attempting to find a way out of your own (we hope, less sticky) jams. The potential for mastery in even so slight and hungry a boy as Pi is inspiring. Read before or while you stew.

For those facing jams of the social variety – such as finding yourself backed into a corner from which there's no dignified escape – we recommend a companion in the mould of Jeeves, the valet in the novels of PG Wodehouse. If you can't afford a real one, the fictional one will do. This smooth-tongued, eyebrow-raising valet, as well versed in Dostoyevsky as he is with the right way to wear a scarlet cummerbund,* is forever getting the hapless Bertie Wooster out of scrapes. Rich in status but poor in good sense and sound judgement (and if you suspect you fall short in this department too, see: common sense, lack of), Wooster knows he wouldn't survive a day without Jeeves or his curative cups of tea – although he'd never admit it. We, like Bertie, find the presence of Jeeves in our lives infinitely soothing – and once you've been introduced, you will too.[†]

Whenever things get hairy, have too many pips or start to bubble too fast – be it with a tiger or a dreadful 'gel' to whom you've got yourself accidentally engaged – imagine what Pi or Jeeves would advise and adjust the temperature accordingly.

SEE ALSO: **stuck in a rut**

jealousy

Venus in Furs
LEOPOLD VON SACHER-MASOCH

Unlike envy, which is the coveting of other people's possessions, jealousy is the tendency to torture oneself with the thought that someone else may take what you have. This results in an urge to cling ever more tightly to that possession, becoming needy and insecure, and full of fury at the potential absconder (see also: hatred). Blind to reason, it's a supremely destructive force, and if left uncurbed will eat away at your self-esteem and ultimately prevent you from having a healthy relationship with the thing you guard with such desperation. Whether it's jealousy among siblings for parental attention (see: sibling rivalry), jealousy over a

---

* Don't.
† You will also have to forgo your scarlet cummerbund, though.

promotion at work, or jealousy over a suspected rival in love from which you suffer, those in its grip would do well to recognise that they are more likely to lose their love-object than would someone free of its taint. Luckily, jealousy – of whatever sort – is self-inflicted, and the person who has created it also has the power to uncreate it.

Our cure, Leopold Von Sacher-Masoch's *Venus in Furs*, shows very clearly the self-inflicted nature of jealousy. Unique for its time (the novel was published in 1870), *Venus in Furs* explores the lure of sexual subjugation. One afternoon after dozing off in front of a magnificent painting entitled 'Venus in Furs', the narrator and his friend Severin share a dream about this deity, and both admit to their predilection for beauty dressed in haughtiness. Our narrator picks up Severin's memoir, which we then read over his shoulder. It describes Severin's relationship to a woman named Wanda – Venus's mortal embodiment. Wanda is a cruel and beautiful tyrant of a woman who alternately loves and abuses Severin – entertaining him, titillating him and philosophising with him one moment, and whipping him, calling him her 'slave', and taunting him with her interest in other men the next.

Severin laps it all up. When she talks about another lover, Severin is seized with passion, a 'sweet madness' – and when we realise that he gave up on a far more gentle relationship for this, we begin to see how unhealthy his love for Wanda is. He wants to be treated badly – the harsher the better – and he obeys her edicts abjectly, his body trembling with resentment. And so begins a series of humiliations, ecstasies and terrors which at one point have him fearing for his life.

Only at the end of his 'confession' (which constitutes most of the book) does Severin stand back and see the relationship for the self-torture it really was. 'Whoever allows himself to be whipped, deserves to be whipped,' is the moral he draws. It's no accident that Masoch gave us the word for this pleasure in pain: 'masochism'. Your jealousy is similarly masochistic – it comes from the lashes of your own crop. Bear witness to Severin's self-hate, then hang up your crop and walk free.

SEE ALSO: **anger** • **bitterness** • **neediness** • **paranoia**

jetlag

SEE: **dizziness** • **exhaustion** • **headache** • **insomnia** • **nausea**

job, hating your

SEE: **bullied, being** • **career, being in the wrong** • **job, losing your** • **Monday morning feeling** • **stuck in a rut**

job, losing your

Bartleby, the Scrivener
HERMAN MELVILLE

Lucky Jim
KINGSLEY AMIS

Losing your job can be a hideous blow, both to your pocket and your ego. The best way to deal with it is to try and see it as an opportunity – a chance to take a break from the daily toil, reconsider your options, and perhaps expand into new territories. Rather than conclude that you were a bad fit for the job, decide that the job was a bad fit for you (see: career, being in the wrong.) If you're not convinced, consider all the occasions on which, in your job, you did not want to do the things you were asked to do. Like Bartleby.

Herman Melville's Bartleby is a scrivener, and when he first arrives for duty at the narrator's law office, 'pallidly neat' and 'pitiably respectable', his employer thinks his sedate nature will have a calming influence on his other employees. And at first Bartleby does seem to be the model worker, industriously copying out letters in quadruplicate. But then he begins to rebel. When his employer asks him to check over his writing, Bartleby gives the response: 'I would prefer not to.' It soon becomes apparent that he will do nothing beyond the most basic elements of his job. If asked to do anything more, 'I would prefer not to' comes the inflexible reply. A dire impasse develops in which his employer can't bring himself to fire the scrivener because he's so meek and seems to have no life whatsoever beyond his desk. And Bartleby will do only what he wants.

Be inspired by Bartleby's act of resistance. To what degree did your job entail compromising over what you really wanted to do? Bartleby's rebellion saw him refusing to leave his desk at all. You, however, now have a chance to move on, and find pastures new.

Perhaps you can even begin to celebrate the demise of your job. When Jim Dixon is appointed lecturer in Medieval English History at a nondescript university in the Midlands in *Lucky Jim*, he has no intention of messing things up. He duly accepts his boss Neddy Welch's invitation to attend an 'arts weekend' in the country, realising that he needs to keep 'in' with Welch. But once there, he can't seem to avoid getting himself into trouble. Farcical scenes ensue, including burning bed sheets, drunken madrigal singing, and various sexual entanglements. It's when he gives his lecture about 'Merrie England', however, that he blows things most spectacularly, delivering the final moments 'punctuated by his own snorts of derision'.

Have a much-needed laugh, then start looking for the job that is even more suited to you. Because there is an unexpected denouement to Jim's very public disgrace. Seeing someone make a pig's dinner of their job – and still come out on top – will boost your morale no end.

SEE ALSO: **anger • broke, being • failure, feeling like a • unemployment**

judgemental, being

The Reader
BERNHARD SCHLINK

Pobby and Dingan
BEN RICE

It is tempting, especially in youth, to go round forming instant and strong opinions about others. To judge, to pronounce, to label – such things can seem to an immature mind to be synonymous with strength and confidence. But having strong opinions must never become a mandate for being judgemental – which is the tendency to judge a thing or person based on one quality or attribute alone. A judgemental person will insist, for instance, that all criminals are terrible people, that all fussy eaters are bad in bed, and all teenagers are naive and judgemental.*

---

* They are right about the last one.

To stamp out your judgemental tendencies, we recommend you immerse yourself in the complex tale of Nazi guilt, personal shame and retrospective horror that is Bernhard Schlink's *The Reader*, a novel that explores the question of how post-war generations should approach the Holocaust and those implicated in its tarry atrocities. Michael Berg is just fifteen when he begins a relationship with thirty-six-year-old tram conductress, Hanna. Their assignations, which often involve bathing together – a hint at a Lady Macbeth-style need to scrub away past sins – also revolve around books, for Hanna likes Michael to read to her (*The Odyssey* in Greek, *War and Peace*), something of which we wholeheartedly approve (see: loneliness, reading-induced; and non-reading partner, having a). Only later, when Michael is a law student sitting in on a war crimes trial, does he recognise one of the faces in the dock. His first love was once an SS guard, complicit in the deaths of hundreds of women. And she has another secret of which she is even more ashamed.

Michael spends his whole life struggling to come to terms with what Hanna did – and what she has done to him. And while she suffers remorse, and even allows herself to be judged for shouldering more responsibility than she actually had, Michael's decision not to reply to her letters from prison causes her pain. Thus Schlink brings the reader into the ethical fray. Do you allow yourself to be moved by Hanna's suffering or continue to condemn her along with her crime? Herein lies your test. May this novel show you that holding strong opinions and being non-judgemental do not by necessity cancel one another out.

If you lack the stomach for such heavy ethics, a gentler cure is available. If ever a novel – or novella – could trick you into dousing your judgemental fire, Ben Rice's slim debut *Pobby and Dingan* is it. Kellyanne, little sister to narrator Ashmol, has two imaginary friends, Pobby and Dingan. As one would expect from any self-respecting older brother – especially one raised in the hard-bitten opal-mining community of Lightning Ridge, Australia – Ashmol has no time for such childish things. Would you, after years of being instructed to set places for Pobby and Dingan at the table and being told you can't come to the pool because, with Pobby and Dingan in the back seat, there's no space for you in the ute?

By the end of the novel, yes. Because when Kellyanne announces that Pobby and Dingan have died, and is made so ill by her grief that she winds up in hospital, Ashmol does a wonderful thing: he goes round town putting up signs offering a reward to anybody who can find his sister's friends ('Description: imaginary. Quiet.'). And from this moment you, too, will want to be on the side of those who buy in to the little girl's fantasy, not those who sniff and sneer.

Remain open. There is good, bad, mad and sad in everyone, and you don't have to condone or believe in every element to be kind to the whole package. This also applies to yourself. If, when you struggle with a new skill, you tend to write yourself off as hopeless at everything (see: self-esteem, low), start by practising a non-judgemental attitude towards yourself.

SEE ALSO: **antisocial, being**

jump ship, desire to

Rabbit, Run
JOHN UPDIKE

When you feel the urge to jump ship – from your relationship, your job, your life – we beg you not to do so until you have read *Rabbit, Run*. The urge to jump generally strikes when the ship we're on appears to be sinking – and it's more likely to feel this way if it started out high in the water. This is certainly the case for Harry 'Rabbit' Angstrom (the nickname is a result of the nervous twitch beneath his 'brief nose'). For Rabbit was once a teenage basketball star, a local if not national hero who now, at twenty-seven, spends his days demonstrating the MagiPeel Kitchen Peeler, married with a son and another child on the way, the best of his life behind him. Or so he feels. Coming home from work one day, Rabbit joins a scuffle of kids shooting balls in an empty lot. Exhilarated to find he still has his 'touch', he decides in a moment of positivity to quit smoking and throw away his cigarettes. But when he gets home, the sight of his pregnant wife Janice slumped mindlessly in front of the TV, drinking, leaves him suddenly infuriated. As he later tells the local vicar, Jack Eccles, he can't stand the fact that he was once first-rate and now – well, 'that thing Janice and I had going, boy, it was really second-rate.' And so he jumps – or, as Updike would have it, runs.

Almost immediately, Rabbit meets someone who knows that running away doesn't work – at least not without a definite plan. 'The only way to get somewhere, you know, is to figure out where you're going before you go there,' points out a gas station attendant when Rabbit admits he doesn't know where he's heading. And later – too late, because by this time tragedy has struck – Rabbit's old basketball coach, Tothero (struggling to formulate the words following a stroke) spells out one last lesson: 'Right and wrong aren't dropped from the sky . . . We make them,' he says. Then: 'Invariably . . . misery follows their disobedience. Not our own.' Rabbit hasn't so much as paused to think about the consequences his running might have on other people.

And he still doesn't now. Tothero's wisdom penetrates us, but it doesn't penetrate Rabbit. He just carries on hating Janice and running away. Sure, we feel sympathy for Rabbit, but we soon see that his problem is not so much that he's trapped by Janice as that he doesn't know how to help her – and thereby himself. Join in with Tothero and tell it to Rabbit, then to yourself: it's better to stay on board that ship, do what you can to plug its holes, then redirect its course. Because if you jump, you jump into the sea. And if you're the one holding the tiller, you won't be the only one who'll drown.

SEE ALSO: **commitment, fear of** • **itchy feet** • **wanderlust**

K

killjoy, being a

Roxana
DANIEL DEFOE

If you happen to stumble on a party – or hear one going on next door – what do you tend to do? Grab a glass, concoct a cocktail and leap into the fray? Or do you recoil in horror from the overly loud music, complain about the folly of letting off fireworks, and frown at the mess and alcohol consumption? Are you, in short, a party-pooper, a sour puss, a spoilsport – one of life's killjoys?

If so, it's time to awaken your inner Roxana, and learn to be the life and soul of the party. Daniel Defoe's most controversial and psychologically complex novel follows the fortunes of a young woman who falls on hard times when her husband absconds with the family's accumulated wealth, leaving her with five children to feed. What, in those days, could a poor girl do but make use of her natural assets? Foxy, fluent in French, and a nimble dancer, Roxana has plenty of offers and – parting from her children 'to avoid having to watch them perish' – becomes a paid mistress to various men. She soon becomes adept at seducing not only new lovers, but entire seventeenth-century ballrooms. Her moment of glory occurs when she appears in full Turkish dress at a ball, dazzling the masked guests so effectively that she's showered with money, attracts the attention of the King, and earns herself the exotic name by which we know her.

Roxana may be forced into her role of party girl; but her

ability to bring a buzz to proceedings even when her chips are down makes her an ideal mentor. You don't have to be in a party mood to begin with; just be willing to plug in and give it your all. The mood will come. Like Roxana, you'll bring smiles to the faces of others – and may even catch the eye of some interesting new friends in high places.

SEE ALSO: **antisocial, being • goody-goody, being a • humourlessness • misanthropy • nobody likes you • teetotaller, being a**

knackered, being

SEE: **busy, being too • busy to read, being too • children requiring attention, too many • exhaustion • fatherhood • motherhood • pregnancy • tired and emotional, being • workaholism**

knocked up, being

SEE: **pregnancy**

L

laziness

SEE: **adolescence** • **ambition, too little** • **bed, inability to get out of** • **lethargy** • **procrastination**

The Member of the Wedding
CARSON MCCULLERS

left out, feeling

Sometimes it can feel as if we are being intentionally excluded, left out of the fun. If we'd chosen not to join in, then it would be alright – not all of us are party people (see: outsider, being an). But when the desire to join in is there yet somehow the welcome hasn't arrived, one can end up feeling extremely sorry for oneself, and begrudging of those selfish, oblivious others who've failed to do anything about our distress. Unfortunately, a common impulse is to try and fix it in one of two misguided ways: to force ourselves upon the group, or to reject the group which has rejected us.

Neither strategy works. Twelve-year-old Frankie, the motherless heroine of *The Member of the Wedding*, one of Carson McCullers's odes to loners and oddballs set in the small-town American South, tries them both. It all starts going wrong when her best friend moves to Florida and her father asks who this 'great big long-legged twelve-year-old blunderbuss' is who's still sleeping in his bed. She takes up some worrying habits after that – shooting her father's pistol in a vacant lot, stealing a knife from Sears and Roebuck, and committing a 'queer sin' with Barney MacKean in the

MacKeans's garage. None of it stops her feeling 'unjoined', and when the neighbourhood kids have a party in the club-house, she listens from the alley behind.

At first she decides the answer is to become a 'we' with her older brother Jarvis and his fiancée. She'll become a 'member' of their wedding, and after the wedding she'll go out into the world with the two of them. When Jarvis and Janice fail to catch on to this idea, she decides to run away instead. But like most twelve-year-old runaways, she doesn't get very far.

The solution, when it appears, brings with it a 'shock of happiness'. *The Member of the Wedding* will strike a chord with all those who feel they're on life's sidelines, whether they're being ignored at work, or left out of a new trend among friends, such as deciding to start a family, or going on a group holiday to Goa. Read it and be reminded: don't force things, and don't – especially if you're only twelve – run away. Have patience. Your ticket to the party will come.

L

239

SEE ALSO: **different, being • foreign, being • loneliness • nobody likes you • outsider, being an • shyness**

lethargy

The Sheltering Sky
PAUL BOWLES

Don Quixote
MIGUEL DE CERVANTES SAAVEDRA

You may have made it out of bed (see: bed, inability to get out of), but you've about as much bounce in your stride as a pregnant hippo. When you're overcome by physical and mental lethargy, dragging your heavy limbs and empty of motivation, it is notoriously hard to shift. Because to combat lethargy you need energy – but where does the initial injection of energy required to reverse the inertia come from?

Our two-part tonic begins by immersing yourself in the sort of stagnant environment in which lethargy thrives. Paul Bowles's inimitable *The Sheltering Sky* – subtle, grave, intense, and filled with a sense of doom – is such a place. Port, his wife Kit, and their 'astonishingly handsome' friend Tunner – Americans who have shunned their homeland yet failed to find anything better – are drifting through the North African desert. A strangely featureless, restless group, they spend their days mostly in avoidance of one another, the local inhabitants, and of any real engagement with life. An unspecified menace seems to exist between them and the Arabs they meet – dark figures that lurk and cannot be trusted. Stones are thrown from unseen hands, wallets are almost pinched. And so the trio move on with no particular destination in mind, an ominous wind at their backs and a 'limpid, burning sky' overhead.

Kit is the most dysfunctional. She has days when she is so filled with a prophetic sense of doom that she cancels any plans she might have had. Tunner, with his bland good looks, bores her, and she finds his morning greetings 'offensively chipper'. For her husband Port, meanwhile, the only certainty is an 'infinite sadness' at the core of his being – reassuring because of its familiarity. When Kit says to Port one day, 'We've never managed, either one of us, to get all the way into life,' she hits the nail on the head. Their lives are like petri dishes in which the bacteria of lethargy breeds: full of languor, uncertainty, miscommunication and alienation. Take a good look at yourself and ask if those petri dishes are present in your life too.

The second half of our cure must be taken as soon as you've turned the last page, as it will zap your body with the electric shock of contrast. Cervantes's loveable, excitable Don Quixote – who styles himself on the knights-errant in the courtly romances to which he is addicted and stays up all night to read – is everything the characters in *The Sheltering Sky* are not. He rises early, he dons his grandfather's spruced-up coat of armour, and he sallies forth in search of adventures – a damsel in distress to rescue and love, a rascal to run through with a lance. Could lethargy grow here? By sooth, we'd say not! While Bowles's disaffected Americans reduce the mystery and beauty of the desert to odd, untrustworthy parts so that it cannot hurt them – denying it the magnificence or epic resonance that would give them a place in history – Don Quixote turns plain roadside inns into castles with silver pinnacles, windmills into an army of giants. And all this with an irrepressibly jaunty, blithesome disposition, immune to the cautions of his trusty squire.

Take it neat, spilling from the pen of Cervantes with its breathless upswing and cavalier call to arms, its romance and zest. For those who are sluggish and slow, it's the most electrifying tonic that literature has to offer this side of the law.

SEE ALSO: **ambition, too little** • **apathy** • **bed, inability to get out of** • **boredom**

libido, loss of

In Praise of the Stepmother
MARIO VARGAS LLOSA

When your sex drive takes a nose-dive, glean inspiration from this wicked little prank of a novel by the Peruvian author Mario Vargas Llosa. Each night, after his fastidious night-time ablutions, Don Rigoberto takes his wife Doña Lucrecia into his arms and murmurs: 'Aren't you going to ask me who I am?' Doña Lucrecia knows the game. 'Who, who, my love?' she implores. And Don Rigoberto – a sensualist, a lover of art, a widower who cannot believe his luck at finding love again in midlife and a stepmother for his teenage son, Alfonso – begins to talk from the point of view of a character in a famous painting.

Because what turns him on is for him and Doña Lucrecia to inhabit the figures in these paintings in their fantasies. One night he is the King of Lydia in a work by the seventeenth-century Dutch master Jacob Jordaens, proudly extolling the virtues of his wife's voluminous buttocks. The next he is aroused and titillated by François Boucher's 'Diana at the Bath', imagining Lucrecia as the goddess of the hunt having her body rubbed with honey and her toes sucked one by one by her female lover. On a more complicated night, it's Francis Bacon's anguished and unprepossessing 'Head I' that gets their juices flowing.

Possibly they take it too far. Cast as Venus in Titian's 'Venus with Cupid and Music', Doña Lucrecia is aroused so much by her husband's descriptions of Cupid tickling her with his wings and 'roll[ing] about on the satiny geography of her body' that she finds herself entertaining dirty thoughts about her angelic stepson, Alfonso. Perched on the cusp of his nascent sexuality, the golden-haired boy is only too keen to egg her on.

There's nothing wrong, though, with borrowing a little inspiration from art and literature to fan the flame of desire in a tired conjugal bed. In the spirit of Don Rigoberto rather than Doña Lucrecia, we offer you this plus a wide range of literary erotica in our cure for orgasms, not enough. We hope you may find something to steam up the windows in your home.

SEE ALSO: **orgasms, not enough** • **sex, too little**

limb, loss of

Peter Pan
J M BARRIE

*The Third
Policeman*
FLANN O'BRIEN

The loss of a limb is an awful bind and will slow you down for a while; but as literature shows there are ways of using it to your advantage. Make a feature of your missing limb, like Captain Hook in JM Barrie's delightful-even-for-grownups *Peter Pan*, and wear a hook or other surprising arm or leg replacement with pride. Not only will you stand out in a crowd, but people will know that you've suffered from your loss and have a more complex personality as a result. Captain Hook's inability to cope with the sight of his own blood and his terror of crocodiles (at least, one crocodile in particular) makes him all the more human to us and Peter Pan.

The one-legged narrator of Flann O'Brien's daft romp *The Third Policeman* is saved from death by his affliction. A one-legged bandit is about to kill him when he notices their common asymmetry and decides to make friends instead.

Be cheered. Life may be different when you lose a limb, but it need not be less hearty, less active or less full of friends.

locked out, being

To pass the time while waiting for the locksmith, you surely need a great detective/crime/spy novel. Keep a stack in your garden shed (where – *ahem* – you should also consider keeping a spare key). You might pick up some ideas for how to break in.

live instead of read, tendency to

READ TO LIVE MORE DEEPLY

It's simply not good enough to say you're too busy getting on with the process of living to spend time reading. Because as Socrates was the first to point out, 'an unexamined life is not worth living'. Books offer a way of turning inward, reflecting, and analysing the life that starts up again as soon as we emerge from the book. And besides, how much living can one person actually do?

Books offer us the lives of a thousand others besides ourselves – and as we read we can live these lives vicariously, seeing what they see, feeling what they feel, smelling what they smell. You could argue that living without books is to live only one, limited life, but with books we can live forever. Without books it is easy to lose direction in life, and to shrink to something small and mean and clichéd. Books develop our capacity to be empathetic, non-judgemental, to accept and honour difference, be brave, extend ourselves and make the most of ourselves (see all the ailments in this book). And they remind us that beyond the minutiae of life, there is another realm of existence common to us all: the mystery of being alive, and what that means. One cannot live fully without spending time in that realm, and books are our ticket there.

**THE TEN BEST NOVELS FOR WHEN YOU'RE
LOCKED OUT**

loneliness

You need never be lonely with a roomful of novels – or even just the one you'd take with you to a desert island – and we all have our favourite literary friends. But there are inevitably times of literary drought when you may have no novels to hand at all, and for these times you must be sure to have pre-populated your brain with plenty of characters, ideas and interesting conversations, gathered from fiction, to ensure your interior world can always be relied upon to keep you company.

One of the best such anti-loneliness vaccines is *Northern Lights* by Philip Pullman, and the other two novels that make up the *His Dark Materials* trilogy. Because in the fictional world that most closely resembles our own – Pullman has created many worlds within the world of these novels – the human characters all have a dæmon, an animal companion that sits on their shoulders and keeps them company throughout their lives. Dæmons are not just companions, though, but representations of a person's spirit. If a dæmon strays too far from their human, both human and dæmon feel physically compromised, and if the dæmon is in any way hurt, the human feels the pain too. Part best friend, part partner, part physical manifestation of one's very soul, a human with a dæmon is never alone.

Terror strikes in this compelling novel when the

'Magisterium' – the religious organisation ruling the land, Cromwell-style – decides to separate children from their dæmons, supposedly for the good of their souls. Lyra, a feisty pre-adolescent, experiences terrible torture as she comes very close to losing her dæmon Pantalaimon, who appears mostly in the form of a pine marten (the form of one's dæmon not settling permanently until one's teens). As you are swept up in Lyra's quest to prevent this atrocity and rescue Roger and the other children from the 'Gobblers' in the frozen North, you will be converted to the absolute necessity of dæmons – and surely will know what form your own would take.

It's hard to believe that Robert Graves was ever lonely, so heaving with intriguing characters are his large and populous novels. Living in an idyllic corner of Mallorca, he wrote his two most successful novels, *I, Claudius* and *Claudius the God* as a means to fund his sociable lifestyle – because he not only hosted a garrulous community in his head, but also in his home. Many glamorous writers, artists and film-stars flocked to his house parties and took part in the theatrical performances he organised. Use his novels to keep the party going in your own head.

I, Claudius is the fictional autobiography of a nobleman who begins life as a stammering fool, derided and ignored by his odious family, only to rise above them all. The sycophants and schemers who surround him make for highly entertaining company; among them the wise Augustus and his conniving wife Livia, sadistic Tiberius and the frankly insane Caligula. With his family at constant war with itself and everyone trying to poison one another all the time, Claudius himself is always in a throng. It all adds up to a fascinating, bustling sense of what it must have been like to live in the Roman Empire in the first century AD. You might actually be quite glad of your solitude once you've put the novel down.

Sometimes when we're lonely we don't have the energy for new friends; it's old, familiar friends we yearn for. In this case, let the residents of 28 Barbary Lane in Armistead Maupin's symphony to San Francisco back into your life (and if you haven't already met them, it won't take you more than a few pages to feel part of the gang). Creations of the late Seventies and early Eighties, Mary Ann Singleton, Mona Ramsey, Michael 'Mouse' Tolliver, Brian Hawkins and their marijuana-growing landlady Mrs Madrigal are still surprisingly fresh. With its episodic form (the experience is as close to watching television as literature gets), this novel and its seven sequels are for keeping in your kitchen along with your cookbooks. Don't eat alone, but with wise-cracking Mona making you laugh as she flips you an egg, sunny side up, Mouse brewing some reassuringly strong coffee, and Mrs Madrigal taking the mug from your hands and replacing it with pearls of wisdom and a joint. Who needs to go out on a Friday night when Maupin's tales of the city are at home?

SEE ALSO: **loneliness, reading-induced**

long-winded, being

The Road
CORMAC
McCARTHY

An exemplary model of short-windedness, and to illustrate its effectiveness as a cure, we, having just re-read it, will say no more.

losing hope

SEE: **hope, loss of**

losing your faith

SEE: **faith, loss of**

losing your job

SEE: **job, losing your**

losing your marbles

SEE: **drugs, doing too many · madness · senile, going**

loneliness, reading-induced

READ IN COMPANY

We all enjoy the pleasure of being left alone with a good book. But sometimes after several hours of immersion we lift our heads and look around, suddenly struck by the quiet, the absence of others. The world outside – and perhaps the world of our book – teems with people interacting with one another. But we are all alone. Something plaintive has entered our soul; we are suffering from reading-induced loneliness.

For some, reading is a way of escaping loneliness in the first place (see: loneliness); feeling perhaps that nobody un-derstands us, we find great solace in the company of a like-minded book. Sometimes we turn to books to escape the people around us, for there can be loneliness within a crowd too. How contrary, then, that the very thing that first cured us of our loneliness has now delivered us into a different sort of isolation.

The solution is to read in the company of other reading people – whether in a public space such as a café or a library, or in your own home, with your reading friend or partner at the other end of the sofa. Next time you look up, you'll see someone else similarly engrossed, and you won't feel alone at all.

Reading can be sociable; if you're at home, try reading aloud with your friend or partner, either at length or just the bits you've underlined. Consider joining a reading group in which everybody takes turns to read from a novel aloud; there are a number of organisations that support these groups and will show you how it's done. Reading a book communally is a wonderful way to share an otherwise inter-nal and solitary experience, and you're likely to come away with a greater insight into and understanding of the book from the reactions of others during and after. It's also a great way to make new reading friends. Maybe at some point one of them might occupy the space at the other end of your reading sofa.

L

247

losing yourself

SEE: **fatherhood** • **identity crisis** • **identity, unsure of your reading** • **lost, being** • **motherhood** • **selling your soul** • **trapped by children**

lost, being

House of Leaves
MARK Z
DANIELEWSKI

Like a terrified character writing notes on a book about an exegesis of a documentary, you may see yourself (as if through a Hi8 video cam) stooping in a dark corner of the page, in a dead academic's room, picking up *House of Leaves* and resting your eyes on the word LOST. And know now, that you really are LOST in a vacillating house/labyrinth/critique/communication theory/isolation chamber/novel about a psychoanalytic deception/house/belief system where your only guide is the flickering light of a printed word against the black infinite void of the white page.

Will Navidson moves with his girlfriend and their two young children into a house on Ash Tree Lane and captures, with a selection of cameras and CCTV footage, uncanny spatial violations in the building (a room larger on the inside than the outside, a door that should open to the garden but leads instead to a long dark hallway). As parallax viewpoints of these anomalies are explored, your reading experience will echo the walk into the dark labyrinth and the psychological implosion of all involved, as meaning disintegrates around you* and a Lovecraftian beast growls at your side. You will be reminded that 'Myth always slaughters reason if she falters; myth is the tiger stalking the herd'.

You could attempt escape by uttering 'the low, eerie flutter of one simple word – perhaps your word – flung down empty hallways long past midnight'. And, by noting the relayed echoes, calculate the size and shape of an unilluminated space, so that, with luck, you will find an archway leading *out*.

---

* So that you realise you are nothing more than some other voice, possessing you with histories you should never have recognised as your own; inventing you, defining you, directing you until every association you can claim as your own is relegated to nothing. Forcing you to face the most terrible suspicion of all, that all of this has just been made up, and what's worse, not by you.

And if you're still LOST, and all that has been revealed is
the 'outline of lives' that are only visible to the imagination,
you'll find, whilst reading this postmodern roller-coaster of
meta narrative and, frankly, blatant lies, that if you give up
on the hope of
c
l
i
n
g
i
n
g
to
the
r
o
p
e

of a linear narrative, you'll find joy in losing yourself in the
footnotes and details, for the investment in such a complex,
time-consuming dazzle of ideas will in the end yield a taste
far superior to anything experienced 'casually' or that being
LOST is just the realisation that ultimately, representation in
all its persuasive disguises[†] is nothing but
a door,
that you would be wiser to
turn the handle
and open.
If you're brave enough

or just escape by leaving *House of Leaves* altogether.
Only to wake next morning
and find
jagged claw-marks
in the wood
by your alarm.

---

† Including this sentence.

love, doomed

Sometimes it's obvious to everyone but you that your love is doomed. Blissed out in your love bubble, you cannot see beyond the shimmering pearlescence that surrounds you. Love born under a maligned star – like Tristan and Isolde's, Cathy and Heathcliff's, Tess and Angel Clare's – is terrible to watch. But the star-crossed pair have no inkling that their bubble will soon pop. Once the membrane is pierced, however, even the doomed lovers will generally realise their folly, and this is the time to take our cure – in the death-throes of romance.

Because however doomed your own romance may be, it cannot be as hopelessly doomed as the ill-fated lovers in Yevgeny Zamyatin's *We*. D-503 (male) and I-330 (female) can only meet in secret because they live in One State, a society run by the 'Benefactor', who controls all human life. Everyone conducts their business within glass walls, so that they can be watched at all times. D-503 and I-330 make their first assignation in the one corner of a building which is opaque.

Gradually, I-330 reveals to D-503 that she is part of an underground operation working to break down the 'Green Wall' keeping their civilisation separate from the outside world. We catch glimpses of free humans in this other world, covered in fur. A plan for escape, fuelled by the intensity of their passion, has us rooting for their future. But Zamyatin was drawing from his experience of Russia in the early twentieth century, where his book was banned for many years – and we know One State is riddled with spies . . . Reading *We* will make you feel better about your own failure to see the end coming.

The love between Lady Chatterley and the gamekeeper Mellors seems completely doomed too. Not only is Connie married – to the paralysed and impotent Sir Clifford with whom she has a mental but not a physical spark – but she is a member of the aristocracy and Mellors a mere 'commoner', to use the term of the day. As if to remind her (or, more probably, us) of the great chasm that exists between them,

Mellors slips every now and then into his broad, Derbyshire vernacular. Quite sensibly, Mellors is 'afraid o' things' once they start their passionate, deeply sexual affair, seeing all the 'complications'. In comparison, Connie's plea for him not to give up on her seems naïve; and the reader can't help seeing that their connection, though deep, is as flawed as her marriage, in reverse. The physical spark is there but they have nothing to talk about.

But DH Lawrence confounds all expectations. Connie, once awakened by Mellors, who touches 'the woman' in her, starts to see her intellectual bond with Clifford as 'just so many words'. And from then on, she doesn't waver. At the end of the novel we are left with them both waiting – Mellors for his divorce to come through, Connie for Sir Clifford to give her her freedom. Their future hovers before them, as yet ungrasped; but Connie is carrying Mellors' child; and having told the world of their love there would seem to be no going back.

And if there's hope for Lady Chatterley and Mellors – well, perhaps you shouldn't be so pessimistic about your love after all. See: pessimism to cure you of this cure.

L

SEE ALSO: **love, unrequited** • **Mr/Mrs Wrong, ending up with** • **wasting time on a dud relationship**

love, falling head over heels in

SEE: **appetite, loss of** • **concentrate, inability to** • **dizziness** • **infatuation** • **insomnia** • **lovesickness** • **lust** • **obsession** • **optimism** • **romantic, hopeless**

love, falling out of love with

SEE: **falling out of love with love**

love, looking for

SEE: **happiness, searching for** • **Mr/Mrs Right, holding out for** • **Mr/Mrs Right, looking for** • **shelf, fear of being left on the** • **single, being**

love, unrequited

Unrequited love is a particular kind of love that can only ever go one-way. To prove our point, we'll borrow Ann Patchett's definition of it in her novel *Bel Canto* (also one of our cures for: Mr/Mrs Right, looking for). Trapped in adjacent seats on an eighteen-hour flight, the young Swedish accompanist to the famous soprano Roxane Cox blurts out a confession of undying adoration that makes the singer wince. Coming out of the blue and without any basis in mutual friendship or attraction, it is too much, too soon – and stinks of recklessness: 'The kind of love that offers its life so easily, so stupidly, is always the love that is not returned,' Patchett writes. How can the object of your love see someone worth loving in return when you are willing to throw yourself at their feet, exposed and bleeding like a piece of uncooked meat?

It's only a matter of time before the accompanist sacrifices himself literally, for the poor sot is well and truly lost to the masochistic destructiveness of his hopeless love. When the terrorists who have taken both the soprano and her audience hostage offer freedom to anyone needing medical help, the love-struck man keeps mum, even though he's a diabetic requiring regular injections of insulin to stay alive. Staying to 'protect' Roxane will mean certain death. Well, thanks a lot, Swedish accompanist, for dumping the guilt of your death on my hands, Roxane would be within her rights to point out. You call that love?

Literature is teeming with similarly tormented, foolish types, dying to die for the love of someone who never asked for it in the first place. And it's not a pretty sight. The worst of the bunch is Werther in Goethe's *The Sorrows of Young Werther*, the sensitive soul whose hopeless love of the peasant girl Lotte – already happily engaged to someone else when they meet – drives him to take his own life in despair. He even has the audacity to arrange for Lotte to send him the pistol that will be the instrument of his death. What cheek! Following this novel's first publication in 1774, sensitive, artistic types from Ostend to Naples began dressing in the signature outfit of young Werther and some killed themselves in copycat suicides with a pistol and an open door. It became known as the Werther effect. Goethe was quick to denounce the overblown emotions of the Romantic Movement – known as *Sturm und Drang* ('storm and stress') – from which his novel had sprung. We do too. If you suspect you're the type to revel in the tragedy of your own unrequited love, we instruct you to steer well clear of *The Sorrows*. Turn to *Far from the Madding Crowd* instead.

This Hardy stalwart, set in the Wessex he loved, is the best novel in the business for showing how to, and how not to, love. Everyone gets it wrong at the beginning. Gabriel Oak – though loveable from the very first line with his beaming smile that reaches to 'within an unimportant distance of his ears' – is somewhat simplistic in his approach to courting. Bathsheba – pretty, marriageable, soon-to-be-rich – is vain and full of herself. She's also a tease, and though this works for Gabriel – for, as we now know a prize worth winning has to be a little hard to get – the Valentine's card she sends in a moment of impetuous silliness to her neighbour William Boldwood is an act of irresponsibility she lives to regret. Hitherto unaffected by the good looks of his neighbour, the card gives Boldwood the idea of loving her, and soon he has plunged head first into a Werther-esque rush of unrequited love, sacrificing himself quite unnecessarily in its depths.

Bathsheba's third suitor, Sergeant Troy, is essentially a good man, though like Bathsheba he thinks a little too much of his looks – never an appealing trait (see: vanity; arrogance). But he has done something even more reprehensible than Bathsheba, having left a pregnant woman in his wake. Gabriel Oak is the only one who proves his worth and he does it by standing firm, by being a loyal friend to Bathsheba throughout the whole messy business with the other two men, and waiting for Bathsheba to see his worth – as well as to prove her own.

If you insist on revelling – just for a while – in the ecstasies and agonies of unrequited love, do it with Turgenev's *First Love*. In this sun-drenched novella, young Vladimir, sixteen, is besotted with twenty-one-year-old Zinaida. She has a whole deck of suitors at her disposal and though she treats him as a young confidante, she does not take his advances remotely seriously. She plays with all her infatuated lovers – and it only becomes apparent at the end who the true object of her affection is. It all, of course, ends in tragedy. Have one last revel in your love along with Vladimir, but decide thereafter to keep your cards close to your chest. Only then will you start winning the suits.

If the love you feel is not returned, pause in your foolish gushing and ask yourself the following question. In your eagerness to love, have you made yourself unloveable, lacking in self-respect? If the answer's yes, you'll be incapable of inspiring more than a guilty 'no'. Buck up. Look yourself in the eye and tot up your worth. Then demonstrate that worth with the sort of behaviour that someone as wonderful as the person you love surely deserves in return.

SEE ALSO: **infatuation** · **jealousy** · **love, doomed** · **Mr/Mrs Right, holding out for** · **self-esteem, low**

lovesickness

The Price of Salt
PATRICIA
HIGHSMITH

In the Middle Ages, literary heroes and heroines regularly pined away from lovesickness. Palamon in Chaucer's *The Knight's Tale* is a prime example, having caught sight of fair Emileye through the window of the tower where he is imprisoned, then nearly wasting away from the effects of seeing but not having her. It is only in our less romantic era that psychiatrists tend to be called in and drugs prescribed. Lovesickness is caused by the absence of the loved one, whether it is through enforced separation, rejection by the love-object (see: love, unrequited), or death of the loved one. Symptoms can be remarkably palpable, including fainting, wasting away, withdrawal from life and addiction to choco-late. All of these afflictions can be most tiresome for one's friends and family (and they should see: family, coping with). Our drug-free cure is a bracing dose of love requited.*

Highsmith's second novel was inspired by an incident in her own life when she was working in a department store selling children's dolls, just like Therese in *The Price of Salt*. She was so bowled over by a customer who seemed to 'give off light' and made her feel that she had seen a vision, that she went home and wrote the bones of the story in two hours. The tale told is one of unexpected passion between two women: Carol, in her thirties, with a daughter and a hus-band she's in the process of leaving, and Therese, nineteen, drifting from job to job but with a flair for set design. It is Therese, the shop-girl, who initiates their affair.

At first Therese is openly besotted, and Carol remains playfully aloof. Therese's boyfriend is disconcerted; she has made no attempt to hide her obsession from him. 'It's worse than being lovesick', he tells her, 'because it's so com-pletely unreasonable,' failing to believe in the possibility of same-sex love. But what is true love but the triumph of emotion over reason? When Carol and Therese take off on a road trip across the States, Carol opens up to Therese and they become fully entwined. Their sensual romance is ex-quisitely described: 'The dusky and faintly sweet smell of her perfume came to Therese again, a smell suggestive of dark green silk that was hers alone . . . She wanted to thrust the table aside and spring into her arms, to bury her nose in the green and gold scarf that was tied close about her neck.' During a period when the two are apart (they believe for-ever), Therese experiences extreme lovesickness: total las-situde and despair in good old medieval style.

'How would the world come back to life? How would its salt come back?' Only Carol can save her from her lovesick state. And she does.

Whatever your sexual persuasion, Therese's endurance

---

* We apologise for giving the game away, but this is a novel that is not spoilt by knowing that the girl gets the girl in the end.

of her lovesickness will give you strength. If you have a Carol in your life, pursue her. The salt will soon come back. If you give up hope, see: love, doomed; love, unrequited; and broken heart.

SEE ALSO: **appetite, loss of** • **broken heart** • **concentrate, inability to** • **death of a loved one** • **dizziness** • **infatuation** • **insomnia** • **lust** • **nausea** • **Obsession** • **romantic, hopeless** • **sentimental, being** • **tired and emotional, being** • **yearning, general**

lust

Girl with a Pearl Earring
TRACY CHEVALIER

Lust has its place, of course. We wouldn't feel alive without it. But when it comes to decisions, let lust take a back seat. Human desire is immensely powerful, but it is also entirely unreasonable, lacking in sense and sound judgement (and if you suffer from this in general, see: common sense, lack of). Letting lust make your decisions in life is, frankly, about as sensible as handing a thirteen-year-old boy the keys to your new Aston Martin and suggesting he takes a spin.

Take a leaf from Griet, the considered, measured maid-cum-muse of Johannes Vermeer in Tracy Chevalier's re-conjuring of the moment behind the eponymous painting. The humble girl captures the painter's interest when he notices that she's arranged her chopped red cabbage and carrots in such a way that the colours do not 'fight', real-ising at once that she has an instinctive, painterly eye. By the time she sits for him, they have come to respect each other, working peacefully in his studio side by side. Griet has begun to refer to him as 'her master' and, more tellingly still, as an unnamed 'he'. Both have taught the other new ways to see. And there's been a significant, highly charged touch: Vermeer places his hand over Griet's to show her how to use the stone, or muller, when crushing a piece of charred ivory to make black paint, causing such a power-ful sexual charge to pass through her that she drops it. The beginnings of courtship, then. And by the time the painting is made, the lust – his, but also hers – is there for all to see, in the glinting whites of the eyes, the moist lips just falling apart, the gently twirled and hitched fabric of the headdress and, of course, the shine from out of the shadowy neck of that incongruous, lustrous pearl.

Griet knows full well that in seventeenth-century Delft a girl from her background can't tangle with a man from Vermeer's class. This is highly dangerous territory, and with the sexual tension blistering on the page, we know Griet's future hangs on the line. Chevalier's careful, concise sentences model the restraint required by both of them. Will they find it, or will lust break through?

Oh lusty reader, when your hormones threaten to prevail over your head, take yourself off to a quiet place with *Girl with a Pearl Earring*. Let those elegant, disciplined sentences temper your passions, rein in your lust. Pause, slow down, re-think. Is your attraction for someone with whom you can share your carrots and cabbages? If not, enjoy the arousal for what it is, then take a deep breath and move on.

SEE ALSO: **infatuation • lovesickness • sex, too much**

lying

Atonement
IAN MCEWAN

Lies come in many colours. But apart from the white ones, uttered to protect someone else from suffering unnecessary hurt, lies are generally spawned by meanness and/or selfishness – a desire to inflict harm, or to protect oneself from shame or punishment. Do not underestimate the damage they can do. Allow yourself to indulge in small infelicities, however seemingly insignificant, and you not only relegate yourself to the category of someone who cannot be trusted (for the disadvantages of which, see: trust, loss of), but you run the risk of causing yourself or others injury to last a lifetime.

Look at what happens to thirteen-year-old Briony in Ian McEwan's *Atonement*. Still smarting, perhaps, from having confessed her childhood crush on Robbie, the son of the Tallis's housekeeper who has been brought up and educated as one of the family, she allows her overly-vivid imagination, her drama-queen tendencies and the idea of herself as a selfless protector of others, to run away with her. When she interrupts Cecilia and Robbie in *flagrante delicto* in the library, her misinterpretation of what was going on could be put down to naïveté. But when she later stumbles on her distressed cousin Lola in the dark, having been knocked down and violated by a shadowy retreating figure, she only considers one culprit. The socially inferior Robbie, with his 'strong, awkward limbs' and 'rugged friendly face who used to carry her on his back' immediately metamorphoses in her febrile imagination into a brute who has abused the family's hospitality horribly, and must be punished.

That Briony is young is no excuse. Trapped in her own delusion, the intricate story she has spun from her own misreadings and imaginings causes her to drown out the voice inside her that knows the truth. Instead, she chooses to shore up her position and expunge her doubt, all for the sake of maintaining the narrative she's embarked on. And so, when she is asked by the inspector whether she saw Robbie clearly, with her own eyes, she lies.

Her lie ruins not just Robbie and Cecilia's lives, but her own as well. As she seeks atonement for her crime, she goes over the details of it in an eternal loop, like 'a rosary to be fingered for a lifetime'. This novel should be read as a vaccination against the temptation to tell an untruth. Read it and let it hover in your mind as a constant reminder.

SEE ALSO: **trust, loss of**

M

madness

The Comforters
MURIEL SPARK

Literature is fond of its lunatics – from Mr Rochester's insane wife in *Jane Eyre*, who scurries round on all fours growling like a wild animal, to the eerie presence that haunts Wilkie Collins's *The Woman in White*. But while these two crazies are harmless, many evocations of mental derangement can be dangerous to the reader who feels that he or she is becoming unhinged. If you feel yourself to be touched in this way, steer clear of Margaret Atwood's *Surfacing*, which tracks the gradual descent into psychosis of its unnamed narrator. Together with her lover Joe and a couple of friends, she travels north to a remote island in Quebec in an attempt to find out what happened to her father, who has gone missing. Perhaps it is grief for her father that undoes her; perhaps it's the emotional void between herself and Joe. Or perhaps it's whatever horrible thing it is that she sees at the bottom of the seabed. But whatever its cause, her increasingly fragmented and ungrammatical narrative does such a good job of conveying her unbalanced mental state that it may well make a few more screws in your head come loose. And despite its title, you will find no comfort in the pages of *The Comforts of Madness*, Paul Sayer's Whitbread Prize-winning novel about a boy so traumatised by abuse that he makes a conscious decision, when his father dies in the bed they share, never to move again. As the boy grows into a man – and is still lying in bed – his interior monologue is mesmerising, heart-rending, and somehow dangerously seductive. See: bed, inability to get out of; and depression, general, for related afflictions which require different cures.

The best novel for those seeking to avoid the loony bin is Muriel Spark's *The Comforters*. Almost all the characters in this novel are mad – in the sense of still functioning in society quite happily, but way up there on the scale. So much so that you will feel right at home, and rather normal, in comparison.

Caroline Rose is renting a flat in Kensington and experiencing mid-century angst around issues of feminism and aesthetics (if you are a modern-day sufferer of this type of affliction, see: malaise, twenty-first century), when she becomes aware of the tapping of typewriter keys. The tap-tap-tap is accompanied by the dispassionate narration of her own thoughts and actions – as if a Greek chorus were intoning the banal drama of her life, off-stage, while someone else was writing it down. At first the Typing Ghost, as she calls it, simply provides a third-person narrative of her day as she lives it. But then it begins to predict her future. Caroline attempts to cheat it – so that when the Typing Ghost predicts she will 'fritter away the day' and be forced to travel to Sussex by car instead of train, Caroline makes a desperate attempt to take the train after all. But, farcically, she can't outwit it.

If Caroline's particular brand of madness doesn't overlap with yours, you might identify more with the diamond-smuggling granny, the Belgian Congolese Baron, the zealous Catholic convert or, of course, the Typing Ghost itself. All the characters are equally delightful – and equally barmy. 'We're all a little mad, Willi,' Caroline confirms to the Baron. 'That's what makes us so nice, dear.' With its gentle and original humour, this novel certifies that there's nothing wrong with being a tad off your rocker – it happens to the best of us, in fact – and we shouldn't fret too much about it. Leave literature's serious crackpots for your friends and family to read, and stick to the deviationist fringe.

SEE ALSO: **paranoia** · **turmoil**

malaise, twenty-first century

The sense of discomfort one feels that is unique to this century comes from a discrepancy between one's desires for a contented, fulfilled, and even adventurous life, and the absurdity of society as we see it unfurling around us: bureaucracy, political correctness, safety legislation, the dysfunctionality of individuals caused by an excessive use of technology . . . The list goes on.

No novel captures this malaise more deftly than Benoît Duteurtre's *The Little Girl and the Cigarette*. Its starting point is the fictional case of Désiré Johnson who, on the verge of being executed for the murder of a policeman, requests that he have a last smoke. His plea throws the authorities into confusion. Désiré's invocation of Article 47 is entirely within his rights, but tobacco consumption is banned within the limits of the prison. The absurdity of his outmoded request, and the obstinacy with which he insists on it, is all too much for their legal capabilities. They decide that only the Supreme Court can make the decision.

Meanwhile, another man is having a different crisis, also involving cigarettes. A technical advisor for the General Services Department of 'Administration City', smoking is this man's secret vice. One day as he enjoys a quiet puff out of the window of the toilets, a five-year-old girl walks in on him with his trousers down. She tells everyone and soon the man is facing charges of child-molestation. A nightmarish satire in the style of Jonathan Swift's *A Modest Proposal*, Duteurtre's inverted vision puts justice in the hands of children. Share your frustration at a world gone mad with Duteurtre. It helps not to be the only one crying out for reason.

In Shteyngart's *Super Sad True Love Story*, Lenny and Eunice live in a world not too distant from our own, in which a data stream constantly updates individuals on their credit scores and social network ranking, while offering up-to-the-minute shopping ideas and the very latest of their friends' gossip. Lenny is thirty-nine, a Jewish immigrant from Russia, who anachronistically still both loves – and reads

– books (particularly Tolstoy, which his friends think is unhealthy). The object of his desire, Eunice, is a young Korean student. Their story is told via their alternate diary entries, Lenny's the old-fashioned way, Eunice's through her Global-Teens account – a kind of all-encompassing version of Facebook – so that we have the fun of Eunice's 'teening' to listen to. Eunices's entries reveal her own angst about the future, and the contentment she keeps finding, to her surprise, with the 'darling little dork' Lenny. Meanwhile, New York is beginning to disintegrate around them, America is at war with Venezuela, and everyone is so in debt to China that the plug may be pulled on resources at any minute. Lenny fears for their future, as individuals, and as a nation.

After Duteurtre's satire, this romp through an oh-so-Media-mad, post-literature world of immortality-seeking 'Nee-groes' (an affectionate appellation for friends of all colours) who check one another out then hold an 'Emote-Pad' to their hearts to learn their feelings, will find you reaching for a 'bound, printed, non-streaming Media artifact' – perhaps some Tolstoy, like Lenny – even if it will bring down your 'PERSONALITY rankings'. Lenny Abramov, last reader on Earth, turns out to be right about a lot of things.

SEE ALSO: **city fatigue** • **disenchantment** • **dissatisfaction**

man flu

Les Misérables
VICTOR HUGO

Infinitely worse than regular flu, and not to be confused with the common cold (which is hard, as the symptoms are identical), man flu is a miserable illness not just for the victim, but for all concerned. Bed rest is essential, and the patient – indeed, the word victim is probably more apt – will require a great deal of sympathy. The victim should be propped up on soft pillows, with mugs of tea, hot water bottles, meals on trays, a TV with remote control, and messages of support and commiseration from family and friends brought to him* regularly; although visitors to the bedside must take great

---

* Scientists cannot explain why this ailment only affects men, but it does.

care when making conversation to stick to the subject of the victim and his suffering. Do not venture onto matters pertaining to the outside world or indeed the domestic sphere (household chores and responsibilities), as this will agitate the victim and prevent him from focussing on his suffering and so begin the long journey back to full health.

Our 'cure' – and this is one of the occasions in this book where we must use the term most loosely – is a two-volume edition of Victor Hugo's classic novel of human torment and suffering, *Les Misérables*. Your patient might consider himself too ill for the application of a novel cure – and in fact urge you to turn to the entry in this book on dying. However, it is important to have a firm hand in administering it, despite his resistance. We assure both you and he that within a few pages he will have lost himself completely in the woes of Jean Valjean and Fantine, Cosette and Monsieur Marius, Eponine and police inspector Javert, recognising his own sufferings in theirs, and taking great comfort as a result.

Because of its great length (the first volume of our edition comes to 713 pages, the second to 524, and the print is small) reading *Les Misérables* may on the surface seem like a punishment. In fact, it will help the victim to find the patience and stoicism to endure his enforced inactivity – for the most pernicious cases of man flu have been known to incapacitate victims for up to a week. Those responsible for nursing the victim, a round-the-clock job, will find him to be less talkative while taking the cure, thus giving everybody a chance to recover and delve more deeply within themselves to find unending supplies of love and sympathy. In the most effective cases, the cure might even enable the sufferer to forget about his symptoms completely, and bring about a return to good humour, vivacity and pleasure in life – even interest in others – which will seem quite miraculous when it occurs. For *Les Misérables* is as gripping as the best soap operas, and as nourishing as chicken soup. (Indeed, we have heard anecdotal cases where those nursing the patient have ended up stealing the novel cure for themselves and leaving the defenceless patient with nothing but a TV!)

If the patient does not finish their medication before

recovering, do not panic. Those prone to man flu are likely to experience recurrences of the illness at regular intervals throughout their life, and an unfinished dose of the medicine is useful to have to hand. Being familiar with the medicine will mean the patient is more likely to be receptive to it, and will likely agree to taking it the instant symptoms appear – a state of affairs which is beneficial to all.

SEE ALSO: **cold, common** • **dying** • **hypochondria**

manners, bad

The Young Visiters
DAISY ASHFORD

Do not attempt to go through life with bad manners. Good manners ensure that you are always a welcome and positive presence. They open doors, carry you through interviews, and land you exciting jobs. They get you good service in restaurants, and complimentary tickets to expensive events. They win you friends, they influence people. In short, they pave your way to a better life.

Of the two eligible men in Daisy Ashford's 1919 novella, *The Young Visiters* – written with devastating aplomb when the authoress was nine years old – it soon becomes clear which one is going to get the girl. It's not just that Bernard has money and an 'ancestle home' (the publishers kept Ashford's juvenile spelling and punctuation, including in the title), nor that he has better clothes, or legs. And it's not that Alfred Salteena is not quite a gentleman. It's about which one has better manners.

Miss Ethel Monticue, the seventeen-year-old whose winsome ways and 'fair hair done on the top' win the hearts of both men, has come to stay with Alfred Salteena. At forty-two, the bewhiskered Salteena is somewhat past it, but he hasn't given up on the idea of love and marriage. Poor Ethel hasn't been in the house very long, though, before she's on the receiving end of his rudeness. 'I shall put some red rug on my face,' she announces with endearing candidness, as they prepare to visit Salteena's friend Bernard. 'You will look very silly,' is Mr Salteena's retort. And that's not all. Though affronted, the girl runs off to fetch her best hat and a 'velvit' coat of royal blue, then gives Alfred a second chance. 'Do I look nice in my get up,' she asks. 'You look rather rash my dear your colors dont quite match your face but never mind ...' comes the regrettable reply.

Of course, Salteena has blown it already. How can any self-respecting heroine accept the attentions of one so poorly mannered? Whether we are aware of it or not, we are judged on our manners at all times by strangers and friends alike. Keep society sweet, and act with impeccable manners towards everyone you meet. Then the goodwill of the world – as well as the Ethels – will be yours, wherever you go.

SEE ALSO: **selfishness**

married, being

The Enchanted April
ELIZABETH VON ARNIM

Being married? An ailment? If that was your first thought when you happened upon this entry, don't read on. You've won life's biggest lottery and found yourself a mate you can live with effortlessly, peaceably and productively. Congratulations.

If, on the other hand, you find that marriage sometimes involves a struggle to maintain your sense of self in the face of constant compromise; if your feel your marriage is stuck in a rut; or if the passing of the years has somehow served to push you and your spouse apart rather than bring you closer, take a burst of luminous inspiration from *The Enchanted April* by Elizabeth von Arnim.

A neglected period piece from the 1920s, the novel tells the story of Mrs Wilkins and Mrs Arbuthnot, two married women who have become jaded and faded by their broken relationships. Both happen to spot the same advertisement in *The Times*: 'To Those who Appreciate Wisteria and Sunshine', it reads. 'Small mediaeval Italian Castle, on the shores of the Mediterranean to be let Furnished for the month of April. Necessary servants remain.' It calls to them both, and in a desperate bid for a gasp of happiness, the two women, though strangers, decide to take the castle together. They invite along a couple of feistier examples of their sex, who yet have relationship issues of their own – the impossibly proper Mrs Fisher and the ethereally beautiful Lady Caroline, who is so sick of drooling attention from both men and women that she has become liberal with the icy put-downs.

Within the purity of San Salvatore's bare white walls and stone floors, the women recover, and slowly begin to rediscover their sensuality and capacity for joy. With the help of juicy oranges, meadows of spring flowers and the ever-helpful gardener Domenico, alchemical transformations occur. Faces puckered by fear and worry smooth out, hearts and minds that have been closed for years break open like buds in full sun. Love floods back in. 'I was a stingy beast at home', declares Lottie (Mrs Wilkins), 'and used to measure and count . . . I wouldn't love Mellersh unless he loved me back, exactly as much, absolute fairness. Did you ever. And as he didn't, neither did I, and the *aridity* of that house! The aridity . . .'

We expect the women to find only themselves in their splendid isolation. But they end up . . . well, let's just say that the husbands don't get forgotten. Marriages are saved and great loves are re-ignited. If your marriage isn't what you hoped it could be, buy *The Enchanted April*. Then book a villa in Italy and read it on the journey out.

SEE ALSO: **children, under pressure to have** • **jump ship, desire to** • **orgasms, not enough** • **querulousness** • **sex, too little** • **sex, too much** • **snoring**

meaning, lack of

SEE: **pointlessness**

melancholia

SEE: **sadness**

memory loss

The Unnamable
SAMUEL BECKETT

The mistake you make of course is to think of memory as if it really exists, in a special place, whereas the whole thing is no more than a project of the moment. But we will let you blunder on until the end of your folly, then you can go into the question again, taking care not to compromise yourself by the use of terms, if not of notions, accessible to the understanding. A little more reflection might show you that you are compelled, in fact, to forget, and that the hour to remember, far from having struck, might never strike. Why not then think of something else, something the existence of which seems to be in a certain measure already measurable, something that is nameable? And now for the 'it', we prefer that, we must say we prefer that, for your attitude towards us has changed, we are deceived, you might be a door taking you to a memory, if only you'll listen, the voice will tell you everything.

You wonder, you don't feel a mouth on you, you don't feel the jostle of words in your mouth, and when you think of a novel you like if you happen to like novels, in a bus, or in bed, the words are there, you don't feel that either, the words falling, you don't know where, you don't know whence, drops of silence, you feel an ear, you feel a nose, though frankly now you don't, you need to make yourself a head.

You think you change you never change you'll be saying the same thing till you die. Where now? Who now? When now? You always forget that, we must resume, you must resume, never stop telling stories to yourself, wondering where you got them from, were you in the land of the living, where do you store those memories, in your head, you don't feel a head on you, you are made of silence, we are made of stories, we'd be you, we'd be the silence, you'd be the stories, you left yourself behind in it, you're waiting for yourself. You must go on, you can't go on, we have carried you to the threshold of your story, before the door opens on your own story, you will be surprised, the door will open, you will be you.

SEE ALSO: **amnesia, reading-associated**

menopause

It may be the end of your monthly cycles, but it doesn't need to be the end of you. In fact, for many women, reaching menopause triggers a desire to dig out the 'you' that was buried or thrust aside by the distractions of the fertile years. Whether you had children early or late or not at all, the deposing of your ovaries from their throne allows you to throw off a certain motherly mantle and cloak yourself in something more exciting instead.

Take as your role model Kate in Doris Lessing's Sixties classic of female self-discovery, *The Summer Before the Dark*. For a number of years, forty-five-year-old Kate has been holding back the tide – tinting her hair, keeping control of her weight, and 'scaling herself down' in order to look and be the part of a housewife and mother from her middle-class London suburb. But the youngest of her four children is now nineteen and ready to leave home, and though she is not yet menopausal, her family – rudely – speak about her as if she is. When a job comes her way – her first, as Kate chose to get married rather than have a career – she leaves her old clothes behind and buys sexy, sophisticated dresses that 'would admit her, like a passport' to a life in which she's no longer Mrs Brown, but Kate Ferreira.

She soon gets bored of this, though. The reason she's so good at her job, she realises, is that she continues to play a diplomatic role – as if she were secreting some sort of 'invisible fluid' that made 'a whole of individuals who could have no other connection'. In short, being everyone's mother. She continues to try on then reject a series of other roles – and clothes – but finds them all variations on the mothering theme, a discovery which sends her spiralling into a breakdown (although fear not, as breakdowns are always purging in the world of Lessing). What shines through from all the confusion is an epiphany she has half-way through her summer of change, that her future will not be a continuation of her immediate past, but will pick up from where she left off as a child – the intelligent, feisty and, yes, sexy, Kate she used to be. If you're looking for a baton, what better one to run with than that?

If you are past caring about your sexiness, and turn with relief to thoughts of art, education, spirituality and self-discovery, *Miss Garnet's Angel* should be your accomplice. A spinster of just past sixty, and still a virgin, Miss Garnet has occasional regrets that she has never been loved by anyone enough to marry. But now that 'the only person she had ever eaten with', her flatmate, has died, all she wants is a little adventure somewhere exotic. Quite randomly she decides on Venice.

Here Miss Garnet opens herself to experiences in a way she never has before, making friends easily, and being sucked into an intriguing art theft, as well as a near-romance. Most importantly, though, she discovers the angel Raphael. Invigorating and wise, and refreshingly free of sex, Miss Garnet's late-flowering will inspire you to higher things in life.

But if you haven't yet done with the reckless adventures of your youth, grab Rebecca Miller's *The Private Lives of Pippa Lee.* From the terrible tedium of a retirement community – albeit for the filthy rich – where Pippa Lee looks doomed to spend her middle age with her more senior husband Herb (eighty-one), we travel via memories of her troubled childhood and speed-crazed twenties into the arms of Chris, a recovering Christian and younger man. Art and angels are an excellent option, but so, sometimes, is postmenopausal sex. Take this novel to bed – because it's never too late for new love.

SEE ALSO: **fifty-something, being** • **headache** • **insomnia** • **libido, loss of** • **sweating** • **tired and emotional, being**

midlife crisis

The Year of the Hare
ARTO PAASILINNA

Do you fantasise about taking off into the sunset in a powerful, throbbing sports-car, sitting proud on leather upholstery, a stiff, shiny gear-stick in your hand? Have you been eyeing up your secretary as a potential passenger? Spare yourself the shame. Slip this slim volume into your overnight case next time you're on a business trip, and refer to it whenever that midlife-crisis urge comes upon you.

One could say that Vatanen, the journalist hero of this picaresque novel, is having the archetypal midlife crisis. He is one of two 'dissatisfied, cynical men', the other being his photographer colleague, 'getting on for middle age'. It is never explained why Vatanen feels the need to leave his home in Helsinki for an adventure with a hare; it just happens. He is on an assignment with the photographer, their car hits a hare, he gets out of the car and discovers the creature has broken a leg. While he nurses it, refusing to answer his colleague in the car, his companion becomes impatient and drives off without him. He doesn't mind; he doesn't feel any great need to go back to Helsinki and his wife anyway.

And so he embarks on a series of adventures that send him all the way up the map of Finland, taking odd jobs along the way. Amongst other things, he is involved in a forest fire; lives alongside a police superintendent in his country cabin who, over a bottle of vodka, shares with Vatanen disturbing evidence that the President of Finland may not be all that he is cracked up to be; and is arrested for looking suspicious when, his hare in a basket, he knocks on someone's door in the middle of the forest, hoping for somewhere to sleep. There are episodes of extreme drunkenness (lasting for eight days in one case), a helicopter ride and a highly dramatic bear-hunt.

All of which is joyously energising and life-enhancing. Reading *The Year of the Hare* will supply you with all the adventures you yearn for, without the destructiveness of enacting them for yourself. Though of course, if you are inspired to take a beautiful wild animal instead of your secretary, you might be able to have your midlife crisis cake and eat it too.

SEE ALSO: **ageing, horror of** • **age gap between lovers** • **career, being in the wrong** • **claustrophobia** • **dissatisfaction** • **divorce** • **extravagance** • **fifty-something, being** • **forty-something, being** • **happiness, searching for** • **jump ship, desire to** • **married, being**

misanthropy

The Holy Sinner
THOMAS MANN

If you are a hater of the human species, try living on a rock in the middle of a lake for seventeen years, like Gregory in *The Holy Sinner*. He has extremely good reasons for his own distrust of human nature. He married his mother, killed his father, and is himself the offspring of a brother and sister. So far, so *Oedipus Rex*. But he decides he must atone for his sins (admittedly unintended), and takes off to live on an island in the centre of a lake. He gets himself shackled to the rock by a leg-iron, just to make his penance more painful. On his limited diet (he suckles from the stone of Mother Earth), he shrinks to the size of a hedgehog over the course of the years.

Meanwhile, the last pope has died, and two bishops have a vision of a bleeding lamb which gives them to understand that the next pope is to be found on an island in the middle of a lake. With great distaste and confusion, the bishops bring the bristly homunculus back over the water. Once he reaches dry land, Gregory is miraculously restored to normal human size again – becoming rather handsome and twinkly, if still a little hairy – and goes on to become one of the greatest popes of all time, admired for his clemency, wisdom and understanding.

If, like Gregory, you tend to stand apart from humanity, despising what you see, consider whether your hatred isn't in fact hatred of yourself. Adopt, like Gregory, the expression '*Absolvo te*,' (I forgive you) – and turn it inwards. Once you've learnt to love yourself, you'll have no trouble falling back in love with everybody else.

SEE ALSO: **antisocial, being** • **cynicism** • **dinner parties, fear of** • **grumpiness** • **killjoy, being a** • **selfishness**

miscarriage

The Time Traveler's Wife
AUDREY NIFFENEGGER

Miscarriage is miserable, bloody and lonely. In some very rare instances it might be a relief, but most often its arrival is greeted with resigned despair. And though logic tells you this foetus was unviable; that thirty per cent of pregnancies fail in this way; that it's just nature's way of doing her weeding, your hormones will be raging and your womb aching. While you recover (hopefully in bed), read *The Time Traveler's Wife*.

Clare has loved the same man all her life. She first met him when she was only six, and he thirty-five. Henry is not a paedophile, but a time traveller, and he knows that in his future, and hers, they will be married.

The haunting and strange tale of their love is both agonising and wonderful to witness. Clare waits for Henry, rejecting suitors from the start. But her lack of control over the romance is stressful: Henry cannot choose when he time travels – sometimes he leaves Clare for months or even years on end – even when they are happily married. Perhaps this is why she becomes an artist, coping with the solitude by channelling it into her art.

The real problems begin when they try to have a baby. Clare goes through five miscarriages before it dawns on them that the foetuses might be inheriting the time travelling gene – and leaving the womb prenatally. Each time it happens, there are blood-soaked sheets, sometimes a 'tiny monster' in Clare's hand, hope and despair hot on each other's heels. Clare perseveres because she is desperate to have a baby, and eventually they find a way round their unique predicament. But she suffers for each loss as you will have suffered, and to bear witness to her grief is deeply cathartic. If you are determined, too, keep trying; and may this life-embracing novel both console and inspire.

SEE ALSO: **children, not having** • **cry, in need of a good** • **failure, feeling like a** • **pain, being in** • **sadness** • **yearning, general**

missing someone

SEE: **breaking up** • **death of a loved one** • **family, coping without** • **homesickness** • **lovesickness** • **widowed, being** • **yearning, general**

missing your children

SEE: **empty-nest syndrome**

missing your flight

SEE: **flight, missing your**

Monday morning feeling

Mrs Dalloway
VIRGINIA WOOLF

If the thought of Monday morning fills you with doom, if you emerge into wakefulness with the weight of a mountain pressing on your chest, pep yourself up with the first page (or two, or three, if you can't then put it down) of *Mrs Dalloway*. For with this masterpiece, Virginia Woolf invented a whole new way of writing, of capturing thoughts in constant flux, and the vitality coursing through the veins of a woman experiencing, moment by moment, a day in June, in the London she loves, after the war has ended. The day is not, in fact, a Monday, but a Wednesday, and Mrs Dalloway is preparing for a party that night.

M

273

She decides to buy the flowers herself. Monday-shirkers take note. You, too, might like to take responsibility for a task – something pleasant, something sensual – which you would normally leave to someone else. The thought of this will help you out of bed. As you eat your breakfast, drink up Mrs Dalloway's – Clarissa's – exuberance, her cut-from-crystal thoughts ('What a lark! What a plunge!') and run with the longer, meandering thought which follows, bending through time, and gathering up sounds: 'For so it had always seemed to her when, with a squeak of the hinges, which she could hear now, she had burst open the French windows and plunged at Bourton into the open air.' What a sentence! What an invitation! Can you not hear that squeak, feel the little shove as the doors give way, taste that clean, cold air?

Then receive, through your eyes and mind and into your body, Clarissa's appetite and love of life. Inhabit her neat and bird-like figure, light, springy, rather upright, as she stands on the kerb preparing to cross. Notice the 'particular hush', the 'indescribable pause' before the tolling of Big Ben. Become aware, as she is aware, of the presence of death – that all these scurrying people will one day just be bones and dust – and carry this awareness with you into your day. Let it heighten your sense of being alive, this particular Monday. Let it help you make the most of your day. Your *Monday*.

Then (making sure you look left and right first – we don't want all your Mondays to end here, and hopefully by this time, you won't either), step out. And . . . why not? Go and buy the flowers yourself.

SEE ALSO: **bed, inability to get out of • career, being in the wrong • dissatisfaction**

money, not having any

SEE: **broke, being • tax return, fear of doing • unemployment**

money, spending too much

SEE: **book-buyer, being a compulsive • extravagance • shopaholism • tax return, fear of doing**

morning sickness

SEE: **nausea • pregnancy**

motherhood

Our Spoons Came From Woolworths
BARBARA COMYNS

I Don't Know How She Does It
ALLISON PEARSON

'"How I dislike the idea of being a Daddy and pushing a pram!" said George. So I said, "I don't want to be a beastly Mummy either; I shall run away." Then I remembered if I ran away the baby would come with me wherever I went. It was a most suffocating feeling and I started to cry.'

This excerpt from *Our Spoons Came From Woolworths*, a soufflé of a novel set in the 1930s, could be printed on packets of birth control pills as a reminder of the realities of having a baby. Once it's there, it's there all the time, and you're responsible for it, whether you like it or not. (Unless, of course, you are the Bolter from Nancy Mitford's *The Pursuit of Love*, who leaves her daughter to be brought up by her sister Emily. Which is one way of coping with motherhood: let other people do it for you.)

Motherhood can't be cured, but it can be treated – and Barbara Comyns's self-deprecating and largely autobiographical novel is an excellent place to start. Sophia is the relentlessly optimistic heroine, who marries far too young, carries a newt called Great Warty around in her pocket, and is utterly ill-equipped for the impending onslaught. She and her young husband are bohemians at heart, cut off from their families and living off various cheques they happen to find in a drawer, or sitting for artists for a small fee, while Charles paints his own pictures. Sophia has not only one but two babies, and Charles's reluctance to make any concessions to fatherhood doesn't bode well for their harmony – he doesn't see why you shouldn't keep a baby in a cupboard, or continue to paint dead fish for several weeks in the room that they all sleep in. Sophia's hideous experiences at the birthing hospital are enough to put many a prospective mother off, but her ability to bounce back after the most appalling setbacks – such as her mother-in-law first swearing not to come to the wedding at all, then turning up with swarms of relatives and expecting to be hosted in the new couple's dingy flat – makes her spirited and positive company. She goes from odd job to odd job, frequently supporting the entire family, while Charles continues to believe he is magnificently talented and should not allow fatherhood to get in his way.

It all adds up to an extreme version of what many new mothers experience; and the refreshingly off-beat humour, combined with Sophia's beguiling voice, will have mothers laughing along with her as she does her best to play house without any help from her spouse. If you're a new mother, you'll save yourself many years of banging your head against a wall by absorbing her survivalist attitude.

For a more modern take on motherhood, Allison Pearson's *I Don't Know How She Does It* is a hilarious dissection of the juggling skills required to hold down a top job, keep a lover, make some pretence at being married, and be a mother. The book begins with Kate Reddy, aged thirty-five, up at 1.37am on the thirteenth of December, 'distressing' mince pies from M&S to make them look homemade. She's determined to at least seem like a 'proper mother', a 'self-sacrificing baker of apple pies and well-scrubbed invigilator of the twin-tub' rather than the 'other sort', so disapproved of in her 1970s childhood.

By day Kate is a fund manager the City firm, where her boss stares at her breasts 'as if they were on special offer' and she keeps long hours, her main entertainment being an email romance with the too-good-to-be-true Jack Abelhammer. She constantly agonises about missing her children's landmark moments ('Today is my son's first birthday and I am sitting in the sky over Heathrow') and rages against the misogynistic world that has put her in this position. Her marriage seems decidedly last-century too, as she bears the brunt of all child-related organisation, domestic chores and school runs, albeit by remote control.

Pearson writes with such humour that reading this will pose a challenge to your post-birth pelvic floor muscles. If you haven't yet entered the realm of motherhood but are curious about what goes on behind the fence, this novel will read as a warning against attempting to 'have it all'. But those already living on that side of the fence will take much roguish delight as Kate Reddy gears up for her next move; still joyfully juggling the balls of marriage, career and kids. Read this, and take heart. You can have it all; just be sure to keep a rolling pin handy to bash your shop-bought tarts.

SEE ALSO: **children requiring attention, too many** • **housewife, being a** • **mother-in-law, being a** • **single parent, being a** • **trapped by children**

mother-in-law, being a

Ladies, please pause to consider. If you are a mother-in-law, do you at least attempt to defy the cliché?* Are you loving and supportive of your son- or daughter-in-law?† Have you accepted them, gracefully, as they are?‡ Do you endeavour to see things from their point of view,§ even taking their side against your own offspring's,§§ knowing that in the end this will strengthen their marriage and, indirectly, help your precious child?

Of the three mothers-in-law (MILs) featured in Joanna Trollope's rigorous exploration of inter-generational in-law relationships, it's Rachel – the mother of three grownup, married sons, and MIL to Sigrid, Petra and Charlotte – who has the longest list of destructive behaviours to her credit. An energetic, efficient, protective 'tiger' mother when her sons were growing up, she has become a forceful, interfering, invasive, controlling old cow now that they're putting their own partners first. Charlotte's mother, Marnie, appears on the surface to be benign – she's generous, and wants to help out the couple financially. But they soon realise there's a fine line between support and suffocation.

If you have brought up your sons never to oppose your wishes; if you phone them repeatedly; if you insist that family gatherings are at your own house, and when they're not, you arrive with the food; if you interrupt their intimate conversations with offers of homemade cake; if you research potential house purchases on their behalf without their consent; if you expect your daughters-in-law to stay with your sons out of gratitude for the way you raised them and reject them when they don't; if you can't allow your daughters-in-law to keep their postnatal depression a secret, when neither they nor your son want you to know about it; and if your response to a daughter-in-law's announcement of her pregnancy is:

M

---

* No-one *is* good enough for your child, of course, but it's still a cliché.
† However little you actually like them.
‡ Though you would not have chosen them yourself.
§ Albeit mistaken.
§§ Even though your darling is always in the right.

'You've only been married ten minutes. Couldn't you have waited?'; if you know that you have committed one or more of these MIL sins, then we'd like you, please, to read this novel.

Then re-create yourself as a second mother to your extra children. It is Sigrid's mother who provides a role model for this. She insists, calmly, that you can only let your adult children go, successfully, if you have interesting, absorbing work – or some other creative outlet – of your own, plus a strong enough relationship with your own partner, if you have one. Only then will you not go begging your children for the time and attention they should be giving their own families.

Be loving, supportive, generous, understanding, kind and fun. But don't have time to interfere.

SEE ALSO: **control freak, being a**

Daughters-in-Law
JOANNA
TROLLOPE

mother-in-law, having a

Ladies, we sympathise. MILs can be forceful, interfering, invasive, controlling old cows, who believe that no-one will ever be good enough for their son/daughter, make no attempt to conceal how little they like you, make it clear that they'd never have chosen you themselves, always take their offspring's side and assume as a default position that you're wrong.

But this doesn't mean you're off the hook. Inter-generational in-law relationships have got to be worked at from both sides. Think about it from the point of view of Rachel, one of the MILs in Trollope's novel. Her identity as a woman is thrown off-balance when her third son, Luke, gets married. Suddenly no-one wants her to do the thing she's good at anymore. Left without agency or power, she panics – and when she panics, as she admits herself, she 'barks'. It's not that she doesn't like you, it's actually that she doesn't like this new person your arrival has forced her to be.

MILs need to be stood up to – and you must never be afraid to do this. The old family dynamic is obsolete and a new one must be built. But while it's happening, be the sort of second child your grieving MIL might like to have: loving, supportive, generous, understanding, kind and fun. And make time to interfere.

SEE ALSO: **Christmas** • **divorce** • **family, coping with** • **murderous thoughts**

moving house

Heligoland
SHENA MACKAY

Consider the snail. His house is on his back, he can slither into it whenever he likes, and as long as no blundering oaf comes by with thoughtless feet, he's always got his home to hand (or rather, proboscis). We, on the other hand, are not so adaptable. When we move house, we require removal vans, checklists, a small forest's worth of cardboard boxes, packers, carriers, in-laws, nannies, dog-sitters and, afterwards, therapists. It's one of the most demanding and stressful events we go through in life, and causes a range of side-effects including angst, hair-loss and conflict within your relationship, as well as throwing your bank balance seriously off-kilter. To avoid these side-effects completely, climb inside a box with this small but perfectly formed novel by Shena Mackay.

Heligoland describes the residents of an unusual shell-shaped house called the Nautilus.* Gleaming 'like a pearl' and with an anchor at its heart connecting it to the seabed of London, the house was built in the 1930s by Celeste and her husband as a place to bring artists and writers together. Now an old woman, Celeste still lives in the Nautilus, though the echoing house is not the hubbub of artistic life it used to be. Its current occupants – including a minor poet and an antiques dealer – are jaded has-beens, one way or another. But there is Rowena too, an orphan of Indian extraction, who has come to be the new housekeeper.

Rowena is a lost soul, drawn to the Nautilus and its intriguing denizens because she craves a combination of the

---

* The perceptive will notice that the house shares its name with Captain Nemo's submarine in Jules Verne's *20,000 Leagues Under the Sea*.

lonely life she shared with her aunt in the Scottish Highlands as a child, and the communal existence of her old boarding school, Chestnuts. As she begins to feel at home in the quirky spaces, Rowena's deep loneliness starts to abate. One day she shyly cooks up an exotic Indian feast in the kitchen without telling anyone what she's doing. Luckily, the fragrances lure them from their shells, and they all appear, dressed for dinner, just like in the house's heyday. Little by little, Rowena brings new life to the Nautilus, galvanising the old crowd to throw a birthday party for her, to clear out the old swimming pool, and discover forgotten areas of the garden.

Mackay's prose, lustrous as the pearly shell she describes, is precise and calm and will de-clutter your mind as you read. And you'll be greatly inspired by Rowena's ability to recreate the idealised dream home she's imagined since her childhood, the Scottish Heligoland of the title: something between an island in unnavigable seas, and a fairground roundabout. Catch, like the other characters, her spirit of optimism as you too create your own 'shelltopia' and start anew.

SEE ALSO: **broke, being** • **exhaustion** • **family, coping with** • **friend, falling out with your best** • **stress**

Mr/Mrs Right, holding out for

The Great Fire
SHIRLEY
HAZZARD

Agapanthus Tango
DAVID FRANCIS

Waiting
HA JIN

Compromise is unavoidable once you're married, but those refusing to compromise *before* they're married – who would rather hold out for Mr or Mrs Right than marry Mr or Mrs Wrong in haste and live to regret it – are opting for a risky strategy. Whole lives can pass by in the waiting, and there's no guarantee that, at the end of it all, you'll find your hoped-for prize. What if you leave it so long that it's too late to have children? (see: children, not having). What if you finally meet your Mr/Mrs Right, but by the time you do you're so set in your bachelor/bachelorette ways that you find you can't stand sharing your house with someone else?

Those holding out need encouragement to keep their nerve – because the alternative is worse. (See: Mr/Mrs

Wrong, ending up with, if you're in any doubt.) Take heart from the story of Aldred Leith in Shirley Hazzard's magisterial *The Great Fire*. Thirty-two but feeling older, Leith is emotionally beached after the trauma of the Second World War and a dissolved 'war marriage' to Moira. He expects nothing from life from here on in. But in the damp hills near Hiroshima where he has come to write a government report, he meets two remarkable children, Helen Driscoll and her terminally ill brother, Ben. The fragile siblings have nothing in common with their oafish father and insincere mother, who represent everything that Leith despises. But together they have created a little haven of intellectualism, reading Gibbon and Carlyle aloud to each other – 'they live in literature and make free with it' – and Leith finds, almost to his embarrassment, that he has met his true love match in Helen. With her small breasts only just showing beneath her dress, he guesses she is no more than fifteen.

At first he puts it down to a need for comfort in an 'entire world' that needs comforting, but real happiness is present when they meet, and Shirley Hazzard makes what might otherwise be an inappropriate pairing (see: age gap between lovers) beautiful and real by the force of her zealously unsentimental prose. Leith and Helen wait for each other, spanning their separation with letters, while also having to cope with the antipathy of Helen's parents and the transplantation of their relationship to a different country. But the certainty with which they recognise – and we, too, feel – their rightness for each other is inspiring to anyone holding out for the same. Their confidence is well placed, in the end.

If you believe you have already met your Mr or Mrs Right, but are forced to hold out for them because *they* fail to see it, we urge you to read David Francis's gem of a novel, *Agapanthus Tango*, set partly in the parched outback of Australia and partly in the green fields of America's horse-racing country. We won't make any promises for a happy ending here; but Day's feelings for Callie are so evidently real, the two of them so clearly suited, that our hearts sit on a cliff-edge as we watch the eighteen-year-old Australian boy being continually rebuffed by the untamed Callie.

Day has run away from home following his mother's death and lands himself a passage to America along with a thoroughbred racehorse. Offering himself as a stable hand to the horse's new owner, it is here he meets the sixteen-year-old Calliope Coates, another runaway. Unreachable, cocky, troubled, smelling of damp hay, and with a cruel streak in her that sees her whipping her horses, she is all that Day wants, from that moment on. Day, recognising another damaged spirit, understands her and accepts her as she is – even when she reveals a pyromaniac side – and simply doesn't give up. Is Day a fool to suffer the wounds and rejections and still hold out hope? Or does he exhibit real emotional bravery? Those finding themselves tempted to be rock-like for someone unavailable like Callie must read right to the end of this exquisitely written novel to find out if such strength of spirit pays off. We'll say this much: only a love as strong and sure as Day's is for Callie is worth the risk.

Be careful, though, that your decision to hold out is not simply a result of indecision or a failure to accept the cards you have been dealt. In *Waiting* by Ha Jin, Lin, a doctor in the city, keeps his girlfriend Manna waiting for eighteen years because first he must divorce Shuyu, the illiterate village girl with bound feet his parents forced him to marry. Each year, Shuyu agrees to a divorce, but each year Lin arrives at the courtroom only to find she has changed her mind. Manna, head nurse at the hospital where Lin works, wastes her thirties waiting for Lin, and her resentment turns her bitter (see: bitterness).

She's not the only one to be damaged by the years of waiting: Shuyu endures a hard, lonely life bringing up their daughter Hua in the countryside; and only belatedly does Lin realise what a poor father to Hua he has been. Eventually, Manna has waited so long for Lin that it becomes too late *not* to keep waiting. Yet by that time Lin's romantic passion for Manna has faded, and his own shilly-shallying has caused him to lose self-respect. 'I know your type,' Lin's roommate tells him. 'You're always afraid that people will call you a bad man.' Lin knows his weakness has ruined all their lives, and even when the waiting is over, there is more waiting on the horizon. Let this novel be a warning: don't let your whole life become one big wait.

We encourage you to hold out, by all means. But make sure you're a realist like Leith and not a grass-is-greener type like Lin. And if you're a Day, holding out for someone who needs to be won round, be ruthlessly honest with yourself. Only do it if he or she is really worth the wait, and if you decide they aren't, see: wasting time on a dud relationship.

SEE ALSO: **change, resistance to** • **commitment, fear of** • **indecision** • **optimism** • **procrastination** • **risks, not taking enough** • **romantic, hopeless** • **wasting time on a dud relationship**

Mr/Mrs Right, looking for

Finding your ideal partner – best friend, lover, companion, bankroller, chef, artfully combined in one winsome package – is generally considered to be the jackpot in the great lottery of life, the best way to secure happiness, good health and longevity. For many, it is the major obsession of their teens and twenties, and, if the search fails, the primary cause of unhappiness in the decades thereafter (see: shelf, fear of being left on the; Mr/Mrs Wrong, ending up with; loneliness). Since the nineteenth century, novels have shared – or reflected, or fuelled, depending on your take – this obsession. Hundreds of searches for Mr and Mrs Right have been presented for our entertainment and edification. But have two centuries' worth of reading about them made us any better at it? Have we, in fact, merely become such perfectionists that we are in danger of seeking an ideal that doesn't exist (see: Mr/Mrs Right, holding out for; happiness, searching for)?

It doesn't seem so. Many of us still follow the terrible example of Linda Radlett in Nancy Mitford's *The Pursuit of Love* who, despite starting out with the conviction that true love comes only once in a lifetime, goes about it using the method by which she later buys clothes: trial and error, marrying two Mr Wrongs before she finds the real thing, at last, with the wealthy French duke Fabrice. Fabrice funds her shopping sprees and for a while makes her the happiest woman in the world. But not, unfortunately, for long. Oh, that she had not been in such a rush and held out for 'the one' at the start!

Of course, we often *do* meet Mr or Mrs Right early on – he or she is sometimes staring us in the face, in fact – but either through our own failings, or theirs, we fail to recognise him or her as such. The former is the case with Jane Austen's Emma, who takes the span of a whole novel to develop enough self-awareness to be struck by the arrow informing her, with absolute, wondrous certainty, that her Mr Right is her neighbour Mr Knightley (*duh!* But who didn't miss it, the first time, too?). The latter is the case with Elizabeth Bennett in *Pride and Prejudice*, whose Mr Darcy has a few character flaws to be ironed out before he can be a Mr Right for her (see: arrogance). And both are the case with the drink-befuddled, damaged pair in Gwendoline Riley's *Joshua Spassky*. After five years of on-off dating and failed sexual encounters, Natalie and Joshua take themselves off to Asheville, North Carolina, where they lie in a motel room and try to work out whether or not they're in love. If you *don't* find it maddening to watch them deliberate, and feel a great sense of relief when the emotionally frozen Natalie finally announces that she feels like a bottle of milk 'that's just been taken out of the fridge' – suggesting an emotional thaw is finally on its way – you're probably equally scared of commitment and should immediately see: commitment, fear of. Don't be too hasty to dismiss the friends in your immediate circle when you're looking for love; many of the happiest marriages are between people who share a similar background and have known each other all their lives.

But sometimes our Mr or Mrs Right is very far away indeed, and life doesn't cause our paths to cross. This is the case for Mr Hosokawa, the boss of a Japanese electronics company, who would surely have gone on believing he could only feel true love for opera rather than another human being if he hadn't been taken hostage while attending a concert in his honour. In one of the best stories we know about love blossoming in unlikely places, Ann Patchett's brilliant *Bel Canto* sees the emergence of three true loves: Mr Hosokawa with the beautiful soprano Roxane Coss, his highly educated translator Gen with a completely uneducated peasant-turned-terrorist, and the French diplomat Thibault who until recently had taken his elegant wife Edith for granted. Transformed by the beauty of Coss's singing – and Patchett writes tremendously about the almost painful, visceral capacity of music to move – and forced to live in the heightened moment by the constant threat of death, the extraordinary outcome for those in the cocoon of the vice president's mansion (where they are being held) is that everyone, hostages and terrorists alike, gravitate to culture and art – to singing, reading, learning, cooking, playing chess and, of course, to loving.

We're not advocating that you should try and get yourself taken hostage. Or indeed that you should stalk the famous person you admire from afar (see: love, unrequited). Literature suggests that searching for your Mr or Mrs Right is a waste of time anyway; they're probably right under your nose. Instead, turn your attention to those things you feel passionate about – be it opera, like Mr Hosokawa, horses (see: Mr/Mrs Right, holding out for) or Hemingway. You'll grow and develop in interesting ways as a person and become happy while you're about it. Then, and only then, will your Mr or Mrs Right find *you*.

SEE ALSO: **happiness, searching for** • **shelf, fear of being left on the** • **single, being**

Mr/Mrs Wrong, ending up with

If you can, avoid ending up with Mr/Mrs Wrong in the first place. The misery the reader feels when the peerless Dorothea Brooke throws herself away on fusty old Casaubon in George Eliot's masterful, groundbreaking *Middlemarch* – a ruthlessly unsentimental examination of marriage and the deplorable consequences that result from an ill-made match – brings home the enormity of such a mistake. Although

Dorothea doesn't think she's making a mistake – for her, Casaubon's 'great soul' is enough, and indeed we can see that in this nineteenth-century world where women are generally trivialised, she has a great need to align herself with an intellectual in order to acquire the label for herself – we know it's only a matter of time before she sees him for the dried-up pedant he is, and that the 'large vistas and wide fresh air' she had dreamed of finding in her husband's mind are in fact 'anterooms and winding passages' leading nowhere.

Luckily, Dorothea is saved from a lifetime of grim servitude by the welcome appearance of the Grim Reaper. But like the dashing young doctor Lydgate within the same novel, you may not be so lucky. He and Rosamond, falling for the romantic ideal that they see encapsulated by the other, face a lifetime of torment when their actual personalities begin to emerge from beneath the façades. Rosamond's spending habits stymie Lydgate's ambitions as a medical reformist, and when Rosamond's motivation for marriage in the first place is exposed as little more than social advancement, bitterness begins to corrode their bond. Lydgate would have been much happier sharing his life and work with the equally socially conscious Dorothea – but divorce was not an option in those days and anyway by then Dorothea is happily married to someone else … Take great care to get to know both yourself and your intended before you tie the knot. If you forge ahead with only a partial understanding of their character, you may have some unpleasant surprises in store.

And if it's too late, and Mr or Mrs Wrong is, at this very minute, annoying the hell out of you as you attempt to hide behind this book (do your best to keep the entry hidden), take heart from Mary, the feisty Scots-born heroine of Oswald Wynd's *The Ginger Tree*. Admittedly her Mr Wrong abandons her when she has an affair with the Japanese count, Kentaro – which is one way of disposing of a disagreeable spouse (see: adultery). But Mary has a habit of picking men who run off with her children as well, and loses two in the course of this novel.

Fortunately, this stoic young woman – marooned first in China by her cold, military attaché British husband and then forced to flee to Japan – is keen to understand and adapt to the cultural differences around her in order to survive. Like the ginger tree of the title, which 'remains the stubborn stranger' in the garden, she manages to maintain a strong sense of self within her alien culture, outcast or not, while doing so. Written in the form of journals and letters to her mother in Scotland and her friend Marie – a writing habit that, surely, helps her keep her sanity through forty years of isolation, two world wars and an earthquake, and one that those in similar predicaments would do well to adopt – this is a novel that will have you shedding the tears Mary rarely sheds for herself. Use it for the inspiration and encouragement to stick to your ginger treeness even if you're married to a turnip. You're in this garden now, so you might as well try to grow as big as you can within it. You may find the garden grows and develops with you, in ways you like better. If it doesn't, at least you won't have wasted your time before, if necessary, finding a door in the garden wall to let you out (see: breaking up; divorce).

SEE ALSO: **dissatisfaction** • **divorce** • **jam, being in a** • **murderous thoughts** • **non-reading partner, having a** • **regret** • **stuck in a rut**

mundanity, oppressed by

When the world seems awfully humdrum, and the only magic in your life is that which is promised on the back of a new cleaning product, you need to discover the transporting capacities of fantasy fiction. And we don't just mean Harry Potter.* Spread your wings with the list below. They will take you into the realm of the miraculous and the marvellous.

---

* We love him too, but there's more to fantasy fiction than Hogwarts and Quidditch.

THE TEN BEST FANTASY NOVELS

SEE ALSO: **boredom** • **disenchantment** • **dissatisfaction** • **malaise, twenty-first century**

murderous thoughts

Thérèse Raquin
ÉMILE ZOLA

M

288

Everyone has them. Even kids. Even cats. So don't pretend you don't. You live with someone. They put their teabags in the sink. They leave long, ginger hairs in the soap. They lean in a bit too close. They make sounds as they eat. And sometimes you want to kill them.

Most of us don't take it any further than a brief internal rant, followed by a period of introverted brooding – at which point we remember the good things about that person and, crucially, the fact that murder is always a really bad idea.

However, some of us do take it one stage further and begin to plot. If you ever catch yourself doing this, Zola's *Thérèse Raquin* is your wake-up call. It describes the abject life of Thérèse and Camille, a married couple who live above their shop in the Passage du Pont Neuf with Camille's mother. Zola lays on the desolation with a trowel: he describes the winter light coming in through the arcade glass roof that should illuminate their shop as throwing 'nothing but darkness on the sticky tiles – unclean and abominable gloom.'

Indeed they are so miserable that we sympathise when Thérèse turns for some passion and excitement to another man, Laurent, gentleman painter and idle sponge. But when she and Laurent decide to kill Camille in order to clear the way for their love, Zola challenges our affinity with the heroine. It's not that we feel any great affection for Camille: Zola deliberately portrays him as a spineless, spoilt sop. But Thérèse and Laurent become progressively less likeable as the novel continues. We won't give away what happens, but the message is clear: killing your relatives will give you bad dreams, bad sex and invariably lead to yet more homicidal thoughts. So stop your plotting. Breathe deeply, and distract yourself with this powerful deterrent. Then see our cures for: snoring; boredom; and married, being.

SEE ALSO: **rage** • **vengeance, seeking** • **violence, fear of**

M

289

N

Napoleon complex

SEE: **short, being**

narcissism

SEE: **arrogance** • **confidence, too much** • **selfishness** • **vanity**

nausea

*Brideshead
Revisited*
EVELYN WAUGH

There are few things worse. Excuse our vulgarity, but since recovery is impossible without letting it all come out . . . that's it. Go on. We won't look.

Shivery, sweaty, shocked? Still a little queasy, perhaps? Go brush your teeth, then come back here and assume a horizontal position, wrapped in a blanket, propped up with pillows, a hot water bottle at your side and your reeling head stilled by the perfectly balanced prose of Evelyn Waugh.

More than any other writer, Waugh can be trusted to put you back on level ground. To take you by the hand – gently, demurely – lift you up to your tiptoes, pause, then bring you down carefully again. Nobody does it better.

From the first paragraph of the first page of his paean to the privileged, *Brideshead Revisited*, observe how Waugh uses repetition to maintain a state of measured equilibrium: 'I had reflected then' is balanced by 'and I reflected now.' A little further down you'll find 'a quarter of a mile' in one clause echoed in the next. Drop your eyes to the bottom of the page and watch alliteration and overlap take over, carrying us forward in precise, dancer's steps: from 'the camp stood', to 'the farm-house still stood', to 'the ivy still supported'. Semi-colons act as brief, unobtrusive pauses – a moment's holding of a pleasing shape, sustaining the upward lift – while commas accommodate the fluency of flow and twirl thereafter. Not for a moment are we left in doubt as to the beat: 'In half an hour we were ready to start and in an hour we started.' Oh, the steadiness, the sureness, the settling of your tummy! This prose is a dance, and Waugh is the graceful, accomplished partner whisking us around the floor.

Whoops! Steady on. If you are afraid of the nausea returning, read on. For Charles, our narrator, whose 'rooms' at Oxford are on the ground floor right next to the quad, forges the most intense relationship of his life because of vomit. Sebastian, the teddy bear-dependent younger son of the lord and lady of Brideshead Castle, 'magically beautiful, with that epicene quality which . . . sings aloud for love', has had too much to drink. And, passing Charles's open window just before midnight, the young aristocrat leans into the room and throws up. Charles is generous enough to see 'a kind of insane and endearing orderliness' about Sebastian's choice, in his moment of need, of an open window, but the roomful of flowers he finds on his return from lectures the next day, and the contrite invitation to 'luncheon', charm him more. Soon he is cast into a world in which hard-boiled plovers' eggs are offered to guests – a world of beauty, intensity and dysfunction that will set his youth aglow then leave him to a lifetime of disappointment thereafter.

But life – and fiction – is made extraordinary by such friendships. If it weren't for Sebastian's nausea, he'd never have gone to Brideshead, or met Sebastian's 'madly charming' sisters, or entered the 'enclosed and enchanted garden' that gives him, at least for a spell, the happy childhood he never had.

Thanks, therefore, be to nausea, his and yours – and to Evelyn Waugh – for making everything better.

neediness

True Grit
CHARLES PORTIS

Are you always asking for help? Unable to do anything on your own? Wanting someone to hold your hand at all times? Asking for help is of course a good thing, but complete dependence is not. There comes a time when you need to learn independence and rely on yourself and yourself alone. As with a slushy road, a dose of grit is your cure.

Set in America just after the Civil War, Charles Portis's novel *True Grit* describes the steely determination of Mattie, a fifteen-year-old girl seeking to bring her father's killer to justice. The killer is Tom Chaney, an employee of her father's, who pulled a gun on him in a fit of drunken pique. Mattie has come to Fort Smith ostensibly to fetch her father's body but, unknown to her family back home, she has her own agenda.

The first thing Mattie has to do is recoup some money owed to her father, then persuade the grittiest ranger she can find to track Chaney down and bring him to justice. Rooster Cogburn is gritty as they come, but she is grittier and wins him round. Next she has to persuade him to take her with him. Cogburn tries to give her the slip, but she won't be left behind; as they plunge into the snowy landscape of Arkansas, Mattie endures hunger, gun-fights and the bitter cold without complaining even once.

Mattie's Presbyterian good sense verges on the pious. But her estimable pluck in the face of outlaws, knives, bullets, snakes and corpses wins our admiration every time, and will encourage an immediate assumption of independence as you read. And although she uses the people around her to help her to achieve her goals, she relies on herself to see her plan through to its conclusion. It is an older Mattie, looking back on this formative chapter in her life, who tells this tale; and her adult self is very much the product of all this hardship and loss. Steel yourself, reader. Say farewell to mush, and welcome a handful of grit into your soul.

SEE ALSO: **coward, being a** • **seize the day, failure to** •
self-esteem, low

neighbours, having

If it's your parents who f**k you up, it's your neighbours who wind you up.

Unfortunately, neighbours can be neighbours for a very long time. Fall out with them and it can make your life a misery. Learn to live with them – and even to like them – and you'll earn yourself an on-the-spot social life. Plus eggs, milk and sugar whenever you need it. Sometimes it's not so much that you've fallen out with your neighbours, but that you've never actually met them. People live cheek by jowl for decades with little more than a formal nod. Our first cure, then, will have you sticking your head over the fence to say hello. Our second will have you knocking the fence down.

In *If Nobody Speaks of Remarkable Things*, Jon McGregor's lyrical first novel, we know the inhabitants of an entire street in a northern city in England, not by name but by the number on their door: 'the young woman from 24', 'the man with the carefully trimmed moustache from number 20'. McGregor's narrative takes flashes of consciousness from these myriad neighbours and builds them into a symphony of sound, a blur of activity, a chaos of unlinked events. Except that they *are* linked. Like the 'quivering flutter of a moth's rain-sodden wings', each tiny happening within this small geographical area conspires to bring remarkable life – and death – to our consciousness. McGregor manages to capture the infinite possibilities of neighbourly interaction, from total indifference to selfless love and sacrifice – all of which are available to us, and the people we live amongst. Throw a street party immediately, and enrich your life.

But what if, when we meet them, we can't stand them? Neighbours could not have less in common than the Pickleses and the Lambs in Australian author Tim Winton's loveable novel, *Cloudstreet*. Which is bad luck for them, or so it initially seems, as they share a 'great continent of a house' in Perth. Sam Pickles, a gambling man, can only afford to install his family in the monstrosity he's inherited if they rent half out. So they build a makeshift fence from old tin signs down the middle of the yard and Lester and Oriel

Lamb and their brood of six move in. Before long, Sam Pickles is looking on in mild astonishment as the Lambs take to their knees on their side of the yard planting vegetables and rearing chickens, and replace their living room window with the shutter of a grocer's shop. Suddenly the house looks like an 'old stroke survivor paralysed down one side' – a maelstrom of activity on the hardworking, God-fearing Lambs' side, and inert lifelessness on the Pickleses'.

As the linguistically inventive Winton moves between each of the main characters' point of view, the line between the two sides of the building starts to blur. Cloud Street becomes Cloudstreet – a single entity, and a symbol of teeming life. And though there is plenty for the two families to fight about – noise, religion, gambling – and the odd slipper is lobbed from one side to another, they take a live-and-let-live attitude. And in the end, neighbours become relations.

Next time you're woken by next-door's teenager playing the drums, think about how soulless it would be if they weren't there. Bring the fence down – metaphorically, if not literally – and feel the warm breeze blow through.

SEE ALSO: **city fatigue** • **misanthropy** • **noise, too much**

neighbours, not having

SEE: **loneliness**

nightmares

If you're prone to being disturbed by bad dreams in the lonesome early hours, a soothing novel will help to reset your psyche. Keep a stash of these river reads by your bed and drift back to sleep in their current.

 THE TEN BEST NOVELS FOR AFTER A NIGHTMARE

The River Why DAVID JAMES DUNCAN
Deep River SHUSAKU ENDO
The Wind in the Willows KENNETH GRAHAME
The River King ALICE HOFFMAN

new books, seduced by

LEARN THE ART OF RE-READING

It's tempting to see books the way we see gadgets: that we need the very latest, most up-to-date version. But just because a novel is new doesn't mean it's any good; indeed, with a new novel being published every three minutes,* the chances that it's good are actually rather low. Far better to wait and see if a novel stands the test of time, and in the meantime read one that's already proved itself to be worth reading. Because the art of re-reading is a neglected one, and arguably even more important than the act of reading the first time round.

Sometimes a novel operates only at the level of the story, in which case a second reading will be a watered-down experience of the first. But the best novels converse with the reader on many different levels, and in our rush to find out what happens we swim over other things. A second reading nets those fish. No longer so blinded by the whats, we can appreciate the hows and the whys. We're more likely to notice the ominous foreshadowing of events before they happen, for instance, and smile with the author at how a character deceives themselves – and the author first deceived us. We're more likely to have a clearer taste of the philosophy underscoring the book by the end. And we'll certainly be more alert to the author's skill at steering the narrative – what was held back, what was told – and how language, dialogue, themes and imagery were used to achieve the atmosphere, momentum and tone.

The revisiting of an especially admired or loved book can become, perhaps, a five-yearly ritual, marking the passage of time in your life, helping you to see how you have changed, and how you have remained the same. Do not go always rushing after the new. Like the best friendships and wine, the best novels get better over the years.

---

* Except on Sundays.

Three Men in a Boat **JEROME K JEROME**
A River Runs Through It **NORMAN MACLEAN**
A River Sutra **GITA MEHTA**
The Guide **RK NARAYAN**
Waterland **GRAHAM SWIFT**
The Adventures of Huckleberry Finn **MARK TWAIN**

ninety-something, being

 THE TEN BEST NOVELS FOR NINETY-SOMETHINGS

The Secret Scripture **SEBASTIAN BARRY**
Through the Looking Glass **LEWIS CARROLL**
Bleak House **CHARLES DICKENS**
Benediction **KENT HARUF**
The Old Man and the Sea **ERNEST HEMINGWAY**
The Stone Angel **MARGARET LAURENCE**
The Book of Laughter and Forgetting **MILAN KUNDERA**
Nightmare Abbey **THOMAS LOVE PEACOCK**
The Grapes of Wrath **JOHN STEINBECK**
The Mating Season **PG WODEHOUSE**

nobody likes you

SEE: **unpopular, being**

noise, too much

When your surroundings are too noisy – maybe the TV's always on, or your fellow commuters are shouting into their phones, or the guy on the treadmill is grunting – seal yourself off in a world of your own with an audio book and a good pair of headphones. You'll find it a treat to be read to – and with these readers, an unforgettable experience.

 THE TEN BEST AUDIO BOOKS

Middlemarch **GEORGE ELIOT** read by Juliet Stevenson
The Great Gatsby **F SCOTT FITZGERALD** read by Frank Muller
The Corrections **JONATHAN FRANZEN** read by Dylan Baker
The Return of the Native **THOMAS HARDY** read by Alan Rickman

nose, hating your

Perfume: The Story of a Murderer
PATRICK SÜSKIND

All noses are pretty weird, if you gaze at them long enough. Some are big, some are dainty, some are ski-jumps, some are craggy outcrops complete with craters – but none, we can probably agree, are particularly lovely. What dictates how others perceive our nose is our own opinion of it, and those with high self-esteem carry their noses off whatever shape and size they are. To learn to love your nose, start not with the organ, but with yourself (see: self-esteem, low).

On the other hand, if you really do have a challenging honker, bury it immediately in *Perfume: The Story of a Murderer* by Patrick Süskind. Within a page, you'll be plunged into a time (the eighteenth century) when there reigned in the streets a stench 'barely conceivable' to us today – a noxious mix of manure, urine and 'spoiled cabbage', of 'greasy sheets' and chamber-pots, of blood, foul breath and 'tumorous disease'. Here, in the most putrid corner of the stinkiest of cities (Paris) is born Jean-Baptiste Grenouille, on the hottest day of the year, his mother squatting amongst the fish guts under a table on which she'd just been scaling a (stinking) fish. He's passed into the hands of a wet nurse, and thence to a cloister of monks – because, the wet nurse complains, the baby has no smell. There follows a description of how babies *should* smell. Their feet are like 'warm stone', or 'curds', or 'fresh butter', the wet nurse says, feeling her way; their bodies 'like a pancake that's been

non-reading partner, having a

CONVERT OR DESERT

If you live with someone who doesn't read books, it can be hard to carve out and protect reading time for yourself – especially if your partner prefers to watch TV, talk to you, or position themselves between you and your book when you're reading in bed. You have two choices: convert them or desert them.

To convert them, browse this book for some ideas then take them to a cosy bookshop and treat them to a new book. If you can't persuade your partner to read what you buy, try reading to them aloud, and having them read to you. This is a wonderful way to share the experience of a book together, and spend time strengthening your bond with books as the glue. See our lists of The Ten Best Books to Turn Your Partner on to Fiction (male and female) for ideas.

If that doesn't work, acquire some audio books to play on long car journeys or while you're involved in domestic chores together – something that both of you will enjoy (see: noise, too much for our list of The Ten Best Audio Books). If he/she gets into a particular novelist, you can give them a physical copy of another book by the same author to follow up.

If your partner still refuses to join in, you'll need to set some parameters to protect your reading time. Decide how many hours you'd like to read per week, and negotiate when these hours will be – Saturday afternoons, perhaps, and the half hour before you go to sleep. Find a place in the house to read where you will not be disturbed – perhaps in your reading nook (see: household chores, distracted by). If you read in bed, retire half an hour before your partner does. If your partner is lost without you (no-one likes to be ignored), work out together what your partner could do while you're reading: grow tomatoes? Learn to play the banjo? Make you some bookshelves?

If none of these things work, and you can see that life with your partner means a life without books, then you have no option. Desert them, and find someone else. See: Mr/Mrs Right, looking for.

THE TEN BEST NOVELS TO TURN YOUR PARTNER (MALE) ON TO FICTION

For mysterious reasons, men don't read as much fiction as women. If you're saddled with a man who hasn't touched a novel since school, give him one of these. (Tell him it's nonfiction in disguise.)

The Wasp Factory IAIN BANKS
Any Human Heart WILLIAM BOYD
The Amazing Adventures of Kavalier & Clay MICHAEL CHABON
Microserfs DOUGLAS COUPLAND
The Name of the Rose UMBERTO ECO
Catch-22 JOSEPH HELLER
Solaris STANISLAW LEM
Flashman GEORGE MACDONALD FRASER
Galatea 2.2 RICHARD POWERS
Breath TIM WINTON

THE TEN BEST NOVELS TO TURN YOUR PARTNER (FEMALE) ON TO FICTION

For equally mysterious reasons, some women don't read novels. If your partner lacks the fiction gene, seduce them with a really good story. Engrossing, engaging, entertaining, these are by some of the best storytellers of modern times.

Alias Grace MARGARET ATWOOD
A Visit from the Goon Squad JENNIFER EGAN
A Room with a View EM FORSTER
To the End of the Land DAVID GROSSMAN
A Thousand Splendid Suns KHALED HOSSEINI
The Hotel New Hampshire JOHN IRVING
The Piano Tuner DANIEL MASON
Schindler's Ark THOMAS KENEALLY
White Teeth ZADIE SMITH
The End of Mr Y SCARLETT THOMAS

soaked in milk', and the back of their heads, the little bald spot left by the cowlick, that bit smells 'best of all . . . like caramel.'

And so, within a few pages, we are vicariously exposed – because good writing succeeds in reproducing the whiffs themselves, or at least the reception of them in our brains – to smells at both ends of the olfactory repertoire. Jean-Baptiste himself, of course, though devoid of personal odour, has the most acute sense of smell in Paris and an indiscriminate, dangerous appetite for procuring new scents, especially those of young virgins. But, on the positive side, he earns a good living from his nose as a perfumier. And if, like him, you make full use of your nose, educating it with full-bodied red wines and freshly ground coffee beans, with subtle *parfums* and jasmine and a few drops of lemongrass essence on the sponge in your morning shower; if you fully appreciate its sensual input in your life then, we guarantee, you'll learn to love and appreciate your sniffer in a whole new way.

SEE ALSO: **vanity**

obesity

For a beautifully simple cure for obesity, follow the advice of Mrs Hawkins, the double-chinned heroine of Muriel Spark's mischievous satire of the publishing industry in post-war London. Mrs Hawkins is liberal with her advice and doles it out on such far-ranging topics as finding a job, writing a book, improving your concentration, getting married, how to say 'no', where to go if you've had a lot of trouble,* and how to deal with too much casual correspondence. But her tip for losing weight is the best: eat half of what you would normally eat. 'I offer this advice without fee,' she says, 'it is included in the price of this book.' We bought her novel, and are now including the advice free in the price of ours.†

Obesity often has a psychological cause, however, and no amount of dieting will help if the psychological cause remains untreated. So it is with Dr Pereira, the portly, widowed editor of the culture page of the *Lisboa*, Lisbon's evening rag, in *Pereira Maintains*. It's 1938 and, under the shadow of Fascist Spain, Lisbon 'reeks of death'. Nobody has the courage to print the real news, and Pereira fills his page with translations of nineteenth-century French literature instead. Each day he cheers himself up by talking to a photo of his

---

* Paris.
† The novel also contains a more complicated cure for obesity, though this isn't included in the price of our book. You will have to read it and work it out for yourself.

dead wife and tucking into an omelette *aux fines herbes* and several glasses of lemonade at the Café Orquídea, washed down with coffee and a cigar.

That the omelettes are having a deleterious effect on his waistline is clear to Pereira, but he finds himself unable to resist. It's only when he meets Dr Cardoso at an out-of-town spa that he begins to understand his need for fatty foods and sugary drinks. Franco is making a mockery of his job, and therefore of him. Salvation arrives in the form of a young couple he meets at the Café Orquídea, who, Pereira eventually realises, are involved with illegal underground activities. Here is a way to fight Franco, and recover the 'chieftanship' of his soul. It's not long before he's ordering seafood salads and mineral water instead.

If you're overweight because you're unhappy, don't padlock the fridge or put yourself on a rigid diet; the diet will fail and you'll only make yourself unhappier still. Try to discover why you are seeking consolation – this book may give you some ideas (try: stuck in a rut; or career, being in the wrong, for starters). Once you've ironed out your relationship with yourself, your relationship with food will self-correct.

If you're large and you like it, embrace the big-is-beautiful world of 'traditionally built' (size twenty-two to be precise) Mma Precious Ramotswe, star of Alexander McCall Smith's famous detective series set in Botswana, best read in order and beginning with *The No 1 Ladies' Detective Agency*. Precious Ramotswe will show you how to be bold and break the rules, to carry your weight with dignity and aplomb, and win the heart of a good man (if you want one) just by being your witty and wise, abundant self.

SEE ALSO: **gluttony** • **high blood pressure** • **lethargy** • **self-esteem, low** • **snoring** • **sweating**

obsession

Death in Venice
THOMAS MANN

The truth is that the obsessed do not want to be cured. What they fear most is an end to their obsession, and to this heightened experience of life. For Aschenbach in *Death in*

Venice, the three or four hours he spends each day sitting on the beach watching Tadzio at play – and then stalking the boy and his sisters through the increasingly fetid streets of cholera-ridden Venice – are 'far too dear to him' to give up. He goes to bed at nine o'clock because, once Tadzio has left the scene, there's nothing to stay awake for; indeed he can no longer imagine life without this grey-eyed boy with his captivating smile. He knows that the responsible thing to do would be to warn Tadzio's mother about the 'sickness' invading Venice, then lay his hand for the first and last time on Tadzio's head and say goodbye. For by not warning her, he is risking Tadzio's death from the cholera epidemic, as well as his own. But he knows that such an act would break the spell, 'restore him' to himself, the reasonable Aschenbach of old, and he will not do it.

Part of what keeps the obsession alive is that Tadzio is Polish and Aschenbach can't understand anything he says. So that what might be the 'sheerest commonplace' is elevated, in Aschenbach's ear, to the realms of music. When Tadzio emerges from the sea, his wet curls lit by the sun, nothing that he shouts out to his siblings on the beach can ruin it. In Aschenbach's eyes he's the real thing, a 'tender young god'.

Moby Dick assumes mythological proportions too. The crew have heard the rumours and seen how the whale possesses their own tormented Captain Ahab for a long time before they encounter the great Leviathan himself. When they finally glimpse him, they see only parts – a hump or a tail, a hot jet of vapour blasted into the sky – while the 'full terrors' of his vast, shadowy bulk remain submerged. Moby Dick's inscrutability gives him power over the crew of the *Pequod*, and Ahab's inscrutability gives him power over them too. Ishmael doesn't even set eyes on the captain until several days into the voyage, and even then it's a 'moody stricken Ahab' he sees, so caught up in his own interior claims as to be unapproachable. But how else other than with sheer charisma could Ahab have persuaded his crew to pursue Moby Dick, even when the boat was full to capacity with blubber already – enough to make them all rich – and when to carry on meant almost certain death?

O

For they are compelled by one that is himself compelled; such is the power of obsession.

To the reader of *Death in Venice*, Tadzio is just a boy. But Moby Dick is never just a whale, and Captain Ahab is never just a man. When Ahab and Moby Dick disappear together beneath the 'great shroud' of the sea, their mutual charisma doesn't die; something vast, tantalising, terrible still remains, just out of reach. And so the power to obsess is transferred from the whale to the novel. Because perhaps more than any other novel in literary history, *Moby Dick* has the ability to hook readers in a way that keeps them coming back throughout their lives. If Aschenbach had been able to know Tadzio; if Ahab had been able to know his whale; if the crew of the Pequod had been able to know Ahab; if the reader of *Moby Dick* were able to *know* Moby Dick, if Herman Melville . . .

But what's the use? You don't want to know how to overcome an obsession. Being already obsessed, you don't want to be cured.

SEE ALSO: **control freak, being a • infatuation • loneliness, reading-induced • love, unrequited • read instead of live, tendency to • reverence of books, excessive • sci-fi, stuck on**

old age, horror of

'Old age has its pleasures, which, though different, are not less than the pleasures of youth.' So said wise old Somerset Maugham, who enjoyed his latter years so much he clung on into his nineties. Most of us can't really see the appeal; and some even go as far as advocating a James Dean-style opt-out, living fast but quitting while you're still able to 'leave behind a good-looking corpse' as the character of Nick Romano put it in Willard Motley's *Knock on Any Door* (also a film starring Humphrey Bogart). The vast majority of us will let old age creep up; being alive, even when feeble, craggy and crabby, generally being preferable to not being alive at all. In order to inspire you to embrace the swansong years that lie ahead in a more positive way, we prescribe two novels that will show you that being a septuagenarian doesn't mean you're past it.

Judge Feathers in Jane Gardam's *Old Filth* is a supremely dignified and still strikingly handsome man with a powerful presence. And despite being given the nickname of the title, he's also very clean – ostentatiously so. His shoes shine 'like conkers', and his clothes have a 1920's elegance; complete with silk handkerchief in his pocket and yellow socks from Harrods. There is no smell of old age in his house – he is rich, and used to having staff to 'do' for him from his days in the Orient. It is not for any lack of personal or domestic hygiene, then, that Judge Feathers is known as Filth and has been for many years; but because, in a phrase he self-deprecatingly coined himself, he 'Failed in London, Tried Hong Kong'.

He and his wife Betty had indeed tried Hong Kong, and been spectacularly successful there. And everyone assumed they would stay. But assumptions made about Old Filth tend to be wide of the mark. For secrets lurk in Old Filth's life and underneath, fuelled by the traumas of his past, is an entirely different man. Beneath the surface, we discover a diorama of projected journeys, a host of people he plans to visit, dreams of redemptive rendezvous – and he's more than capable of making them happen. (Most importantly, he will leave behind a good-looking corpse.)

Think about it this way: when you're old, you won't have to let the professional facade of your middle years stand in your way any more. You'll be able to let your inner Judge Feathers out – though hopefully not his driving skills.

The elderly Mrs Monro in *The Skeleton in the Cupboard* also casts old age in a refreshing light – this sharp, witty narrator is merciless in her observations of her nearest and dearest. All she desires is to see her son Syl settled and married before she dies – and indeed the wedding day is imminent. Her reflections on her loving but mean son, her dead and faithless husband, and her inappropriately young and self-denying prospective daughter-in-law, make for a wonderfully unsentimental drama. What's more, the wicked Mrs

Monro actively looks forward to death, experiencing a burst of 'unimaginable joy' when she glimpses the point at which the temporal meets the eternal, where 'eagles might clash with angels and the ice-bright light, shattered like gems, would scatter and dissipate.' As a vision of the afterlife it's certainly more interesting than most.

This is the first in Alice Thomas Ellis's *Summerhouse* trilogy, in which each novel tells the same story from a different point of view and each narrative supplies the answers to questions raised in the last. But this novel also stands alone, and is a fine testament to the ability of the old to join in with events when they choose to, retreat into benign-old-lady/man mode when they don't, and supply a biting commentary from the sidelines all the rest of the time. Don't be horrified by old age – it is just a different point of view on the same story.

SEE ALSO: **amnesia, reading-associated** • **ageing, horror of** • **baldness** • **memory loss** • **senile, going**

one hundred, being over

 THE TEN BEST NOVELS FOR THE OVER ONE HUNDREDS

A Little of What You Fancy HE BATES
Solo RANA DASGUPTA
The Confessions of Max Tivoli ANDREW SEAN GREER
Oldest Living Confederate Widow Tells All ALLAN GURGANUS
The Glass Bead Game HERMANN HESSE
The Hundred-Year-Old Man Who Climbed Out the Window and Disappeared JONAS JONASSON
Immortality MILAN KUNDERA
Winnie the Pooh AA MILNE
Dracula BRAM STOKER
Gulliver's Travels JONATHAN SWIFT

optimism

Candide
VOLTAIRE

Incurable optimists sometimes need to bite the maggot in their apple in order to temper their expectant orifice with a taste of reality. While we embrace the optimist to our hearts, we also feel the need to warn them of being *too* blithely cheery in the face of the inevitable injustice and pain in the world. For one cannot always assume the best motives behind the actions or words of others. And what if you need to flee, or fight back? Between optimism and naïveté, sometimes, lies a lot of unnecessary strife.

Candide is a case in point. Brought up in an idyllic Eden with Pangloss as his teacher, Candide has been taught that 'everything is for the best in the best of all possible worlds.' So when he has his first taste of the world beyond his childhood walls, he is in for a bit of a shock. The illegitimate nephew of a baron, he falls heavily in love with the baron's daughter, Cunégonde. But the Baron has other plans for Cunégonde; and when he catches them kissing, he expels Candide, whose prospects are limited, from his castle. This is bad enough, but there's worse to come.

Forcibly conscripted into the Bulgar army, Candide witnesses a horrific battle. Then, after wandering off from camp for a walk, he is brutally flogged as a deserter. The trials and tribulations continue, but through them all the young man resolutely maintains his optimistic outlook. Only towards the end, after he has been robbed of his fortune and finds himself living with a much altered Cunégonde; after his beloved Pangloss has been hung, dissected, and beaten to a pulp (but that is not the end of his story); after Cunégonde has wondered aloud if it would be worse to be repeatedly raped by hordes of Bulgars or to be here doing what she's doing (nothing), does he begin to waver. You too will surely see the folly of grinning benignly as the catastrophes rain down.

But if your optimism is even harder to shift than Candide's, *Never Let Me Go* by Kazuo Ishiguro is guaranteed to blast it out of its foundations. Growing up in the mysterious Hailsham House, Kathy, Tommy and Ruth are encouraged to express their imaginations, create art, and develop relationships. But at the same time they are curiously repressed and separate from the world. We won't give any more away. Suffice to say that we're so sure this cure will work we'll give our right arms if you still believe in the best of all possible worlds by the end. And in case this takes you *too* far down that road, see: pessimism to bring you back to centre.

organised, being too

On the Road
JACK KEROUAC

An unfortunate side-effect of a busy life is that we can become so adept at organising our time, parcelling up our days into half-hour segments allocated to a particular use – work, sleep, exercise, meal-time, errand, shopping, social – that we forget to allot any portions to those aspects of living that won't fit under a heading. Because what about: just sitting around? What about: taking off spontaneously on a bicycle, without a plan? What about: meeting someone at random on the street and going for a coffee? If you want to avoid the realisation, on your deathbed, that you ticked off everything on your list but never actually just stepped out your door and let life come to *you*, spend some random amount of time in the company of Sal Paradise and the 'great amorous soul' of Dean Moriarty in Jack Kerouac's hymn to the generation that knew how to hang, *On the Road*.

O

308

Nobody in *On the Road* does anything more than make a very vague plan. And when they go, they go fast, jumping on a bus or onto the back of a flatbed truck, hearing a 'new call', an 'ode from the Plains' in the general direction of the West. They don't take much with them – just a few things in a canvas bag, plus a sheer, Benzedrine-fuelled exuberance and a love of life's infinite possibilities. Because Sal and Dean and Dean's new 'beautiful little sharp chick' Marylou are on a wave, a 'wild yea-saying overburst of American joy' that sweeps them across the country in a spirit of reckless excitement, improvising to the beat of bebop, and yelling and talking all the time. They are people that 'like every-thing', who want to get caught up in 'the whole mad swirl' of whatever it is they find, and when they get to Denver, or Chicago, or New Orleans or wherever it is they're going, they'll do whatever it is that people do in those places, once they're there. Because: 'Hell, we don't know. Who cares?' They'll find out soon enough.

Take it from these boys. Being organised, planning ahead, deciding things in advance – these are not the holy grail of existence. If you want a truly intense, Kerouacesque kind of life, get yourself a shot of *On the Road* at the start of each day, and let the beat play out.

SEE ALSO: **anally retentive, being** • **control freak, being a** • **goody-goody, being a** • **reverence of books, excessive** • **risks, not taking enough** • **seize the day, failure to**

organised, not being

SEE: **carelessness** • **cope, inability to** • **find one of your books, inability to** • **overwhelmed by the number of books in your house** • **risks, taking too many**

orgasms, not enough

Can one ever have enough? One might well ask. It used to be thought that having too many orgasms drained one's chi and shortened one's lifespan – but now, experts seem to think that the more you come, the more you'll keep on coming, in every sense. For some, though, an inability to reach orgasm with ease – or at all – can mar an otherwise happy intimate relationship. Known as anorgasmia, the condition is more common among women than men, and though science is unsure of the cause, repression stemming from a lingering belief that female sexual expression is somehow 'wrong' – a hangover from Victorian days – is often mooted. We suggest, therefore, that those afflicted should moderate their literary diet accordingly: no more euphemistic or avoidant Victorians (we name no names*). Instead, loosen yourself up with novelists who tend towards the explicit.

For many of today's adolescents, it's vampire novels with their dark, unrealised yearnings that bring newly sexual beings to their first literary climax. Virginia Andrews's incestuous captives in the *Flowers in the Attic* series still

---

* Dickens.

continue to fascinate; with more explicit sexual encounters offered by the likes of Ellen Hopkins et al. Adults get their rocks off in literature in so many different ways that we can barely moisten the tip of our finger before feeling the need to insert a long and varied list – both of novels that suggest ways of achieving orgasm, and novels that are so erotically compelling that you may need no more than the text itself, mulled over at your own pleasure. But we'll limit ourselves to a choice few. John Cleland's 1748 novel *Fanny Hill* – generally considered to be the first pornographic novel in English – will surprise you with its young female prostitutes indulging in mutual masturbation, discussion of penis size and sexual romps that last several days at a time. In the twentieth century *Lady Chatterley's Lover* led the way – for those who could get their hands on a copy – with a brazen, earthy sensuality and overt references to male and female genitalia that had not laced the pages of literature for a hundred years (for more on this novel, see: love, doomed). Once *Lady Chatterley* became widely available in the Sixties, the floodgates opened and everybody joined in. *Gravity's Rainbow* by Thomas Pynchon sports an actual orgy on board the *Anubis* – outlandishly erotic, with its nautical setting adding to the hilarity. A public spanking culminates in all on board climaxing simultaneously. Bloom's masturbatory fantasies in *Ulysses* may do it for the boys, while Molly's reminiscences about how her afternoon of sex with Boylan made her 'feel all fire inside' may work for the girls. In *Doing It* by Melvin Burgess we get the chance to re-live the complicated and fraught sexual fumblings of teenagers; while Alina Reyes's *The Butcher* describes one summer an adolescent girl spends working in a butcher's shop and is drawn into an exploration of flesh that is not just about offal. (What is it with butchers and sex scenes? Kate Grenville also could not resist their siren call in *The Idea of Perfection*, which has more sweaty couplings in butcher's overalls.) The heroine of *The Private Lives of Pippa Lee* by Rebecca Miller precociously achieves orgasm in her teens by doing the breaststroke (of the swimming variety) and Nikki Gemmell's anonymously-published *The*

Bride Stripped Bare has its heroine taking time out from her recent marriage to explore her inner whore and dominatrix. Pauline Réage's *The Story of O* unleashes a sadomasochistic fantasy about a sex slave that harks back to the inaugural work of this genre, the late nineteenth-century *Venus in Furs* (for more on which, see: jealousy); have whips at the ready for these two. Meanwhile, lesbian and gay literature has been making up for the years of repression with fulsome abandon: Alan Hollinghurst's *The Swimming-Pool Library* is a rich source of gay male erotica – happily brandished hard-ons are the order of the day here. Emerging homosexuality is explored in Edmund White's *A Boy's Own Story*, a paean to young gay male love, while a more agonised male-on-male take explodes with floral metaphors in *Our Lady of the Flowers* by Jean Genet. Girls can add costume drama to their repertoire with *Fingersmith* by Sarah Waters, queen of lesbian erotica. Sufferers of situational or complete anorgasmia should keep these novels by their bedsides, applying their suggestions alone, or with a friend.

SEE ALSO: **dissatisfaction** • **married, being** • **seduction skills, lack of** • **sex, too little** • **single, being**

orgasms, too many

SEE: **sex, too much**

outsider, being an

Oscar and Lucinda
PETER CAREY

The outsider is one who doesn't belong. He or she is not left out (see: left out, feeling), because they were never in in the first place. And though he or she is certainly different (see also: different, being), he or she is also transplanted. Because the outsider has left the place where there are others of its kind, or never found it to start with; and roams the world as the perennial observer, looking in, but never, ever, stepping inside. If this describes you, you will cheer all the more exultantly at the eventual meeting of outsiders

overwhelmed by the number of books in the world

SEE A BIBLIOTHERAPIST

The fact is, one simply cannot hope to read every book that exists. Or even every good book. If thinking about the size of the reading mountain out there sends you into a blind panic, breathe deep. Extreme selectivity is the only solution. Reading time is hard to come by, and you don't want to waste any of it on even a mediocre book. Reach for excellence every time.

The Novel Cure is a good place to start when picking a more discerning path through the literary jungle. Consider also booking a consultation with a bibliotherapist, who will analyse your reading tastes, habits and yearnings, as well as where you're at in your personal and professional life, then create a reading list tailored especially for you.

For optimal health, happiness and book satisfaction, see your bibliotherapist at least once a year, or whenever you feel the need for an overhaul. A good book, read at the right moment, should leave you uplifted, inspired, energised and eager for more. With so many books to choose from, what's the point of reading even one more that leaves you cold?

overwhelmed by the number of books in your house

CULL YOUR LIBRARY

Sometimes the sheer volume of books in your house can get out of hand. Not only have books taken over your walls, but they are piled by your bed, and on the end of each stair. There's a stack in the toilet, and they're filling up the windowsills, the boot rack, the bed. Sometimes you have to remove them from the sink before you can do the washing up.

Reader, cull your books. Do it every six months, and aim to cut your library by at least ten per cent each time. Give away any books you failed to finish – or forced yourself to finish (see: give up halfway through, refusal to). Take to a charity shop those books that disappointed you. Keep only books that fit into the following categories: books you loved, books which are beautiful objects in themselves, books you consider to be important, edifying or otherwise necessary, books which you might return to one day, and books to keep for your children. Everything else is just bits of paper taking up space.* This way, you will keep your library fresh and make room for new additions.

---

* As Susan Hill says in her lovely *Howards End is on the Landing*, 'You don't have to pay its rent just because it is a book'.

extraordinaire Oscar and Lucinda in Peter Carey's 1988 Booker Prize-winner.

Oscar Hopkins is such an outsider that he doesn't even know there is an inside. Brought up in the tiny Devon village of Hennacombe, his botanist father, though loving, is a member of an evangelical sect called the Plymouth Brethren who interpret the Bible literally, 'as if it were a report compiled by a conscientious naturalist'. He begins to sense that they are different when the servant Fanny Drabble makes him a Christmas pudding and his father, being against Christian feasting, calls it 'fruit of Satan' and makes him drink salt water until he brings it back up. But he does not question his father's beliefs or realise how much of an oddity his upbringing has made him until he's at Oriel College, Oxford, and his 'ignorance' becomes a talking point.

When fellow student Wardley-Fish – a member of the 'fast set' – bangs on Oscar's door looking for somebody else, he invites Oscar to the races even though Oscar is known as 'the Odd Bod' as far as Trinity. Oscar does go to the races with Wardley-Fish and, winning his first bet 9-1, develops the pathological relationship to gambling that threatens constantly to uncollar him when, later on, he becomes the Reverend Hopkins (we direct Oscar, and anyone else partial to a flutter, to our cure for gambling). But when, on board a boat to New South Wales, he meets Lucinda Leplastrier, an heiress and owner of a glass factory with similarly uncontrollable hair, it becomes a cause for celebration – for Lucinda is just as much an outsider as Oscar, and happens to share his addiction. Coming to him for confession, she tells him in a voice so tiny 'you could fit it in a thimble' of her seemingly unquenchable thirst for a game of dice, or poker – or even a cock fight. Oscar can hardly believe his ears. Holy thoughts soon shoved aside, he knows he has met the person who can make him belong.

What Lucinda and Oscar do with their bond is for those of us who've read it to know and those of you who haven't to find out. But the healing is there, in the scene on board the *Leviathan*, where Lucinda looks into Oscar's eyes and sees herself 'mirrored' in them. Oscar, the outsider, has been recognised. As long as he's with Lucinda, he's an outsider no more.

Board a ship, and find your other outsider half.

SEE ALSO: **different, being** • **foreign, being** • **left out, feeling** • **loneliness** • **shyness**

overwork

SEE: **busy, being too** • **busy to read, being too** • **career, being in the wrong** • **cope, inability to** • **exhaustion** • **insomnia** • **nightmares** • **stress** • **tired and emotional, being** • **workaholism**

P

pain, being a

SEE: **adolescence** • **antisocial, being** • **Daddy's girl, being a** • **cynicism** • **grumpiness** • **humourlessness** • **hypochondria** • **killjoy, being a** • **lovesickness** • **man flu** • **misanthropy** • **neediness** • **querulousness** • **teetotaller, being a** • **teens, being in your** • **vegetarianism**

pain, being in

The Death of a Beekeeper
LARS GUSTAFSSON

No life is free of it. And though modern medicine offers various ways to numb it, and literature can help you to escape it (see our list of The Ten Best Escapist Novels, below), it is harder to find suggestions in literature on how to bear it and live with it.

The Death of a Beekeeper provides just that. Through the experience of Lars Westin, a divorced ex-school teacher who lives on the beautiful, remote peninsular of North Västmanland in Sweden with his dog and his bees, we explore the world of physical pain – its various pitches, frequencies and decibel counts – and what it is like to endure pain without drugs. Lars's pain is from cancer. He discovers at the beginning of the winter thaw that he will likely not live to see the fall, and decides not to go to hospital in the city and have the pain removed, but to stay where he is – because this is his life and he wants to live it while he still can. And so, taking his dog, he goes on long walks through the grey February landscape with its bare trees and boarded-up summer houses, and learns to live with pain.

At first, he is aware of the pain mostly at night, dreaming of it before it wakes him – and in his dreams he finds he is trying, literally, to turn his head away from it. The pain makes him more aware of his body – that he *is* a body. But he also projects the pain outward. On his walks, the landscape sometimes assumes his pain for him – so that a tree becomes the tree where his back really hurt, and a fence post becomes the place where he strikes his hand when passing – and where he can somehow leave the pain 'hanging on the fence' and walk on without it.

But as the pain gets worse, conjuring memories from his marriage and childhood, he enters a stage where the pain is so 'absolutely foreign, white hot and totally overpowering' that he struggles to cope. And this is when he realises that the art of bearing pain is just that – an art, like music, or poetry or eroticism or architecture, except that its 'level of difficulty is so high that no-one exists who can practice it'. He does though – as others do, every day.

If you are unfortunate enough to experience pain at this level, think of yourself as an artist practising something so demanding and hard that you are elevated to a master by the act of your endurance. And let the beekeeper accompany you there. For as he discovers, blaming others for your pain, or even grumbling about it to others, doesn't help. With the beekeeper, you will discover a terrible but wonderful truth: that pain makes you more alive.

☞ **THE TEN BEST ESCAPIST NOVELS**

When you need to forget the pain in your head, heart or body; when you're waiting for a bus that never comes; when you want to press 'eject' on the daily grind, decamp with one of these.

Hondo LOUIS L'AMOUR
Captain Corelli's Mandolin LOUIS DE BERNIÈRES
Jamrach's Menagerie CAROL BIRCH

panic attack

Shane
JACK SCHAEFER

There is only one thing more frightening than thinking you might be about to have a panic attack, and that is having the panic attack. Of course knowing this, and worrying about it, makes the possibility of having the panic attack even more likely. Those caught up in this chicken and egg situation need to keep a flask of literary tranquility to hand and take a long, slow draught – either by reading or quietly reciting passages committed to memory – whenever you're in a panic that you might panic. Do it often enough, and in time just the title alone will have your heart rate abating. The novel for the job is *Shane*.

Shane rides into the valley dressed in black. When he politely asks for water for himself and his horse, all three members of the Starrett family are drawn to him – for he exudes something powerful and mysterious. They persuade him to stay with them, offering him work as a temporary farmhand, even though it is clear that farming is not his trade. It becomes rapidly apparent that Shane is the essence of calm. A man of few words, he has a strong sense of justice; although his strength and power could easily overwhelm another man, he clearly holds no truck with aggression. He keeps his gun under his pillow rather than on his belt, as other men do.

The first thing Shane does when he comes to live with the Starrett family is to take an axe to the ironwood stump in the yard that has been niggling at Joe Starrett ever since he first cleared the land. The stump is big – big enough to serve dinner on to a family twice their size – but, as Shane cuts it, the clear ringing sound of steel on wood strikes young Bob as no sound ever has before, filling him with warmth. At that moment Shane becomes the hero that Bob needed in order to grow up 'straight inside, as a boy should'. For Bob needed an example from outside his family unit – someone he could emulate. Determined, graceful, just, with sorrows we know nothing of, and who will always do the right thing, Shane is that mentor – and not just for Bob, but also for his father, Joe.

Install this fierce, hard gem of a man in your heart. Your blood will pump as steadily and calmly as that clear ringing axe on the obstinate stump. Let panic be the tree stump you know you can conquer.

SEE ALSO: **anxiety**

paranoia

The Crying of Lot 49
THOMAS PYNCHON

This novel is all about you. You'll find your name in it. Try page 49.*

parent, being a

SEE: **children requiring attention, too many • fatherhood • motherhood • mother-in-law, being a • single parent, being a • trapped by children**

parents, ageing

SEE: **ageing parents**

---

* Actually, it's about something far more interesting than you. It's about perpetual motion, entropy, LSD, an underground postal system, and an era in American cultural history that we wish we could have experienced ourselves. But read on. Because we will cure you of your paranoia by proving to you, during the act of reading this novel, that if you look hard enough for something, you will find it. Rather than look for the conspiracy theories you want to find, therefore, let Pynchon's fantastically complex and curious worldview take you on a journey into the curious mind of Oedipa Maas as she investigates her own conspiracies. By the time you've run round San Narciso with this maiden in search of a knight of deliverance, you'll be hooked on her story rather than your own false terrors, and looking out, instead of within.

perfectionism

SEE: **anally retentive, being** · **control freak, being a** ·
organised, being too · **reverence of books, excessive** ·
risks, not taking enough

pessimism

Robinson Crusoe
DANIEL DEFOE

'A man's fate is his character,' said Heraclitus, many years ago. Society in the West took a grand detour from this idea, believing in medieval times that God, or fate, held the reins and the individual was a mere pawn. If an individual couldn't shape his or her own destiny, what did personality matter? But then, suddenly, God (or fate) took a back seat. A successful life depended on an individual's ability to make it so – and hey presto, the psychology-driven novel was born.*

Robinson Crusoe was the first demonstration in literature of the power of optimism to turn a life around. At first, Crusoe's situation looks unremittingly bleak. The sole survivor of a shipwreck, he finds himself on a barren, uninhabited island with nothing but a knife, a pipe and a little tobacco in a box. In 'terrible agonies' of mind, he runs around like a madman, convinced he's about to be eaten by a ravenous beast.

As we all know, it's hard to achieve anything when you're in such a state (see: broken heart; depression, general). What saves Crusoe is forcing himself to think positive. He plunders what remains on board the ship before it sinks, finds a pen and paper among the booty, and sets down 'the good against the evil' of his situation – in other words, he writes a list of good old pros and cons. By doing this, he discovers something simple but life-changing: that the pros cancel out the cons, and because he can't imagine anything worse than his predicament, he concludes that there's 'scarce any condition in the world so miserable but there was something . . . positive to be thankful for in it'. Hurrah to that!

---

* Following this line of argument, the novel was born (with Robinson Crusoe) in 1719. On other days, though, we follow other lines of argument.

And so, buoyed by looking on the bright side, Crusoe does all the things necessary to survive: he hunts, rears goats, plants crops, adopts a parrot, makes pots and does his own DIY (and is good at it, but if he wasn't, we'd direct him to: DIY). He goes on to become a self-sufficiency expert on the island for twenty-eight years.

A successful life is about finding your inner resources, and never more so than when times are hard. If you refuse, in your darkest moments, to give in to pessimism and despair, but instead dig up some optimism and a cheery outlook, you'll not only have discovered the best in yourself but you'll become your own best friend. We'll go as far as saying, with optimism to hand, it almost doesn't matter what happens. Bring on the shipwrecks. Keep Crusoe by your side. As Heraclitus might have put it if he'd thought of it first: choose optimism over pessimism and you'll have a much nicer life. [†]

SEE ALSO: **cynicism** · **depression, general** · **despair** · **faith, loss of** · **hope, loss of** · **pointlessness** · **trust, loss of**

phobia

SEE: **agoraphobia** · **claustrophobia** · **homophobia** · **xenophobia**

piles

SEE: **haemorrhoids**

PMT

Your legs ache. You've got the chills. You don't want to move very fast. Anything too challenging may reduce you to tears. Cosy up under the duvet with a hot water bottle and a good girly read: an all-enveloping analgesic.

[†] But don't take it too far. See: optimism.

THE TEN BEST NOVELS FOR DUVET DAYS

SEE ALSO: **bed, inability to get out of • cry, in need of a good • headache • irritability • pain, being in • tired and emotional, being**

pointlessness

Life: A User's Manual
GEORGES PEREC

We know what you're thinking. What's the point of prescribing a cure for pointlessness? In fact, what is the point of prescribing anything for anything? It's all meaningless, devoid of purpose, right? Not once you've read Georges Perec's novel, *Life: A User's Manual*.*

The novel opens with an apartment block in Paris, frozen in time just before 8pm on 23 June 1975 – seconds after the death of one of its inhabitants, Bartlebooth. Another resident, Serge Valéne, has set himself the task of painting the entire apartment block 'in elevation' – with the façade re-

---

* In fact, it is perhaps a series of novels, or even – you've guessed it – a very manual for existence. Perec liked games – mathematical ones, circular ones, unanswerable ones. *Life* is full of them (which is one of the points of the novel). A member of the group Oulipo, from the French *Ouvroir de Littérature Potentielle* (which can be roughly translated as: *Workshop of Potential Literature*) he and the other members gave themselves deliberate constraints which they then followed when writing. See if you can work out the constraints Perec placed upon himself in writing *Life: A User's Manual*. We will give you a small clue: there are ninety-nine chapters in the book, which describes an apartment block in which there are ten floors, and ten rooms on each floor; and the narrative structure of the novel is dictated by the 'knight's tour', which sees the novel as a chessboard.

moved – revealing all the inhabitants, and their possessions, in perfect detail.[†]

It transpires that the recently deceased Bartlebooth, a wealthy Englishman, had devised a (pointless) plan to dispose of his immense fortune – and thus occupy the rest of his life. The plan was for the painter Serge Valéne to teach him to paint and for Bartlebooth to then embark, with his servant Smautf, (another inhabitant of the block), on a decade-long trip around the world, painting a watercolour every two weeks, with the ultimate aim of creating 500 paintings. Each painting would be sent back to France, where the paper would be glued to a support and cut into a jigsaw puzzle by another resident of the apartment block, Gaspard Winckler. On his return, Bartlebooth would solve the puzzles, recreating the scene that he himself painted. Each completed puzzle would then be sealed back together and removed from its backing to leave the scene intact. Precisely twenty years to the day after each painting was made, it would be sent back to the same place where it had been painted, at one of hundreds of places around the globe, then placed by an assistant stationed there in a special solution that would extract all colour from the paper; then returned by post, blank, to Bartlebooth.

A pointless task, some would say. And to make it even more so, Bartlebooth goes blind during the process, so that it's increasingly difficult to finish the puzzles. And in the end, when he lies dead at his puzzle with one space in the shape of a 'W' still to fill, and in his hand a piece in the shape of an 'X', we cannot help wondering what has been the point of it all.

And yet, the journey to this point in the novel has been remarkably rich. Perec has provided us with a wealth of stories, ideas and opportunities for laughter – and herein lies the clue to the point of pointlessness. Pointlessness itself can be a source of great joy, if we cease to worry about its pointlessness, revelling in the life, the quirks, the marvellous minutiae, the sheer excuse for stories, that this very

---

[†] The point of this is never made clear.

pointlessness offers. And this is precisely the point – or one of its many points.‡ But its ultimate point is that the point of existence is simply that despite its pointlessness – despite the fact that the last piece of your last puzzle does not fit – the journey towards that wrongly-shaped hole is full of fascination and delight.

SEE ALSO: **cynicism** • **despair** • **happiness, searching for** • **pessimism**

pregnancy

A Dance to the Music of Time
ANTHONY
POWELL

Girls, it's one mother of a journey. One minute, you're a happy-go-lucky solo player with ordinary things to worry about – like what colour to dye your hair, whether to go to Mongolia or Milan for your next major trip, and whether to wax or shave – then the next thing you know you are ballooning out a pair of stretchy jeans, having to sleep with a pillow between your knees and reading books which tell you to shove cabbage leaves into your bra cups.

While your ligaments soften and stretch, and while blood is being diverted to various complex tasks of internal creation, we suggest you make the most of your brain before full-on 'mummification' sets in. Ignore the siren calls of your house to be re-decorated. Milk your state by seizing this moment to read. Because pregnancy is a real chance to take on something long and engrossing; something that, in years to come, will define this expectant period of your life. And what better, as you contemplate your own current steps in the dance of time than the twelve-novel cycle of Anthony Powell's *A Dance to the Music of Time*.

Inspired by Nicolas Poussin's painting of the same name, Powell's saga follows its narrator Nicholas Jenkins from his schooldays during the First World War right up to the 1970s, so that as well as running the gamut of a life, it is a portrait of a century. Marriage, infidelity, voyeurism and even

---

‡ There are points all over the place in this masterpiece; it makes more points in more ways than almost any novel we have read.

necrophilia are all in the mix but creativity is the unifying theme – as Moreland composes, Barnby paints and Trapnel and the narrator write. Stack the twelve novels by your bed and devour them one by one as you nourish the burgeoning life inside you. You will delight in being lost to this bohemian world in the company of stylish people, ready to begin a new dance yourself.

SEE ALSO: **bad back** • **bed, inability to get out of** • **childbirth** • **haemorrhoids** • **motherhood** • **nausea** • **tired and emotional, being**

pretentiousness

SEE: **arrogance** • **brainy, being exceptionally** • **confidence, too much** • **extravagance** • **vanity** • **well-read, desire to seem**

procrastination

The Remains of the Day
KAZUO ISHIGURO

Why do today what can be left undone until tomorrow? Because every day that you leave a task undone, it grows bigger, and the motivation for doing it gets smaller.

Procrastination, or the art of avoidance, has nothing whatsoever to do with laziness, or even busyness. Its causes are emotional. Quite simply (and, one could argue, quite sensibly), the procrastinator avoids those tasks which, consciously or subconsciously, he or she associates with uncomfortable emotions, such as boredom (see: boredom), anxiety (see: anxiety) or fear of failure. The problem with allowing an uncomfortable emotion to stand in your way is that, once avoided, tasks that were probably quite achievable to begin with grow larger both in our imaginations and (often) in actuality – until they loom over us in such an oppressive way that they become worth procrastinating about. And while we're busy procrastinating and avoiding those uncomfortable emotions, untold opportunities for happiness and success – whole lives, in fact – pass by. It is this sense of a life half-lived, and the intense regret that follows, that we should be trying to avoid; not a few unpleasant emotions that will in any case quickly pass. What procrastinators need, therefore, is a lesson on the catastrophic consequences of running away whenever an unpleasant emotion threatens to ruffle our ponds. And who better to provide us with this than the very English, buttoned-up butler of Darlington Hall in Kazuo Ishiguro's *The Remains of the Day*.

Mr Stevens is an arch avoider of emotions – *all* emotions. As such, he has the perfect job. Because he believes that what separates a great butler from a merely competent butler is the ability to repress one's real self and inhabit a purely professional front at all times – holding up as an example the butler who 'failed to panic' on discovering a tiger under the dining table (see: stiff upper lip, having a). His repression thus justified and protected, he spends his life focussing only on being the best butler he can be – even when it is clear that his boss, Lord Darlington, is a Nazi sympathiser, and even when his own father is dying. So it is that when his father wants to say his final goodbye, all Mr Stevens can think of is hurrying back upstairs to serve the port. And when Miss Kenton, the house-keeper, tries to show her interest in him, he rebuffs her with coolness and distance from behind the fortress of his butler self.

It takes him twenty years to realise what he has missed. By failing to act on those 'turning points' in his relationship to Miss Kenton as they presented themselves – those precious moments in which, had he been brave enough to make himself vulnerable, he might have let down a drawbridge into his fortress and allowed himself to feel his feelings – he has lost the chance of a happy married life, for both of them. Instead he has lived as if he had before him 'a never-ending number of days, months, years in which to sort out the vagaries of [his] relationship with Miss Kenton.' Now, of course, it's too late. He is left with the poor scraps of what remains of 'his day'. Even someone with a lip as stiff as Mr Stevens has a heart that can break when he realises this.

Procrastinator: you do not have a never-ending number of days in which to accomplish the tasks you are so intent on avoiding. By procrastinating, you are allowing your negative emotions to become obstacles to an otherwise productive and forward-flowing life. Whether it's anxiety or fear that accompanies the contemplation of the task at hand, put out that hand and greet your emotions one by one. Invite them to come in and sit down, and make themselves comfortable. Then begin your task in their company. Once you begin, you'll find they don't hang around very long; in fact they'll probably get up and leave immediately. And when you're close to finishing, you'll look up and discover far more pleasant emotional companions sitting in their place, waiting to celebrate with you when you're done.

SEE ALSO: **indecision** • **seize the day, failure to** • **starting, fear of**

queasiness

SEE: **nausea**

querulousness

Death and the Penguin
ANDREY KURKOV

There are plenty of things to complain about in life. If you agree with this statement, you're one of them. Because you are one of those annoying people who suffer from querulousness, or a constant urge to grumble and complain, which is not only self-perpetuating – a determination to see the world in black and white being the surest way to bleach it of colour – but it also precludes you from noticing life's bounty in the first place.

Viktor, the would-be novelist in Andrey Kurkov's *Death and the Penguin* – written with the deadpan concision of an obituary itself – has plenty of things to complain about. His girlfriend left him a year ago, he's trapped in 'a rut between journalism and meagre scraps of prose', he has just come home to a power cut, and his only friend is his pet penguin, Misha – who is himself depressed. And yet Viktor doesn't complain. He receives his lot with a sort of dumb acceptance that makes it unlikely that anything will ever get better.

But then it does. The editor-in-chief of *Capital News* offers him $300 a month for creating an index of 'obelisk jobs', or obituaries, while the subjects are still alive. Viktor's first reaction is alarm – it sounds like real work. But once he begins, he finds he enjoys it. Soon, however, he becomes aware of the downside: that after a hundred obelisks, he hasn't yet had the pleasure of seeing his work in print. His subjects are all, stubbornly, still alive. When a contact of the editor's – a man who shares the name of Viktor's penguin, Misha, and so becomes known as Misha-non-penguin – pays him a visit, the urge to moan about this gets the better of him: 'Here I am, writing and writing, but nobody sees what I write,' he can't help protesting out loud.

That's when the VIPs start to die.

Don't grumble to anyone else. You might receive the wrong sort of help – and you'll certainly bring others down with you. But also, don't grumble to yourself. Once people start dying around him, Viktor's life improves in many ways, but by then the habit of accepting what life has given him is gone, and he's querulous about the good things instead. Those who catch the habit of querulousness and find them-selves constantly peeved about life may, like Viktor, fail to spot happiness even when it's delivered to them on a plate.

SEE ALSO: **dissatisfaction · irritability**

Q

R

racism

Anyone on the receiving end of racist attitudes or behaviour – or those still inclined to lay the blame for racial tensions at the door of the beleaguered minority – would do well to read Ralph Ellison's extraordinary and radical novel, *Invisible Man*. The writing and publishing of it was a feat of heroism on the author's part, and when it exploded onto the literary scene in 1952, America was still a country bound by segregation and fraught with racial prejudice. Rosa Parks had yet to refuse to give up her seat on a bus. Martin Luther King, Jr had yet to give his speech. Suddenly, here was a novel that offered a whole new black aesthetic: elegantly written in an ironically laid-back voice (the novel quickly acquired the label 'the literary extension of the blues') but opening with an act of shocking black-on-white violence that yet did not throw down a gauntlet. Because here we had a highly educated black narrator for whom the tendency of other people not to notice him is sometimes convenient (he uses it to live rent-free in the basement of a building reserved for whites) and sometimes, in a wry understatement typical of his voice, 'wearing on the nerves'. When a tall man with blue eyes and blond hair bumps into him and then insults him in the street, the Invisible Man grabs him by the lapels, brings the man's chin down sharp against his own head, then kicks him repeatedly, demanding an apology. He refuses – to us – to take responsibility for the man's near murder. 'I won't buy it . . . *He* bumped *me, he* insulted *me.* Shouldn't he, for his own personal safety, have recognised my hysteria, my "danger potential"?' And so we are shown the geyser of rage that exists inside him – built up over the years, handed down from preceding generations.

Attitudes – and laws – have improved since 1952, both in America and elsewhere. But *de facto* segregation still persists far and wide, and statistics suggest vast inequalities in wealth, education, opportunities and the treatment of racial minorities. Those experiencing racism will find Ralph Ellison's courageous, groundbreaking novel to be a bracing tonic – both as a literary achievement in its own right, and a non-polemical examination of one man's struggle to define himself in relation to a disrespecting world. Those who know that racism resides in their hearts will, we hope, find a way to see themselves for what they are – and others for who they are. And whatever your race and the colour of your skin, know that it's an act of cowardice (see: coward, being a) and shame (see: shame) *not* to join the fight against racism whenever you infer its presence in the world.

SEE ALSO: **hatred · judgemental, being · xenophobia**

rage

Cry, the Beloved Country
ALAN PATON

Rage consumes. It's the hottest, fieriest emotion there is. Your vision turns red and you cannot think logically. You become a tsunami, wreaking havoc on everything around you. You don't care what you destroy.

The problem with giving vent to your rage is that you not only might hurt yourself or someone else, or break something valuable to you (in the event of which, see: broken china), but your rage will frighten those who witness it, and may make those who love you feel unsafe around you. Moreover, rage is deeply exhausting and wounding to the soul. Repeated outbursts will deplete you, leaving you a little more broken, a little less noble in heart, than before.

It should be nipped in the bud at its first appearance, and before it becomes a habit.

Our cure, *Cry, the Beloved Country*, is a novel about a man who has more reason to rage against the world than almost any in literature, told in language that soothes and calms. It shows by example that even when confronted with the most appalling calamity, it is possible to contain your rage and choose a different way. 'There is a lovely road that runs from Ixopo into the hills. These hills are grass-covered and rolling, and they are lovely beyond any singing of it . . .' So, with beguiling lyricism inspired by the language patterns of Zulu, begins this deeply moving account of a country parson's search for his errant son, Absalom, in Johannesburg. It is 1946, and Johannesburg is a frightening place for Stephen Kumalo. Unlike in his native village, Ndotsheni, where 'every bus is the right bus', there are countless ways to lose oneself, both morally and physically. Following one word-of-mouth sighting after another, the gentle *umfundisi* (parson) and his wise friend and colleague Msimangu, discover that Absalom, like countless other vulnerable black, discriminated-against young men in South Africa during Apartheid, has been swallowed up in a criminal underworld, and by the time they find him, it is too late. The boy has shot and killed a white man – a man who, to complicate matters, had devoted his life to campaigning for the rights of the black underclass. The *umfundisi* is forced to watch his only son stand trial for the murder of a widely admired and respected man, and we in turn must watch Kumalo become more and more bowed and frail as his heart breaks under the enormity of his grief.

There is no happy ending for Kumalo. Instead, what Alan Paton gives us is an extraordinary evocation of one man's endurance through suffering. Kumalo thinks and acts slowly, in the 'slow tribal rhythm' into which he was born, and Paton monitors the old man's emotions as he struggles against his rage and grief with each new assault. Sometimes his rage wins out – for Paton's characters are nothing if not human – and Kumalo submits to the desire to wound with

R

words. But he is always quick to remove himself, and later to go back and apologise.

Cry, the Beloved Country is a novel about having the courage to say what needs to be said, about apologising when rage wins out, and about how hard and bitter words do not lead to a resolution but to more anger and hurt. Kumalo's sufferings will put your own in perspective. Paton's language will quiet your raging soul. And the wisdom of Paton and his cast of suffering characters will show you how it is possible to live with your pain – and, even, to laugh again.

SEE ALSO: **anger** • **broken china** • **road rage** • **turmoil** • **vengeance, seeking** • **violence, fear of**

rails, going off the

Goodnight, Nebraska
TOM MCNEAL

Though it occurs most often in adolescence, vulnerable people can go off the rails in their twenties, thirties or even older. If someone you know is heading that way now, it can be hard to know how to help; they're likely to present you a toughened, prickly façade, and push away the hand you reach out. And if you're heading off the rails yourself, how do you stop yourself careering fast towards destruction? You fall in love with one of literature's wayward souls is how, and Randall Hunsacker is your boy.

When Randall, at thirteen, loses his father in a horrific accident at home (see: DIY), the loss is more than he can know. Shy, awkward, his fragile relationships with his mother and sister nose-dive further when his mother takes up with a new man, Lenny. And when Randall discovers Lenny enjoying a compromising moment with his sister, he finds a vent for the hatred he's been nursing ever since his father's death. Randall careers off the rails in spectacular fashion, involving a gun, a stolen LeMans, two severed fingers and juvenile hall. It's his football coach who comes to the rescue, despatching him to a new life in the small town of Goodnight, Nebraska. Here, hurting and alone, he intimidates the locals with his 'obstinate sullenness' and alarms his peers at school with his recklessness on the football pitch.

To disclose that he catches the eye of a popular local girl suggests a Hollywood plain-sail ending, but McNeal is a braver writer than that. He takes Randall, and us, on a realistically bumpy – and moving – journey in which nothing turns out as you expect. Whether you're concerned about someone else going off the rails, or think you might be heading that way yourself, this novel will help you to see the sensitive, wounded person beneath the angry exterior. Just because someone acts tough doesn't mean they don't, deep down, want to be rescued. A fall from grace generally begins with a loss, an absence or a neglect, and a hitherto healthy human being becomes disaffected when there's no-one to catch them when they fall. Be there for your tumbler. Catch them and hold them. And if it's you that's falling, take heart from Randall's story. Someone will be brave enough to see who you are beneath that hardened skin. Let them in and, like Randall, you'll find your way back.

SEE ALSO: **adolescence** • **alcoholism** • **drugs, doing too many** • **rage** • **risks, taking too many**

recklessness

SEE: **adolescence** • **alcoholism** • **carelessness** • **drugs, doing too many** • **gambling** • **rails, going off the** • **risks, taking too many** • **selfishness** • **twenty-something, being**

redundant, being made

SEE: **anger** • **bitterness** • **broke, being** • **failure, feeling like a** • **job, losing your** • **unemployment**

regret

Bright Lights, Big City
JAY MCINERNEY

If only.

Beware these two little words. They may sound innocent enough, but give them half a chance and they'll stick their steely hooks into you, winch you off your feet and leave you swinging – ineffectually, miserably – for years. Because

read instead of live, tendency to

LIVE TO READ MORE DEEPLY

'The regular resource of people who don't go enough into the world to live a novel is to write one.' So said Thomas Hardy of his fellow authors in *A Pair of Blue Eyes*. If you would rather read than live, you are in danger of missing out on the real McCoy. Actual experience is necessary if you've any hope of understanding and doing justice to your books. How can you feel the pain of Anna Karenina if you've never taken a risk – only to find the ground whipped out from beneath your feet?

A good way to tell if you've got the balance right is never to spend more hours of your spare time reading than living. Go forth and put some of the life-lessons you've learned from novels into practice. Go and see someone instead of posting them a letter – like Harold Fry in *The Unlikely Pilgrimage of Harold Fry*. Take a trip on a camel, like Aunt Dot in *The Towers of Trebizond*. Throw caution to the wind like Pop Larkin in *The Darling Buds of May*. Read to live, don't live to read.

R

*These is My
Words: The
Diary of Sarah
Agnes Prine*
NANCY TURNER
....

regret derails; it paralyses and prevents. And what's more, it's often misdirected. For who's to say that we would have been better off if the thing that we wish hadn't happened *hadn't* happened, and the thing we wish *had* happened *did* happen after all? If you feel regret over things you never got round to doing, see: procrastination. But if you feel regret for things you did get round to doing, and wish you hadn't, read on.

The protagonist of Jay McInerney's *Bright Lights, Big City* – who is, actually, *you** – certainly seems to be setting himself – or rather you – up for regret. You mess up your job, you make absolutely sure to cut off all avenues back to it, then you stand up the only decent woman who's approached you in years. None of which does anything to slow your stride as you and your notorious friend Tad pursue your mission of having 'more fun than anyone else in New York City'. You still manage to end up in bed with a lovely girl.

Some would say the novel is amoral; others would counter that life is just endlessly available. You may have abused your twenties, screwed up in your thirties, and spent your forties on the psychoanalyst's couch – but no matter. Regret? Pah! There are more things ahead, this novel tells us, so just keep going.

That said, few in literature have more cause for regret than Sarah Agnes Prine, the narrator of *These is My Words*. Having upped sticks once and travelled the Oregon Trail to New Mexico, Sarah's papa decides to sell up a second time and head to greener pastures still. It is a disastrous decision. Not only does the youngest son, Clover – 'a top notch fellow after he got out of diapers' – die from a rattlesnake bite on the way, but they are attacked by Comanche Indians who steal their entire herd of horses. Sarah, not yet eighteen, witnesses gruesome deaths among the families travelling with them (Mr Hoover takes an arrow 'plum' in the throat), the multiple rape of a friend, and has the blood of two white men and five Indians on her own hands. Meanwhile her older brother Ernest loses a leg. By the time they get to their

---

* Conveniently for our purposes, the novel is written in the second person.

promised land, they find there's nothing for them there – it's hot and scorched, 'deader' than where they have come from. And then, within a week of arriving, Papa himself dies from a gunshot wound – and Mama promptly loses her marbles.

'Couldn't we turn back and go home,' Sarah asks her papa, understandably enough, while they are still on the road. But Papa puts his hand on her arm and says, 'Girl, there's never any turning back in life.' Mr Prine – may he rest in peace – is right. Turning back won't bring Clover back, nor Ernest's leg, nor eradicate the traumas from their minds, and the only thing that can bring Mama back to her senses is the passage of time. Instead, one has to allow oneself to be made stronger by one's experiences, and move on. Readers of this novel will see clearly how Sarah is transformed by the sorrows and hardships she undergoes. And without the pluck and resilience of character she acquires, would Captain Elliot, the droopy-moustached Cavalry soldier, have noticed her?

Take heart from this novel. We can either spend our time looking back mournfully at the door that just closed behind us – or we can emerge from that door tougher for it. The wisdom and strength we've gained will help us through the door that comes next. At least this way we won't make the same mistakes twice. And what awaits us through the next door may very well be better than what we wish we'd never left behind.

SEE ALSO: **bitterness** • **guilt** • **shame**

relationship issues

SEE: **adultery** • **age gap between lovers** • **commitment, fear of** • **jealousy** • **love, doomed** • **married, being** • **Mr/Mrs Wrong, ending up with** • **non-reading partner, having a** • **wasting time on a dud relationship**

resentment

SEE: **anger** • **bitterness** • **cynicism** • **dissatisfaction** • **hatred** • **jealousy** • **rage** • **regret**

restlessness

SEE: **anxiety • claustrophobia • itchy feet • jump ship, desire to • skim, tendency to • wanderlust**

retirement

The Enigma of Arrival
VS NAIPAUL

The Spire
WILLIAM GOLDING

For many, the moment of hanging up your hatchet is a terrifying one – if not for you, then for your partner. What will you get up to in the next few decades? Set off on a round-the-world adventure, build your own folly, learn Sanskrit, or get under the feet of your family and neighbours by being constantly, annoyingly, *there*?

Retirement offers the first opportunity for reflection that you'll have had in a long time, and to start you off, read *The Enigma of Arrival*, VS Naipaul's fictionalised meditation on his own life – how he came to leave his native Trinidad and live his latter years in Dorset, England. Naipaul studied at Oxford University as a young man, then travelled the world extensively, exploring Africa, India, America and the Islamic nations. Naipaul now turns his outsider eyes on the ancient heart of olde England, a place where he was 'truly an alien', yet where he finds he's been given a second chance – a chance for 'a new life, richer and fuller than any I had had anywhere else'. For the first time, he is 'in tune with a landscape': the hips and hawthorns of England suit his temperament better than the lush tropical vegetation of Trinidad. It's a surprising and inspiring discovery for someone at this stage in life. Have you, too, yet to find the landscape with which you most resonate?

Bucolic and tranquil, *The Enigma of Arrival* will encourage you to take stock of your life and enjoy the unfolding of new possibilities. Try focussing, as Naipaul does so beautifully, on the minutiae of life – such as when he notices that the grass on the path through an orchard has been mown in two directions, 'one swathe up, one swathe down . . . the two swathes showing as two distinct colours.' Just because you're retired, it doesn't mean you can't learn to see the world in new ways – especially now that you have the time.

Sometimes the change from working to not working can be too fast and sudden, leaving you feeling you're in free-fall or that there's no meaning to your days (see: dizziness; pointlessness). Perhaps, you think, retiring was a mistake. Perhaps you weren't quite ready to quit. If you find yourself tempted to jump back into the fray, we urge you to hesitate long enough to read *The Spire* by William Golding. Dean Jocelin will not rest until he has built a 404-foot spire for Salisbury Cathedral, an act of religious and personal hubris. The fulfilment of his vision exhausts everybody, except him, and his blinkered determination to see the job completed against all odds leads to terrible suffering for others. It's an excuse for some brilliant writing about the desire for beauty in the world – 'Everywhere, fine dust gave these rods and trunks of light the importance of a dimension. He blinked at them again, seeing, near at hand, how individual grains of dust turned over each other, or bounced all together, like mayfly in a breath of wind.' But by the end, the folly of the endeavour is all too apparent. Think twice before embracing work once more – especially if it's to leave a last monument to posterity. Realise how lucky you are to be away from all that stress. Sign up for a literature course instead.

SEE ALSO: **boredom**

revenge, seeking

SEE: **bitterness** • **hatred** • **vengeance, seeking**

risks, not taking enough

Biggles Defies the Swastika
WE JOHNS

Thundering rattlesnakes! Are you the kind of stay-at-home, lily-livered coward who malingers on your lounge chair until the Hun come round to lock you up? Some of the Bosch are decent chaps, we know, but they do have a habit of disposing of the enemy if you don't look lively and get out while you can. If you make a swift survey of the weaknesses of your position, you will quickly come to understand the necessity of taking risks. Seize the right moment for action; that moment

reverence of books, excessive

PERSONALISE YOUR BOOKS

Some people won't turn down the pages. Others won't place the book face down, pages splayed. Some won't dare make a mark in the margin.

Get over it. Books exist to impart their worlds to you, not as beautiful objects to save for some other day. We implore you to fold, crack and scribble on your books whenever the desire takes you. Underline the good bits, exclaim 'YES!' and 'NO!' in the margins. Invite others to inscribe and date the frontispiece. Draw pictures, jot down phone numbers and web addresses, make journal entries, draft letters to friends or world leaders. Scribble down ideas for a novel of your own, sketch bridges you want to build, dresses you want to design. Stick postcards and pressed flowers between the pages.

When next you open the book you'll be able to find the bits that made you think, laugh and cry the first time round. And you'll remember that you picked up that coffee stain in the café where you also picked up the handsome waiter. Favourite books should be naked, faded, torn, their pages spilling out. Love them like a friend, or at least a favourite toy. Let them wrinkle and age along with you.

may never be repeated. Otherwise, you might end up letting down not just yourself, but your country. You yourself are not important, but your code of honour should dictate that you do what is best for your comrades, and your nation.

The only way to ensure that you too can fly your aircraft through a squadron of death-spitting devils and come out unscathed is to follow the example of squadron-leader James Bigglesworth. He would never abandon his chums, and his first thought is for the rules of conduct in his aeronautical world. There are times when he must become a machine, a part of the aircraft itself, focussing only on the goal ahead. And it simply wouldn't occur to him to leave Ginger and Algy behind in the soup, even if rescuing them is near impossible.

There's no point in courting calamity, but you'll never get anywhere if you hesitate. The last thing you should do is to sit around passively. With Biggles as your mentor, leading you down a path of excitement and danger, you will soon find that people always leave keys in their cars and fuel in their tanks, and your last desperate measures to escape are bound to pay off. You may find yourself tight-lipped with concern, but you will walk tall, acting as if everything is bound to work out for the best, and sure enough one of your chums will swing by at the last minute in the very vehicle that you thought was about to run you over, ready to drive you to safety. You will find the courage to look disaster in the eye, pancaking your aircraft into the treetops rather than tangling in the telegraph wires.

Any of Captain WE Johns's ninety-six Biggles books will galvanise your risk-taking instincts, as you will be drawn to follow his lead as he successfully battles against international conspiracies, rescues both fellow fighters and damsels in distress, and selflessly saves the day before breakfast. We particularly love *Biggles Defies the Swastika* for Biggles's debonair propensity to dress up as a Nazi, and bluff his way through sticky situations – including an excellent mid-air wrestling match for the controls of a tumbling fighter-plane, rescuing his mates from the jaws of disaster and providing us with an utterly spiffing tale.

R

341

SEE ALSO: **coward, being a • goody-goody, being a • organised, being too • procrastination • seize the day, failure to**

risks, taking too many

If you are a natural daredevil, prone to giving your nearest and dearest the heebie-jeebies by skiing off piste with yaks, crossing undulating rope bridges in a zorbing ball or white-water rafting through military war-zones, you need to temper these tendencies with some daring, yet ultimately sensible literature.

Start with *Breath* by Tim Winton. A novel about the desire of adolescent boys to push their limits, this takes the friendship of two young men as its focus. Bruce Pike (Pikelet) looks back on his teenage years with Loonie, with whom he used to dive into the local river, competing to see who could stay under the longest, and enjoying the panic this generated in anyone watching. Then one day they meet Sando, an older man whose obsession is surfing. 'How strange it was to see men do something beautiful,' muses Pikelet, who is drawn to the grace of the surfers as a direct antithesis to his fisherman father's inability to swim. The boys take up surfing too, with Sando egging the boys on to greater and greater feats of daring. 'In time we surfed to fool with death – but for me there was still the outlaw feeling of doing something graceful, as if dancing on water was the best and bravest thing a man could do.'

One day Pikelet pushes himself out on his board into a terrifying riptide, with no-one around to rescue him. He knows he is not ready for it, but is powerless to resist the urge. Surviving his ocean baptism, he befriends Sando's wife. An ex-surfer herself with a permanent injury, she plays her own dangerous games with him, flirting with other alarming activities as a substitute for the thrill of the waves. It's a novel that will fulfil your desire to push your limits vicariously. With several near-death experiences, let it serve as a warning about what happens when you go too far (see: regret).

In direct opposition to this Australian outdoor tale of reckless youth, read Fyodor Dostoyevsky's amalgam of tragedy and satire, *Notes from the Underground*, in which he illustrates the consequences of a man's radical denial of his own natural drive. In this novel, short in length but huge in its implications for world literature (containing as it does the seeds of *Crime and Punishment* and *The Gambler*), Dostoyevsky inhabits the disintegrating mind of a man who has deliberately chosen to do nothing with his life at all.

Writing from his present existence as a bitter and misanthropic forty-something, the unnamed narrator looks back at his younger self, when an encounter with a prostitute named Liza could have changed everything. 'I used to imagine adventures for myself, I invented a life, so that I could at least exist somehow . . .' he writes. But he is a man who thinks instead of living and who 'consequently does nothing'. A purveyor of paradoxes, he puts forward a convincing argument for the pointlessness of taking any action at all, let alone risks (and if you have a tendency towards this nihilism, see: pointlessness). We're not suggesting that you follow his example and reject a life of action altogether, but rather achieve a half-way point between your audacious leanings, and complete inertia. Between Winton and Dostoyevsky lies a middle path; armed with these extremes you can walk this path without fear.

SEE ALSO: **carelessness** • **confidence, too much** • **gambling** • **optimism** • **regret** • **selfishness**

road rage

Instead of jumping out to assault the incompetent driver in front, stick one of these novels in your stereo. Angry, exhilarated, loud, to dissipate and divert your fury; others invite quiet meditation and reflection.

 THE TEN BEST AUDIO BOOKS FOR ROAD RAGE

Crash **JG BALLARD** read by Alastair Sill
2001: A Space Odyssey **ARTHUR C CLARKE** read by Dick Hill
Heart of Darkness **JOSEPH CONRAD** read by Kenneth Branagh
Hopscotch **JULIO CORTÁZAR** read by Kevin J Anderson

The Revised Fundamentals of Caregiving JONATHAN EVISON read
    by Jeff Woodman
On the Road JACK KEROUAC read by Matt Dillon
Zen and the Art of Motorcycle Maintenance ROBERT M PIRSIG read
    by James Purefoy
Anywhere But Here MONA SIMPSON read by Kate Rudd
Fear and Loathing in Las Vegas HUNTER S THOMPSON read by Ron
    McLarty
The Miracle at Speedy Motors ALEXANDER MCCALL SMITH read by
    Adjoa Andoh

SEE ALSO: anger • rage • violence, fear of

rolling stone, being a

SEE: wanderlust

romantic, hopeless

The Go-Between
LP HARTLEY

Do you scatter rose petals on your bed every night, expect
your suitors to climb up to your balcony bearing chocolates,
and leave love notes inside your partner's fridge? Would you
travel thousands of miles to pick the first alpine strawberry
of the season to present to your soul-mate for breakfast?
And expect him/her to do the same for you?

If the answer is yes to any of these questions, then you
are indeed a hopeless romantic. We applaud you and lament
you in equal measure. Because although we love a hopeless
romantic, we fear for your heart, and hope it will not be too
frequently broken (see: broken heart). As a first defence for
the inevitable heartache that will come your way, we urge
you to turn to *The Go-Between*. Read at the beginning of
spring each year (when romance is most likely to blossom),
it will protect you from complete heartbreak by pre-shatter-
ing just enough to prevent full-scale wreckage later on.

In the novel's prologue, we meet Leo Colston as an old
man, stumbling upon a diary that he wrote in 1900, when
he was twelve. The little book triggers a terrible sense in
Leo that he has wasted his life, as something that happened

to him during the year of his Zodiac-decorated diary has marred his ability to have a happy relationship forever after. And so the story unfolds. Leo, an only child, was invited to stay with his school friend Marcus Maudsley for a few weeks in the summer holidays. When he arrives at Brandham Hall, he is ill-equipped for the aristocratic milieu in which he finds himself, and his clothes are too hot, itchy and tight. But he slowly adapts to his new environment – helped by his hosts who buy him a new, lightweight suit. Over the course of his stay, he is drawn into the relationship Marcus's older sister Marian is having with local farmer Ted Burgess, becoming their go-between, delivering letters from one to another that help them meet up. Leo, in his naïveté, is completely unaware of the social consequences of this affair of the heart until he is too enmeshed in the web. The deadly nightshade in the woodshed that so fascinates and repels him is a symbol of the secrets at the heart of the novel, lurking in the dark and working their poisonous magic on their unwitting satellite.

We know from the prologue that Leo will be at least partially destroyed by the events of this stifling summer. But we only discover at the end that he is still, at his core, a hopeless romantic. Rather than scaring him off romance for life he continues to idolise and worship the idea, treating the players in the story like the gods of the Zodiac, with himself as Mercury the messenger. This is why his life has not worked. He is like the driver of a car with a shattered windscreen, unable to see where he is. Don't make the same mistake. Bury those romantic ideals, along with your diaries. Take a hammer to the glass, and move on.

R
....
345

SEE ALSO: **sentimental, being**

rut, stuck in a

SEE: **stuck in a rut**

S

sacked, being

SEE: **bitterness** • **broke, being** • **job, losing your** • **murderous thoughts** • **rage** • **unemployment**

sadness

The Beastly Beatitudes of Balthazar B
JP DONLEAVY

When we are sad, our bodies move towards our bookshelves with the same irresistible, invisible force by which the tides are drawn by the moon, or migrating birds are lured back home. To land with inexorable precision on *The Beastly Beatitudes of Balthazar B.* A novel so steeped in sadness, so embodying its lilting melodies, that the emotion seems to seep from the page by osmosis and mingle with our own, providing comfort in the inescapable knowledge that, in this world, deep sadness exists. Because no-one understands this better than the Irish American writer JP Donleavy. Who drops his pronouns and active verbs as naturally as the melancholy drop their false cheer when they come inside and close the door. Who poses questions without question marks, and observes the subtle changes in the light with exquisite brevity ('And this evening a fresh green darkness over Paris'). If you are sad, immerse yourself in the warm, tender humour of this novel. To begin the long, slow uplift out of sadness that it effects.

Born into wealth in 'the big house off Avenue Foch' in Paris, Balthazar B is a famously shy, elegant young man whose life is littered with loss and an endless search for love. His father dies, leaving him to his neglectful mother (see: abandonment) and a 'reservoir of riches'. And so he attaches himself to 'nannie', her cheeks round and smiling, and Uncle Edouard, mad balloonist and adventurer, who regales the wide-eyed boy with tales of narrow escapes from bears and how he once persuaded a hot-air balloon to go up by venting his bowels over the sixteenth arrondissement. Despatched in his white stockings and buckled shoes to a heinous English boarding school, where boys rise shivering 'clutching towels' in the mornings, and where his blue stuffed elephant Tillie is torn to shreds before his eyes, solace comes in the shape of carrot-headed Beefy, his only friend. Beefy stitches Tillie together and comforts Balthazar with thoughts of margarine and marmite for breakfast, and how they'll put salt in the masters' coffee, and how they will survive the beastliness of life by doing, whenever possible, the *in*decent thing. And then Beefy is expelled, and Balthazar is alone again.

There are wondrous joys along the way, but it is the ever-present, ever-gentle humour that keeps us going, including Uncle Edouard's advice on how to live – 'lighthearted on the boulevard, gay in the café, a good shot at the shoot', with a flower in the buttonhole every day and the 'roar of a lion' with every morning bowel motion. Keep this novel on a shelf by your bed, and dip into its well of sadness whenever your own is threatening to overflow. By mingling your sadness with that of the emotion's grand master, you will come to know it, as he knows it, as a painful but tender, and sometimes funny thing.

SEE ALSO: **cry, in need of a good**

scars, emotional

Crustaceans
ANDREW COWAN

We all have them. What varies is how deep they run, and how well you keep them hidden – both from yourself and others. And what is the best thing to do with your wounds, anyway? To air them at every opportunity so as to speed the healing process and keep the scars from forming in the first place? Or to lick your wounds in private and keep them buried, the better to protect the sanctity of your sufferings?

Paul, the narrator of *Crustaceans*, does something in between. His wounds – big ones – spur him to take a drive to a small resort on the Norfolk coast on his son Euan's sixth birthday. On the way, he tells Euan about the day he was born and the early years of his life – the first step, the first word, the first time he sat naked on the floor and watched himself pee. Then he goes back in time to how he and Euan's mother Ruth met, and then further back still to the death of his own mother when he was a boy, and the terrible hush that descended on that death.

And then we realise that Euan is not in the car. As the scale of Paul's wounds becomes clear, we realise that this remembering, this telling – with every precious detail preserved in words – is part of a vital, cathartic process. Whether we confide in one or two understanding friends, to ourselves on a piece of a paper, or even to an empty car, the careful telling of stories marks the beginning of our healing. Choose your listener – imaginary or real – with care. Make it someone who will care about you and look after you afterwards. This way you can keep the scar tissue from forming too thick a layer, while still treating your wounds with due respect.

SEE ALSO: **demons, facing your • haunted, being**

scars, physical

Skin Tight
CARL HIAASEN

If you're unlucky enough to have a serious scar on your person, you may spend time fretting over how to conceal it. Vitamin E cream, cover-up cosmetics, temporary or permanent tattoos – even plastic surgery – may be options you have considered. Fret no more. Artful positioning of a novel – tipped nonchalantly, for instance, over that unsightly flaw on your chin – will either hide or steal all the attention away from your scar, especially if the title is intriguing enough.

Observers will be far more interested in seeing what you are reading than in the underlying blemish.*

However, we digress. Our novel approach to healing your scar is Carl Hiaasen's *Skin Tight*. Like all Hiaasen's novels, it's set in Florida among the tourists and criminals of the Everglades. The anti-hero is Chemo, a man whose skin has erupted into horrific Rice Krispie puffs after an unlucky electrolysis incident. Chemo enters into a bargain with a plastic surgeon: facial reconstruction in return for the disposal of an inconvenient witness to the accidental death of one of the surgeon's other unfortunate patients.

At six foot nine, Chemo is not the most discreet of hit-men. He's also not gifted with enormous intelligence. To make matters worse, Rudy Graveline, the unorthodox plastic surgeon without a certificate to his name, has a backlog of mysteriously unfinished, dead or otherwise unsatisfied patients. There is one woman, however, whose anatomy even the unscrupulous Rudy Graveline won't tamper with, an actress named Heather Chappell whose body is as perfect as bodies get. Heather does not think so, however, and wants a boob job, a tummy tuck, rhinoplasty and a chin implant. Her desperation to improve her non-existent faults serves as a reminder that we often see flaws where observers do not.

A hilarious black comedy involving the gruesome and unlikely disposal of bodies and socially challenged evil-doers getting their just deserts, this novel is guaranteed to keep you safely away from the surgeon's knife. Learn to love your scars. They are a part of your history and the narrative that lives on your skin.

---

* The following titles are particularly good at distracting your interlocutors from your scars (this strategy, sadly, will not work with e-books): *I Still Miss My Man but My Aim is Getting Better* (Sarah Shankman); *The Perks of Being a Wallflower* (Stephen Chbosky); *John Dies at the End* (David Wong); *The Hundred-year-old Man who Climbed Out of the Window and Disappeared* (Jonas Jonasson); *Gun, with Occasional Music* (Jonathan Lethem); *Wait Until Spring, Bandini* (John Fante); *Do Androids Dream of Electric Sheep?* (Philip K Dick).

sci-fi, fear of

One of the most common absences in the reading galaxy of an otherwise well-rounded reader is that cluster of novels that fall under the banner of science fiction. For reasons that are not entirely clear, the term has the capacity to send a chill down the spine. Perhaps it conjures images of aliens, spaceships and intergalactic warfare – with no human hearts in the throng. Perhaps the non-sci-fi reader is unable to see how unreal worlds could possibly relate to the world outside their own door.

Or perhaps readers are put off by an umbrella term that fails to communicate the range and quality of the genre. Instead of science fiction, think of it as 'speculative' fiction, as Margaret Atwood puts it – fiction that explores the possible directions in which the human race could go. Writers of speculative fiction have famously predicted our present: Ray Bradbury, Arthur C Clarke and John Brunner all envisaged the gadgets of today, fifty years ago. The writers of such fiction now will predict, and in some ways shape, our tomorrow – and continue to serve as an early warning system. Think, for instance, about how literature has pointed up the dangers of genetic engineering (*Oryx and Crake*), bio-engineering (*The Day of the Triffids*), and social engineering (*Nineteen Eighty-Four*). If, as readers, we consider ourselves students of what it is to be human, shouldn't we be as interested in our future selves as we are in our selves of the past?

In many ways sci-fi is a natural progression from the magical worlds we inhabited as children.* Speculative fiction opens up parallel universes to which we can escape and exercise our love of all things beyond our ken. Close off these speculative worlds at your peril.

☞ THE TEN BEST NOVELS FOR SCI-FI BEGINNERS

Transcending the bounds of their genre, these books have run AWOL to classic status. Almost without realising it, you will be converted to brave new worlds – within yourself as well as in fiction.

The Hitchhiker's Guide to the Galaxy DOUGLAS ADAMS
The Year of the Flood MARGARET ATWOOD
The Drowned World JG BALLARD
Neuromancer WILLIAM GIBSON
Brave New World ALDOUS HUXLEY
Never Let Me Go KAZUO ISHIGURO
A Wrinkle in Time MADELEINE L'ENGLE
The Left Hand of Darkness URSULA K LE GUIN
Nineteen Eighty-Four GEORGE ORWELL
The War of the Worlds HG WELLS
The Chrysalids JOHN WYNDHAM

sci-fi, stuck on

DISCOVER PLANET EARTH

You only ever read sci-fi. There is not a single book jacket in your house that doesn't glitter with an alien glow. Sci-fi has become a reading black hole, and you have fallen in. While we applaud your imagination, and your ability to take mental leaps with the laws of physics, we urge you to apply such well-exercised minds to artistic representations of the planet outside your front door. Because there are other literary universes out there. We suggest you take a tour of this unchartered territory.

Begin with Tolstoy's *War and Peace*, the great Russian epic that, like *Dune* by Frank Herbert, spans three generations of war and politics while never losing sight of the individuals caught up in the spokes of the wheels. Move on to *The Glass Bead Game* by Hermann Hesse, a novel reassuringly set in the twenty-fifth century but concerning itself with philosophical and spiritual matters. Next read Michel Faber's *Under the Skin*, a genre-crossing novel that will suck you in then zap you with a powerful shock. Allow *The Infernal Desire Machines of Doctor Hoffman*, Angela Carter's exuberant magic-realist extravaganza, to introduce you to reality-distorting machines that mess with your mind. And Jeanette Winterson's genre-defying *The Passion* will leave you probing the underbelly of site-specific fiction. From here it's only a short step to all those other novels set in unfamiliar parts of our own planet. Now work your way through our list of The Ten Best Novels to Cure Wanderlust (see: wanderlust). By the end you'll be officially cured of your space-lust.

schadenfreude

A Happy Man
HANSJÖRG
SCHERTENLEIB

Schadenfreude is an exquisite German word which we English admired so much we decided to steal. But once attached to a person it's not so pretty. If you're guilty of schadenfreude, you are not merely oblivious to the suffering of others (see: empathy, lack of) but you take great delight in watching their suffering play out. In short, you are someone we hope never to meet. Dig your schadenfreude out by the root, like a verruca. By reading *A Happy Man*, a little every day, you will gradually learn how to feel pleasure in another's joy instead, and look for the opportunity to prompt that joy, whenever it lies within your power.*

A Happy Man is a novel about a man who is really and truly happy, and with good cause. He plays trumpet in a jazz band; is married to a potter who makes cups capable of containing light and music; and has a daughter who, at fourteen years old, is complicated but loving. The story takes place during a few days in Amsterdam, where This Studer (yes, 'This' is his name – it works better in German) is performing with a band whose members he has known since his twenties. The descriptions of This's easy relationship with his best friend Henk provide glimpses into the trajectory of the lucky man's life so far – including the time he and Henk entertained commuters in a sweltering train, playing air guitar and making them laugh with their antics. He is aware of his luck, and this makes him a *'geluksvogel'*, or Fortune's darling. He knows how to handle the fruits of his fortune too: he and his wife still make each other laugh. 'Who am I speaking to today?' she asks him flirtatiously each morning. 'Today, I'm Saccharine Saccharus!' he proclaims. He still yearns for her, loving the coconut scent of her skin.

If you're expecting the 'but', there isn't one – at least, not for This. Such unmitigated happiness in a fictional life is rare indeed. 'Not that we would delight in another's unhappiness, but we need it in order to bear our own,' is how

S

---

* If our cure fails, apply duct tape to the mouth (which, applied to the afflicted part of the foot, is quite a good cure for a verruca too).

Schertenleib puts it. So can a happy story be a good story? With this Schertenleib proves it can. This's relishing of his own fortune is eminently uplifting and will put the most *schadenfreudig* gloater in his or her place. Ruminate on happiness with this novel. Teach yourself to celebrate it when you see it in others. Become a champion of the happy life – both in art and reality.

SEE ALSO: **misanthropy**

seduction skills, lack of

History of a
Pleasure Seeker
RICHARD MASON

Of all life's skills, those pertaining to the gentle art of seduction are perhaps the hardest to come by – while also, surely, being some of the most crucial for a happy and satisfying life. But where do we turn to acquire them? We observe our parents with horror, our friends with amusement, and Hollywood movies with disbelief. Can literature come to our bedside rescue?

The answer is yes, of course – for seduction is explored from Ovid to EL James, by way of Anaïs Nin and *Les Liaisons Dangereuses*. But you have to pick and choose with care, as not all of the ardent lovers in these novels use strategies we'd care to encourage. For the best all-round handbook, offering a skill-set that poses the least risk to self and others, we suggest Richard Mason's racy tale of sexual and social conquest, *History of a Pleasure Seeker*.

Piet Barol has many natural, physical advantages that make him attractive to women – and, in fact, many men (and this arch seducer is not one to let gender mess with his mojo). He's unafraid to use them, too – but he doesn't rely on looks alone. His mother was a singing teacher and, from his earliest youth, taught the boy to read the emotions and thoughts of others. As he accompanied her students on the piano, he used the lessons to practise these silent skills, holding the gaze of the prettiest pupils while they sang.

In fact, much of Piet's seductive charm comes from his knowledge of music. Although not a great pianist himself, he knows when to choose a flirtatious Bizet over an abstract

Bach, and when he applies for the job of tutor to young Egbert at the house of Jacobina Vermeulen-Sickerts, he remembers his mother telling him that the 'only key for love is E flat major'. And so his seduction of Jacobina begins.

Piet has ample opportunity to flex his skills, for there are two daughters in the household, as well as Jacobina, and Jacobina has not been touched by her husband for a decade. His impressive draughtsmanship, his ready wit, his awareness of the nuances of manners and clothing, all stand him in very good stead. Even a fellow staff member, Didier, becomes enslaved. Neither does he restrict himself to the Vermeulen-Sickert household. On an impulse, he emigrates to South Africa on the lavishly appointed *Eugénie*, where he encounters even more opportunities to seduce.

Throughout the novel, there is a recurring motif of a man on a tightrope, balancing precariously. It's perfect – for seduction is a high-risk art, and one is always close to falling. Take lessons from Piet: use your natural advantages, step boldly where others (eg husbands) fear to tread, and know when it's time to (gracefully) retreat. Oh, and like Piet, you'll need complete conviction in your own irresistibility.

SEE ALSO: **orgasms, not enough** • **self-esteem, low** • **sex, too little** • **shyness**

seize the day, failure to

A Month in the Country
JL CARR

The Hundred-Year-Old Man Who Climbed Out of the Window and Disappeared
JONAS JONASSON

We live only a limited number of days. And the number of days within that precious time span on which something or someone special comes along are few. Hesitate, or lack the courage, to grab what fate has offered, and we may live to regret it for ever.

We know of no novel in which the hero – and in a superlative act of osmosis, the reader too – is more haunted by the ache of knowing that he failed to seize the day than JL Carr's Eighties classic, *A Month in the Country*. It is the immediate aftermath of the First World War and, carrying with him a terrible stammer and a twitch picked up at Passchendaele, Tom Birkin arrives in the village of Oxgodby in full anticipation of a 'marvellous', recuperative summer. He has been contracted to excavate a medieval fresco on the ceiling of the village church, living in the bell-chamber while he does so. The experience is every bit as healing as he hopes – for in this 'haven of calm' he spends his days in blissful solitude at the top of his ladder, living off bully-beef and Mrs Ellerbeck's currant teacakes, making friends with fellow front-line survivor Charles Moon, and falling in love with Alice Keach, the vicar's lovely young wife.

He doesn't expect anything to come of it. Alice visits regularly – but so does young Kathy Ellerbeck, and somehow it is all part and parcel of the gift of the summer that he wishes could go on for ever. One day, up in the bell tower, they lean together as Tom shows her the meadow where Charles is digging and her breasts press against him. He knows it's now or never. What stops him? A certain habit of unhappiness he's acquired in the last few years, perhaps. English propriety. An assumption he makes about Alice. One leaves the experience of reading this novel a sadder person – unless, of course, you turn it into a commitment never to let the same thing happen to you.

If you suspect that, like Tom, you have a tendency to be more of a passenger than a pilot in your life, you might need a lesson in how to do it. Someone who navigates admirably through their long and eventful life is the geriatric hero of Swedish writer Jonas Jonasson's *The Hundred-Year-Old Man Who Climbed Out of the Window and Disappeared*. Allan has always lived his life lightly, with more curiosity than conviction, yet has somehow been instrumental in many of the key events of the twentieth century. On the eve of his one hundredth birthday party in the Malmköping Old People's Home, to which the press, the mayor, and the staff and guests have been invited, Allan decides that the home won't, after all, be his last residence on Earth, and that he will die 'some other time, in some other place'. He is not only blithe, but lucky, as one of the first things he does after escaping is land a suitcase full of money.

What follows is a retrospective romp through Allan's life, from his birth in 1905 to his new beginnings aged 101 in Bali, with a younger woman (eighty-five) at his side. On the way, he helps to create the atom bomb, and advises various world leaders, including Winston Churchill and Mao Tse-tung. His adventures in the present continue, taking him and his suitcase, via several accidental murders (Allan doesn't have much cop with morality), to many glorious places. And Jonasson's message is clear. If you find yourself asking 'Should I?', the answer is always 'Yes'.

SEE ALSO: **apathy** • **coward, being a** • **indecision** •
procrastination • **risks, not taking enough**

self-esteem, low

The Shipping News
ANNIE PROULX

A Kestrel for a Knave
BARRY HINES

Rebecca
DAPHNE DU MAURIER

It's not surprising that Quoyle, the hero of *The Shipping News*, has low self-esteem. He spends his childhood being told he's a failure by his dad, his favoured older brother Dick beats him up, he's fat and has a freakishly enormous chin, his wife can't stand him and sleeps around, he's underpaid by his employers, his parents get cancer and kill themselves, his wife leaves him, taking their two daughters (who, by the way, are called Bunny and Sunshine, which can't help), he gets the sack, his wife is killed in a car crash – oh, hang on, that's a positive bit. Anyway, you get the gist. Number of reasons to feel good about himself by the end of the first few chapters (yes, this all happens at the beginning, so we haven't spoiled anything): frankly, zero.

And so, 'brimming with grief and thwarted love', Quoyle decides to follow his aunt's advice and start a new life in the somewhat unpromising environs of Newfoundland, where his father was born. This he does, with the aunt and two requisitioned, delinquent daughters in tow, and what follows is surely one of the most remarkable comebacks in literature. Those low in self-esteem should read this novel not just as a literary and curative experience in and of itself, but as a how-to manual. Do as Quoyle does, step by step. If you do not possess the relevant passport or visa requirements to live in Newfoundland, substitute with another inhospitable and inaccessible location such as Iceland, the Outer

Hebrides or Northern Siberia. After acquiring a generous life insurance policy, arrange for the death in a car crash of the partner who torments you and —

Just kidding. But we do suggest that you at least go and stay for a while in the place your family comes from, however much you hate it, or them. While you're there, research your ancestors. You may, like Quoyle, uncover less than pretty facts about your lousy forebears – the crimes and wounds that, passed down from one generation to another, did for your own self-esteem in the first place. With luck you'll be able to break the hereditary cycle, as Quoyle does, and move on.

Of course, it's not always the fault of dead relatives. Sometimes it's the fault of relatives who are still, unfortunately, alive. In what remains one of the most devastating social critiques of its generation (1968), *A Kestrel for a Knave* by Barry Hines shines an unflinching light on the way a community can demoralise and stunt a youthful spirit by depriving him of love, trust, stability, encouragement and praise. Not to mention breakfast.

Growing up in a bleak, depressed Yorkshire mining town, Billy has to fight his elder brother Jud for everything from space in the bed to their mother's scant affection. No-one sees any promise in him – except Mr Farthing at school who hears Billy talk about the kestrel he keeps in the garden shed. Through Kes, Billy discovers a quality that no-one else has shown him, for the beautiful, still-wild hawk 'just seems proud to be itself'. Kes means everything to Billy, and when he takes the hawk out to fly it – using a lure to control its sweeps and loops, watching it eat a sparrow, receiving the bird's weight on his gauntlet when it lands – Billy becomes transformed from a boy with no future except to go 'down the pit' like his brother, into an eloquent, confident lad full of passion and potential.

But the promise is only there as long as the hawk. The lesson for anyone also needing to escape the limitations of their upbringing or the poor expectations of others, is to find your equivalent of a kestrel and become an expert. It doesn't matter what you are an expert in. Just to have knowledge that no-one around you has will boost your self-esteem and draw you to the attention of others – like Mr Farthing – who are in a position to help you to a better life.

Sometimes, of course, you've got no-one to blame but yourself. If you subject yourself to constant criticism, undermining your belief in yourself and your own opinions, you'll recognise a kindred spirit in the narrator of Daphne du Maurier's *Rebecca* – who, by the way, remains nameless, underscoring her lack of belief in her own right to exist. From the minute she assumes her role as the second Mrs de Winter, mistress of Manderley – the beautiful country estate owned by her older and more sophisticated husband Maxim – she becomes gauche in the extreme, forever dropping her gloves, knocking over glasses and stepping on dogs, blushing and apologising and biting her nails as she tiptoes around. Inadequately dressed and coiffed and knowing it, she has no idea how to run a big house with servants and does nothing to help herself learn, naïvely handing over her authority to the housekeeper, Mrs Danvers – a spiteful spectre of a woman who 'adored' the first Mrs de Winter and is only too happy to encourage the young woman's self-sabotage. 'Second-rate', 'odd', 'unsatisfactory' – these are all ways in which, directly or indirectly, she describes herself. Unsurprisingly, when Mrs Danvers suggests she throw herself from the bedroom window, she very nearly agrees to do it.

The heroine of *Rebecca* is an orphan – so, once again, we could blame her dead relatives for her lack of self-esteem. But watching her put herself down, compare herself unfavourably to the elegant, clever, beautiful Rebecca, her husband's first wife, becomes hard to stomach after a while, so clearly does she make things worse for herself. Anyone with the same tendency to cripple themselves with self-criticism will blush in guilty recognition on reading this novel, and swear to put an end to such self-destructive behaviour once and for all.

SEE ALSO: **failure, feeling like a** • **neediness** • **shyness**

selfishness

*One Flew Over
the Cuckoo's
Nest*
KEN KESEY

Being selfish has been re-branded as a positive personality trait. Look after your own needs first, the self-help books exhort. Make sure it's you that gets to the top. Putting yourself first may well bring you lots of money and land you a CEO's swivel chair, but it's never going to make you friends – or at least, not the sort of friends you'd want. Unless you find it fun to watch people around you having a miserable time (in which case, see: schadenfreude), being selfish will never make you happy.

It's time to take inspiration from one of our favourite characters in literature, Randle P McMurphy, the bold and brassy Irishman in Ken Kesey's 1962 exposé of psychiatric institutions, EST and lobotomies, *One Flew Over the Cuckoo's Nest*. With his 'big wide-open laugh' and absolute refusal to be cowed, McMurphy storms into the lives of the Acutes and the Chronics of the loony bin – damaged men, abandoned by the society that created them – and changes them forever.

McMurphy is not selfless in the tedious way of saints and martyrs. As the admissions doctor reads on his records, he's probably feigning psychosis to get out of doing chores on the 'work farm' where he was previously held. Primarily, McMurphy is after a good time. And as he goes round the ward introducing himself, insisting even on shaking the hands of the Wheelers and Walkers and Vegetables, it appears that he's simply asserting his dominance over the group. But McMurphy's irrepressible spirit soon starts having an effect on the men. When he laughs, it's the first laughter Chief Bromden – the apparently deaf-and-dumb American-Indian narrator of the novel, who has been there longest of all – has heard in years. McMurphy knows that in this place of cowedness and fear, where the tyrannical Nurse Ratched rules, none of the men are going to get better. 'Man, when you lose your laugh you lose your *footing*,' he says.

And so, subtly and perhaps only half-consciously, McMurphy begins to build his fellow inmates up, winking and joking in group therapy meetings to 'wheedle a skinny laugh out of some Acute who'd been scared to grin since he was twelve,' persuading the doctor to let them play basketball in the corridors, listening to the 'big-as-a-damn-mountain' Chief Bromden to find out why he feels so small. When, one day, he takes twelve inmates out on a deep-sea fishing trip with a couple of 'aunts' (aka hookers), he rewards them for their courage in coming by teaching them how a bit of bravado can help, even if you have to pretend. What follows is a glorious, heart-breaking day in which the laughter swells the men up, and reminds them what they could be.

McMurphy didn't have to take any of them out with him on the boat. He didn't have to share his spirit. He didn't have to bring one of the hookers, Candy, to the party, and he certainly didn't have to delay his escape so that the young stuttering Billy Bibbit could spend his first night with a woman. He pays a terrible price.

But that's the thing with selflessness. It's not about you, it's about everyone else. And what would you rather be remembered for, bringing joy and laughter to everyone else's lives, or just making sure everything's dandy in your own? Forget about number one. Think about numbers two and upwards from this day on.

SEE ALSO: **empathy, lack of** • **greed** • **manners, bad**

self-satisfied, being

SEE: **arrogance** • **confidence, too much**

selling your soul

Doctor Faustus
THOMAS MANN

Those who barter their literary souls tend to do so in return for eternal youth, knowledge, wealth, or power. In real life, this translates as losing your artistic integrity, preferring pots of money to having time to breathe, and turning your back on old friends. But the outcome is the same: you lose yourself. And what's the point of living while you're only half *there*?

Arch-consumer John Self in Martin Amis's *Money* believes himself to be a big-shot in the film world. But he has signed his life away – not to the devil, but to debtors. Kurtz in Conrad's *Heart of Darkness* is less interested in the trappings of Western civilisation than in power and control. He has sold his soul for sovereignty over his fellow men and, in doing so, reduced himself to an animal. But the best template for the glory and catastrophe of selling your soul remains Thomas Mann's masterpiece, *Doctor Faustus*. In this version of the Faustus myth, it's a composer the devil ensnares. In return for twenty-four years of unparalleled artistic achievement, his soul will belong forever to Mephistopheles.

It is not the first time Adrian Leverkühn has resorted to drastic measures. Before meeting the embodiment of devilishness, he deliberately contracts a case of syphilis with the idea that the madness it will bring him will deepen his artistic sensibilities. It's during a bout of syphilitic derangement that a vision of Mephistopheles appears. The devil warns him that he shouldn't assume he is hallucinating.

Unsure and terrified, Leverkühn returns to his work – and immediately starts creating masterpieces. He 'invents' the radical 'twelve-tone system', is hailed as a genius, and becomes the most celebrated musician of his generation. But there is something disconcerting about him, something cold which friends and audiences notice – and which they can only describe as an absence, as if one's feeling towards him 'dropped soundless and without trace'. It is no coincidence that the novel is set when Germany was itself heading into the inferno.

Hold on to your soul. You may not get your four and twenty years of fame – or whatever earthly riches you so desire. But who wants to be – or to know – a person with no soul?

senile, going

The Hearing Trumpet
LEONORA
CARRINGTON

At the start of this surreal, wonderful novel, ninety-two-year-old Marian, 'a drooling sack of decomposing flesh' and a little deaf, is living happily with her son Galahad. She is in perfect bliss in fact, feeding her cat on the bed, living largely off chocolate and soup, and regularly meeting up with her best friend Carmella to discuss plans for their trip to Lapland. But when her relatives can no longer bear her toothless exclamations and cat-fur-covered clothing, she is moved to an 'extremely sinister' institution known as the Well of Light Brotherhood. Carmella gave her a hearing-trumpet shortly before her move, and this gift transforms Marian from a victim of deafness to the heroine of a brilliant, if slightly fantastic drama. Unfettered by her age to the point where she thinks nothing of scaling the roof of a house if it's the only way to find out what's going on inside, she has always had a sense of limitless possibility. But the hearing trumpet enables her to engage with the world once more – so much so that she masterminds a nine-day-long hunger strike in which the ancient residents of the home subsist on nothing but chocolate biscuits smuggled in by Carmella (who likes nothing better than to come to the rescue).

With this group of nonagenarians, anything could happen, and indeed a new and more positive world order does seem to be taking over by the end. Read it, and you will be skipping into your senile years with ear trumpet in hand.

SEE ALSO: **ageing, horror of** • **amnesia, reading-associated** • **memory loss** • **old age, horror of**

sentimental, being

A High Wind in Jamaica
RICHARD HUGHES

Once upon a time, being sentimental simply meant being in touch with your emotions, and therefore being more appreciative of literature, music and art. But the word has moved on, and now it denotes untrustworthy emotions – a saccharine world of teddy bears and schmaltzy Hollywood endings (and if you're not careful, it can tip over into hopeless romanticism, see: romantic, hopeless). We strongly urge the cessation of all such shallow emotions, coming as they do at the expense of deeper, more subtle feelings. The sentimental are requested to self-administer a dose of Richard Hughes's excellent tale of piracy, kidnap and death, *A High Wind in Jamaica*. So searingly unsentimental is this novel that after reading it you will find you no longer well up at an image of a starving child. Instead, you'll send a food parcel, or volunteer to help.

This bracing tonic begins with five expat children leading an idyllic and semi-feral existence in Jamaica. After surviving a minor earthquake and a major hurricane, Emily and her four younger siblings, the neglected offspring of emotionally absent parents, are shipped off to the Mother Country for a bit of education. But on the way to England, their boat is seized by pirates. As the siblings become embroiled in the pirates' way of life – which, though threatening, involves little violence – the eldest girl, Emily, inadvertently becomes instrumental in their misdeeds. Before long the siblings are more attached to the pirates than they ever were to their stiff, English progenitors.

And this is not because the pirates are particularly charming. Emily's actions are reprehensible. At first she acts in self-defence, then in pure obedience to her elders, without realising the horror of what she's doing. And there is much musing within the novel on the different way that children think – closer to cats, fishes and snakes, muses the narrator, than to adults. And when their instinctive, self-preserving behaviour is compared to various adult moralities – that of the pirates, and of the British, as demonstrated here by their legal system – neither is any more admirable.

What is so powerful about the novel is the children's own total lack of sentimentality. When one of their number disappears, they appear to forget him almost at once, and put him out of their minds. On the boat, the ratio of fear flips at one point from the children being more afraid of the pirates to the opposite. As it turns out, the pirates are right to quake in their boots. This novel, with not a whisper of sentimentality in it, should effect a complete and permanent cure. Read it, then throw your teddy bears in the bin and go out with a firm new upward tilt to your chin.

SEE ALSO: **romantic, hopeless**

seventy-something, being

 THE TEN BEST NOVELS FOR SEVENTY-SOMETHINGS

Mr Bridge EVAN S CONNELL
Mrs Bridge EVAN S CONNELL
The Summer Book TOVE JANSSON
The History of Love NICOLE KRAUSS
Moon Tiger PENELOPE LIVELY
Love in the Time of Cholera GABRIEL GARCÍA MÁRQUEZ
The Best Exotic Marigold Hotel DEBORAH MOGGACH
The Sea, the Sea IRIS MURDOCH
State of Wonder ANN PATCHETT
Jane and Prudence BARBARA PYM

sex drive, low

SEE: **libido, loss of**

sex-life, issues with

SEE: **coming too soon** • **libido, loss of** • **orgasms, not enough** • **seduction skills, lack of** • **sex, too little** • **sex, too much**

sex on the brain

SEE: **lust**

sex, too little

*The Thousand
Autumns of
Jacob de Zoet*
DAVID MITCHELL

If you're not seeing enough action in the bedroom department – resulting in frustration, sadness and a thwarted desire to celebrate your physical side – we urge you to compare your suffering with those of the monks and nuns in David Mitchell's multi-stranded *The Thousand Autumns of Jacob de Zoet*. Set on an island off Japan on the cusp of the nineteenth century, it tells of two single-sex communities so sexually deprived that they invent strange and disturbing rituals to alleviate their duress. You'll be so relieved you're not living *that* life that you'll embrace your own with more equanimity. If you're single, brush up on your seduction skills (see: seduction skills, lack of) and hot-foot it to your local library to see what – and who – else you can pick up. If you're already coupled up, present your partner with a suitably titillating novel (and for ideas on what to choose, see our cure for libido, loss of, and orgasms, not enough).

SEE ALSO: **libido, loss of** • **married, being** • **orgasms, not enough** • **seduction skills, lack of** • **single, being**

sex, too much

The Life and Loves of a She-Devil
FAY WELDON

Women
CHARLES BUKOWSKI

Yes, it is possible to be over-sexed.

Men who feel they are unduly fixated should pour a bucket of cold water over themselves in the form of Fay Weldon's *The Life and Loves of a She-Devil*. When Ruth's good-looking husband Bobbo leaves her for petite, dainty Mary Fisher – a cliché of femininity straight out of the best-selling romances Fisher pens – Ruth decides to embrace her inner devil (see: vengeance, seeking). She sleeps around until sex means nothing to her, then uses it to get what she wants – ripping Bobbo and Mary's lives apart with devastating aplomb. If you're married and tempted to stray, this novel will make you gulp and think twice. And married or not, you'll find Ruth's conclusion that pretty women use sex to control their menfolk sobering stuff. A good long celibate stint will start to look as enticing as a wink after this.

Women in need of a turnoff will find it in the pages of Charles Bukowski's voracious *Women*. The narrator Henry Chinaski – based more or less on Bukowski himself – is a randy fifty-year-old whose craving for sex never lets up. A pint of whiskey, a vomit before breakfast, and he's latched on to the next pair of tight blue jeans, kissing and fighting – then wondering if his stomach's too upset for oral sex. There's soul here, and a crude and vulgar beauty that'll fascinate some – particularly if you have an ear for rhythmic prose, but it'll definitely make you want to leave your sexy underwear in its drawer.

SEE ALSO: **bad back** • **exhaustion** • **pain, being in**

shame

The Help
**KATHRYN
STOCKETT**

Shame is a deep, primitive emotion – one of the earliest to erupt in innocent, carefree hearts. The shamed feel a natural, instinctive need to run away and hide – deep in the laundry basket, or to another country – where no-one can find them. Take our cure into the laundry basket with you, and by the time you emerge, you'll see the wisdom and necessity of facing the music.

Set in Jackson, Mississippi, in the Sixties, just as the civil rights movement was getting underway, *The Help* describes the very public shaming of generations of wealthy white families who used and abused cheap black labour in the form of maids, known as 'the help'. The catalyst and facilitator of the shaming is a young white woman, daughter of one of those wealthy families, and guilty by association.

Eugenia – or Skeeter, as she is known – has high ambitions of becoming a writer, but is unsure of her material. 'Write about what disturbs you, particularly if it bothers no-one else,' advises the New York editor who mentors her through her first journalistic attempts. It is a brilliant piece of advice. For just beginning to emerge within twenty-three-year-old Skeeter's chest is a vague sense of unease about Constantine, the black maid who raised her – and who disappeared abruptly from her family's home. She realises that the story of Constantine and hundreds of others – told for the first time, in their own words – would make for fascinating reading. Of course, she is met by terror and suspicion. Because who will employ these maids once they've spilled the beans (see: beans, temptation to spill the)?

In the end she gets more than she bargained for. Aibileen (who has raised seventeen white children but lost her own son in an accident at work), and the outspoken Minny are brave enough to get the ball rolling. And so, jeopardising the fragile balance of a society built on injustice and racism, Skeeter opens up a Pandora's box.

We don't generally encourage taking revenge (see: vengeance, seeking), but when the guilty fail to own up to their

S

shame, reading-associated

CONCEAL THE COVER

Caught red-handed reading *Flowers in the Attic* while waiting at the school gate? Shy of being seen sniffing over *One Day* while on your security-guard night shift? Embarrassed to pull out Proust while under the dryer? And what if your students spot their blue-stockinged Eng Lit professor gawping over a vampire novel on the bus?

Go digital. Discretion is the e-reader's gift. Either that, or crochet a book cover. Nobody need know the source of the words causing your mouth to drop open, your eyes to shine. Your novels are your pleasure and yours alone.

shame, tit-for-tat shaming becomes justified. The impeccably just punishment meted out on Hilly Holbrook – instigator of an initiative to enforce separate toilets for blacks and whites – is perfect. And when Minny joins in by giving her appalling employer her just desserts, Hilly gets something far, far worse than humble pie. Boosted by so much bravery, come out of that basket and own your shame. Like guilt (see: guilt), you cannot move on until it is expunged. Tell whoever you need to tell, and then say sorry. And whatever you do, don't leave it for someone else to expose on your behalf.

SEE ALSO: **guilt** • **regret** • **shame, reading-associated**

shelf, fear of being left on the

The Idea of Perfection
KATE GRENVILLE

The fact that Douglas Cheeseman and Harley Savage get together in the course of Kate Grenville's novel, *The Idea of Perfection*, gives hope to anyone who fears failing to find a partner with whom to share their life. Both middle-aged and dragging a dead-weight of emotional baggage behind them, Douglas has zero confidence and a face that makes him 'look stupid'. Hayley has eye teeth like 'fangs' and is convinced from her third husband's suicide that she's not only a 'dud' but actually dangerous to be with.

But get together they do. And in a novel that's all about learning to accept imperfections – first in oneself and then in others – it points out a possible way in which you might be sabotaging your chances beyond that first date. Read it and keep the novel's epigraph (from Leonardo da Vinci) in your mind: 'An arch is two weaknesses which together make a strength.'

SEE ALSO: **Mr/Mrs Right, looking for** • **single, being**

shopaholism

Tender is the Night
F SCOTT FITZGERALD

The modern compulsion to spend, spend, spend has seen many an over-excited acquirer of nice things go under, credit card gripped between their teeth. Either we end up in debt (see: broke, being), or strapped to the hamster wheel of earn,

earn, earn in order to stay afloat (see: workaholism). One of our favourite shoppers is the beautiful, damaged Nicole in F Scott Fitzgerald's *Tender is the Night*, whose ability to spend – wantonly, guiltlessly – cannot but be admired. And while we are the first to admit that the sheer act of purchasing can give a high, it's not hard to see that if women such as Nicole – the 'It' girls of their era – were less dependent on looks and dresses for a sense of their own worth, they might not need to spend quite so recklessly. See: self-esteem, low.

The profusion of designer labels splattering the pages of *American Psycho*, Bret Easton Ellis's ground-breaking and nerve-shattering foray into the head of a mass-murdering psychopath, is presented as an early warning sign of a world that has lost its values. And indeed if you are brave enough to read this novel (and we should stress that you need to be *very* brave) it will put you off designer goods forever.

Patrick Bateman is a stickler for the rules. You have to be manicured, coiffed and perma-tanned, hard-muscled from the gym, and you have to have the right clothes. A wool and silk suit by Ermenegildo Zegna, ideally, with cuffs by Behar, a Ralph Lauren silk tie, leather wingtips by Fratelli Rosset-ti, and horn-rimmed glasses by Oliver Peoples (of course). You have to eat and be seen to be eating at only the hottest restaurants (Dorsia, Barcadia, Orso) and the difference be-tween success or failure in life is whether you have enough clout to get a good table.

It creeps up on us only slowly that Pat Bateman is telling the truth when he mutters in the presence of his girlfriend Evelyn that, far from being the 'boy next door' as she likes to call him, he is in fact a 'fucking evil psychopath'. And once we start to witness this for ourselves, with random, hateful killings, mutilations, torturings (again: be warned, these scenes are horrific and will stay with you for a lifetime), it is a chillingly convincing extension of the contemptuous, controlling, inhumane façade we have seen thus far. At one point Bateman makes a list of things he intends to buy – Christmas gifts for his Wall Street colleagues – and if you're anything like us you'll not be able to look a silver-plated wine carafe, or anything else from this psychopath's list, in the eye again.

Don't get huffy. We're not suggesting you're a psychopath too. But watch those spending habits. Don't fix your gaze so much on the starry labels that you lose sight of what really matters. And beware that man with the Tumi leather attaché case from DF Sanders, the one with the perfect nails who's refusing to eat the eggplant because it hasn't been cooked the right way . . . yes, him. Actually, he won't bother you because you're not wearing the right colour socks.

SEE ALSO: **book-buyer, being a compulsive** • **broke, being** • **extravagance** • **greed** • **tax return, fear of doing**

short, being

The Tin Drum
GÜNTER GRASS

The Hobbit
JRR TOLKIEN

If you're vertically challenged, few things can be more gratifying than reading a classic novel about someone short, powerful and immensely charismatic. We give you not one but two such heroes, whose stories will thoroughly stamp out any issues you may have about your succinct stature.

Oskar Matzerath in *The Tin Drum* is a bundle of compressed energy, a man who makes up for his curtailed growth by becoming a galvanic force of myth creation. His subject is himself. The novel is narrated by Oskar from within a mental asylum, where he has been incarcerated for the murder of Sister Dorothea. He is, we quickly realise, an unreliable narrator, claiming as he does that he was fully cognizant at his own birth. On his third birthday, three pivotal things occurred: he deliberately ceased to grow; he was given the titular tin drum, from which he henceforth refused to be parted; and he stopped speaking, communicating now only by drum.

This drum becomes Oskar's voice through the next twenty-seven years, and although he is a character with many faults, he gives off an energy as compelling as a jazz solo. But it's his mastery over his physical destiny that sets him apart. His self-willed shortness stands as a symbol of strength – and defiance.

The quiet, dignified essence of Bilbo Baggins in *The Hobbit* could not be more different. Bilbo belongs to a race of creatures about half the size of your average human, with big, hairy feet and soles so thick they make footwear redundant. Hobbits love comfort, warmth, and at least six meals a day; and much prefer the predictability of staying at home. Bilbo, however, is destined for an epic adventure. When thirteen dwarves come to his door and ask him to help them in their quest to regain their rightful treasure from the dragon Smaug, something awakens in Bilbo's breast, something pertaining to magic and madness, which comes from his ancestry.

Take heart, O ye of little loftiness, and consider these sturdy heroes. They may be scant of skeleton, but they are huge in heroism and influence. Never let it be said that to be short is to be slight.

SEE ALSO: **self-esteem, low**

shyness

*The Dud
Avocado*
ELAINE DUNDY

Being shy can be a paralysing condition. School, work, social occasions, even shopping can become events which sufferers dread and do their best to avoid. Left untreated, shyness can lead to agoraphobia (see: agoraphobia), hermit-like tendencies and eventually misanthropy (see: misanthropy). Adults suffering from shyness often hide behind hats or jobs. Children retreat into books, TV or solitary play.

While we wholeheartedly encourage the obsessive reading of novels as a valid way of life, we are aware that burying your nose in a book is not the best way to break free of shyness – and that it may in fact be a symptom of it. We suggest you restrict your reading hours, therefore, and use novels to prepare yourself for social events (see: dinner parties, fear of) and to reward yourself after having made the effort to go out. One character that will help remind you that there are other ways to be is the *jolie* heroine of *The Dud Avocado*, Elaine Dundy's Fifties classic. By the end of this novel, you'll have relaxed into your own skin.

Not many women who have an orgasm in a café in Paris while holding the hand of a man they barely know can be accused of being shy. Sally Jay Gorce is a champagne cork of a woman who flies through life with a gush of bubbles in her wake. At twenty-one she has come to Paris, having made a deal with her Uncle Roger who told her to go and discover herself, then come back and tell him all about it. She makes the most of it by dyeing her hair a rainbow of colours, becoming a mistress to Teddy the married executive, working as an extra on a film set, posing nude for an artist, and losing her passport in circumstances that lead her to discover that she can't trust all the menfolk in her life. Her voice is arch, knowing, and cool; she is a woman on her own in a beautiful city just after the second world war. And she is clear about one or two things: that she's here to fulfil her childhood dreams ('staying out late and eating what she likes'); that she'll meet people she hasn't been introduced to; that she'll live in a house 'without a single grown-up'; and that when she walks around Paris no-one will know where she is. She aims to get to a point where she can 'guess right about people' (which, by the by, is a useful skill for a shy person to acquire, as you're less likely to be wrong-footed or caught unawares).

French phrases are scattered throughout, giving a Parisian flavour to Sally's take on life: 'Teddy really was madly attractive *dans sa façon*'. Together with Sally's sardonic tone and disdain of convention, this makes for a hilarious read and fabulous company for the shy. After spending 300 pages in her company you'll adopt Sally's breezy attitude to life. *A l'enfer* with what people think of you. Learn to believe in *toi-même*. 'If you hadn't existed I'd have had to invent you,' says Max to Sally. 'Don't you believe it, I invented myself,' she retorts. *Inventez-vous* right now, *portez les robes de soirées dans le matin,* and *ne donnez pas un* hoot for what *tout-le-monde* thinks of you.

SEE ALSO: **blushing** • **dinner parties, fear of** • **loneliness, reading-induced** • **seduction skills, lack of** • **self-esteem, low** • **words, lost for**

sibling rivalry

Literature heaves with squabbling siblings, young and old. Little siblings in unrequited adoration of big siblings, siblings competing for parental attention, siblings who abuse, siblings who betray, siblings who love too much, siblings who are just irritating to one another because they're siblings.

A little bit of competition between siblings is par for the course, but beware the example of Cain, who let it go too far. We mostly know this archetypal tale of fratricide from the Bible, but in José Saramago's novel, *Cain*, we are given a fuller picture. The brothers start out the best of friends; but as grown men and farmers, the competitiveness reaches dangerous heights. One day they make offerings to God: Abel the flesh of a lamb, Cain a bunch of vegetables. The Lord doesn't think much of the vegetables and shows it. Cain experiences such intense sibling rivalry over Abel's success that he takes the jaw-bone of an ass and slays his brother in a cave. He immediately feels terrible remorse – and blames God for not intervening. (Frankly, we think he has a point.) For the rest of the novel, Cain seeks revenge on God by meddling with the Almighty's plans, sticking a spanner in the works of the Old Testament stories, from Sodom and Gomorrah to the Flood. The results are delightfully entertaining.

God is the all-too-human parent in Saramago's novel – inconsistent, unreliable and favouritist. The children of similarly unskilled parents need to do something challenging indeed: rise above the bad example they've been set and love one another regardless of the different way they are treated. Ultimately, therefore, the failure lies with Cain. Don't fall into the same trap, and blame your siblings for the errors of your progenitors.

Mr Tulliver in George Eliot's *The Mill on the Floss* tries setting a good example: he tells his own sister, Mrs Moss, that she doesn't have to pay back the money he loaned her in the hope that Tom will take heed and show similar kindness to his sister Maggie one day. But Tom's refusal to forgive

Maggie when she forgets to feed his rabbits (and they die) reveals a cruel streak. Here is an elder brother who, basking in his little sister's adoration, continually denies her the approval she craves – and so keeps her dangling forever. One can't tell someone in Maggie's position to stop loving their elder sibling quite so much. But one can suggest they try and hide it. If Maggie could have found an ambition for herself other than to 'keep house' for Tom one day, she may have succeeded in turning the tables and winning his admiration in return.

Certainly, literary siblings seem to get on better when they're united in battle against someone or something – and when it's not a parent they're fighting, it's usually poverty, or bullies. The siblings in Leif Enger's *Peace Like a River* are very nice to their dad, Jeremiah Land, but are bonded together by hardship, hunger and small-town suspicion in Roofing, Minnesota. Left motherless when their father downsizes from doctor to janitor (unimpressed, she leaves), eight-year-old Swede valiantly tries to generate a Christmas spirit by making Santa Claus cookies with frozen peas for the eyes and macaroni for the beard. Elder brother Davy crunches right through one, beard and all, managing a 'flawless display of gladness and enjoyment' that even convinces the other brother, eleven-year-old Reuben. Alienated siblings should definitely try emulating this inter-sibling generosity at home.

Loyalty becomes problematic when it breaks the bounds of morality, though. Davy defends his siblings somewhat over-zealously when he shoots the two town bullies, making an outlaw of himself. These are siblings who love without thinking, despite themselves. Emulate this love up to a point, but not to the extent that it becomes destructive.

S

375

What if there are neither hardships nor annoying parents to make allies of you – and you and your siblings have nothing in common? Your only option is to learn to love one another anew when you're adults. Study the interactions of Meg, Jo, Beth and Amy in Louisa May Alcott's *Little Women*. If any siblings had reason to wonder how they could have derived from the same gene pool (or pen), then the March sisters do: responsible Meg, tomboy Jo, goody-two-shoes Beth and spoiled Amy could not be less alike. But rather than despise one another for their differences, the March sisters (bonded by a near-death experience for one of them) develop a genuine understanding and appreciation of one another's strengths that – if you can cope with the old-fashioned girliness of it all (and you should; it's all part of the novel's charm) – is very much worth absorbing.

Siblings are for life. Treat them well – even if it means ganging up against your parents, or moving out of the family house. Say goodbye to the dynamic you formed as kids, and embark on a new relationship, as adults, with these grown-up brothers and sisters who, thank heaven, are completely different from you.

SEE ALSO: **Christmas** • **family, coping with** • **irritability** • **jealousy**

single, being

Bridget Jones's Diary
HELEN FIELDING

Wednesday 2nd January
7.17am New Haven, our house. Wake up before the child. Miracle. Lie there for half an hour beside the snoring husband thinking, must get up before the child. Do it. Make it past his room without waking him. Wonder when started treating the child as if he is an invasive and potentially dangerous species. Creak downstairs, make coffee.

7.29am Interrupted by bloodcurdling scream from master bedroom. Rush up to discover child standing upright with all limbs in appropriate places and no visible sign of blood or vomit. Child pointing at empty space on my side of bed. 'MAMA YOU WEREN'T THERE!' Consider backing away. Note that husband's eyes are closed. Presume turned deaf overnight or else has died in sleep. Child thrusts book in face. 'BREAKFAST! AND RUNAWAY BUNNY. NOW!'

8.15am Enjoy moment of peace eating porridge with the child. Notice gratefully how he cannot speak and eat at same time. Thought interrupted by top-volume hideous shrill squealing of alarm clock followed by shouted obscenity from the husband. Then silence. Conclude alive and able to hear after all.

8.35am Thoughts interrupted by repeated battering over head with *The Runaway Bunny*. Suggest the child does something less annoying such as painting a picture instead.

8.36am Eyes fall on ancient copy of *Bridget Jones's Diary* propping up shortest leg of table.

8.45-9.45am Spend entire hour under table re-reading *Bridget Jones's Diary* while the child uses me as abstract art canvas. Chuckle at Bridget fending off enquiries about love-life ('Why can't married people understand that this is no longer a polite question to ask? We wouldn't rush up to *them* and roar, "How's your marriage going? Still having sex?"'). Also at flirty prehistoric email-equivalents from Daniel Cleaver at work ('Message Jones: You appear to have forgotten your skirt'). Laugh so hard that hit head on underside of table. Suddenly filled with nostalgia for being thirty-something singleton, guzzling bottles of Chardonnay in emergency de-briefing situations with Best Friend and spending entire weekends exfoliating elbows in anticipation of candle-lit dinner with emotionally unavailable man. Can't believe spent so much time yearning to be a Smug Married and am now Married But Not Smug. Realise table leaning precariously and shove copy of *How to be Happy Though Married* under shortest leg. Note to self: read that one too.

10am. Despair. Reading *The Runaway Bunny* in continuous loop under table.

10.30am Interrupted by child shouting 'MAMA WHY HAVE YOU STOPPED?' Tell the child I was thinking. 'WHAT ABOUT?' asks the child. Hear myself say that I was imagining stabbing the Runaway Bunny with a knife, setting fire to its tail with a match, then running away myself. 'WHY,' asks the child. 'Because when I was single I could have done anything and didn't,' I say. 'WHAT'S SINGLE?' says the child. 'It is what I was before I met Daddy and had you.' 'BUT WHAT DID YOU DO?' asks the child. 'I did what I wanted, when I wanted and with whom I wanted, within certain socially acceptable limits,' I say. 'Except that I didn't do it enough.' 'CAN I BE SINGLE?' asks the child. 'No,' I say. 'WHY CAN'T I BE SINGLE?' wails the child.

10.34am Make excuse to go to toilet. Text BF asking her if she knows why the hell we didn't appreciate being single in our twenties/thirties. Gaze out the window thinking of all the things we could have done instead of staring at the phone waiting for it to ring. Interrupted by beeping phone. 'Because we were looking for Mr Right,' BF has replied. 'Because we were worried about being on the shelf.'

10.46am Interrupted by the husband walking into bathroom without knocking. Says, 'Are those your knickers?' and 'Are there any eggs?' and 'What is that burning smell?'

10.47am Race downstairs while yanking up old grey knickers closely followed by the husband to find child under table holding lit match to copy of *The Runaway Bunny* which is staked through with knife. The child says, 'MUMMY AM I SINGLE NOW?'

10.49am Interrupted by husband asking, 'How did the child get hold of a box of matches?' and 'Did you say yes or no to eggs?' and 'What's this about being single?'

10.50am Interrupted by the child shouting, 'MAMA!! WHAT ARE SOCIALLY SUSHEPCHONAL LIMITS?'

10.53am The husband opens cupboard and peers in. Says, '*Eggs!*' and smiles. Says, 'So did you get lots of work done this morning?' and 'Shall we have sex later?' and 'I read this really interesting article this morning about electoral systems in emerging democracies. Shall I tell you about it?'

10.54am I stare at husband. Think: Eggs? Democracy? *Sex?*

S
....
378

SEE ALSO: **dinner parties, fear of** • **happiness, searching for** • **loneliness** • **Mr/Mrs Right, holding out for** • **Mr/Mrs Right, looking for** • **sex, too little** • **sex, too much** • **shelf, fear of being left on the**

single-mindedness

The Hunters
JAMES SALTER

We used to be in favour of single-mindedness. In fact, you could go as far as saying we were single-minded in our belief in single-mindedness. We believed that single-mindedness was a useful trait because it got things done. We have, in the past, been single-minded in our pursuit of various things, many of which we achieved, which surely had something to do with us having been single-minded about them in the first place. We were of one mind about it.

But then we read *The Hunters*, and found ourselves believing that our approach to single-mindedness had been somewhat single-minded. *The Hunters* is about the single-mindedness of fighter pilots, and how the only thing they care about is becoming an 'ace'. You have to shoot down five enemy planes to become an ace, so naturally one runs a great risk of being killed in the single-minded pursuit of becoming an ace. One can see from this that sometimes single-mindedness can kill you.

But that's not the only reason our faith in single-mindedness was shaken. While on leave from his single-minded pursuit of becoming an ace, Cleve Connell (thirty-one years old, a man of few words, honest, intelligent, brave – in other words, someone we wanted to see fall in love and live happily ever after) meets the daughter of a Japanese artist who was an old friend of Cleve's father's. The girl is only nineteen but has extraordinary poise, and we could see immediately that she was good enough for Cleve. We also saw that if Cleve were to survive the war, he would come back to find her, and they would live happily ever after.

But in order to survive the war, Cleve would have to swap one single-minded pursuit for another. He'd have to swap the single-minded pursuit of becoming an ace with the single-minded pursuit of *staying alive*. Because one cannot pursue two single-minded objectives in direct conflict with one another. The problem is that to swap one single-minded pursuit for another, one has to be open-minded. And one cannot be open-minded when one is already single-minded.

S

379

The crux of the issue, as we saw it, is that single-mindedness is the opposite of open-mindedness. And we had long ago sworn allegiance to open-mindedness in our lives, as open-mindedness allows for growth. We therefore found ourselves concluding that it was necessary to take a negative stance towards single-mindedness. We would even go so far as to say that we became single-minded in our stance against single-mindedness; not just because we were *of one mind* about it, but because we could not say that we were exactly open-minded about single-mindedness any more. Of course, this stance immediately came to seem too single-minded, because one couldn't ignore the fact that *The Hunters* itself would not exist were it not for single-mindedness – not just because it is *about* single-mindedness, but because what novel could possibly be finished were it not written in a state of single-mindedness – and we were indeed happy that the novel existed, and indeed all the other novels that we have written about in this book, and many of the ones that we haven't. Would we have wanted to cure James Salter of his single-mindedness had we been given the opportunity? *Could* we have cured him of single-mindedness, prior to him having written the novel which was the cure for it? Such circuitous thinking was in danger of cracking our single minds into many fragments, a state which would surely need another cure to bring us back to a state of single-mindedness again, and so we decided the best thing to do was to leave this entry unfinished and to remind our readers that the most important thing was to keep

S
....
380

SEE ALSO: **anally retentive, being** • **change, resistance to** • **obsession**

single parent, being a

The Last Samurai
HELEN DEWITT

Silas Marner
GEORGE ELIOT

No-one said it would be easy. And unless you can afford not to work, or have a live-in nanny or a hands-on granny, trying to be there for your offspring emotionally and physically while simultaneously earning a living, running a house, and having a sniff at a social life is challenging even to the most stoic human being. Literature has a great and disproportionate appetite for single parents, and there is a lot to be learnt from the range of parenting strategies on display. At one end are the botch jobs, providing you with an excellent list of 'don'ts': the alcoholic, abandoned Bojan in *The Sound of One Hand Clapping* by Richard Flanagan belongs on this list (though he gets a chance to redeem himself as a granddad); while the father in David Vann's *Legend of a Suicide* wins top spot for the worst divorced dad in the business (see: depression, general; and optimism if you have kids and happen to suffer from a similarly disastrous mix). As for single mothers, literature generally takes the line that the more alternative the approach, the better – see Aunt Penn (who, though not strictly a single mother, might as well be) in Meg Rosoff's *How I Live Now* for some impressively hands-off parenting techniques. Her fourteen-year-old Edmond might smoke and drive the family car, but he displays the sort of maturity and sensitivity that every mother dreams about kindling in her boys.

Our stand-out favourite single mum, though, is Sibylla in *The Last Samurai*. Mother to the super-intelligent Ludo, she doesn't have enough money to heat the house, regularly spending whole days riding the Circle Line on a continuous loop to keep the two of them warm. But Sibylla doesn't let poverty come between her and high achievement. Choosing to home-educate, Sibylla teaches Ludo to read by the age of two, and by three he is tackling Homer – in the Greek.

No stranger to genius herself, Sibylla is undaunted by Ludo's lust for languages – and in the next few years Hebrew, Japanese, Old Norse and Inuit are added to his CV. The one thing she will not do is introduce him to his father, opting to depend on the classic Kurosawa film, *Seven Samurai*, for male role models instead. This doesn't stop Ludo embarking on a search for his real dad himself – but will any of the contenders match up to the samurai? It's a brilliant conceit and executed with the love of language one might expect from an author who gave birth to such a multi-lingual pair. The conclusion will bring a silent cheer to the heart of any single mum struggling to raise children in the absence of a committed father.

Being left holding the baby is most commonly the woman's lot – but sometimes men find themselves in this character-building predicament too. Whatever your gender, George Eliot's utterly moving *Silas Marner* will ensure that you see it as a blessing, in case you're in any doubt. Embittered and lonely, shunned by the other inhabitants of Raveloe (people of Raveloe, see: judgemental, being), Silas Marner has nothing to live for except his accumulating gold, which he hoards beneath the floorboards. One day he finds a mysterious child asleep at his hearthside. Gradually, Eppie melts his heart, teaching him how to love and bridging the gap between Silas and the local people. If single parenthood wasn't something you planned and you're struggling to adjust to, this novel will give you great heart.

But it's Atticus Finch in Harper Lee's *To Kill a Mockingbird* who gets our vote for the best single father in the business. For how to treat your children with respect, for how to give them freedom to play and discover the world for themselves, for showing them the importance of standing up for what you believe is right, and having the courage to take action against wrong (for more on which see: coward, being a), look no further. Build a house with a porch and put a rocking chair on it. Sit there, smoking a pipe. Read *To Kill a Mockingbird* once a year, first to yourself, and then out loud to your kids. Be strong. And be there for your children. The rest will come.

SEE ALSO: **busy, being too** • **busy to read, being too** • **cope, inability to** • **fatherhood** • **motherhood**

sixty-something, being

 THE TEN BEST NOVELS FOR SIXTY-SOMETHINGS

Things Fall Apart CHINUA ACHEBE
The Sense of an Ending JULIAN BARNES
The Unlikely Pilgrimage of Harold Fry RACHEL JOYCE
The Diviners MARGARET LAURENCE

skim, tendency to

READ ONE PAGE AT A TIME

If your eyes are apt to skip ahead, scanning for dialogue or drama, sex or scandal, leaping rudely over passages of description, it may be that you are reading a bad novel. In which case, use this book to guide you to a better one. But it may be that your capacity to delay gratification has been eroded and you need to retrain your brain to slow down and digest.

Your therapy is to read a novel one page at a time – no more, no less. A page before you go to sleep, a page when you wake in the morning, a page as you eat your lunch. The best novel for the purpose is one in which every page glistens with intelligent insight: Robert Musil's *The Man Without Qualities* is ideal. But you can take your pick. The point is to allow whatever you read to trigger your thoughts, and then to spend time with these thoughts, penetrating to deeper and deeper seams within yourself. We agree that finding out what happens next is important. (And so is sex and scandal.) But do you want to live your life on the surface, just picking the icing off the cake? Sometimes chewing on a piece of really good bread is the most satisfying part of the meal. It's certainly the part that will fuel you through the rest of your day.

S

383

sleep, too little

SEE: **busy, being too** • **depression, general** • **exhaustion** • **insomnia** • **nightmares** • **pregnancy** • **sex, too much** • **snoring** • **stress** • **tired and emotional, being** • **workaholism**

sleep, too much

SEE: **adolescence** • **ambition, too little** • **apathy** • **bed, inability to get out of** • **depression, general** • **lethargy** • **seize the day, failure to** • **unemployment**

sleepwalking

The Sleepwalkers
HERMANN BROCH

When we dream, the brain imagines all sorts of vivid wanderings. For most of us, the wires transmitting the intention to move from brain to body are blocked by sleep – we lie still, with no outward manifestations of our inner journey other than, perhaps, a twitch, a sob or a squeak. In children and, it seems, the elderly – plus a few odd bods in between – the wires malfunction every now and then, letting the intentions of the brain loose on the body and transforming a dreamer into a meandering somnambulist who will scare the living daylights out of any other members of their household who happen to be passing on the landing. Eyes glassy, the somnambulist will be completely unaware they are padding around barefoot – and if you wake them to tell them, you're likely to scare the living daylights out of them too.

We advise you to reconsider your use of the term 'sleepwalker'. From now on, begin to see it metaphorically, as does Hermann Broch in *The Sleepwalkers*. In this great experimental, modernist epic – which is in fact three distinct novels each written in a different style – Broch uses the term to represent those caught between two sets of ethical values, old and new, as the nineteenth century becomes the twentieth.

In the first of the trilogy we have Joachim von Pasenow (the romantic), a highly-codified Prussian aristocrat who ardently espouses traditional values – so much so that he enters into a suitable but loveless marriage with the emotionally distant Elisabeth. But Pasenow is also passionately involved with the sensual Ruzena, a Bohemian prostitute with whom he's ashamed to be seen in public. In the second, there is August Esch (the anarchist), a steady, responsible accountant who chucks it all in to go and work as a manager of a circus – only to find that that doesn't suit him either and he becomes an accountant again. And finally, in the third novel, in which Pasenow and Esch return, we have Huguenau (the opportunist), a man who cheats, murders and rapes to get what he wants, without receiving any comeuppance. During any given epoch we are trapped, philosophically speaking, between different ways of living – like somnambulists who are not quite asleep and not quite awake. Are we living our lives deliberately, guided by a set of principles, or are we chasing after whatever false god we happen to favour in any given moment, be it art, politics, business or pleasure, with an eye only for the object, and no consideration of the consequences? In other words, how should we live?

Trust an Austrian modernist to devote himself so openly – in fiction – to the exploration of a philosophical thesis.

And while, somnambulists, you wrestle with the philosophical, psychological, existential, grammatical, transcendental, translational (we could go on) questions evoked by the metaphorical condition of sleepwalking, one of three things will have happened. Either you will have discovered an inner conflict of your own, one part of you sanctioning your way of living, the other not – the resolution of which will curb your night-time wanderings forever. Or you will have exhausted your brain by reading this dense, often moving, always fascinating, sometimes abstruse, definitely long trilogy, so that you will sleep in the deepest part of the sleep cycle in which no dreams, or sleepwalking, occur. Or you will have fallen asleep mid-sentence, this door-stopper of a tome still weighing on your chest where, dreams or no dreams, it will have you pinned to your bed till morning.

smoking, giving up

Smoking these days is not really an option; shorn at last of its final glimmer of glamour, it's now bad for you in every conceivable way. But that doesn't make it any easier to give up. A good novel can be as effective as a nicotine patch in terms of injecting a buzz – see our list of The Ten Best Novels for Going Cold Turkey. But don't attempt to quit the ciggies without the help of the following two novels. The first allows you to revel in the accessories of smoking without actually inhaling. The second delivers a short, sharp punch to the thorax that will put you off destroying your lungs forever.

Slipping *Still Life with Woodpecker* into your pocket will almost certainly give you a thrill – imitating as it does a packet of Camels. The publisher's justification for this shameless brand-borrowing is that the heroine, red-headed Princess Leigh-Cheri, meditates on these iconic pyramids and palm trees for countless hours while her outlaw boyfriend Bernard Mickey 'the Woodpecker' Wrangle, is in prison – his only company also being a pack of Camel cigarettes, identical to hers. As she feels the psychic connection, facilitated by their shared icon, she decides she can't actually smoke them, because to open the pack would be to destroy her imaginary world. 'A successful external reality depends upon an internal vision that is left intact,' she muses; but she does go travelling by camel with the traders, Bedouins and sheiks she meets in the desert beyond the packet. Through her meditation, the reader thus learns fascinating facts about pyramids, redheads and the purpose of the moon, as well as pondering the innate wisdom of inanimate objects.

Towards the end of the novel, Leigh-Cheri and Woodpecker Mickey Wrangle are trapped inside a genuine, newly built pyramid, believing they are entombed there forever with nothing to eat but wedding cake and champagne. They make use of Mickey's gunpowder expertise, and share a joint hallucination in which they fall into yet another pack of Camel cigarettes. This is so much more fun than actually smoking a cigarette that you will be very glad it's this novel causing the bulge in your back pocket, rather than a real pack of Camels.

Asylum is a novel that will catch your breath, compress your lungs and constrict your throat at a moment of unbearable horror. If you haven't quite managed to quit the habit yet, this will convince you you must. The action revolves around Stella Raphael, whose husband is a forensic psychiatrist in an asylum. It's 1959 and the asylum is a maximum security outfit in an old Victorian prison – just far enough from London for Stella to become isolated and mildly depressed in her new life. She begins a misbegotten affair with Edgar Stark, an attractive inmate who is charming, intelligent and cultivated, but known to have had violent episodes. Stella chooses to skate over his lurking sadism.

Once back in London, Edgar finds a studio where he can work on his obsessive, brilliant clay busts. We sense danger, as his behaviour becomes more and more erratic. But Stella is drawn deeper and deeper into his dark interior world. To cope, she smokes almost constantly, punctuating her days with long, deep pulls on her cigarettes.

There comes a moment in the novel when Stella is at her lowest. And one day, when her son Charlie talks her into coming on a school trip, something appalling happens. Stella could have intervened, but at a vital moment she looks away, her attention focused entirely on her cigarette. 'With one hand she clutched her elbow as her arm rose straight and rigid to her mouth. She turned her head to the side and again brought the cigarette to her lips and inhaled, each movement tight, separate and controlled.'

It is this moment, with its terrible chill, that will have you extinguishing your last cigarette by crushing it resolutely into the ground.

SEE ALSO: **anxiety · cold turkey, going · grumpiness · hunger · irritability**

snoring

Sleeping with someone who snores can be a nightly torment. At best you end up in separate beds and facing a less physically intimate future. At worst you spend your days in a fug of irritability from your shattered sleep, and your nights hating the emitter with a vengeance (see: murderous thoughts). To save your sanity and your relationship – if not your partner's life – invest in a set of headphones or an audio device designed to slip beneath your pillow, and keep a stack of soothing audio books by the bed. Mellifluously read, tranquil in tone, these books are guaranteed to drown out your partner's snores while not keeping you from your sleep. Play all night if need be, drifting in and out. For optimal sleep conditions, familiarity with the book is a bonus.

 THE TEN BEST NOVELS TO DROWN OUT SNORING

Sense and Sensibility JANE AUSTEN
Essays in Love ALAIN DE BOTTON
A Little Princess FRANCES HODGSON BURNETT
Our Mutual Friend CHARLES DICKENS
The French Lieutenant's Woman JOHN FOWLES
The World According to Garp JOHN IRVING
The Wings of the Dove HENRY JAMES
Ulysses JAMES JOYCE
English Passengers MATTHEW KNEALE
Anne of Green Gables LM MONTGOMERY

SEE ALSO: **divorce** • **insomnia** • **noise, too much**

social climber, being a

Vanity Fair
WILLIAM
MAKEPEACE
THACKERAY

When invited to a party, do you first ask, 'Who's going to be there?' Do you drop the names of your famous acquaintances more often than you drop your keys? And do you consider marriage an opportunity to advance your career? If so, you'll recognise yourself in Becky Sharp, who springs from Miss Pinkerton's Academy for Young Ladies with her talons out and at the ready. She pounces first on her best friend Amelia's brother, who is duly warned off, but her next prey,

Rawdon Crawley, the son of a baron, is not so lucky. He's caught and quickly hitched (though we don't mind, because he's no better himself). From then on her rise is meteoric – she sucks up to the source of the family cash, Rawdon's spinster aunt, makes a profit out of Amelia's brother when he panics over the looming Napoleonic war, considers absconding with Amelia's husband, then claws her way up in Paris and London until she's cavorting with a marquis – and a prince – at the top. And for what? Read and find out. But we'll tell you this much: it may be fun at the top, but there's not much room and plenty of other contenders eager to knock you off the spot. If raising your social status is your goal, be warned by this cautionary tale. When you've backstabbed your way to the top, who's going to want to catch you when you fall?

SEE ALSO: **ambition, too much**

speech impediment

Black Swan Green
DAVID MITCHELL

The most insightful exploration of the trials and tribulations of having a speech impediment that we know – in this case, the stammer of thirteen-year-old Jason Taylor – is to be found in David Mitchell's *Black Swan Green*. Jason thinks a lot, and intelligently, about his stammer, which struck aged eight – around the time his parents' marriage began to founder. Jason has noticed, for instance, that 'the Hangman', as he calls his stammer, particularly likes to hijack words beginning with 'N' (though it later moves to 'S-words' – the thickest section in the dictionary); that the best way to 'outfox' the Hangman is to scan one sentence ahead for 'stammer-words' and change what you wanted to say for something you *can* say; and how stammerers can never win an argument with a quick retort or wise-crack, 'cause once you stammer, H-h-hey p-p-presto, you've l-l-lost, S-s-st-st-utterboy!'

As tension rises at home and his stammer worsens, the dreaded bullying begins (see: bullied, being). It starts off mild but crescendos to excruciating heights and we share Jason's pain as we watch him cling on to his tattered reputation. And then something magical happens: Jason discovers poetry. And with the help of Mrs de Roo, his speech therapist, and an exotic local woman called Madame Crommelynck who makes sure his anonymous submissions to the parish magazine appear in print, he begins a new relationship with words, learning to love them and harness them to tell his truth. As Jason's narrative becomes increasingly studded with lyricism – an impressive sleight of hand by Mitchell – he begins his metamorphosis from someone filled with envy for people able to say 'what they want at the same time as they think it' to someone for whom words are, at last, a beautiful tool.

Jason's cure may not be your cure, as all speech impediments are different. But watching him reach the point where he can create an 'appalled silence' in class by delivering a shocking riposte with metronome-slick timing will bring a glow to your heart. Anyone whose tongue gets in similar tangles must take two things at least from this novel: you, like Jason, will be the more mature for having had this extra battle to fight. And – again like Jason – blunted in one direction, you'll probably find you flower in another.

SEE ALSO: **different, being** • **self-esteem, low** • **shyness** • **words, lost for**

speechlessness

SEE: **words, lost for**

spinelessness

SEE: **coward, being a** • **selfishness**

spouse, hating your

SEE: **adultery** • **divorce** • **DIY** • **midlife crisis** • **Mr/Mrs wrong, ending up with** • **murderous thoughts** • **snoring**

stagnation, mental

The Blue Flower
**PENELOPE
FITZGERALD**

Like dogs, brains require regular exercise in order to stay in tip-top shape. If yours has fallen into a stagnant state from lack of use – or from being too much in the company of other stagnant brains – we suggest you shock it back to life with a mental defibrillator in the form of *The Blue Flower* by Penelope Fitzgerald.

The Blue Flower tells the story of the incandescently brilliant real-life German poet Friedrich von Hardenberg (who later became known as Novalis), and his bemusing adoration of Sophie von Kühn, a twelve-year-old girl with an unmistakably mediocre brain. Being in the company of the von Hardenbergs is constantly amusing: Fritz's eccentric siblings all deliver their lines with such a crisp, dry wit that each utterance glistens on the page. But the main reason to read *The Blue Flower* is to experience Fitzgerald's own brain writ large. It's partly what she puts in – making observations with devastating clarity, then moving on as lightly as a fly – and partly what she leaves out. She'll make geographic or spatial leaps between one sentence and the next that would have most novelists passing out in a panic. She'll give a character a simple tilt of the chin that contains a lifetime's dignified concealment of a broken heart. So much that's important remains unsaid, and we are kept mightily busy filling in the gaps.

By the end your synapses will be thrumming at the same high frequency as Fitzgerald's own. To sustain a bristling intelligence, we recommend re-reading *The Blue Flower* every five to ten years.

SEE ALSO: **boredom** • **career, being in the wrong** • **housewife, being a**

starting, fear of

DIVE IN AT RANDOM

You have a brand new novel in your hands. You have read the reviews, it has been recommended by people you trust, you're sure you're going to love it. You may have been saving it for just this moment, knowing that you now have uninterrupted hours ahead of you to read, perhaps in the bath, or on a train. But you hesitate. You've read and loved books by this author before – what if this one does not live up to his/her last? Are you committed enough to give it a chance? Can you be the reader this book needs you to be?

Do not be shy. Open the novel at random, and read whatever sentence catches your eye. Intrigued? Flick ahead and read two more paragraphs. Then close your eyes, karate-chop the book, and where it falls open, read a page. Finally, throw the novel on the floor (gently if it's a nice edition), then pick it up with a thumb inside. Read the page your thumb caresses, and turn over and read the next. By now you have opened several windows onto the book. You have glimpsed its interior and know a few of its secrets. Curious to know more? (In case you haven't noticed, you've already started. Now go back and start at the beginning.)

stiff upper lip, having a

Where Angels Fear to Tread
EM FORSTER

Stiff upper lips – a peculiarly English facial modification – are caused by the repression and withholding of emotions. One's lip remains rigid as cardboard in the face of all calamities, from heartbreak and the death of pet dogs to the caving-in of ceilings. Those of this stern persuasion will dust the debris off their hair, make a relevant quip, and suggest a good strong cup of tea among the devastation of their kitchen for all affected, rather than give any clue to what they might be feeling. And though we admire that self-control, though we know that keeping calm and carrying on is the definition of Britishness, undoubtedly helping us get through two world wars, particularly the Blitz, many would say that the famous British froideur is on the wane.*

Forster's beautiful but tragic novel, *Where Angels Fear to Tread* – written at a time when the stiff upper lip was in its heyday – illustrates just how dangerous the lip can be to the lives of others, especially if they don't share it. Lilia, the widow of Charles Herriton, is a trifle too flighty for the tastes of her in-laws, and they have encouraged her to travel to Italy as a means of distracting her from a new and inappropriate liaison. Supplying her with a suitably sober and spinsterish travelling companion, Caroline Abbott, they wave her off with every hope that the experience will prove ameliorative. As her brother-in-law Philip Herriton condescendingly remarks, 'Italy really purifies and ennobles all who visit her.'

Unfortunately purification, in Herriton terms, eludes her. Because almost immediately Lilia falls head-over-heels in love with Gino – a beautiful, passionate, feckless Italian, devoid of any title. 'A dentist in fairyland!' exclaims Philip, who loves all things Italian, except passion, and the low-born sons of dentists. The Herriton rescue party is despatched once again – but arrives too late. Lilia has already married Gino, and soon produces a son.

For reasons that cannot be divulged, Philip and his sister Harriet eventually find themselves face-to-face with Gino.

---

* Indeed some say it died forever, with Lady Di.

And in the confrontation that ensues – the expressive Italian unafraid to be vulnerable and show his feelings, in particular his love for his son – we can see that the restrained English way, all buttoned up and disregarding, is terribly flawed. For a moment Philip sees the lure of the Mediterranean way, and wavers. But Harriet, her lip kept very stiff indeed, brushes it off as sentimentality and forces everyone's hands. It leads them all to a place of irrevocable damage. Let those lips wobble, let them tremble, let them open wide. And let those big, wet, messy emotions spill right out.

SEE ALSO: **emotions, inability to express**

stress

The Man Who Planted Trees
JEAN GIONO

Your heart is pounding. Your breath comes fast and shallow. Your fists are clenched and your eyes and ears are straining for information that may save your life.

No, you haven't just come face-to-face with a bear. You're waiting for the train to work, or making toast, or deciding which toilet rolls to buy – just some ordinary, everyday thing. Except that you're suffering from one of the most debilitating epidemics of the modern age: stress.

We prescribe a novel that is so slim and undaunting in appearance that we guarantee it will not add to your stress.* *The Man Who Planted Trees* will soon have your soul slipping into a state of serenity. It's a simple tale: a shepherd lives in a stone house in a desolate part of France. He is surrounded by what he needs and no more, his buttons neatly stitched to his shirt, his gun oiled, his washing-up done. Three years earlier, it had struck him that this part of the country was dying for lack of trees, and 'having nothing much else to do he decided to put things right'. He has since spent his evenings sorting acorns, good from bad, and his days planting them in the ground.

The lush forests of oak – then beech, then birch – that spring up in the fields around him transform the region

---

* In fact, if we're honest, it's barely a novel at all. But, being stressed, you don't need to know this.

into one which can support, nourish and bring joy to more than 10,000 people. But it's not the results of his labours that bring tranquillity of mind to the shepherd. It's the labour itself – the walking, digging, planting, watching, and waiting.

It's more or less impossible not to feel peaceful in the company of the shepherd. And when you've finished and chuckled at the postscript, put it down and step outside. The first way to overcome stress is by reading the right novel. The second is to do some exercise. Put a trowel in your pocket and go for a good long walk.

SEE ALSO: **anxiety** • **busy, being too** • **busy to read, being too** • **concentrate, inability to** • **cope, inability to** • **headache** • **high blood pressure** • **insomnia** • **libido, loss of** • **nightmares** • **workaholism**

stubbed toe

A Portrait of the Artist as a Young Man
JAMES JOYCE

The agony of a stubbed toe has to be endured; nothing can cure it. Thankfully, like a blow to the nose, the pain is short-lived. Expletives are usually one's only resort.

To prevent public outrage and embarrassment, we strongly suggest you arm yourself with the literary equivalent of a venting expletive: a quote that comes easily to the lips and which is staccato, memorable, alliterative, musical, evocative, distracting – that is, the first paragraph of this most approachable of Joyce's novels, *A Portrait of the Artist as a Young Man*. We will here supply only the opening words – for if it is a novel that is not already in your possession, you must get hold of a copy immediately, and commit to memory the first seven lines. Then, when you next stub your toe, be ready to exclaim:

'Once upon a time and a very good time it was there was a moocow coming down along the road and this moocow that was coming down along the road met a nicens little boy named baby tuckoo . . .' and so on until 'lemon platt'.

Then read the rest of this edifying novel, wisening up with Stephen on how best to avoid life's obstacles and find your wings.

stubborn, being

SEE: **single-mindedness**

stuck in a relationship

SEE: **Mr/Mrs Wrong, ending up with**

stuck in a rut

*The Towers of
Trebizond*
ROSE MACAULAY

When you're feeling stuck in a rut, what you need is an
eccentric aristocratic aunt in possession of a camel – one
just such as belongs to Laurie, the narrator of *The Towers
of Trebizond*. 'Take my camel, dear,' begins one of the most
beguilingly daft novels we know – and the best admonition
to step out of your rut and start behaving in a capricious,
plucky and effervescent fashion. Let Laurie's Aunt Dot inspire you to live life as a true eccentric. You will never find
yourself anywhere near a rut again.

Where others might lose their nerve and falter, Aunt
Dot is unfailingly enterprising. So when Laurie, the thirty-
something narrator, accepts an invitation from her Aunt Dot
to travel around Turkey with the aim of founding an Anglican mission and emancipating the Levantine women from
their subservient lives, we know that she is set to have an
entertaining time. Along too comes an opinionated septuagenarian clergyman called Father Hugh Chantry-Pigg, who
travels with a portable altar on which to conduct impromp-
tu mass, and the camel – a white Arabian Dhalur (single
hump). With its tendency to cast spiteful looks and masti-
cate with that 'unpleasing sideways motion of the lower jaw'
that dromedaries have, it gets them into a lot of trouble, but
it also high-foots them out of it (see also: jam, being in a).

It's when Father Hugh and Aunt Dot disappear together
into Russia, bequeathing the camel to Laurie, that the novel
turns from semi-farcical travelogue to soul-searching soliloquy. Because Laurie, a private girl, has been having an affair
with a married man, a relationship she cannot hope to reconcile with her Anglican faith. She opens her heart to us and,
with the camel as a catalyst, soon becomes as eccentric as

her aunt, indulging her passion for fly-fishing at every opportunity and acquiring an ape which she teaches to play her at chess.

The ending of the novel is heart-breaking and sombre, thus balancing out the uproariously silly start. Be encouraged to break off by yourself, to let your personality emerge in its full, quixotic glory. Perhaps you have been stuck in a rut because you are living in someone's shadow – or the shadow of the person you thought you ought to be. Hear Dot's invitation to take her camel. Climb up. Let it take you to places you've never been, and do things you've never before allowed yourself to do.

SEE ALSO: **career, being in the wrong** • **change, resistance to** • **jam, being in a** • **Mr/Mrs Wrong, ending up with**

superhero, wishing you were a

*The Amazing
Adventures of
Kavalier & Clay*
MICHAEL CHABON

*This Book Will
Save Your Life*
AM HOMES

Wait – don't tell us. You imagine the red and blue Lycra. You wonder which superpower you'd choose. Just a bit of you still believes in Wonder Woman's bullet-stopping tiara, her powers of telepathy and her typing speed (160wpm, if you're curious). You don't completely write off the possibility that you might one day own something similar, if not identical, to Batman's Batmobile. And occasionally when you go about your daily life you imagine '*Woosh!*' '*Bam!*' '*Kaboom!*' or '*Pzzow!*' in little bubbles over your head.

Well, that's OK. Some children grow out of it; you didn't.

You'll have already read and adored *The Amazing Adventures of Kavalier & Clay*, Michael Chabon's epic tale of comic-book makers Josef Kavalier and Sammy Clay. Riding the wave of the golden age of comic books, the duo create a series of superheroes, beginning with the Escapist who 'comes to the rescue of those who toil in the chains of tyranny and injustice' in 1939, fighting the war against Hitler with pen and ink. Joe and Sammy do not become superheroes themselves, though; and if you are looking for a how-to literary mentor, we know someone who does.

Richard Novak, in AM Homes's *This Book Will Save Your Life*, was left emotionally numb by a divorce thirteen years ago and he left a four-year-old son, Ben, behind in New York when he moved to California. His life now represents everything artificial about modern-day LA: he lives in a glass box house on a canyon wall, splendidly sealed from the world with a noise-cancelling headset and interacting only with his housekeeper, his nutritionist, his masseur and his personal trainer. One day, he starts to *feel* again – beginning with an overwhelming and undiagnosable physical pain – and gradually people start coming into his life: Anhil, the owner of the donut shop, Cynthia the put-upon housewife, and his 'startlingly sexy' movie star neighbour, Tad. The next thing he knows, he's breaking his rules: drinking coffee ('Real coffee?' asks his nutritionist, aghast. 'With regular milk?'), snacking on donuts, bursting into tears, taking naps . . . and he wants to 'be more, do more . . . to be heroic, larger than life – rescue people from burning buildings, leap over rooftops.' Be a superhero, in other words.

Richard's various heroic acts – one of which involves our favourite highway car-chase in literature – will have you aglow with superhero awe. It takes his quack doctor, Lusardi, to point out that maybe all this saving of other people is really about saving himself. When his son Ben, now seventeen, finally pitches up on his doorstep, Richard is ready to try and rescue the most important relationship of all.

The truth is, you can't become a superhero if you haven't suffered first. Richard notices the needs of others, but it's his desperate need to make things right with Ben and recover some of what he's lost that really drives him. If you are motivated by correcting past wrongs and improving the lives of others, you can be a superhero too.

sweating

The Snow Child
EOWYN IVEY

Sweating can be a great pleasure. But there are limits. When dark circles appear beneath your armpits, and you begin to exude an odour that even you can detect, you've crossed that fatal threshold from healthy glow to full glandular swither. Pick up this snowflake of a novel and let it caress you with cold like a winter sprite.

Mabel is so lonely and full of despair at her childless state that she deliberately walks out onto the unreliable surface of the freshly frozen Wolverine river (see also: children, not having if her sadness rings bells for you). The ice makes a 'deep, resonant crack like a massive champagne bottle being uncorked' – but unexpectedly it holds and she crosses safely, returning to her cabin with a renewed sense of hope. Soon afterward, in the first flurry of new snow, she and Jack make a snow-child together, its face whittled by Jack's pen-knife. But by the next morning it has disappeared – along with the hat and gloves they gave it. Footprints run from, but not to, the site of the sculpted snow child.

As this magical child weaves in and out of their lives – leaving them when it's warm, and returning in a flurry of ice-crystals when it's cold – Mabel worries about her 'Faina' disappearing. When your body heat rockets, return to a mental image of this wild and icy spirit, in whose hand snow flakes do not melt. Let her pervasive cold encroach your body. Lose yourself in the enchantment of these Alaskan forests. Catch moose with Jack and Faina, and lynx with Garrett, the man who loves her. Sketch snowflakes with Mabel. By the end you'll be so chilly that sweating will be a distant memory.

T

taste, bad

If you have poor taste, don't be ashamed. It's probably because you've spent your life doing something practical, scientific – or good. Computer geeks wear famously bad sweaters. Footballers reside in architectural eyesores. Saints are oblivious of their hairdos. But should you desire access to the haloed world of the arts, you may want to give your eye an aesthetic education. Literature suggests it's never too late to learn. Many a philistine within white borders has learnt to dress in the fashions of the day – and to affect good taste even if they don't possess it. Look at the example of Julien Sorel in Stendhal's *The Red and the Black*. As the son of a carpenter, he knows little of the world of high art. Luckily he's blessed with a naturally refined sensibility, though, and when he encounters beauty he faints. With a little help from books and a photographic memory, he impresses his employers no end when he becomes tutor to a fashionable family and hangs out with the aristocratic elite.

It's interesting to note that literature doesn't align an aesthetic sensibility with worldly success very often – and *The Line of Beauty* is no exception. Nick Guest is a bachelor aesthete who has a taste for high living, but lacks the means to achieve it. He becomes a lodger in the home of the MP Gerald Fedden, the father of his best friend from university. Their Victorian mansion is full of beautiful and desirable *objets d'art* but, as Hollinghurst delights in making clear, they treat art more as a symbol of their wealth and power rather than possessing innate good taste. While looking for ways to survive in this world of people richer than he can ever hope to be, and half-heartedly finishing a doctorate on Henry James, Nick gravitates towards the status – and physical beauty – of Wani Ouradi, a young millionaire whom he meets at one of the Fedden's parties (see: social climber, being a).

Soon he and Wani – the son of a Lebanese supermarket mogul – have a plan to start an arty magazine. It will be named 'Ogee' – after the S-shaped curve found to be present in many artistic standards of beauty, such as Islamic and Gothic architecture and Germanic clocks. (Hogarth called it 'the line of beauty' – hence the novel's title.) For Nick, this line is most sensually expressed in the curve of a young man's back, at the point where it cleaves to his buttocks. Things start going wrong when various of the characters' sexual proclivities are exposed, with cataclysmic repercussions for Gerald Fedden. And though Nick, the cuckoo in the nest, plays a part in Fedden's fall, his genuine aesthetic sensibility ultimately redeems him. As you read this novel, listening attentively to Nick as he waxes lyrical on music and art to the less finely tuned members of his milieu, your own sensibilities will open like a daisy in the sun. It's not that we want you to throw away your reindeer cardigan; but you might find yourself noticing that sinuous curve of beauty – in art, music and perhaps the small of your lover's back.

tax return, fear of doing

Christie Malry's Own Double-Entry
BS JOHNSON

The January 31st deadline is looming. Once again, you've left it to the last minute. You stare at your filing cabinet in horror, then back away from it as if from a rabid dog.

Fear of doing one's tax return is a debilitating condition that affects one in five of the self-employed.* Leave it untreated and you not only risk incurring hefty fines from the Inland Revenue but you put yourself at risk of accepting a

---

* Based on a rough head-count made in August. We dread to think what the statistics would be for January.

full-time job on a pay-roll (think: windowless office, air conditioning, strip lighting and a boss who forbids you your personality). This, as everybody knows, leads to loss of hope (see: hope, loss of), zestlessness (see: zestlessness) and, before you know it, old age.

Sufferers must forge an entirely new relationship with their finances (and by extension their filing cabinet); one that is non-threatening and even friendly. This can be achieved by reading of the shockingly toxic accounts kept by the simple, disaffected young man in avant-garde author BS Johnson's novel, *Christie Malry's Own Double-Entry*. Besieged by a sense that life is unfair, Christie Malry hits on the 'Great Idea' of keeping track of the ways in which he has been slighted by others. According to the rules of double-entry bookkeeping as codified by the Tuscan monk Luca Pacioli in the fifteenth century – said to have laid the foundations for modern capitalism – every debit must be balanced with a corresponding credit. And so Christie balances his accounts by taking revenge on the world – acts that start small (scratching an unsightly line down the side of an office block) but quickly spiral out of control.

Christie takes pleasure from keeping his accounts in tidy order, and you should extract all you can of this sentiment as you squeeze this bitter, brief novel into your soul. By the time he enacts his most far-reaching act of vengeance, you'll see that the keeping of emotional accounts is the only real beast in the filing cabinet. Your own finances can then be seen for what they are: an entirely harmless set of figures that won't bite when you open the drawer. Read about Christie Malry then breathe easy. Armed with a clear head and a calculator, your accounts are safe to approach.

SEE ALSO: **procrastination**

tearful, being

SEE: **cry, in need of a good** • **PMT** • **tired and emotional, being**

tea, unable to find a cup of

The Hitchhiker's Guide to the Galaxy
DOUGLAS ADAMS

We all know – or, to be more precise, those of us who are British know – the need for a good cup of tea. It traditionally hits at four o'clock, when our energy slumps. Luckily it's usually fairly easy to make one. But what do we do when there's no kettle, boiling water, teabags or milk to hand?

Pick up a copy of *The Hitchhiker's Guide to the Galaxy*. Because your need cannot be greater than Arthur Dent's, after one particularly trying Thursday. The day begins with Arthur prostrating himself before a bulldozer intent on demolishing his house. His protest is interrupted by his friend Ford Prefect – actually, we discover, an alien from the planet somewhere near Betelgeuse – who insists he comes to the pub and downs three pints to anaesthetise him against the imminent destruction of planet Earth. Made duly blotto, they 'hitchhike' onto a passing Vogon spaceship, where they're tortured with poetry, and escape to another ship (belonging to Zaphod Beeblebrox, ex-president of the Galaxy). It's when Arthur, still in his dressing gown, is blearily watching a binary sunrise over the legendary planet of Magrathea and wondering what on Earth – except there isn't one any more – is going on, that the need for a cup of tea hits.

The only source of hot drinks on the ship is a Nutri-Matic Drinks Synthesizer, a machine so sophisticated it claims to be able to produce a drink tailored precisely to your tastes and metabolic needs. But when Arthur requests a cup of tea, it produces a plastic cup filled with liquid that is 'almost, but not quite, entirely unlike tea'. Arthur throws away six cups of the stuff before finally, desperately, telling the machine everything he knows about tea – from the history of the East India Company to silver teapots and the importance of putting the milk in first. Only after the ship is all but destroyed do they find a small tray on the delivery plate of the Nutri-Matic Drinks Synthesizer with three bone china cups and saucers, a silver teapot and a jug of milk. It's the best cup of tea that Arthur has ever tasted.

All of which will help you bide the time between when the urge for tea hits, and the moment at which you are reunited with kettle and teapot. Even if you've had to wait, at least you can sip your tea in the luxurious knowledge that the Earth, along with the contents of your kitchen and, come to think of it, you, haven't been demolished. Yet.

teens, being in your

 THE TEN BEST NOVELS FOR TEENAGERS

The Absolutely True Diary of a Part-Time Indian SHERMAN ALEXIE
Other Voices, Other Rooms TRUMAN CAPOTE
Ender's Game ORSON SCOTT CARD
The Perks of Being a Wallflower STEPHEN CHBOSKY
Le Grand Meaulnes ALAIN-FOURNIER
Looking for Alaska JOHN GREEN
The Prime of Miss Jean Brodie MURIEL SPARK
The Color Purple ALICE WALKER
A Boy's Own Story EDMUND WHITE
The Book Thief MARKUS ZUSAK

SEE ALSO: **adolescence**

teetotaller, being a

Farewell, My Lovely
RAYMOND CHANDLER

T

We know that being on the water-wagon is no bad thing. Life on the straight edge gives you a clearer, purer view, and many health practitioners, unless they're French, advocate abstinence. But being a teetotaller in a world of drinkers is terribly dull. There are only so many mocktails you can get through before one of your companions will surprise you with a Death in the Afternoon. And what of that tricky moment when your future father-in-law suggests a man-to-man moment with a malt whisky? Do you decline and still get his daughter? And how do you raise a toast to your great grandmother on her one hundredth birthday? With a limp-wristed 'Lemonade for me'?*

---

* Yes, if you're a recovering alcoholic. In which case this cure is not for you. Please skip and go instead to: alcoholism; and dinner parties, fear of.

Literature's drinkers are generally more fun. And none more so than the great Philip Marlowe in Raymond Chandler's detective novels. Our favourite is *Farewell, My Lovely*, though any one of the eight will reacquaint you with the undeniable link between liquor and a certain louche, effortless cool as demonstrated by Marlowe at his most impressive: 'I needed a drink, I needed a lot of life insurance, I needed a vacation, I needed a home in the country. What I had was a coat, a hat and a gun.' People who find themselves pursued by Marlowe give him smiles that are at once 'cozy and acid', because they know he'll extract compromising evidence from them somehow. But he does it with such panache that the baddies are almost honoured to be found out. Living as he does by his own sense of justice – only handing the culprits over to the police if he knows them to be irredeemable – he manages to be a force for good but never a goody-goody (see: goody-goody, being a). And it's partly down to drink.

Of course you mustn't overdo it – if you do, you won't be interesting at all. Marlowe drinks elegantly, and with restraint. Rye whisky is his weakness; occasionally he uses it medicinally to help him get to sleep. And he uses a shot of whatever's going to encourage his suspects to spill. If you tend to be an abstainer, hang out with Marlowe for a novel or two. You'll find the wily sensibility of this quietly heroic detective will slip into your bloodstream like a rye whisky highball. Drink as you read, and your thoughts will become so hard-boiled and smart and dry that you'll soon be dodging around your neighbourhood as fast as a cat, wondering what you had been using for brains all your life, without actually getting out of your chair. You'll have those mobsters safely locked up before you know it, and blondes will be giving you smiles that you can feel in your hip pocket.

Follow Marlowe's example, and don't take your cure too far. If you feel you're going the other way, see: alcoholism.

T

SEE ALSO: **goody-goody, being a** • **killjoy, being a**

tension

SEE: **anxiety** • **stress**

thirty-something, being

 THE TEN BEST NOVELS FOR THIRTY-SOMETHINGS

London Fields **MARTIN AMIS**
The Tenant of Wildfell Hall **ANNE BRONTË**
Middlesex **JEFFREY EUGENIDES**
The Sun Also Rises **ERNEST HEMINGWAY**
The Best of Everything **RONA JAFFE**
Of Human Bondage **W SOMERSET MAUGHAM**
The Rector's Daughter **FM MAYOR**
The Jungle **UPTON SINCLAIR**
Miss Mackenzie **ANTHONY TROLLOPE**
All the King's Men **ROBERT PENN WARREN**

tinnitus

Freedom
**JONATHAN
FRANZEN**

Sufferers of tinnitus – a constant and generally incurable hiss or ringing in the ears, sometimes likened to the clamour of cicadas on a summer night – are often advised to block it out with an alternative wall of sound. The idea behind this is that the brain finds this second wall of sound both more acceptable and more instantly recognisable as 'background' noise, happy then to relegate both layers to background status, or noise which the brain doesn't need to 'hear'. The problem with this is that most alternative walls of sound are more maddening than the tinnitus itself – the dreaded new-age shush of waves washing up on a shore being the best example. So what is the sufferer who is discerning about his or her sounds to do?

Our suggestion is to erect an interior wall of sound, inside the head, by reading Jonathan Franzen's *Freedom*. Here is a novel which has trawled contemporary American society for its current preoccupations, trends, obsessions and anxieties and built them into a document of the sort that one might seal in a capsule and deliver to aliens in space. For Franzen's technique is to put everything in, leaving nothing out, so that the couple at the centre of the story, Patty and Walter Berglund, together with the apex of their marital triangle, Richard Katz, become rich repositories of the sort of characteristics we all recognise – but which it takes someone of Franzen's genius to pluck from reality, boil down into one quintessential moment, and reproduce on the written page.

Patty and Walter are 'young pioneers' of Ramsay Hill, spearheading its gentrification, and though we are told straight out that there 'had always been something wrong with the Berglunds', we cannot at first see what. She is pony-tailed and bouncy; he rides a bike to work. They are the golden couple with two children, Joey and Jessica. But such apparent perfection does not, of course, come without its own shrill, interior vibration, poised as it inevitably is on the edge of cracking. And when the crack comes, out come all the vices.

This is a busy novel, delivered to us in Franzen's characteristic voice – an unremitting jabber laced with street slang, brands and references to world events, filled out with internal soliloquy and sparkling with metaphor that is often funny and always exact. As such it is the perfect wall of sound to drown out the tinnitus hiss: there's no brick missing, not a crack in the cement. That one of the characters, Richard, actually suffers from tinnitus himself – a result, one assumes, of years of 'vicious' assault by his punk band The Traumatics – is more an example of the thoroughness of Franzen's trawl than a pointer to a possible cure. We're just sorry for Richard that, being a part of the novel, he can't make use of it as a cure himself. But then that's tinnitus for you. It's on the inside, and though one can find temporary relief, there's ultimately no way out.

T

SEE ALSO: **noise, too much**

tired and emotional, being

The Friday Night Knitting Club
KATE JACOBS

When you're tired and emotional, what you need is a comforting, warm and well-told yarn – the literary equivalent of a hand-knitted afghan wrap. *The Friday Night Knitting Club* is that yarn.

Georgia is the owner of a knitting shop, 'Walker and Daughter', in downtown Manhattan. The single mother of beautiful, engaging Dakota, who is just beginning to spread her adolescent wings, Georgia was abandoned by the charismatic but unpredictable James when she fell pregnant. So when he makes a re-appearance in her life, wanting to make up for all the lost years, she is not exactly thrilled. She's far more interested in ensuring her business stays afloat, and that her Friday night group are all happily looked after and fed (with Dakota's wondrous cookies and muffins).

Because clustered together in Georgia's shop every Friday evening are Darwin, the compulsive documenter of women's feminist movements; Anita, a seventy-year-old widow engaged in a late romance; Petra, a law-student turned handbag designer; and a richly diverse mix of others. Back into this comfortable world rocks her ex James, an architect, whose family are suspicious of Georgia because she's from a different background. Partly to avoid him, at one point Georgia and Dakota cast off to misty Scotland, where Georgia introduces the girl to her grandmother, providing an opportunity for examining the weft of family ties.

Yes, the yarn metaphors come thick and fast, but to read this novel is to be cable-stitched into a great warm skein of wool. The gentle nudges towards granny-ish wisdom will set you back on course to recovery. As Jacobs says, 'Just grasp that yarn between your fingers and twist. Just start. It's the same with life . . .'

SEE ALSO: **cry, in need of a good**

tome, put off by a

CUT IT UP

If you are daunted by books the size of bricks, you'll be missing out on some of the most absorbing reading experiences known to man (see: The Ten Best Big Fat Tomes, below). To overcome your block, break the book up into more manageable chunks. If it's a hardback, stand the book upright and peer down: you'll see that the pages are divided into a number of 'signatures', which are then stitched together. Make your divisions between one signature and the next. The pages of paperbacks are glued to the spine and can be attacked in a more random fashion; you'll need to carry a supply of clothes pegs with you to keep the loose leaves together. Suddenly the big fat tome has metamorphosed into a dozen slim tracts – each about the size of a long short story, and no longer intimidating at all. And don't be too precious about the loose pages, by the way. Once you've read them, throw them away. We're fond of the notion of blithely letting the pages fly one by one out the window of a fast-moving train (although to recommend such littering would be irresponsible). Either way, shrink the book as you read and thus gain the upper hand. Far better a copy of *A Suitable Boy* existing in non-corporeal form inside your head than left intact but destined to spend its life propping open a door.

 THE TEN BEST BIG FAT TOMES

The Brothers K DAVID JAMES DUNCAN
Lanark ALASDAIR GRAY
The Sea of Fertility YUKIO MISHIMA
À la recherche du temps perdu MARCEL PROUST
Gravity's Rainbow THOMAS PYNCHON
A Suitable Boy VIKRAM SETH
Vanity Fair WILLIAM MAKEPEACE THACKERAY
War and Peace LEO TOLSTOY
Kristin Lavransdatter SIGRID UNDSET
Infinite Jest DAVID FOSTER WALLACE

tonsillitis

Gone are the days when they whipped them unceremoniously out. Now it's all about endurance, penicillin and sweat. Apparently you need to keep those beastly organs in the back of your throat so that you can open your mouth and wobble them about if you ever find yourself in a cartoon and need to scream.

When the dreaded tonsillitis strikes, here's a smooth, ice-creamy novel to slip down your throat. *The Empress of Ice Cream* begins in Florence in the seventeenth century when Carlo Demirco, a young boy of lowly origins, comes to assist Ahmad, the Persian ice maker with his craft. Ahmed's secrets have been passed down from his family, and he sticks to the traditional recipes: only four basic flavours (orange, rose-water, mastic, cardamom) can be used to create four different kinds of ice – *cordiale*, *granitte*, *sorbetti* and sherberts.

The magic of ice in those days can barely be imagined. Back then it was carved from glaciers or harvested from frozen rivers and lakes, then ingeniously preserved in ice-houses built for the purpose. In order for the ice cream to reach a low enough temperature, it was mixed with saltpetre. This was quite a science – more a matter of engineering than culinary genius. Carlo is to all intents and purposes a slave, not a servant, with no prospects of rising up the ranks. But he is ambitious, and learns avidly, conducting his own experiments with syrups and fruits: 'Nothing was too outlandish or ridiculous for me to try.' Carlo makes ices from wine, from *pesto genovese*, from almond milk, crushed fennel, and every different kind of cream. He attempts to unlock the deepest, most frozen secrets lurking within ice. Then he takes these secrets into the innermost chambers of the court of Charles II, where sex, sorbets and politics make a potent mix.

Make the continued existence of your tonsils something to celebrate. When tonsillitis strikes, cool them with this syllabub of a story, eating spoonfuls of ice cream as you read.

SEE ALSO: **pain, being in**

toothache

Anna Karenina
LEO TOLSTOY

If you're suffering the exquisite pain of toothache – an ache all the worse for being inside one's head – you will empathise with Vronsky in Tolstoy's *Anna Karenina*: 'He could hardly speak for the throbbing ache in his strong teeth, that were like rows of ivory in his mouth. He was silent, and his eyes rested on the wheels of the tender, slowly and smoothly rolling along the rails.'

What cures Vronsky, in the very next moment, is the displacement of the physical pain by a searing emotional pain; – a memory that sets his 'whole being in anguish' and makes him forget his toothache completely. Looking at the rails, he suddenly recalls *her*, or at least 'what was left of her', when he had found her sprawled on the table in the railway station cloak room, among strangers, her body bloody and limp, the head lolling back with its weight of hair, the eyes awful in their stillness and openness, the mouth still seeming to emit the 'fearful phrase' that she had said when they had quarrelled: that he would be sorry.

If this image of Anna's broken body hasn't done the job, think of another shocking tableau from the pages of literature (for our own favourites, see the cure for hiccups). Then meditate on it while you put a call through to your dentist.

SEE ALSO: **pain, being in**

traffic warden, being a

SEE: **nobody likes you**

trapped by children

The Millstone
MARGARET DRABBLE

Notes from an Exhibition
PATRICK GALE

Sometimes, when we find ourselves seeking refuge in the cupboard beneath the stairs, our children rampaging around the house, we read Margaret Drabble's *The Millstone*, kept there for just such emergencies. Because even the happiest of parents can feel trapped by their children at times.

Rosamund Stacey is catapulted into motherhood by her

very first sexual encounter. She nevertheless has a brisk approach to her pregnancy, and then life with her unplanned child. Because though not initially thrilled to be pregnant – she makes vague, botched attempts to get rid of it (gin, a hot bath) – in the end she 'fails to decide not to have it'. And though she has plenty of other calls on her attention, she becomes utterly devoted to the beautiful creature she produces. So much so that she never feels the millstone around her neck that her friends predict. Suddenly, in our cupboard beneath the stairs, we realise we are not trapped by children, but by love.

You'll find more of this sudden, unexpected joy in Patrick Gale's *Notes from an Exhibition*, in which we meet bipolar mother Rachel. Rachel's way of being a mother is unique. She spends months locked away in her studio, painting and more or less ignoring her children, but then on special days such as birthdays, plunges in with total body and soul, keeping them off school and letting them choose the pleasures of the day. On top of this, she is most inspired artistically when she's not on her medication, and loves being pregnant – when she's forced off the drugs – for this reason. And so through her children, and children-to-be, she heads to her biggest highs.

Of course it's not as easy as that. After the highs come the lows, and the consequences of those live on in the bones of her children. But there's an encouragement here to live more intensely with our children than we, perhaps, always remember to do – to delight in them and celebrate them for whole days at a time.

SEE ALSO: **children requiring attention, too many** • **claustrophobia** • **fatherhood** • **identity crisis** • **jump ship, desire to** • **motherhood** • **single parent, being a**

trust, loss of

In the Cut
SUSANNA MOORE

First of all we have to decide if someone is worthy of our trust or not. Most of us have a fairly good idea of this after one meeting. Trust this first impression. After that, continuing to trust someone when things get bumpy is an act of generosity. When in doubt, remember this: the degree to which you are prepared to trust is a measure of the degree to which others can trust you. Give up on people too easily, and they'll know that you will let them down too.

When you're a single girl in New York with a gift and appreciation for the combative one-liner, you're making decisions about who to trust all the time. When you have an interest in risqué sex, making the right decision can mean the difference between life and death. Frannie teaches English in a special city programme for teenagers with 'low achievement and high intelligence'. A collector of words from Middle English to New York street slang, she enjoys telling her students that she doesn't want to see them spelling motherfucker *mothafucka* – not until they've learnt to do it right. Then, like jazz, they can do what they like and break the rules. She enjoys, too, the fast-talking, anecdote-rich conversation of Detective Malloy who calls on her to investigate the murder of a young actress in her neighbourhood.

Her attraction to Jimmy Malloy is immediate, despite his cheap drug-store cologne, despite the fact that he wears a gold watch stolen from a DOA (dead-on-arrival), despite the ring on his little finger with two hands holding a heart that she dismisses as 'Mick shit'. And she likes the way he 'put[s] it right out there' when he chats her up in a bar.

As Frannie becomes involved with Malloy and meets his colleagues at the homicide bureau, including his partner Detective Rodriguez who carries a yellow plastic water pistol in his holster, the first murder is followed by a second, and the tension ratchets fast. Test yourself with this novel: who would you trust, and when and why would you stop trusting? It's worth getting good at it. As Frannie's fate testifies, one day your life might depend on it.

SEE ALSO: **lying**

T
....
413

turmoil

Home
**MARILYNNE
ROBINSON**

To be in turmoil is to be in a state of great and terrible disturbance. Perhaps you're at a fork in the road and you don't know which way to turn. Overwhelmed and confused, you need to find calm and clarity – the still centre at the eye of the cyclone. Lucid, clear and cool, Marilynne Robinson's prose is that eye.

At the age of thirty-eight, Gloria – Glory to her family – has returned to look after her dying father, a Presbyterian minister, after a disappointment in love. Once she's there, she begins to think the lifestyle suits her, and she discovers some much-needed peace. But then her brother Jack also turns up, after a twenty-year absence.

Jack's prodigal return fills his father with delight – he is a strong, silent type, and has a calm about him. But his silence is a complicated one: dark secrets lurk within it, things that cannot be discussed in front of their dogmatic father, and Glory becomes increasingly troubled by what may or may not come out. However, Glory finds some comfort in his presence too – she remembers how, as a child, Jack taught her the gentle word 'waft' while breathing on a feather. When Jack entered the room, the 'stir of air' had floated the feather out of her hand. He stood in the doorway and watched the feather circle against the ceiling in the air, then caught it lightly in his hand and gave it back to her.

While you let the prose of this novel do its work on your troubled psyche, notice how turmoil coexists with calm in the world it describes. *Home* is that still room in which a single feather can waft unharmed, floating on a gentle current of air, then return to your hand. An elegy to forgiveness, your inner turmoil will be calmed.

SEE ALSO: **anxiety** • **cope, inability to** • **stress**

twenty-something, being

 THE TEN BEST NOVELS FOR TWENTY-SOMETHINGS

Old Man Goriot HONORÉ DE BALZAC
L'Étranger ALBERT CAMUS
The Mysteries of Pittsburgh MICHAEL CHABON
I Cannot Get You Close Enough ELLEN GILCHRIST
The Buddha of Suburbia HANIF KUREISHI
The Group MARY MCCARTHY
Goodbye, Columbus PHILIP ROTH
Requiem for a Dream HUBERT SELBY JR
The Secret History DONNA TARTT
Sexing the Cherry JEANETTE WINTERSON

U

unemployment

Those out of work should make sure to read some quintessential Murakami. Because Murakami, the most popular Japanese novelist to be translated into English, and the most experimental, specialises in passive protagonists (generally male, though gender is irrelevant here), with a lot of time on their hands and a tendency to get themselves mixed up in a series of adventures which may or may not be dreams, hallucinations, or a futuristic cyberpunk mystery plot. *The Wind-Up Bird Chronicle* begins with Toru Okada, who has left his legal job for no particular reason, doing the sort of things one does when unemployed in suburban Tokyo; cooking spaghetti at ten o'clock in the morning, listening to a radio broadcast of Rossini's *The Thieving Magpie*, and fending off his wife Kumiko, who calls to tell him about jobs for which he's unsuited and wouldn't enjoy. He goes out to look for their lost cat, Noboru Wataya, named after Kumiko's brother, with whom he shares the same 'blank stare' (and whom Toru hates, believing him to have sold out to the working world).

The search for the cat leads Toru to two strange women, down a dried-up well, and into the arms of a third strange woman. But none of these things really matter – at least for the purposes of this cure. What matters is Toru's response. Because however bizarre and unconnected the events that happen to Toru, he accepts them with neither surprise nor comment – as we too become trained by the novel to do. And though the meaning of everything eludes him (and us), so what? Perhaps it'll make sense later on (we hope so too).*

Our cure will divide its readers into two camps. If you identify with Toru, delighting in the bizarreness and liberation of the journey, then you are made in the mould of a Murakami hero, and being unemployed suits you well. Enjoy the spaghetti, the Rossini, the dried-up well. Good luck with the search for the cat. Luckily, you have a partner who's employed and can keep you both (though be sure to give her/him some attention or she/he may, like Kumiko, go the way of the cat). But if Toru's unquestioning passivity winds you up like the bird of the title, and you want to know what you're doing down a well and what it all means, then dust yourself down, bid the world of Murakami goodbye, and go back with renewed determination to the 'wanted' ads. Like Noboru Wataya, you're made for the world of work – but take note of what happens to him, and don't sell out (see: selling your soul).

SEE ALSO: **ambition, too little** • **bed, inability to get out of** • **boredom** • **broke, being** • **job, losing your** • **procrastination** • **seize the day, failure to**

unhappiness

SEE: *The Novel Cure* ELLA BERTHOUD AND SUSAN ELDERKIN

unpopular, being

SEE: **traffic warden, being a**

---

* It doesn't.

vanity

The problem with being vain is it makes you selfish and stupid. Scarlett O'Hara, the Southern belle at the heart of *Gone with the Wind*, is so aware of her green-eyed beauty that all she can think of is pretty gowns and winning the heart of not just the man she wants to marry, Ashley Wilkes, but of every young man in the vicinity (much to the annoyance of every other young woman). When she hears that Ashley has become engaged to his cousin Melanie – an undeniably plain girl – she can't believe it. Obsessed as she is with outward beauty, she doesn't rate Melanie's other qualities – or see the need to nurture them in herself. And so she remains stuck as a spoiled, petulant teenager, continuing to use her looks to get what she wants. And, as oblivious to the importance of kindness as she is to the deeply entrenched racial attitudes she sees around her (a quality she seems to share, unfortunately, with the author, and indeed the sympathetic portrayal of slavery is something the reader has to take a big breath and stride over if he/she* is to enjoy this otherwise wonderful novel), she runs roughshod over everyone, including her husband Rhett, before the truth finally dawns. Her friend, the flawless Melanie, has retrospectively won her admiration, respect and love for the same reasons she won Ashley's all those years ago. And it has nothing to do with looks.

---

* Let's not kid ourselves. *She.*

Vanity also makes you ugly in the end. When the incandescently beautiful Dorian Gray starts to realise that everybody loves him for his looks, he becomes so worried about losing them that he pledges his soul for eternal youth (see: selling your soul), arranging that the handsome portrait painted of him by Sir Basil Hallward deteriorates instead. He then embarks on a life of heedless hedonism under the tutelage of Lord Henry Wotton, and when a young actress whose heart he breaks commits suicide, an ugly sneer appears on the portrait. For our face bears testimony not just to the passing of the years, but to the evolving character of the person behind it – and as Dorian's disregard for others leaves more and more human detritus in its wake, his portrait becomes correspondingly hideous.

The inescapable truth is that beauty is on the inside. Treat others as you would like to be treated yourself, and you'll keep blooming into your nineties.

SEE ALSO: **arrogance** • **well-read, desire to seem**

vegetarianism

Cold Mountain
CHARLES
FRAZIER

Every now and again you bean-lovers need to get down off your high horses and admit that death is an undeniable part of life. Eating only living things that grow from the soil is all very worthy, but the body cries out for blood every now and then. And although we admit that much modern meat is farmed in reprehensible ways, there are times – not least when you find yourself out in the wild without a picnic – when it might just be imperative to snack on a beast.

This is something that Inman, the fantastically masculine protagonist of *Cold Mountain*, knows better than most. Inman's odyssey takes him from the Confederate Military Hospital in Petersburg across America to North Carolina, where he hopes to be reunited with the woman who holds his heart. He walks all the way, avoiding roads for fear of reconscription into the Confederate army. He needs to eat, and his adventures largely spring from his attempts to procure himself a meal: stealing a basket of bread and cheese from women washing at a river, saving a widow's hog from the Feds and eating its brains, and shooting a bear cub whose mother has died (which leaves him with the taste of regret).

Halfway through his travels he meets a 'goat woman' who has lived in a rust-coloured caravan surrounded by her herd for twenty-five years. Her relationship with her animals is one of total symbiosis, and when she strokes the goat she cradles in her arms, then gently slices its throat, its dying is portrayed as a completely natural part of the cycle of life, by no means cruel or wasteful, but loving and respectful. Inman leaves the goat-woman's caravan with a belly full of two-toned goat, and forges on towards his beloved Ada clutching a drawing the goat-woman gave him of a carrion flower plant. The carrion flower emits a stink of rotten flesh in order to attract its pollinators – carrion-eating beetles and flesh flies – and serves as a reminder of the tricks nature plays on itself to survive. With this, Frazier puts us carnivores firmly into the natural order of things.

vengeance, seeking

Wuthering Heights
EMILY BRONTË

Taking revenge is always a bad idea. It sets in motion a chain reaction of revenge and counter-revenge that inevitably escalates in severity and becomes extremely hard to stop.

Such a domino effect is played out in full, terrible glory on the tormented, windswept moors of Emily Brontë's *Wuthering Heights*. When Mr Earnshaw, lord of Wuthering Heights, brings the orphan Heathcliff into his home, his own children, Hindley and Catherine, resent it (see: sibling rivalry). And when Mr Earnshaw starts favouring Heathcliff over Hindley (while Catherine and Heathcliff fall in childish love), Hindley is even more put out and takes revenge on Heathcliff. Seeing this, Mr Earnshaw takes revenge on Hindley by sending his son away to college, and shortly afterwards he takes revenge on all of them by dying. Hindley inherits Wuthering Heights, and immediately sets about taking revenge on Heathcliff by re-installing himself (and his new wife Frances) at Wuthering Heights and sending Heathcliff out to work in the fields. Frances dies giving birth to a boy named Hareton* and Hindley becomes a gambler and hits the bottle, and in his drunkenness takes revenge on Heathcliff even more. At about this time, Cathy, despite loving Heathcliff, marries Edgar Linton, who lives with his sister Isabella on the other side of the moor at Thrushcross Grange, and Heathcliff takes revenge on Cathy by running away. Then he comes back and takes revenge on Hindley by arranging for Hindley's son Hareton's education to be discontinued, so that the boy grows up illiterate. He also lends money to Hindley so that Hindley gambles and drinks even more and eventually dies. Heathcliff inherits Wuthering Heights and then gets his revenge on Cathy for marrying Edgar by marrying Edgar's sister Isabella, which means he's in line to inherit Thrushcross Grange should Edgar die. He is vile to Isabella as a way of getting revenge on Edgar for marrying Cathy. Then Cathy, who lives at Thrushcross Grange, gives birth to a daughter named Catherine and dies† and Heathcliff runs over the moor wishing he had not taken revenge on Cathy, or she on him, and shortly afterwards Isabella takes revenge on Heathcliff by running away to London and giving birth to a boy named Linton.‡ We then fast-forward thirteen years to when Cathy's daughter Catherine crosses the moor from Thrushcross Grange to Wuthering Heights and meets Hareton, Hindley and Frances's illiterate son. Then Isabella dies§ and Linton goes to live with Heathcliff at Wuthering Heights. Heathcliff is horrible to him, presumably in revenge against everybody. Then Catherine meets Linton at Wuthering Heights and they fall in love, although it turns out that Heathcliff has talked Linton into seducing Catherine because if Linton and Catherine marry, Linton will inherit Thrushcross Grange

V

---

* Frances's dying could be interpreted as her taking revenge on her newborn child for the pain he inflicted on her. It's just an idea.

† Cathy's death could be interpreted as an act of revenge on Heathcliff for taking revenge on her by marrying Isabella.

‡ Interestingly, Isabella does not die after giving birth. This could be interpreted as her taking revenge on Heathcliff. However, she does die later.

§ See?

as well as Wuthering Heights and Heathcliff's revenge on Edgar Linton will be complete. One day Heathcliff holds Catherine prisoner at Wuthering Heights until she marries Linton. Soon after, Catherine's father Edgar Linton dies and then so does Linton, perhaps in revenge on Heathcliff for forcing him to marry Catherine. Heathcliff therefore inherits Thrushcross Grange and forces Catherine to live at Wuthering Heights with him and Hareton.* While Catherine and Hareton fall in love, Cathy's ghost continues to take revenge on Heathcliff by driving him mad and one wild night Heathcliff dies, presumably in revenge on Cathy, but also in revenge on himself. Hareton and Catherine inherit Wuthering Heights and Thrushcross Grange and decide to get married and the reader takes revenge on Emily Brontë (who had intended to write a novel about the madness of taking revenge†) by gunning for Heathcliff all the way through because of his overwhelming love for Cathy, despite the fact that he's been vile and taken revenge on absolutely everybody ever since Hindley first took revenge on him for something that wasn't, in fact, his fault.

Do you see? Don't do it. The revenge that comes back to you will be worse than the revenge you inflicted in the first place – and it may start a cycle of vengeance that goes on all your life.

SEE ALSO: **anger** • **bitterness** • **murderous thoughts** • **rage**

* We are not sure if this is an act of revenge, or if it is, who it is an act of revenge against.
† This is not actually true. However before you take revenge on us by hurling your copy of *The Novel Cure* out the window, we should point out that it's thought that Brontë intended the novel to be a warning against loving too deeply, and if this is the case, then the fact that the reader guns for Heathcliff because he's such a romantic still means that Brontë's intention has backfired and the claim that the reader is therefore taking revenge on Brontë for writing about love so well still stands.

violence, fear of

There is violence from without, and violence from within. Let's deal with the latter first. Most of us are aware that every now and then in a flash of rage we have a brief fantasy of committing a violent act. Most of us quash it immediately. But if you find the urge to lash out physically hard to resist, and harder to stop thinking about, this novel will allow you to explore your inner violent streak vicariously.

Stevenson's famous novel is a deep excavation of the latent possibility of violence within us. Dr Jekyll, a respectable doctor and experimental scientist living in London, has long been fascinated by the opposing natures of man, and decides to divide his own two natures using a home-made drug. The temporary schism will allow his dark side to operate independently of his moral, respectable self. And because he looks completely different when he transforms into Hyde – shorter, hairier, younger – Jekyll need not answer to the consequences of Hyde's actions.

Most of what Hyde gets up to we don't actually witness – his ominous disappearances, sometimes lasting several months, remain shrouded in mystery. But we soon gather that he is a monster, capable of the utmost depravity. As Hyde begins to dominate Jekyll, making it harder and harder for Jekyll to maintain his respectable façade, the potion that changes the doctor from one to the other starts to run out. Soon he can no longer control whether he's Jekyll or Hyde.

The message is clear: allow your inner violence an inch and it will take a mile. This novel will fill you with disgust for the urge to hurt another human being. Read it and stamp out any potential for violence within you once and for all.

If it's the violence of others you fear, acquire the strength of a samurai by osmosis. Eiji Yoshikawa's epic novel *Musashi* is about the noble pursuit of samurai swordsmanship – a nine-hundred-page masterpiece that takes you on a journey from punishing mountain-top training rituals with Zen Buddhist teachers to the battlefields of sixteenth-century Japan and thence to the discovery of love, humility and wisdom.

V

Our impressive hero eventually realises that actually committing a violent act is the last thing he ever wants to do. But the knowledge of his inner strength means that he'll never need to. Absorb the legend of Musashi. Let his fearlessness – if not his martial art prowess – rub off on you. If you can emulate his inner confidence and unconquerable demeanour even to a tenth of a degree, would-be aggressors will leave you well alone.

SEE ALSO: **confrontation, fear of** • **murderous thoughts** • **rage**

W

wagon, falling off the

SEE: **alcoholism**

waiting room, being in a

*The Stars My
Destination*
ALFRED BESTER

Waiting rooms mean hospitals, doctor's surgeries, dentists, train stations, bus depots, airports. Joyless, drab, stained with worry, echoing despair. It is crucial to be armed for this dead zone with the perfect novel cure.

Which is Alfred Bester's hugely influential 1956 novel *The Stars My Destination*, precursor of William Gibson's *Neuromancer*, and anticipator of the cyberpunk movement of the 1980s (characterised by the cybernetic enhancement of the body, the power of metacorporations, and a generally bleak view of the future). What makes it perfect fodder for a waiting room, however, is Bester's unique addition to this cyberpunk mix, the 'jaunte'. Developed unintentionally by a man named Jaunte, it describes the technique of transporting yourself to another location – as long as you have the co-ordinates of where you are now, and where you are going to, and can visualise your destination. You can jaunte anywhere on this planet, either instantly or, if your jaunting ability is distance-limited, in stages. The only limits are space – it is impossible to jaunte through a vacuum. Because jaunting is all about the mind. It works by focussing very clearly, and *willing* the leap through longitude and latitude. At least until

Gully Foyle comes along, who will eventually challenge the entire system with his dauntless roaming through the galaxies.

The novel is set in the twenty-fifth century when Gully, the sole survivor of an unexplained catastrophe, is clinging to life in the only airtight room left intact in the wreck of his spaceship the *Nomad*. His locker is four feet wide, four feet deep, and nine feet high – a 'lightless coffin' in which he's been incarcerated for five months, twenty days, and four hours. When a ship appears in space that could save him, Gully is galvanised into action – but the *Vorga* passes him by. Gully swears vengeance, and this is what drives him to survive. When we next see Gully, he is at a jaunte training school back on Earth, playing AWOL with his co-ordinates and going whole countries further than he is strictly allowed.

As you read this in your waiting room, be grateful that it is a little bigger than 'four by four by nine'. Harness the power of your mind and feel possibilities surge through you as you imagine all the places you would jaunte to if you could. You may not get your jaunte certificate, but you may discover, like Gully, new skills waiting to be used in the chambers of your mind.

SEE ALSO: **anxiety** • **boredom**

wanderlust

The Alexandria Quartet
LAWRENCE DURRELL

So you are gripped by the desire to go to Africa.* For the sake of argument, let's say that you want specifically to go to Egypt.* And within Egypt, the city that enthrals you, calls to you, is Alexandria,* the city founded by Alexander the Great.*

Reader, consider the expense. First of all there's all the things you will have to buy in advance: the luggage, the

---

* Replace as required with relevant country/city/founder/transport method/tourist attraction/climate, and with the relevant novel cure from the Ten Best list. Please note that these novels have been chosen for their length (i.e. their capacity to incapacitate for a fortnight or three weeks at a time), as well as their ability to transport the reader without leaving home.

digital camera, the safari trousers, etc. It all adds up. And then there's the cost (and let's not forget the environmental cost, too) of the flight. At either end there will be trains, taxis, trams, camels,* feluccas.* Then there are the hotel bills – and if you're anything like us, you'll convince yourself you should stay in the nicest room that you can find, so you can make the most of it, splash out a bit, now that you've come all this way. And we haven't even begun to add up the cost of the food – three meals a day, in restaurants and cafés – and the mosquito repellent and medicines. And what about the shopping? You will almost certainly want to buy an expensive shawl or rug or bowl, as a souvenir. And go on excursions – to the pyramids,* the Red Sea,* the desert.* Again, now that you've come all this way.

Consider, also, the discomfort. Alexandria* in the height of summer is stiflingly hot.* And at night it can be freezing cold*. And that's not even to start on the winds.*

And finally consider the strain of all this on your relationship with your travelling companions. Hot, tired, perhaps suffering from digestive trouble, you will be at your most irritable – and so will they. Only the naïve would expect to come home from such a trip with their marriage/friendship intact.

Now consider the alternative. Stay at home and read about Alexandria in the first three volumes of the *Alexandria Quartet*: *Justine*, *Balthazar* and *Mountolive* (skipping, for now, the fourth, which is set in Corfu). Together with the narrator Darley, your guides to the city will be Alexandrian natives: the vain, goddess-like Justine, magnificent with her dark skin and white dresses, every particle the Alexandrian society woman; her husband, the humourless but faithful Prince Nessim; the fragile, sickly Melissa; the serene, solitary artist Clea; and Balthazar with his 'deep croaking voice of great beauty', yellow goat-eyes, and monstrous hands. Darley himself, an itinerant schoolteacher, falls in love with them all.

W

427

And, as you visit every corner of this dusty city in their company, wandering aimlessly from the cafés to the sandy beaches in the fast-fading afternoon light, so will you. The best way to know Alexandria is to know its people – Durrell believed we are formed by the place we're from, but also that we then inform that place further – and Justine's temperament is part of the city's microclimate. Luxuriate in the layers, then, of the characters and the city they cannot exist without. By the time you emerge, you will understand this ancient city a thousand times better than if you had taken a two-week package tour, spent your money on tourist tat and come home with sunburn and a case of VD.

 THE TEN BEST NOVELS TO CURE WANDERLUST

Save the planet and your pocket by travelling the world from your armchair.

Guyana: The Sly Company of People Who Care RAHUL BHATTACHARYA
Burma/India: The Glass Palace AMITAV GHOSH
Spain: For Whom the Bell Tolls ERNEST HEMINGWAY
Japan: Snow Country YASUNARI KAWABATA
Australia: Kangaroo DH LAWRENCE
Trinidad: Is Just a Movie EARL LOVELACE
Libya: In the Country of Men HISHAM MATAR
USA: The Razor's Edge W SOMERSET MAUGHAM
France: Good Morning, Midnight JEAN RHYS
Honduras: The Mosquito Coast PAUL THEROUX

SEE ALSO: **itchy feet**

wardrobe crisis

Fabulous Nobodies
LEE TULLOCH

Many of us face this ailment at the start of every day. Gazing at a chaos of bobbly, hole-ridden, ill-fitting and faded relics, alongside a few classy numbers completely unsuitable for everyday wear, we shiver in our undies trying and discarding random alternatives one by one. As we slip resignedly into whatever we had on the day before, we dream of that ideal outfit, the one that's comfortable yet well-made, flattering yet relaxed – and can take us anywhere. Or, even better, a perfectly thought-out collection of stunning, co-ordinated pieces for every occasion, plus lots of clever accessories. If this fantasy strikes a chord, *Fabulous Nobodies* is the novel for you.

Reality Nirvana Tuttle has a huge responsibility. As fashion enforcement officer at the Less Is More Club in Manhattan, she must let in the fabulous, and turn away the unfabulous. Reality, known as Really to her friends, is incorruptible when it comes to fashion fabulousness. Anyone wearing angora, acrylic or peach chiffon is *out*. Anyone wearing Thierry Mugler or an old Pucci print is *in*. And on top of that, Reality has to recognise the Somebodies who look like unfabulous Nobodies, and let them in too – because we all have days where we look unfabulous even when we are, actually, fabulous.

Reality could come across as an insufferable fashion victim, but for her endearing love affair with frocks, and her genuine concern for her style-challenged acolytes. She calls her dresses by name, and communes with their different personalities: Françoise, with *haute couture* status, is always the first to want to party, and the first to want to come home; Gina is a vivacious Italian with red and white polka dots, cinched waist and shoestring straps; and Anita, Really's miracle dress, is eminently reliable while also enjoyably flirtatious.

You'll learn a lot from Reality Tuttle. Not only will she steer you through common fashion mistakes, but she'll open your eyes to the potential for the clothes in your wardrobe to be your friends. As with friends, you'll need to choose well – and then look after them, appreciating their special qualities, and finding ways to support and encourage what they do best. Ultimately the novel acknowledges the folly and absurdity of fashion; but clothes are a fact of life. Get to know your own wardrobe inside out. Identify and source any omissions. Throw the useless ones away.* With Reality as your guide, you'll never be at a loss first thing in the morning again.

W

---

* Actually, don't. Remember, each frock has its own voice, and what doesn't work for you will work for someone else. Take them to a charity shop instead.

wasting time on a dud relationship

The Transit of Venus
SHIRLEY HAZZARD

It is deeply painful watching a character you have come to love throw themselves away on someone unworthy. We grieve for the loss of their potential, and for their self-inflicted pain – because anyone in love with someone undeserving of them is bound to suffer eventually – and we yearn to see them come to their senses and move on. And yet, for reasons that are often unclear, we are often just as prone to the same error. Though at some level we may feel grief for ourselves, we often fail to act on it, to rescue ourselves as we would rescue others.

We require victims of this sorry predicament – and you'll know who you are – to fall in love with Caroline Bell, a grave, raven-haired beauty, and watch her suffer in the inferior embrace of Paul Ivory. Caro, as we come to know her, is one of two orphaned Australian sisters who have emigrated to 1950s London to take up new lives – Grace into a conservative marriage and kids, Caro into a government job and independence. Caro is loved – devotedly, hopelessly – by Ted Tice, a working-class academic with an unfortunate line in Fair Isle jumpers (see: taste, bad). But it is the tall, graceful and upper-class Paul to whom she succumbs – a dashing young playwright tipped for great things, whose easy manner and pleasure in his own good health and good looks makes him bound to outshine his red-haired rival.

When they meet Paul is engaged – and soon marries – Tertia, heiress to a castle. But he is drawn to Caro's 'sombre glow', and their mutual attraction is over-powering. We know from the start that he is not good enough for Caro. Dazzled by his own success, his shallowness evidenced by his marriage to the empty-eyed Tertia, they both know Caro sees through him, and that her love is mixed with contempt. A better man would insist she get on with her life, that their affair can come to nothing (see: adultery); but she cannot seem to resist the visceral pull to his city bedsit.

What drives home the anguish we feel for Caro's wasted years is Shirley Hazzard's extraordinary prose: dense to the point of ellipsis, it requires all one's attention to read.

You will find yourself forced to submit, and learn, as from a teacher of great authority. Hazzard is a masterly writer who dissects emotions with surgical precision, and will elevate you to new levels of emotional understanding. By the end of *The Transit of Venus* you will be a more sophisticated person than you were at the start – just as Paul saw his capacity to feel extended through association with the deeper, more substantial Caro.

There'll also be no more self-deception. With your new standards of honesty, new ranges of emotion, you'll see your dud relationship for what it is. Ache for Caro as you read, but as soon as you've turned the last page, ache for yourself. Then cut your losses and run before it's too late.

SEE ALSO: **love, doomed** • **Mr/Mrs Right, holding out for** • **Mr/Mrs Wrong, ending up with**

wedding

SEE: **broke, being** • **children, under pressure to have** • **jealousy** • **single, being** • **shelf, fear of being left on the** • **wardrobe crisis**

widowed, being

The Same Sea
AMOS OZ

The Widow's Tale
MICK JACKSON

Major Pettigrew's Last Stand
HELEN SIMONSON

Do not underestimate the enormity of what you are going through. To lose one's life partner is to see set in motion a series of seismic shifts in every department of your life. Before, you had a companion; now you live alone. Before, you were – perhaps – one half of a set of parents; now you are parenting alone. Your relationship to your child or children will undergo some changes. As will the relationships with your friends. And you will also have to build a new relationship to yourself. Because without that other person to prop you up, fill you out, add whatever it was they added to your sense of self, you will sometimes wonder who you are.

To help you navigate these sad and difficult times, we offer you Israeli author Amos Oz's transcendentally beautiful prose-poem, *The Same Sea*. Written in short, gentle

well-read, desire to seem

While we sympathise with your desire – a well-read individual, particularly of novels, is likely to be more balanced, more mature, and of course more interesting to talk to* – we do not condone this pitiful failure of integrity. Like Nick, the narrator of *The Great Gatsby*, who after embarking on a career in the city buys 'a dozen volumes' that promise to unfold the secrets of 'Midas and Morgan and Maecenas', you probably have every intention of reading the books you claim to have read already. And maybe you will. But the chances are you'll be bluffing next time too.

The good news is that you don't have to have read *that many* books in order to seem well-read – and even strikingly so. You just have to pick the right ones. The following ten will stand you in excellent stead for a lifetime of good first impressions. With luck, by the time you read to the end of this list, you'll have acquired the taste for more.

THE TEN BEST NOVELS FOR SEEMING WELL-READ

The first five are simply essential; the second five will imply the existence of vast literary landscapes in your head.

Essentials
Wuthering Heights **EMILY BRONTË**
The Great Gatsby **F SCOTT FITZGERALD**
The Magic Mountain **THOMAS MANN**
Moby Dick **HERMAN MELVILLE**
War and Peace **LEO TOLSTOY**

Icing on the cake
The Recognitions **WILLIAM GADDIS**
Independent People **HALLDÓR LAXNESS**
The Radetzky March **JOSEPH ROTH**
Voss **PATRICK WHITE**
Beware of Pity **STEFAN ZWEIG**

* Not that we are biased or smug.

vignettes, it tells the story of Albert Danon, a 'mild' account-ant whose wife Nadia has died of cancer. Their only son, Rico, has taken himself off to Tibet, thinking the world needs some sorting out, leaving his girlfriend Dita to look in on his dad. Albert, to his shame, does not have an entirely platonic reaction to pretty, bold Dita in her short orange skirt, and when she suddenly finds herself homeless he invites her to move in to his spare room. Meanwhile Albert's friend Bet-tine – herself widowed for twenty years – keeps a watchful eye on the pair, not without a vested interest.

In times of grief and loneliness, we must take life moment by moment. And this is how Oz proceeds, captur-ing with wondrous clarity the time-suspended moment be-tween Albert turning off the computer and going to bed; or the moment when Nadia, woken in the night by a blackbird, wonders who she will be when she dies; or the moment when Bettina lays her cards on the table. Oz gives equal attention to the banal and the beautiful, the touching and the inap-propriately lustful, side by side. For sensitive, understanding company that allows you access to the vast and complicated terrains of emotion inside your heart, *The Same Sea* can't be beat.

The Widow's Tale by Mick Jackson offers an opportu-nity to reflect on this remaking of the self by examining the past – this time from the widow's point of view. The widow herself remains unnamed, but through diaries and interior monologue we know her every thought. Wry, humorous, and mildly aggrieved, she is angry at the way her husband died and directs her anger, uselessly, at him. Her way of dealing with it is to flee to the Norfolk coast, where she rents a cot-tage and, under the pretence of being a birdwatcher, begins spying obsessively on the house of a former love, fantasis-ing about the life she could have had with this other man.

Her behaviour may seem bizarre – but her stint as a stalk-er turns out to be cathartic. In her attempt to re-awaken a largely fictitious affair it makes her realise the good things she had in her marriage, and purges her of the negative emo-tions that were threatening to swamp her memories. Let this novel encourage you to examine both the good and the bad in your years of marriage, accepting and forgiving the past and leaving you with an honest, open heart.

Because new beginnings are always possible, however jaded we might feel. In *Major Pettigrew's Last Stand*, Major Pettigrew – a retired military man in the stiff-upper-lip mould – is about as rigid in his habits as a man can get. But when, after losing his wife, he also loses his brother, the sixty-eight-year-old major is so tripped up by grief that he begins to see the familiar in a different light – including the kindly Mrs Ali, the woman who runs the village shop. On the surface the two could not be more different, but they're drawn together by their mutual widowhood, clashes with their similarly small-minded families and a shared love of books, particularly Kipling. Anyone reading the book that you are holding in your hands will appreciate this as a basis for a new relationship – and it may encourage you to leave the door open, just a crack.

SEE ALSO: **death of a loved one** • **loneliness** • **sadness** • **single, being** • **yearning, general**

wind, having

SEE: **flatulence**

words, lost for

Lolita
**VLADIMIR
NABOKOV**

If you're lost for words because you're in shock, wait for the shock to pass and the words will return. If the words won't come because you have a stutter or a stammer, see: speech impediment. But if you're lost for words because eloquence is not your strength, and the right words seem to desert you whenever you need them most, then take as your companion the narrator of *Lolita*, Humbert Humbert, a man who is as far from being afflicted with this ailment as a person can get.

By rights Humbert Humbert – or HH as we shall call him – should be the one shamed into silence. He has used a young girl for the selfish pursuit of his own illicit pleasures.

But instead, as he waits in prison for the trial that will determine his fate, words are his greatest friend. In fact HH can't wait to speak. Here, in prison, he no longer has to keep secret the despicable self he has been repressing all these years. At last he can indulge in the rapturous specifics of what, and who, he has loved.

And one of those things is language. To HH, words are a plaything: he loves allusions and double meanings, and finds in them both a catharsis and outlet for his humour. But they are also a tool of seduction – and this time it's the reader who's being seduced. From the very first paragraph, with its sensuous dismantling of her name into its three delectable syllables, 'Lo-lee-ta', we are as entranced by his descriptions of Lolita as he is by the girl himself. We want more of this 'exasperating brat' because we want more of the language in which she's revealed to us. Thus ensnared into the rhapsody, tainted by the joint titillation, how can we condemn HH without condemning ourselves? Such is Nabokov's cunning game. By the end, we are captivated by this confession of rape, murder, paedophilia and incest, with its 'bits of marrow sticking to it, and blood, and beautiful bright-green flies'. Nabokov has made a sordid thing into a work of art.

What separates you, tongue-tied and anxious-eyed, from Humbert Humbert – erudite, literary, a French speaker with a predilection for *le mot juste* as well as little girls – is that this loquacious criminal has an unwavering sense of his right to speak. Borrow that right from HH. Steep yourself in his elegant rhythms – though not his inelegant activities. Think of words – though not nymphets – as your playthings, as sources of private and shared amusement. Let his charm – though not his charming of young girls – become your charm, tripping off your tongue from the palate to the tip 'to tap, at three, on the teeth', giving your anxious tongue licence, at last, to speak.

workaholism

When life has shrunk to the size of your desk and all you seem to do is meet deadlines, tick off tasks (see: organised, being too) and put yourself in recovery position in readiness for the next day, you need to immerse your desiccated soul in something very simple, very rustic, very small. We suggest Hardy's gentlest, most innocent novel, *Under the Greenwood Tree*. The members of the Mellstock parish choir are a motley crew. Gathering in rain or shine with their fiddles to sing and play – a labour of love not money – they have not forgotten the important things in life: a little music, a little cider, a gathering of young and old alike.

Life is about more than work. Step outside your office and take a look. And once you're outside, take a life lesson from a character who is the antithesis to all things overly laboured: Snufkin, the unacknowledged hero of the Moomintroll novels. Snufkin is the mysterious wanderer/poet/musician who appears in Moominvalley every spring, complete with hat and harmonica. Moomintroll always waits for him, and feels that spring has only really arrived when Snufkin comes. But he is not someone you can count on. 'I'll come when it suits me,' says Snufkin, and 'perhaps I shan't come at all. I just may set off in another direction entirely.'

An idler extraordinaire, Snufkin's philosophy is irresistible. He travels light; his suitcase is almost empty. He would rather get to know an object thoroughly, then leave it behind, than carry it around with him. He will pitch his tent wherever the fancy takes him. Go out on the open road with your feather in your cap, like Snufkin. The world is a 'wonderfully splendid' place, with a lot more in it besides desks.

SEE ALSO: **busy, being too** • **busy to read, being too** • **cope, inability to** • **exhaustion** • **high blood pressure** • **obsession** • **selling your soul** • **stress**

work, not having any

SEE: **unemployment**

worry

SEE: **anxiety**

writer's block

I Capture the Castle
DODIE SMITH

The remedy for writer's block inflicted upon the novelist-father in *I Capture the Castle* is nothing short of genius. But – darn it – to tell it would be to give away one of the plot twists in this unutterably charming novel. Mortmain, as he is known by his second wife Topaz, achieved great critical success with an experimental novel called *Jacob Wrestling*. But he has not been able to put pen to paper since an unfortunate incident involving a next-door-neighbour who foolishly intervened when Mortmain brandished a cake-knife at his first wife while they were having tea in the garden. He ended up spending three months behind bars, writer's block set in, and the family has been penniless ever since.

While Topaz and the three children struggle to feed and clothe themselves and their ruined castle crumbles around them, Mortmain drifts around reading detective novels and the Encyclopaedia Britannica, and staring into space. He's ditched all his friends and more or less stopped talking to his family. Eventually Rose, the elder daughter, can stand it no more and decides to marry her way out of poverty. But the younger, wiser narrator-daughter Cassandra soon realises it's time to force their father's writing hand. Her plan – which involves a Freudian regression to the moment at which the block began – works to a T.

Sufferers of this unfortunate condition should not necessarily attempt to copy Cassandra's cure. It is somewhat extreme and in any case would not work with your own consent. But read between the lines of this book and a fuller, more complete picture of how Mortmain's block disperses will emerge. As you read, gather the things you need around you: a person of like mind, someone to do the cooking and, yes, the Encyclopaedia Britannica.

Feedback on the success rate of this remedy would be greatly appreciated.

xenophobia

If you find yourself fearing or even loathing those from countries other than your own, bathe in these books from foreign parts. Written by authors native to the settings, they reveal the essential sameness of us all beneath the skin, and will remind you of the humanity common to us all.

 THE TEN BEST NOVELS TO CURE THE XENOPHOBIC

Once Upon a River BONNIE JO CAMPBELL
See Under: Love DAVID GROSSMAN
The Blind Owl SADEGH HEDAYAT
Waltenberg HÉDI KADDOUR
Cities of Salt ABDELRAHMAN MUNIF
Q&A VIKAS SWARUP
Harp of Burma MICHIO TAKEYAMA
House of Day, House of Night OLGA TOKARCZUK
Cutting for Stone ABRAHAM VERGHESE
The Garlic Ballads MO YAN

Y

yearning, for home

SEE: **homesickness**

yearning, general

Silk
**ALESSANDRO
BARICCO**

To long – painfully, endlessly, fruitlessly – for something which you believe will satisfy a need in you that won't go away, is a painful, endless, fruitless way to spend your life, and irritating to all who have to witness it. Life is too short for such things. Luckily, we have a cure so short that we needn't spend much time prescribing it, and you won't spend much time administering it.

It is not that Hervé Joncour doesn't appreciate his loving wife Héléne, who waits for him patiently when he makes his annual, hazardous trip by land and sea to the Japanese village of Shirakawa to smuggle back silkworm eggs – an illegal trade at the time. It is just that were it not for the yearning he feels for the young concubine who captures his heart in Shirakawa – and with whom he exchanges only missives written in Japanese – he would have appreciated her even more. Do not prize what you do not know above what you know. Love your real life companion (see: married, being, if that feels hard) rather than your distant, impossible dream.

SEE ALSO: **dissatisfaction**

Z

zestlessness

Ragtime
EL DOCTOROW

Zestlessness is a notoriously difficult ailment to diagnose. Easily confused with boredom (which is really a failure of the imagination, see: boredom) and apathy (which manifests as physical sluggishness though it too has an emotional cause, see: apathy), zestlessness can appear, to the untrained eye, to be simply a case of having a dull personality. Left untreated, it can ruin entire lives – and we're not just talking your own. To live without zest is to live without an appetite for new experiences; to miss out on the spice, the juice, the edge that makes life thrilling. It is to live with deadened, flattened senses, with your passions unaroused and your curiosity untapped. It is to depress the hell out of those around you – and, frankly, us too. Do us all a favour. Read this novel and switch yourself on.

Ragtime takes as its subject the dawn of the twentieth century in America – a time when the entire nation was in the exhilarated grip of commotion, invention and change. Sparkling new railroads sprung up across the country. Model T Fords spilled off the assembly lines. Twenty-five-storey buildings shot people skywards, and aircraft zoomed them away. Telephones and the press were abuzz with new ways of communicating. Skyrockets and cherry bombs exploded in the skies. In ordinary homes, sneezing powder and squirting plastic roses tickled people's noses and made them laugh.

In amongst all this is the story of a well-to-do family in New Rochelle, New York. The son (known simply as 'the little boy'), is fixing his gaze on a bluebottle crossing a fly screen one day when Harry Houdini crashes his car outside and is invited in for tea. Soon after, Mother discovers a black baby in the garden, and takes the child in – so breaking the first of several cultural and gender taboos. When Father returns from an expedition to the Arctic to find her running his fireworks business, he becomes increasingly alienated from the domestic scene, and the family begins to fall apart.

By turning his lens from vivid close-up to great, sweeping vista and allowing real and fictional characters to meet at the junctions of a vast, complex cobweb, EL Doctorow injects the novel – and the reader – with enormous zest. As immigrants from Italy and Eastern Europe, such as Tateh and his beautiful daughter, pour into squalid tenements on the Lower East Side, the financier JP Morgan sets new standards of wealth and power, and Houdini defies death with more and more terrifying feats. Freud puts America on the couch, and the boy's uncle, known as Mother's Younger Brother, stalks the country's first sex goddess, Evelyn Nesbit.

As you read, notice how Mother and the little boy say 'yes' to progress and change. Watch how Father, conversely, says 'no', refusing to move with the times. Like Tateh, let the tumult and tumble of Doctorow's startling sentences remove you from what is familiar and failing. Board the train to a new life. Take with you the boy's curiosity for recent inventions. Appropriate Grandad's joy at the sight of spring (though take care, if you're over seventy, that you don't slip and break your pelvis, as he does, doing a spontaneous jig). Be in a place where change is a given, and feel the zest flood back in.

SEE ALSO: **disenchantment**

EPILOGUE

The Reader had just opened a new book – Malory's *Le Morte d'Arthur*, perhaps, or Spenser's *The Faerie Queene*, as it was Medieval Literature that first term – when there was a knock at the door. 'Come in!' she called, a little absently, for she was gone with the gentle knights and damsels. Somewhat rudely she did not look up when the door opened but kept her eyes trained on the page. But then a joyful 'He*llo*!' broke her reading bubble. There, in a kaleidoscope of mismatched colours and patterns, stood the Other Reader. She held a steaming mug in each hand.

The first – and for a while, the only – thing the Reader noticed about her were her eyes. Swathes of turquoise, pink, green and gold spanned outwards from her eyes to her brows as if she were an iridescent fish. A fish that was delighted to see her – that was in fact bestowing on her the sort of crazed smile one generally reserves for one's Siamese twin, tragically detached at birth but who has now, eighteen years later, unexpectedly moved into the room next door.

In an instant, the Reader decided to love her back.

'I see I've interrupted you in the middle of *The Faerie Queene*,' said the Other Reader, handing her a mug of black coffee (she took it black from that day on). 'Do you feel you're lacking in Virtues? Good *god*.'

Her eyes, which of course had been scanning the bookshelves, had come to rest on a copy of *If on a Winter's Night a Traveller* which had been strategically positioned at one end (next to *The Unbearable Lightness of Being*, *The Bell Jar*, *The House of the Spirits* – you get the picture) so that its title could be seen by anyone casually passing the open door. The Other Reader put down her coffee, took the Calvino and turned it over lovingly in her hands. 'The horror of not being able to finish the story – of being interrupted just at the moment when it is at its most gripping – that feeling of complete desperation at wanting to know what happens next – ' she began.

The Other Reader looked at the Reader, breathlessly. The Reader could only nod, solemnly – because this had become, suddenly, the first really important moment of her life involving someone to whom she wasn't, in fact, related. She reached out her hand and the Other Reader passed the book to her, and she flipped through until she had found the bit she loved the most, the bit that describes all the different categories of books in a bookshop, the 'Books That If You Had More Than One Life You Would Certainly Also Read but Unfortunately Your Days Are Numbered', and the 'Books That Everybody's Read So It's As If You Had Read Them, Too' and the Other Reader said, 'Yes! Yes!' and began to laugh, and so she laughed as well, and the Other Reader grabbed the book back, and flipped through until, increasingly desperate, she too found the bit she wanted, the bit where the way we circle a book before we read it is described, scanning the blurb, touching the cover, how that's like the foreplay before sex, and this projects us into the consummation, which is of course the act of reading itself. Reading it aloud, the Other Reader burst out laughing again, because she found the sexual metaphor somewhat embarrassing considering the short duration of their friendship, but the Reader was laughing too and she snatched the book back again because she hadn't finished reading the bit about the bookshop, the bit that, she felt sure, the Other Reader would love as much as she did, where it describes the way all the books you *didn't* buy look at you tragically as you leave with a different book, like the rejected dogs in the dog pound. And in her determination to reclaim the book, she pulled a bit too hard, and for a moment the book threatened to tear along the spine between them, and they were both struck, simultaneously, with what a strange irony this would be, if the book were to be separated into two halves and could no longer be read, interrupted just before the climax, or just after, just as the books within the book can no longer be read . . .

Their eyes met over the tortured book.

'Of course, "One reads alone, even in another's presence,"' the Other Reader said.

'But "what is more natural than that a solidarity, a complicity, a bond should be established between Reader and Reader, thanks to the book"?' the Reader replied.

The Other Reader nodded. She was about to hand the book back, when something seemed to occur to her. 'But are books a "defence you set up to keep the outside world at a distance", "a dream into which you sink as if into a drug", or "bridges you cast towards ... the world that interests you so much that you want to multiply and extend its dimensions through books"?'

The Reader already knew her answer to this question. 'All three,' she replied. 'But particularly the drug.'

The Other Reader nodded. She understood. She slid *If on a Winter's Night a Traveller* back into the bookcase, in the middle this time.

They would use the drugs together from then on.

INDEX OF AILMENTS

INDEX OF READING AILMENTS

INDEX OF LISTS

INDEX OF AUTHORS AND NOVELS

ACKNOWLEDGEMENTS

Thank you to our team of readers, who valiantly tested our literary cures and reported on their efficacy: Becky Adams, Miranda Alcock, Nichole Beauchamp, Chris Berthoud, Colin Berthoud, Lucy Berthoud, Martin Berthoud, Tim Bates, Josh Beattie, Veronique Biddell, Amanda Blugrass, Gael Cassidy, Sarah Cassidy, Sarah Constantinides, Belinda Coote, Stephanie Cross, The Danny House Book Group, William Davidson, Sandra Deeble, Mel Giedroyc, Gael Gorvy-Robertson, Teresa Griffiths, Gill Hancock, Jane Heather, Belinda Holden, Charlie Hopkinson, Grahame Hunter, Clare Isherwood, Lou James, Tim Jones, Sarah Leipciger, Annabel Leventon, Rachel Lindop, Hilary Macey-Dare, Sam Nixon, Emma Noel, Anna Ollier, Patricia Potts, Joanna Quinn, Sarah Quinn, Janaki Ranpura, Lucy Rutter, Carl Thomas, Jennie Thomas, Morgan Thomas, Clare Usiskin, Pippa Wainwright, Heather Westgate, Rachel Wykes.

For G&Ts, nurturing and hands-on help we would like to thank Damian Barr, Polly and Shaun at Tilton House, Pippa Considine, Tim Jones, Natalie Savona, Laurie Tomlinson and Olivia Waller.

Thanks to our Bibliotherapy Advisory Board for ideas and suggestions over the years, including Terence Blacker, Rose Chapman, Tracy Chevalier, Abi Curtis, Nick Curwin, Ashley Dartnell, Geoff Dyer, Piers Feltham, Patrick Gale, Sophie Howarth, Alison Huntingdon, Nicholas Ib, Lawrence Kershen, Caroline Kraus, Sam Leith, Toby Litt, Anna McNamee, Chiara Menage, Stephen Miller, Tiffany Murray, Jason Oddy, Jacqueline Passmore, Bonnie Powell and her Facebook friends, Charlotte Raby, Judy Rich, Robin Rubenstein, Alison Sayers, Anna Stein, Chris Thornhill, Ardu Vakil, David Waters, SJ Watson, Rebecca Wilson, Carrie Worrall and Charmaine Yabsley.

Special thanks go to our colleague and friend Simona Lyons at The School of Life; and Morgwn Rimmell, Caroline Brimmer, Harriet Warden, Clemmie Balfour and all those at The School of Life who supported us throughout the period of writing the book.

Thanks also to our bibliotherapy clients past and present, who gave us ideas for books we had not yet read, and allowed us to practice our medications on them.

Thank you to our agent Clare Alexander, our editor Jenny Lord and all at Canongate, plus Colin Dickerman, Liesl Schillinger and all at Penguin US.

A posthumous thank you to our tutor at Cambridge, David Holbrook, who set us on our way.

And most of all to our families: Martin, Doreen, Saroja, Jennie, Bill, Carl and Ash, for their love and support throughout this process; and to our children, Morgan, Calypso, Harper and Kirin for putting up with our mental absence.